Sports Idols' Idols

First Heroes of Our Heroes

Scott Lynn

authorHOUSE®

AuthorHouse™
1663 Liberty Drive
Bloomington, IN 47403
www.authorhouse.com
Phone: 1 (800) 839-8640

This book is a work of non-fiction. Unless otherwise noted, the author and the publisher
make no explicit guarantees as to the accuracy of the information contained in this book
and in some cases, names of people and places have been altered to protect their privacy.

Published by AuthorHouse   11/17/2015

ISBN: 978-1-5049-4777-0 (sc)
ISBN: 978-1-5049-4776-3 (e)

Library of Congress Control Number: 2015918493

Print information available on the last page.

Any people depicted in stock imagery provided by Thinkstock are models,
and such images are being used for illustrative purposes only.
Certain stock imagery © Thinkstock.

This book is printed on acid-free paper.

Because of the dynamic nature of the Internet, any web addresses or links contained in
this book may have changed since publication and may no longer be valid. The views
expressed in this work are solely those of the author and do not necessarily reflect the
views of the publisher, and the publisher hereby disclaims any responsibility for them.

For Sharon, Adam and Kelsey

CONTENTS

PREFACE

Over the last few years, I had the opportunity to speak with nearly 200 sports figures about their first childhood idols. While many professional athletes avoid unnecessary interaction with the media, I found that nearly every athlete I approached was willing to discuss the people that meant most to them when they were young. Perhaps it was because the question seemed to instantly propel them back to the days of his or her youth. Whatever the reason, I found most athletes were quite willing to share stories of their childhood idols and what it was like for them the first time they came face-to-face with their heroes. In many cases, those initial meetings were unforgettable—surreal in nature, a memory to cherish. As many of the athletes shared their stories, they smiled and their eyes twinkled. I could tell they were thinking back to a more innocent time in their lives, a time when they were dreaming of a life as a professional athlete.

However, a few discussed the disappointment they felt when a childhood idol shunned them. It had a devastating impact. During the telling of those stories, there were no smiles, no twinkling eyes. Having experienced both the joy and heartache of good and bad interactions with my own heroes, I could empathize with those who had been crushed by receiving a brush-off from someone they had once idolized. I realized that while meeting one's hero is an important moment to most everyone, it doesn't always go as planned.

With only a few exceptions, I attempted to begin each interview by asking some variation of the question, "Who was your first childhood idol?" While the question seems simple, it soon became clear that it could be interpreted many different ways. More than a few considered the query about their "first idol" to mean their first sports hero. Others responded by naming a family member—a mom or dad, a sibling, grandparent, cousin or uncle. There are those who immediately thought of a former coach. It quickly became clear that a story of someone's "first idol" was going to be a matter of interpretation.

If you search for *idol* in a dictionary, you might read that an idol is a greatly admired or loved person or perhaps a worshipped god, icon or object. It is clear the four-letter word *idol* can mean different things to different people.

I have always considered former St. Louis Cardinals' star Stan Musial my first boyhood idol. He was the first sports figure I followed passionately. I imitated his batting stance when I played Wiffle Ball. No doubt about it, he was my favorite player. But, does being a favorite player make that player an actual idol? Some would say yes; others would say no. Let's be clear. In most cases, our idols/heroes should be our parents. However, most of us did not understand that our parents were the ones most deserving of our praise and admiration. We were more drawn towards people we saw on television, heard about on the radio or read about in magazines and newspapers.

We now know our idolatry has sometimes been misplaced. Today's more inquisitive press and the never-ending stream of information on social media has revealed that many of our childhood heroes are not necessarily of the highest character. Some are cheaters and liars. Others are drunks and drug-users. Some have been convicted of serious crimes. Yet, some things never change. Many sports fans continue to cheer for stars of their favorite teams even though they understand those stars might not be perfect human beings. I should point out that a few of the people in this book—or some of the childhood idols they mention—have been alleged to have broken rules or laws. It is for you to decide what to make of these transgressions—alleged or otherwise.

The book is primarily about heroes and idols. But, as you'll learn as you make your way through this oral history, many of the athletes also discuss special moments in their careers or lives. I am confident that you will enjoy reading this book because we all had heroes. Hopefully, your idol is among the many athletes who share their stories in the following pages.

*   *   *

My only regret about this book is that I cannot tell you with absolute certainty who my first sports hero, Stanley Frank Musial, idolized when he was a boy. By the time I got around to calling the Musial home in September of 2010, Stan was in poor health. His wife, Lil, told me that Stan was not able to come to the phone, so I asked if she happened to know who Stan considered his boyhood idol. Mrs. Musial wasn't sure, but said she knew that he had always loved baseball. Lil said I probably would not get a chance to talk with Stan because he was no longer feeling up to speaking with anyone. Mrs. Musial had me contact Stan's longtime administrative assistant, Pat Anthony, who had worked closely with Musial for decades. Lil thought Pat might be able to provide valuable insight.

When I spoke with Pat Anthony in September of 2010, she had been Stan Musial's secretary for 48 years. She had certainly been in position to hear many stories from Musial, so I tend to believe her when she said she knew who Stan had idolized as a child. Anthony told me that Stan's boyhood idol was former Pittsburgh Pirates' star Paul Waner, the Hall of Fame outfielder. She indicated Waner was the player Stan always talked about and had really liked as a youngster.

Trying to confirm the information Stan's longtime assistant had passed along, I contacted George Vescey, who wrote the Musial biography, *STAN MUSIAL: An American Life,* in 2011. I asked Vescey if the subject of Stan's boyhood idol was ever discussed during his book research. He had not talked with Musial specifically about his childhood heroes, but he did know that Musial had been a huge Pirates' fan. Musial had grown up in Donora, Pennsylvania, only twenty miles downriver from Pittsburgh.

Paul Waner played for the Pirates during the exact time Musial was growing up. Waner played in Pittsburgh from 1926–40, as Musial went from being a young boy, through his teen years and into early adulthood. Musial was just five years of age when Waner broke into the major leagues. Little Stanley was six when Waner won his first batting title. It makes sense that a child just learning about baseball would be attracted to the star player on his favorite team. Therefore, it seems likely that Musial would probably say "Big Poison"—Paul Waner—was the player he considered his first childhood hero.

There is no way for me to be absolutely certain who Stan would have identified as his first boyhood idol because I had waited too long to ask. That tiny piece of information is now lost forever. I wrote this book so that you might learn about your idol's childhood hero before too much time slips away.

* * *

The format for this book is simple. For each of the athletes I spoke with about their childhood heroes, there is a short introduction to the athlete, followed by—*in italics*—my personal association, comment or observation about the athlete. Then, just prior to my interview with the athlete, I share with you the date of the interview because in some cases certain circumstances might have changed since the interview was conducted. The interview then follows with my questions in **bold** font. Following the athlete's last response, I include a few notes about the athlete's career.

Please understand that I transcribed the quotes directly from the athletes' responses during our interviews, but I did not attempt to fact-check all names, dates and other information for historical accuracy.

The quotes are accurate. While each interviewee answered the questions based on his or her memory, the information provided might not be 100% accurate. Few of us have total recall of things that happened decades ago.

1

Six Seconds And Six Stitches

Phil Esposito was one of the greatest scorers in National Hockey League history, amassing 717 goals and 1,590 points in his 18 seasons with the Chicago Black Hawks, Boston Bruins and New York Rangers. After hanging up his skates, the Hockey Hall of Famer later coached the Rangers for parts of two seasons and worked as general manager of the Rangers for three years. He later founded the Tampa Bay Lightning franchise and served as the team's president and general manager.

I never really knew what to expect when I asked an athlete about meeting his or her childhood hero. I certainly didn't expect Phil Esposito's response when he told me what happened when he met his boyhood idol for the first time. How could anyone anticipate that a guy would find himself in the penalty box with his idol after getting into an altercation moments after meeting him on the ice?

I talked by phone with Phil Esposito on July 10, 2015.

Thinking back to your childhood, did you have a boyhood idol?

Absolutely. It was Gordie Howe. Actually, I had two. I had Gordie Howe and Jean Beliveau. I played against both of them. I played All-Star Games *with* them, and I played *against* them for years. I can tell you a story. It was my second game in the NHL. The first game, I played one shift. The second game, we're in Detroit Olympia. I'm not playin'. I guess I'm 21 years old. I just was called up. It was the third

1

period, and Coach Billy Reay says, "Esposito, get the hell out there. Go out there with (Bobby) Hull and (Reggie) Fleming. And, let Bobby take the face off." As I skate out there, I look around and there's Gordie Howe, my idol and future Hall of Famer. Holy Christ! There's Alex Delvecchio—Hall of Famer. Pierre Pilote—Hall of Famer. Bobby Hull, Glenn Hall, Terry Sawchuk, Billy Gadsby. Holy Christ! All of a sudden, Bobby said to me, "Hey, kid! You got that old son of a bitch?" Gordie smiled because they were good friends. I look at Gordie, and I said, "I got him." As soon as the puck is dropped, Gordie gave me an elbow in the mouth. I'm telling you I saw stars because he got me right below the nose, and I ended up with six stitches. I go back to him, and I went, "You old son of a bitch." And, I swung my stick at him. In those days we swung it around the hips 'cause that's the only place we had protection. So, that's where I swung it, and we both get a penalty. I'm on the ice six seconds. *Six seconds!* I got a penalty and six stitches from Gordie Howe!

In those days, we'd go into the penalty box and a cop or an usher sat between you because many times they had fistfights in the penalty box. This time it was an usher. Anyway, I'm trying to stop the bleeding. I went in first because I'm the visitor. So, as we settle in, I lean over, and I said to Gordie, "And you used to be my f***in' idol." And, he says, "*What* did you say, Woppo?" I went, "Nothing, Mister Howe. Absolutely nothing." (Laughs) At which point, the conversation was over. When I met him years later, he said to me, "You know? I tested everybody that came into the league. Everybody! And, if you didn't respond, I owned you." He said, "You responded." He never bothered me again. He and I became good friends.

It might have been my first All-Star game in '69 or '70. I'm playing with Bobby Hull and Gordie. I was a First All-Star, and they were First All-Stars. I'll never forget. We were in St. Louis. I go out and the first faceoff was to the left of the goaltender, and Gordie said to me, "Where do you want me, kid?" I looked at him, and I said, "Anywhere you wanna go." And, he says, "Look. You're the centerman. Where do you want me?" And, I said, "Preferably on the bench." And, he started to laugh. We became fast friends after that.

Jean Beliveau was the class of hockey. I can remember a Game Seven. I'm with the Black Hawks. He beats me for a faceoff clean, and they score and win the Stanley Cup. Boy, oh boy! I'll tell you. I've never forgotten how I lost that faceoff. And, guess what? I didn't lose too many after that.

You were an idol for so many people through the years. I talked with former Tampa Bay Lightning player Brian Bradley, and he told me that you were one of his guys. Back in your playing days, did you think about the fact that you were a hero for a lot of young kids?

Absolutely, but I was surprised to learn that Brian Bradley considered me one of his idols. When you're the boss, and you take a guy like Brian Bradley in the expansion draft, you know, you're just trying to survive. You got a bunch of players that nobody else wants, and you put them together and try to make a team out of them. Brian Bradley was absolutely spectacular. I gotta give my brother all the credit in the world for that because Tony said, "We gotta take this kid. He can skate. He's fast. We're in the Western Conference, and that's what it's all about." We were in the Western Conference that first year, and it was all speed, speed, speed. Brian became our best player. Without a doubt, he was our best player from the beginning.

But again, back when you were playing, you were an idol for many. I'm curious. Was getting an autograph a big deal? Did kids badger you for autographs? And, did you ever seek someone's autograph?

I never refused anybody an autograph, but I never asked anybody for one. I just didn't. Actually, the only guy I ever asked for an autograph was Jesse Owens. I asked Jesse Owens for an autograph at a big banquet in Sault Ste. Marie. I said—like a lot of people do—"I'm getting this for my sister." (Laughs) A lot of people say that.

In fact, at ten minutes to twelve, I got a phone call from Bobby Hull telling me that he heard I was traded. I went, "What?" Sure enough, I was traded to the Boston Bruins ten minutes before you had to have your protected list in. I wasn't going to be protected by the Hawks even though the first year of playin' in Chicago in '60, I ended up 11th in the league in scoring. The next year, I was ninth; the third year, seventh. And, they traded me. Then, of course, my first year in Boston, I ended up second in the league in scoring. Then I won five scoring titles in the next six years.

I want to ask you about the Lightning winning the Stanley Cup in 2004 and then getting back to the Cup Finals this year in 2015. Since you were the founder of the franchise, what sense of pride do you have about this team's accomplishments in such a relatively short period of time?

Oh, huge! I gotta tell you. It's been great from the beginning! Winning the Stanley Cup in 2004 was great, and it felt like my kid had graduated from college. But, we had a lockout so we couldn't capitalize. There was a strike—a lockout—whatever you wanted to call it. We couldn't capitalize on anything that we did. People sort of forgot about us. You know what I mean? They just forgot about us. I can tell you that this past season was—outside of that very first year 'cause we knew we couldn't win and weren't gonna be good but had so much fun—this year was the most fun I've ever had. It's all due to Jeff Vinik, Steve Yzerman, Steve Griggs, Tod Leiweke and management. And, the players were fabulous. They treated me fabulously. They treated me with respect. I can't say that in 2004 I got that.

You and your brother, Tony, are both in the Hockey Hall of Fame. Your sweater number 7 was retired by the Bruins, and I know it was an emotional night for you when they retired your number.

It's pretty clear from the career that you had and the people that say they idolized you when they were growing up that you've had a pretty special life.

Well, of all the things I've ever done in the game, my biggest accomplishment is getting the Tampa Bay Lightning—without a doubt. I mean, as a player, I was a good player. God gave me some talent to play. I exploited it and ended up doing what I did in the game as a player. But, as a businessman, I never had any formal education to speak of. I never had any business acumen to speak of, but I was able to put things together because I got good people around me. That is the sign of a great manager—when you put good people around you. Basically, they do the work. I never forgot that. Yes, Tony and I are in the Hall of Fame together as players. To tell you the truth, personally, I should be in the Hall of Fame as a builder because of what we did down here in Tampa Bay. If I had to choose, I would go into the Hall of Fame as a builder and be taken out as a player *tomorrow*.

Career Notes: Phil Esposito led the NHL in goals scored six consecutive years (1970–75), and he led the league in points scored five times (1969, 1971–74). He was once featured on a bumper sticker in Boston which read in large letters "JESUS SAVES" then, in smaller letters underneath, "and Esposito scores on the rebound!" Esposito teamed with Bobby Orr to help the Bruins win the Stanley Cup in 1970 and 1972. Esposito won two Hart Trophies as the NHL's MVP. Interestingly, when Esposito retired in 1981, he trailed only his boyhood idol, Gordie Howe, in NHL goals and total points.

*   *   *

2

Jimmy Goes Home With Us

Carl Erskine pitched for the Brooklyn/Los Angeles Dodgers from 1948 to 1959 and helped the Dodgers win six National League pennants. The right-hander was affectionately called "Oisk" by the Brooklyn fans. That's how "Ersk" sounded when spoken with a Brooklyn accent.

One of the players prominently featured in Roger Kahn's outstanding book *The Boys of Summer*, Erskine has authored two books—*Tales from the Dodger Dugout* and *What I Learned from Jackie Robinson*.

I can tell you with absolute certainty that the most important thing in Carl Erskine's life is his family—his wife, Betty, and their four children. Carl and Betty have been devoted parents to all of their children, but particularly so to their youngest son, Jimmy, who was born with Down syndrome. Carl's pride for Jimmy's accomplishments in life far exceeds how Erskine feels about anything he accomplished playing baseball. Every interview I've conducted with Erskine through the years has included a discussion of his son, Jimmy. He is one very proud father.

I spoke on the phone with Carl Erskine about Jackie Robinson in 2005 and about his boyhood idol on June 15, 2011.

Carl, thinking back to your earliest days, can you recall your very first boyhood idol?

Well, I would have been about ten years old. It was probably our high school coach, who just won two state championships in basketball in 1935 and 1937. His name was Archie Chadd. He could have run for president after winning two basketball championships in the state of Indiana. He was the first kind of big name that I looked at with awe. I went into high school a few years later, and I actually did play under Mr. Chadd for a couple years before he moved on to be school superintendent.

What was the first practice like for you? Were you at all intimidated by this legendary coach?

What actually happened was when I went into high school—I was probably 13 years old—and I got a note to go to Mr. Chadd's office. I had zero idea what Mr. Chadd would want with me. I just went into high school mid-term. I was a mid-termer. The coach's office is over in the gymnasium. It's a famous gym in Indiana called the Wigwam— because the team mascot is the Indians. We're the Anderson Indians. Years ago, we used to pack the Wigwam with eight or nine thousand people. Well, Mr. Chadd's office is in the gymnasium. I went over there very intimidated because, "What would Mr. Chadd want with me? Maybe I'm in trouble." I had no idea. So, I went in his office. Mr. Chadd was a wonderful man, but he was a stern personality. To a kid, the coach looked very stern. He said to me, "Son, I want you out for baseball this spring." Well, that was a shock to me. How did he know anything about me playing in the park league? We didn't have Little League in those days, but our city park in Anderson had a kids' program for baseball. I played in that—started when I was about nine years old—and I played three or four years in the park league. I was a pitcher, and I could throw hard as a kid. So, Mr. Chadd had done his scouting of kids coming into high school, I guess. He just turned and said to me, "Son, I want you out for baseball this spring." Then, he explained to me that since I was a mid-termer, that if I post-graduated in my senior year, I would have five springs in school. He said, "You cannot letter five times in high school." I had never heard of what a redshirt meant, but that's basically what he did. He said, "I want you on the team. You'll make all the trips with us, but I can't play you this year." So, actually, other than my own dad, Mr. Chadd gave me my first real push toward a career in baseball. I lettered four years, but I did have the experience of five high school baseball seasons. Mr. Chadd also coached the American Legion team in the summer after school was out, so I played a couple years for Mr. Chadd on the Legion team. Then, he moved on to Superintendent, and we had a different coach. To a kid, Mr. Chadd looked very stern, but I got know him later in life, and he was really a nice person.

Beyond Anderson, Indiana, was there someone who captured your attention?

The *national* hero, and probably my baseball hero, was Babe Ruth. He was the one that got all the hype. Baseball was *the* sport in those days. Pro basketball, football, hockey—none of that was on the screen yet—but all boys played baseball. So, Babe Ruth of the 1930s was the big name.

But, an interesting thing happened. They had a pitcher on the Yankees named Herb Pennock. I never met him. I never saw him pitch. I never knew anything about him at all except that I read that he was a real gentleman and a tough competitor. As a kid, that impressed me. I was like, "That's what I'd like to be." He was very much respected as a real gentleman, but when it came to competition, he was tough. I thought that was a great combination. As a kid, that really impressed me. One time, somebody asked me that question and my answer got in the newspaper. I got a letter from a granddaughter of Herb Pennock. She was so impressed that I thought that much of her grandfather—who I'd never met and I wasn't close to.

Did you ever have a chance to talk with Babe Ruth?

I never met Babe Ruth. But, I had an interesting experience. In the 1949 World Series, I had my family come to New York. I was only in my second year in the big leagues, and we were all awestruck by New York. I took my mother and dad to Toots Shor's Restaurant, a famous New York restaurant in those days. While we were eating, a gentleman came to the table and said, "Aren't you Erskine with the Dodgers? There's a lady at a table right behind you that would like to speak with you." I guess someone pointed me out. I was just a kid. I was a rookie. I was 22 years old. So, I turn around to speak to this lady, and it was Mrs. Babe Ruth. She was a gracious lady—a Southern lady—and she said, "Young man, I heard you were here. I think you'd like to know something." Now, when I went up to the Dodgers in 1948, Babe Ruth was in the hospital. He had throat cancer. He died later that year. But, Mrs. Ruth said to me, "Since you're here, I'd like to tell you something. Babe, of course, is deceased now, but while he lived in New York, Babe saw every game that was telecast in New York. He saw you come up as a rookie, and he made a couple comments like, "There's a kid that's gonna make it." (Laughs) I said, "Really?" Boy, I was just ecstatic. It was unreal. I won my first five games in the big leagues. I got off to a great start. I was five-and-oh, and I didn't come up until mid-year. I think Babe Ruth died late summer. I don't think he lived too much longer after I came up. No, I never met Babe Ruth, but I came close.

Carl, when you were pitching for the Dodgers, you were a hero for a lot of kids in Brooklyn. Did you think about that—that you were more than just a face on a bubble-gum card? You were, in fact, an idol for these kids?

I think you recognize it since you were a kid yourself not too many years before. I used to go to Cincinnati and stand at the gate where the players came through. I just had my eye balls bulge out seeing these good-looking men—dressed first-class—come through the gate going in to get dressed for the game. I was twelve. Then eight years later, I was walkin' through that gate as a major league player. Kids were there just as they had been when I was a kid. I think you do know that, and I think players—in various ways—feel an obligation. We were just kids ourselves—20, 21, 22 years old and in the major leagues. I think you're still so close to your own days as a youth that you do relate to that.

Knowing that young kids were watching you, did that make a difference in how you lived your life?

Yeah, I think I was sensitive about the kids. We always had two sponsors, at least two sponsors. One was a beer company, and one was a cigarette sponsor. Now, I never drank beer, and I never smoked. But, we would have chances to endorse products—especially a cigarette brand. A few guys didn't smoke; but to have a thousand or 15-hundred dollars just handed to you when your own salary was about $15,000, a lot of guys signed to endorse cigarettes because it was a little payday. Jackie Robinson and I were the only two players I know on the 1950's Dodger teams that refused to sign up for cigarette ads. I didn't smoke. It wouldn't have been honest. I had two little boys of my own. I did not want any kid to be influenced that way. Jackie didn't smoke, and I remember that Jackie said he wasn't going to do it either. I was always sensitive about kids. A lot of kids always waited around after games.

Mail? I still get a lot of mail from kids. My wife says, "Why do you answer all that mail?" I say, "Read some of these letters. These kids don't have a clue who I am. They've only *read* something about me." They write and say, "It must have been wonderful to play in that era and to play with Jackie. I'm doing a report in school. Could I ask you a few questions?" You can't throw that letter away.

I think that says a lot about the kind of person you are. I've talked with you maybe a half-dozen times through the years, and you are always gracious and very generous with your time.

I can sum up my life in one word—thankful. I am very appreciative of what transpired in my very modest home life. I married a little girl from high school. We've been married 64 years and had four kids. We've had our ups and downs, but in the main, we can't get up in the morning without being grateful. That's kind of my take on my life. I think people have been a lot better to me than I've been to them. (Laughs)

I went to Duke Snider's funeral out in California, and a guy from the Hall of Fame, (National Baseball Hall of Fame and Museum President) Jeff Idelson drove Betty and me to Fallbrook from San Diego. I told Jeff after the whole thing was over, I said, "You know, I'm not in the Hall of Fame, but the only thing missing is a plaque. I get treated like a Hall of Famer, so what's the difference?" (Laughs)

Have you had major league players approach you to say you were their idol as they grew up? Has that happened on occasion?

I did have it happen. It always floored me. I can tell you a real fast story. I coached Anderson University baseball after I got out of baseball—only by default. I didn't plan to do it. They asked me to fill in for a coach that had taken another job so that they could search and find a coach. I stayed a few years coaching college baseball. We won our way to the NAIA World Series in St. Joseph, Missouri. When we got there, the hot prospect was a guy named Clyde Wright. Clyde ended up playing for the Texas Rangers. He was a left-handed pitcher, but he was also a very good hitter. Well, the scouts were just en masse down there to look at Clyde Wright. He was an outstanding player, but I never met him at the time. Now, years passed, and I went to an Old-Timers Game at Yankee Stadium. Previous to the game, I went up the steps to check in at the Commodore Hotel, and Red Ruffing and Bill Dickey—two Hall of Famers—came walking across the lobby. Bill Dickey said, "Hey, Carl! How ya doin'? Do you know Red? Shake hands with Red. Red, this is Carl Erskine." They chatted a minute, and then they went on. I thought to myself, "Holy Columbus. I'm on a first-name basis with Bill Dickey and Red Ruffing. That's pretty amazing." So, I'm at the Old-Timers Game at Yankee Stadium. We dressed inside and came out through the visitors' dugout. I go out to the dugout, and Clyde Wright happens to be dressed in his uniform in the Rangers' dugout. As I went through the dugout to go on the field, I said, "Oh, Clyde Wright. I'm glad to see you. I watched you play in the NAIA World Series. You've had a fine career, Clyde. I'm really pleased to shake your hand." Well, he looks at me, and he says, "I don't believe this. You call me by my first name. How can I be on a first-name basis with you?" And, thinking about what had just happened to me with Dickey and Ruffing, I said, "Let me tell you a story." (Laughs)

But yeah, I've had younger players come in the league and seek me out. Of course, if some guy on the other team—some rookie—got a hit off of me, he always looked me up. He'd say, "I'll never forget you, Carl. I got my first hit in the big leagues off of you." (Laughs)

It's always a joy to talk baseball with a fine gentleman like yourself. One of my greatest regrets is I never got to talk with my boyhood idol, Stan Musial, about his childhood heroes. You pitched against Stan, who many consider one of the finest gentlemen baseball has ever seen. Did you get to know him very well?

Stan and I got to be acquainted. I pitched over 200 innings against the Cardinals. By some stretch of good fortune, I had a very good winning record against the Cardinals. But, Musial and I were acquainted through mutual respect to begin with. We knew each other through competition.

I was with Stan one night at a big baseball bash. We ate dinner together with him and his wife. Al Hirt was playing the music for this little private dinner of baseball guys, mostly Hall of Famers. Anyway, Stan pulled a harmonica out of his pocket, and I said, "What are you gonna do with that?" Stan said, "Well, I'm gonna play with Al Hirt in a minute. He comes to my restaurant in St. Louis, and I get up and play with him." I said, "No kidding! I wish I had brought my harmonica." He pulls one out of the other pocket, and he says, "Here." (Laughs) He gave me a harmonica. So, we got up and played *Oh, Dem Golden Slippers*—an old tune—with Al Hirt. I told Stan afterwards, "You're a lot easier to play *with* than *against*." (Laughs) He could have been a hero of *mine* if he hadn't got so many hits off me. No, I like Stan a lot. Most people do.

We've corresponded over the years. I talked to Stan a few months ago, and his health is not good. It's sad. But, he left a great impression in baseball. I'm glad I got to know him personally, aside from playing against him. It was amazing to meet people who seemed bigger than life and find out that they're real people.

Carl, you were a great friend of Jackie Robinson. You even wrote a book about the lessons you learned from Jackie—lessons that actually had very little to do with baseball. You had a special bond with Jackie, didn't you?

The first guy to my locker on the first day that I joined the Brooklyn Dodgers was Jackie. I played nine seasons with him. Not only was he a great player, but I watched all the things that he endured—and his character and the self-control that he demonstrated. Gee, I didn't know until I got old enough to realize what I'd seen and been through how much I'd learned from Jackie.

I know that you drew on the strength and the character you had seen from Jackie when your son Jimmy was born with Down syndrome.

Oh, yeah. I had three healthy kids when I retired. Jimmy was born April 1st, 1960, my first year out of baseball. The shock waves went through our local hospital like you wouldn't believe—"Oh, the Erskine baby..." In those days, the term was Mongoloid. The term Down syndrome has come along and is a much softer, more compassionate term. But, in those days, society did not understand how to deal with somebody as different as a Down's person. So, the customary thing was to have the doctor recommend the baby be put in an institution—"Don't let it interrupt your family. You got three wonderful kids. Just take Jimmy [to the institution]. He'll have good care." Well, that was not to be done. Betty, my wife, carried this little guy for nine months. She was not *about* to abandon him. She said, "Jimmy goes home with us." Well, he has gone home with us, and he's been home with us. (Laughs)

Believe me; what I saw Jackie do in terms of facing social rejection and having no opportunity was paralleled in our lives. There were no special schools in the early '60s. There was no Special Olympics. But, all those kinds of things came along the way—just as they had for Jackie—when society began to see people in a different light. They began to see that Jackie deserved to be a major leaguer and that he deserved to be a first class citizen. So, he *became* that. Well, Jimmy has too over time. So, I see this wonderful parallel in our society, and I salute our society for being willing to say, "Hey. We've been doing this the wrong way." Jimmy works at Applebee's restaurant. He's in Special Olympics. He's completed school. He has friends. I say that if Jimmy ever ran for office, he'd get a lot of votes because he knows so many people. (Laughs) He's been totally accepted.

Jackie faced social rejection in the beginning, and that all changed through his perseverance, his patience, self-control and seeing the big picture. To win a small fight wasn't worth it, so he didn't fight. He knew the bigger victory was to encompass society in a willingness to recognize the dignity of every individual. Now, Jimmy has benefitted from that. When he wins a gold medal in Special Olympics, I think of my old teammate, Jackie. I think Jackie had something to do with that. While Jackie can't be credited with *every* civil rights accomplishment, I think he started a momentum. That momentum—through sports—he earned it right in the public in the bright lights of a major league field, and I think Jimmy has benefitted from that. You might say, "Well, you're a romantic, Erskine." Yeah, I am. I think there's romance in that. I think there is love, affection and sensitivity in that story.

Even in your hometown, people have had their eyes opened by the life Jimmy has been able to lead.

Well, people had to learn, and that's the beauty of what happened. They did learn. In the beginning, there was rejection and resistance—to group homes, for instance. There was resistance to special education. People said, "These kids can't ride the buses. They can't participate in physical education." There were just a lot of negatives. It was natural that they were on the sidelines. They were never given a chance. When they gave a chance to Jimmy—and others like Jimmy—you know what? Those people began to be surprised. Inside this body that's hampered by some birth defects, there's a real person in there. There's a loving and a caring, sweet personality in that person. Once people began to get exposed, it was just like Jackie. When people met Jackie, they couldn't help but like him. When people meet Jimmy—and people like Jimmy—you can't help but like them because there's a dignity there. I just salute society for finally recognizing that.

You speak with such excitement—not only about your baseball career—but about the life you've lived experiencing the wonder of your son, Jimmy.

I think the lasting, really significant part of my career was the privilege of playing and living with Jackie—being a close friend—and watching what he accomplished in American society. Then, I have the privilege of living with my son Jimmy through all the stages of his development. I was an average kid—just a skinny kid in Anderson, Indiana—throwing a baseball, and I could throw it pretty hard. I got a chance to do the things in baseball. Then, I got to have this marvelous experience with Jimmy. In one lifetime, you don't often get the chance to have that much of a dramatic and dynamic experience.

I have a couple World Series rings. When I look at those rings—and then I look at a gold medal that Jimmy won in swimming, golf or bowling—I say, "Really, we were *supposed* to win these rings. We had talent. We had a lot of Hall of Fame guys." So, we were supposed to win. Jimmy was never supposed to be a gold medalist in anything, but he is. The true yardstick in life is getting the most out of what we have individually—not against the clock or the guy in the next lane—but what have I done with what I've been given? When you measure it that way, Jimmy's gold medal has to be a bigger achievement than that '55 World Series ring of mine.

Career Notes: Over his 12-year big league career, Carl Erskine won 122 games and lost 78. He appeared in 11 World Series games. He won two and lost two. Erskine started three games in the 1953 World Series and set a single-game strikeout record by fanning 14 Yankees in Game 3. (His record was broken by Dodger Sandy Koufax ten years later.) Of the seven National League no-hitters pitched in the 1950s, Erskine threw two of them. He turned the trick against the Cubs on June 19, 1952, and against the Giants on May 12, 1956.

*　　*　　*

3

Blanket Babies

Rick Barry was special when it came to putting the ball in the basket. Few have done it better than the 6-foot-7 Hall of Fame forward. Barry led the nation in scoring in 1965 when he averaged 37.4 points per game for the University of Miami. He is the only player to lead the NCAA, the now-defunct American Basketball Association (ABA) and the NBA in scoring. He averaged an NBA-best 35.6 points for the Warriors in 1966-67 and a league-best 34.0 while leading the Oakland Oaks to the 1968-69 ABA title.

Rick Barry had many individual highlights during his career, but I have to think he must truly treasure being named MVP of the star-studded 1967 NBA All-Star Game after scoring a game-high 38 points to lead the Western Conference to a 135-120 victory over the East. Receiving special recognition for his performance in that game was a testament to Barry's basketball abilities. Barry's Western Conference teammates that day included fellow future Hall of Famers Elgin Baylor, Nate Thurmond, Dave DeBusschere, Lenny Wilkens and Jerry West. There were nine future Hall of Fame players on the losing East squad—Wilt Chamberlain, Bill Russell, Oscar Robertson, John Havlicek, Bailey Howell, Willis Reed, Hal Greer, Chet Walker and Jerry Lucas. No doubt Barry was very pleased when he was recognized as the best of the best in the All-Star Game at San Francisco's Cow Palace on January 10, 1967.

Since Barry spent a few years as a broadcaster working basketball games for different networks, he understands both the needs of the media and the value of being interviewed. Unlike many current and former athletes who attempt to avoid the media, I have always found Rick Barry to be fairly accessible. He loves to talk and tell stories, and I have enjoyed every one of my conversations with him. I've heard some people say they consider Rick to be rather cocky. Make no mistake about it. Rick Barry understands just how good he was on the court. But, man, the guy could really play, and part of his game was his supreme confidence. As far as Barry's perceived arrogance, I think you could say—in today's parlance—Rick Barry has always displayed a fair amount of swagger. Years ago, Walter Brennan used to say on the TV western, "The Guns of Will Sonnett, "No brag, just fact." Well, Rick Barry had game, and that's no brag, just fact.

I talked by phone with Rick Barry on January 23, 2014.

Who was your very first boyhood idol?

My first one was Willie Mays. That's why I wear number 24. I have great stories about Willie that are pretty unbelievable. I was a young kid, and baseball was my sport growing up. Here's this rookie that comes to the Giants, and all of a sudden he's catching fly balls with a basket catch—which is how my dad taught me to catch. I said, "Well, that's my guy right there." I never saw anybody doing that in Major League Baseball except this guy. But, my dad had taught me how to do that when I was playing baseball.

Did you ever meet Mays when you were a kid?

Actually, yeah! It was kind of cool. I was in parochial school in grammar school. They had a Police Athletic League day trip to the Polo Grounds to go watch the Giants play. I thought, "Oh, my God!" I cut school to go on the PAL trip to the game. It was an early game. In the Polo Grounds, when the players were done, they would go out to centerfield and go up these steps to go to the clubhouse. So, when the game was over, I jumped over the wall out in left field. I just sprinted out on the field to go see Willie Mays. I ran up to him and got to shake his hand.

We got back on the bus. Then, I get back home, and my brother was there. He said, "How was the game?" I said "What do you mean? Why are you talking about the game? I was in school." He said, "No, you weren't. You were at the game." I said, "I wasn't at the game. I was in school." He said, "No, you were at the game. I saw you on television." I said, "What?" He said, "Yeah, at the end of the game the cameras focused in and zoomed in on this kid that jumped over the wall to go shake Willie Mays' hand. That was *you*!" I said, "Oh, my God! Don't tell Mom and Dad!"

So, what a great country, right? Willie's my hero. I wear his number, and I actually get to become friends with my boyhood hero. Willie and I are now friends. In fact, when he had his 70th birthday at Bally's, they invited me to be on the dais. I'm on the dais with all these amazing great, great Hall of Fame baseball players. I was the only basketball player. I mean, I was the only guy from another sport up there. They said, "Rick, we would like you to be one of the guys to talk, and they want you to go first." I said, "What, really?" They said, "Yep." So, I get up in this packed ballroom with all these people there, and the first thing I say is, "Okay. I know what every one of you is thinking, 'What the hell is *he* doing here'?" (Laughs) I told them the story that I just told you, and it was really cool.

What was he like? Was he everything you expected in real life when you became friends?

Yeah. I mean, he was Willie Mays for God's sake. It was great. It's not like I would go out to dinner with him lots of times, but I did a lot of things. I did stuff for his foundation that he was doing things with— Say Hey Foundation—and I used to do a lot of things. C'mon! How could there be anything wrong with your boyhood hero? (Laughs)

Rick, you were a boyhood idol for many basketball fans in the '60s and '70s. Did you think about the fact that you were an idol for a lot of young kids?

No, I didn't. I had a lot of people come up to me and tell me how much they enjoyed my play, and I felt great about it. I did learn one thing growing up. I do think that you are a role model. I do think you have a responsibility to act in a manner which is conducive for kids who would follow you to follow. You have to set a good example. I think that's part of being a professional athlete.

I learned at an early age that one thing I would never want to do is disappoint kids. Again, when I was a kid I was a baseball fan, right? The Giants came over to do something in New Jersey. They were playing some exhibition or doing something over there at a field near where I lived. I went over there to see that. After the game, I didn't get a chance to get to Willie Mays, but I got to Monte Irvin. I asked him for an autograph, and he refused. I was crushed. I went back home, and I remember telling my mom and dad, "If I ever get to be a professional baseball player, I will never do that to a young kid." It had a real impact on me.

Of course, sometimes a fan asks you for an autograph and you just can't do it. If I was out on the court doing stuff, I would never try to start signing for someone because then you start a whole big rampage. It's not fair to sign for just a couple and not for the rest of them. Leaving the arena on the road was always a problem because there would be a bunch of autograph seekers waiting. I always took a long time to cool down because I never wanted to shower right after a game. I'd just start sweating again. So, I sat there until I cooled down. My teammates didn't like it because it would take a little bit longer for us to get on the bus. When I went out to get on the bus, if somebody was there, I would start signing as much as I could. But, then it got to a point where I'm holding everybody else up, so it was hard for me to try to sign for everybody. I always felt badly, and I would say, "I'm really sorry. I would stay and sign these, but they're all waiting for me. It's not fair for me to hold up my team." And, to be honest, I always felt badly about that. I didn't do it to avoid signing autographs. I did it because that was my way after games to cool down. But, at home, whoever waited for me until I came out, I would sign for them.

Were you the boyhood idol of any your basketball-playing sons?

Oh, God! No! What? Are you kidding me? I'm their *father*. What the hell did I know? (Laughs) Growing up, Drew loved Jamaal Wilkes—you know—Keith Wilkes. Brent loved Clifford Ray. In fact, Brent had one of those small Nerf baskets, the small hoops that kids used to have. Brent would imitate Clifford Ray. He'd hunch over, make this look on his face, and go up and just throw the ball through the hoop like Clifford would dunk the ball. I have a video of it, and it's absolutely hysterical.

Both Drew and Brent were blanket babies. They loved their blankets. I went to both Clifford and Jamaal and said, "Guys, do me a favor. My boys are too old to have these blankets with them all the time. Could you please ask them if you could have their blankets?" Each of them asked the respective boy, "Can I have your blanket?" And, both boys gave up their blankets! Clifford and Jamaal hung the blankets in their lockers. It was so cool.

Rick, you shot 90% from the line during your NBA career, and you did so by shooting your free throws underhand. Was that shooting technique at all inspired by the basket catch used by your baseball idol, Willie Mays?

No. My dad used to shoot that way, and he's actually the one that got me to make the change. It worked pretty darn well.

Career Notes: Rick Barry was the 1966 NBA Rookie of the Year and All-NBA First Team after averaging 24.7 points in his first season with the Warriors. Barry left the Warriors and played four seasons in the rival American Basketball Association before returning to the NBA where he led the Warriors to the NBA championship in 1975. Barry was the '75

Finals' MVP. He was an All-Star 12 times—eight times in the NBA and in all four of his ABA seasons. Barry was named All-League First Team nine times (five in the NBA, four in the ABA). When he retired, Barry ranked sixth in NBA/ABA scoring with 25,279 career points. He averaged 23.2 points in NBA games and 30.5 points in four seasons in the ABA. Rick Barry was recognized as one of the 50 Greatest Players in NBA History in 1996.

*   *   *

Brent Barry is one of Rick Barry's boys that—like father, like son—fashioned a lengthy pro basketball career. Brent remains close to the game today by working as an NBA analyst for TNT and NBA TV. Barry played four years of college basketball at Oregon State University. In 1995, he was the Beavers leading scorer and was named to the All-Pac-10 First Team after he had averaged 21 points, 5.9 rebounds and 3.9 assists.

I first met Brent Barry in the early 1990s when he was playing at Oregon State. I was the sports director of the radio station that aired the Beaver basketball games in Portland, and I also hosted a sports talk show. I occasionally interviewed the well-spoken Barry and also interviewed his father from time to time. Nicknamed "Bones" because of his slender build, Brent Barry is one of the good guys in sports. I am happy for him that he had a long and productive NBA career as a player and that he remains involved with the game working as an analyst on the national stage.

I don't know if Brent Barry ever realized that his dad asked Clifford Ray to gain possession of that baby blanket Rick Barry told us about, but I found it interesting that—unsolicited—Brent told his version of the story when he responded to my boyhood idol questions via email on January 28, 2015. With the exception of a few very minor changes, Brent's responses shown below are exactly as he sent in his email.

Who was your very first boyhood idol?

If I go back to the very first person that I can remember in the way someone outside of my parents impacted me and my life, an individual I looked up to—and in this case, quite literally—was Clifford Ray. When I was a very young boy my father was playing professionally for the Golden State Warriors, and I have vivid memories of interactions with a teammate of my father in the form of a six-foot nine-inch, two hundred and thirty pound teddy bear of a man whom I fell in love with. I was around 5 years of age. Clifford had joined the Warriors during the season they had won their only championship in 1975, and I had severe separation anxiety from my blue blanket. My parents kept preaching to me that I was too old to be carrying it around anymore and that I needed to move on from it—keeping me from going places without it. Throw it away? Never. Someone had to take care of it for me. Someone special. After weeks of deliberation—a word I only know now by definition—I decided who I would bestow my young life's prized possession on. To this day, Clifford Ray still has my blanket.

Why was Clifford Ray so important to you?

He was special to me because he smiled when he saw me. He hugged me bigger and tighter than anyone besides my parents. He picked me up and put me on his shoulders and carried me to my highest heights. He laughed. At 5 years old, isn't that everything?

But, as far as the idol question tends to go, as I grew older and began to find a young boy's passion for sport, basketball became my love. Honestly, it has been and always will be. But my view of the game and my love for the Warriors brought me to admire the way Chris Mullin mastered the floor. Maybe it is my Catholic upbringing that doesn't allow me to use the term "idol," but Chris impacted me in so many ways as to how fundamentals, work ethic and tremendous skill could still be recognized at the most elite levels. I met Chris several times in high school, attending Warrior games whenever I got homework done and could be done with practice on time. Longtime Warriors team physician Bob Albo was the doctor for the team during my dad's playing days, and he would offer tickets up occasionally to my mom that me and my brothers would often fight over—just add that one to the list. These were brief after-the-game encounters, ones that I would grow all too familiar with, but meant the world to me. To shake hands, see that Mully squinty-eyed smile and hear that thick New York accent mutter the words, "How ya doin'?"—I wanted to be in the NBA.

But it was years later, when I would return home from Oregon State University for the summers, that Chris truly impacted my belief in what I could accomplish as a player. He invited me to join him. Now when most guys tell you that you can come workout with them, it usually means an hour or two in the gym and mostly you are rebounding and working on your passing. Not with Mully.

I ate breakfast with him. Got on treadmill. Went to the gym to weight train. Eat lunch. Go to a small gym that he had finagled the key to shoot for an hour and a half. Back to the house for a dip in the pool. Dry off, snack and ride to Saint Mary's College in Moraga (my grandfather Bruce Hale once coached there) to play 2 hours of open gym. Tim Hardaway. Chris Webber. Rod Higgins. Lamond Murray. Jason Kidd. It was heaven.

He became my big brother in many ways and a very special person in my life. I penned a letter to Chris a few days after I was drafted and told him that there was no question in the deepest parts of who it is on the inside that represents me as a player, he was the biggest reason I was a professional player. We played on the same court several times over the next 5 seasons, and they were all very special nights in my career.

When you played at Oregon State and then later in the NBA, there were youngsters who loved to watch you play. Did you ever consider that you were being idolized by kids similarly to the way you had looked up to your boyhood hero?

I have never given much thought to the idea of younger players that happened to see me play through the years. Mostly because I don't want to think that I am in that category yet, although most certainly I am. But, without question, because of Chris, I have been and will always be approachable and available to young players that are seeking the very thing I was at that impressionable age—to maximize your potential.

Career Notes: Brent Barry played 14 years in the NBA with the Clippers, Heat, Bulls, SuperSonics, Spurs and Rockets. He was the 1996 NBA Slam-Dunk Champion. His most productive season came in 2001-02 when he averaged 14.4 points, 5.4 rebounds and 5.5 assists as the starting point guard for Seattle. Barry won a pair of NBA championships with San Antonio (2005, 2007). He and his father are among the few father-son combinations to win NBA championships as players.

*   *   *

Jon Barry, another basketball-playing son of Rick Barry, also played in the NBA. Like his brother, Brent, Jon is now a broadcaster. He works as an NBA game analyst for ESPN.

Prior to playing in the NBA, Jon Barry played one year at the University of Pacific. He then transferred to Paris Junior College in Texas. After one season in the Lone Star State, Barry moved on to play two seasons at Georgia Tech. For the Yellow Jackets, he averaged 15.9 points in 1990-91 and 17.2 points and 5.9 assists in 1991-92. As a senior, Barry led Georgia Tech to a pair of victories in the NCAA tournament before the Yellow Jackets fell to Memphis State in the Midwest Regional Semifinals.

I first became aware of Jon Barry when he was playing at Georgia Tech. I appreciated his ability to create opportunities for himself and his teammates while helping his team win. I watched him in 1992 when the Yellow Jackets won a couple games to advance to the regional semifinals. Working in Portland—Pac-10 country—I was surprised when the 7th-seeded Yellow

Jackets slipped past 2-seed Southern California 79-78 in the Round of 32. The next game, Barry played magnificently and scored a game-high 29 points against Memphis State. However, Barry missed a potential game-tying three-point shot with 20 seconds left. Georgia Tech fell 83-79. Anfernee "Penny" Hardaway led Memphis State with 24 points in the game that ended Jon Barry's collegiate career.

I have enjoyed Jon Barry's work as a broadcaster. He does a very solid job and brings interesting perspective to his analysis. Rick Barry spent a short time as a broadcaster, but he was not nearly as good a broadcaster as he was as a player. I think his sons, Jon and Brent, have a chance to be even better broadcasters than they were players—and they were solid pros. Add the name Barry to the expanding list of families that have had multiple members working in broadcasting (think Albert, Buck, Caray, Brennaman).

I talked with Jon Barry in Portland, Oregon, on April 16, 2014.

Who was your very first boyhood idol?

Yeah, the first guy was Chris Mullin. I think it was when he was on the 1984 Olympic team. My dad was a broadcaster, and he came back with a binder of all the players—their bios, pictures of them and all kinds of articles. I remember reading them all, and I picked Chris Mullin. I was like, "This is my guy." He wasn't a super athletic guy, but he could just shoot the lights out. He was smart. Something about him—that was my guy. And, then I got to play with him with the Golden State Warriors.

That had to be unbelievable to be able to play alongside your boyhood idol?

It was. I wore 17 when I got in the NBA my first three years in Milwaukee because that was Chris Mullin's number. Then, I went to Golden State my fourth year and got to play with him. Now he's my friend and colleague. We work together at ESPN. (Mullin has since become the men's head basketball coach at St. John's.) Now we're friends, and I can call him and say, "What's up?" It's still tough to act normal around him. You know, I'm like a 12-year-old kid. That's my guy that I wish I could play like, and then, to have him become my friend, it's wild.

Did you ever tell him that?

Yeah, he knows. He knows. I didn't want to boost up his ego too much. He's just a guy whose work ethic I respect. I mean, this guy spent so much time in the gym and just perfected his craft. One of the best shooters ever—a Hall of Famer, a Dream Teamer—and he did it because he understood the game. He worked at it. He didn't have the physical tools like most of the guys that we played against. That's what I really respected about him.

You were a great college player and had a nice NBA career. Now you're an ESPN announcer. I'm sure there are kids that looked up to you as an idol.

I don't know about that. I was very fortunate to be able to make it 14 years in the NBA. I feel like I should have an Oscar for the acting performance I put on, but I'm just very fortunate. This is what I wanted to do. When I was in the eighth grade, I said I wanted to be a broadcaster. The NBA kind of got in the way for 14 years. It's a testament that anybody can do anything they really put their mind to. You have an opportunity to do that. Sometimes you're not fortunate enough to do that, but if you put the time in—and you have the work ethic—you give yourself a chance.

Career Notes: Jon Barry played 14 seasons in the NBA with the Bucks, Warriors, Hawks, Lakers, Kings, Pistons, Nuggets and Rockets. A role player for much of his pro career, Barry's most productive season came in 2001-02 with Detroit when he appeared in every game and averaged 9.0 points and 3.3 assists.

* * *

4

Tough At The Top

Nancy Lopez is one of the most important people in women's golf history. At a time the LPGA was struggling for recognition in the late 1970s, Lopez burst onto the scene and grabbed the headlines. Born in Torrance, California, and raised in Roswell, New Mexico, Lopez won 17 tournaments in her first two full years on the LPGA Tour. Her torrid start was just the beginning of a marvelous career that resulted in her inductions into the LPGA Hall of Fame and into the World Golf Hall of Fame. After bringing much-needed attention to the LPGA Tour during her playing career, Lopez continues to promote the women's game and remains one of the LPGA's most vocal supporters.

Having interviewed Nancy Lopez numerous times in my career, I can tell you that she is the sweetest, most gracious athlete I ever encountered. Although she was a fierce competitor on the golf course, Lopez has always been a kind, thoughtful woman who is passionate about the things that matter most to her—family, friends and women's golf.

One of Lopez's biggest disappointments came at the 1997 U.S. Women's Open at Pumpkin Ridge Golf Club near Portland, Oregon. Alison Nicholas won the tournament, though Lopez became the first woman to shoot four rounds in the 60s in a U.S. Open. Lopez never won a U.S. Women's Open title. Lopez became somewhat emotional when responding to questions asked by reporters—including me—during a news conference in Portland, Oregon, during her Farewell Tour in 2002.

Nancy, you have accomplished so much, but was one of your biggest frustrations that 1997 U.S. Women's Open that got away from you late in the final round?

Oh yeah. Pumpkin Ridge is a great place for me. I play very well there. It was a wonderful time for me to play that well in the U.S. Open. Unfortunately, it was very devastating when I didn't win it because I thought for sure it was gonna be mine. It took me awhile to get over it. I've finished second many times, but *that* second really hurt. It was really hard to get over. It took me six or seven months. I cried every time somebody asked me about it. (Laughs)

(Lopez was asked by a reporter how she wanted to be remembered.)

Well, after 25 years of competing, I would love to be known as one of the best players that ever played, but [also] one of the nicest players. I think that has done more for me as a professional athlete—having the friends and fans that have followed me—than winning 48 tournaments. I think the support of the fans—and being friends with them—has been, I guess, more fulfilling because I don't have to celebrate my wins by myself. And, whenever I've struggled, the fans have been there supporting me. (Lopez starts to become tearful)

From "Rookie Sensation" to "Farewell Tour", has it gone by quickly for you? Does it seem like it's been 25 years?

Um, it's gone by quickly. (Lopez pauses for five seconds with tears in her eyes). Um, (another long pause) when I first came out and played out here my first year, it was thrilling—and a lot of fun. (With her eyes moistening and her voice breaking). And, I think, um, what I'm going to miss the most is the players (Lopez pauses with tears flowing) because I know my first few years on Tour, there was a little jealousy on the Tour towards me. (Lopez takes a deep breath) I knew that I could win their friendship, and that was important. I think we need friends that are out here all the time because we're like a family. I respect all of the players. Each one of them has a talent and a personality all their own. I get disappointed that the world doesn't see the LPGA Tour the way I see it. I think it's a great Tour. We have some really great players, and they're not given the credit they deserve. I know Tiger Woods has brought a lot of people to golf, but Annika Sorenstam and Carrie Webb have brought a lot to golf, too. I know they're not Americans. It's probably harder to watch LPGA golf because fans want to see Americans winning. But, they have brought a lot to the LPGA Tour, and they've done just as much as Tiger has. I don't know if it's just because we're women and people don't care about us as much, but I could bet anybody—if they come out to watch the LPGA Tour—that if they had a choice, they'd always come watch the LPGA Tour. They just need to try us a few times. You know, my friendship with the players, I will truly miss them. I love them all. There's a few that I have complications with—internally. They don't know that. I just want them to represent this Tour with a lot of pride because it's a great organization and a great bunch of people.

(Lopez was asked by a reporter to try to explain why she felt the other players were jealous of her during her first few seasons.)

Well, I was beating them a lot. (Laughs) And, I really didn't get to see them a lot. I think that they thought I was stuck up. I was never in the locker room. I would play my round of golf, and then the press would take me right off the golf course into the press room. Then when I was done in the press room, I would go hit balls. So when I went in the locker room, there was nobody there. I was always alone. I never saw the players—*ever*—those first few years. I was always going golf course—press room—practice. Then as I started to not win as much, (laughs) I was in the locker room a little bit more, and I got to spend more time with them. I think they got to know me better. I think they just really didn't know me those first couple years on Tour because I was never there for them *to* know me. I felt like I always said hi to them. I never walked by anybody without saying hi. I may not have known their name, but I always said hi. I think that was part of it. They didn't know me as a person. They only knew me as a competitor. I never really got to talk to them very much.

I interviewed Nancy Lopez one-on-one on September 25, 2013. Prior to this phone conversation, it had become obvious to me that many current LPGA Tour players had great respect for what Lopez had done for women's golf.

Nancy, so many of the players I've talked with have indicated you were someone they looked up to. For example, Lorena Ochoa, Brittany Lincicome, Natalie Gulbis and Paula Creamer have all told me that you were a person they grew up idolizing. What does it mean to you to hear you meant so much to so many other women golfers?

Well, first of all, I'm glad that I could help in any way. The thing for me is how much I love the game. If I can, I help a young person that comes in on our Tour to give them insight to love the game because that's what my dad always taught me. He wanted me to enjoy what I was doing. To me, the future of the LPGA is all these young players. It helps if you can give them a tip and help them to get through a very, very tough career because it's not easy. I relate with a lot of these girls because I have daughters their age. (Laughs) I learned a lot from my daughters. When I'm giving advice to these young girls on Tour, I know when to step away, and I feel like I know when to step in. It's funny because I always let them know to reach out to me if they ever need anything anytime.

I really love these kids. I want them all to be successful. If I can touch them by playing good golf like what they saw before—and give them good advice—then I'd like to be able to do that. It's all about the LPGA Tour. It was the Tour that gave me a wonderful career and a wonderful life. I think that it's important to keep building that because—as we always say—we want to leave whatever we're in better than it was when we were there. When we leave, we want it to be better. So, that's important to me—to see these players play the game and with integrity, too—not to be a club-thrower, not to let their temper get them. Just play the game, and love it the way that I did and the way that my dad taught me.

Beth Daniel told me you were rivals first, not friends. You became friends later. Back in 2002 on your Farewell Tour, you got pretty emotional as you talked about how it wasn't easy for you when you first came on the LPGA Tour and seemingly won all the time. There was jealousy and envy. You didn't have a lot of close friends at that time. When did that start to turn around?

It probably was when I wasn't winning as much. (Laughs) I think there was jealousy because the players really didn't know me. They only knew me as a competitor. My rookie year, I won nine tournaments. I practiced. I played. When I was done, I went in the press room. From the press room, I went to practice. I never could practice right after I was done. I always had to go to the press room because I was playing so well. I went to the press room. I went to practice. By the time I got done and went into the locker room, nobody was there. So, nobody really ever got to know me. That first year and the second year, it was talk with the press—golf—practice. I never had a relationship with any other players because I was never in the locker room. Then, I didn't win as much and wasn't in the press room as much. Still, there were times the press would bring me in when I shot a terrible score, and I was like, "You all need to be talking to the leaders, not to me." I really got to spend more time in the locker room when I stopped winning as much. I still won sometimes, but at least I was in the locker room when there were players in the locker room. I got to socialize with them some, when *before*, I never got to. I think that's why there was jealousy more than anything because here I was winning all the time and I didn't give them the time of day because I didn't *have* the time of day to give anybody—except what I was doing with my career.

Nancy, the first question I usually ask when interviewing athletes for this book is, "Who was your very first childhood idol?" Who pops into your head when I ask you that question?

JoAnne Carner was my idol when I was growing up watching women's golf whenever it was on television. She was just an exciting player to watch. A lot of people say we don't have much personality on our Tour when you're watching the players, but JoAnne, she was enthusiastic. You didn't really know how she was playing because she had such a great attitude. She never gave up. She was fun to watch. She had lots of expression. I really liked watching her play. Then, of course, when I got on the Tour, we were head-to-head many times. But, when I played with her as an amateur—like in the U.S. Open—I really wanted to kind of show off. I wanted to play really well when I played with her. It seems like every time I play with her, I play well. But, even though she was my idol, I wanted to beat her. I always admired her and looked up to her because of her comportment on the golf course and how she was as a player. As I watched her, I was always said, "Gosh, I'd like to be like that one day if I ever turn professional." It was just fun watching her.

I mentioned some of the players who told me they idolized you growing up. Several of the Asian players on the LPGA Tour told me they grew up idolizing Annika Sorenstam because she appeared in many Japanese and South Korean magazines. The impact Annika had on women's golf was pretty similar to the impact you had a generation earlier, don't you think?

Yeah, I think Annika definitely touched a lot of players' lives—even now when we go out to watch the players. The Korean players, I feel like I have a good relationship with them. I always encourage them because when they came over here, they didn't speak English and that was a big deal. I'll see an interview of a Korean player, and I'll go up to them and say, "That was a great job." You want to influence them in a positive way to make them feel comfortable—that when they speak English, it doesn't matter if it's broken. They're very proud players. They don't want to speak English unless it's correct. But, I always tell them it's okay because the world loves watching them *try* to speak English. It really means a lot—especially to fans in the United States. We have so many Korean players that are winning now that, when they make the effort to speak English, it means a lot. I always encourage them and tell them thank you for doing what they're trying to do because they're really excellent players and really super people.

Lorena Ochoa, who has meant so much to fans in Mexico, talked with me about always keeping in mind that she has been an idol to many Hispanic youngsters. I know you were born in California, but did you think about the young girls in Mexico and in the United States that were paying close attention to what you were doing on the LPGA Tour?

Absolutely. When I was growing up, there were hardly any Hispanic kids playing the game because it was too expensive. I went back to Roswell when they named my grade school after me. It was Flora Vista Elementary. Now, it's Nancy Lopez Elementary. As I sat there talking to all those little kids, they were wide-eyed, and they just really want to see you and learn what you're all about. To me, being able to touch their lives and make them realize that if they work hard—no matter what color their skin is—they can go far. That's what my dad always told me, "Nancy, you have to do the best you can and work hard—and have a good heart. It doesn't matter what the color of your skin is. People will love you." And, that's very true. As I talk to young kids about that, I tell them, "My dad never said, 'Oh, poor us.' because we're Hispanic. He never did that." You have to teach these kids not to respond to life in that way. You've got to work hard and do what you can to become successful. You can be successful no matter what kind of background you have. I think that's so important to teach any kids—black, Indian, Mexican—even white kids that are poor. Let them know they can do much better in their lives if they just work hard and have integrity and learn to be honest; do things the right way in their lives.

Did you make a conscious decision to be nice to people or was it just a part of your DNA?

Well, I learned a lot from my dad. My dad was a businessman who owned his own business—an auto body repair shop. When I was with my dad, I would watch him and the way he was with people. I think he had a lot of integrity when he did his job. I know when people would come back with a problem, they'd say, "Domingo, this just doesn't seem quite right." He would go, "I'll do it again. We'll make sure it's right." He never said, "Oh, no. I've done it." He didn't have an ego that—if you're gonna attack him, then he was gonna tell you, "Yeah, I did it right," when he didn't. He was always good with people. That's why he had so many customers. He was good to them, and if he didn't do something right, he wanted to correct it. When I worked during the summer at his shop—being there with my dad, just answering the phone and cleaning windows—I got to see what he was all about. I think I learned a lot from him.

I never threw a club. I just wasn't going to be violent. I'm very stubborn, of course, but I think those are a few things that helped me to win golf tournaments. He wanted me to always play golf—to not throw clubs and to not be angry. Those are things he taught me as I grew up playing the game. I think it will definitely rub over into your life in what you become and how you are with people if you're nice or if you're not nice. I'm not perfect emotionally, but I'd rather be happy than be mad. (Laughs)

Throughout your playing career, you did a lot of things that people remember. For instance, in 1997, you were playing at the U.S. Women's Open at Pumpkin Ridge. It looked like you were going to win your first Open title, but things didn't work out for you late in the final round. As you came off the 18th green, a disabled man dropped a handful of ballpoint pens he was trying to sell. Despite your disappointment with coming so close to winning the U.S. Women's Open, you stopped and picked up the pens for him.

35

You were so gracious, and that was a moment that he will always remember. Do *you* remember that?

Well, I'm writing a book, too. It's coming out next year about Mother's Day, and we talk about that in my book. Yes, I do remember. I didn't remember it until it was brought up, and then I remembered it. You don't really remember moments in time unless somebody reminds you. Then, you do remember because you remember the feeling of what was happening at that time. I do remember that. I sure do.

The Nancy Lopez Golf Achievement Award has been given to a deserving LPGA player since 2007. What does it mean to you to have an award named after you because of your approachability, leadership, passion and giving—basically all the things that define you as a player and a person?

It's a great honor. I look at the players that have won it, and their goal is to *win* it. If that means that much to them, then, hopefully, that will make them a better person. You know, I was just talking to a lady from ESPN. As your golf game leaves you and you're not playing as competitive, you don't get very many awards any more. It's really an honor, especially to have your name on an award, but also to *receive* awards. espnW and ESPN Deportes just voted me the number one influential Hispanic Female. That's an honor for me because it means you're not forgotten. I think what means more to me than anything is not being forgotten. That was what I always wanted to do. I wanted to be that golfer and hoped that everybody would remember who I was, and I wanted to, hopefully, lead other people to golf to love the game the way that I did. That's important to me. That's a legacy I want to leave when I'm gone.

Career Notes: Nancy Lopez won 48 LPGA tournaments, including three LPGA Championships. She was a four-time LPGA Player of the Year. Despite playing in a less profitable era, Lopez still earned nearly $5.3-million on the LPGA Tour.

*   *   *

Annika Sorenstam is regarded by many as the greatest female golfer of her generation and perhaps the best of all-time. The native of Sweden won 72 LPGA tournaments including 10 majors during her Hall of Fame career. Sorenstam was ranked number one in the world from February 21, 2006, (the first official world ranking) to April 22, 2007.

There is no doubt in my mind that Annika Sorenstam ranks as one of the two or three best women's players in history. Sorenstam was so good that she was even invited to compete in a men's PGA Tour event in 2003. Her career numbers are staggering—especially when you consider that she retired in 2008 at age 37. Sorenstam was still one of the best players in the game when she stepped away from the Tour to focus on her business interests and her foundation.

I spoke on the phone with Annika Sorenstam on January 29, 2014.

Who was your first childhood idol?

It was Bjorn Borg. I played tennis. I competed in tennis for many years. He was a national hero, and I wanted to be like him. I would say him, for sure.

As a kid, were you captivated by all the winning or was it the way he played? Can you explain what it was about him that you liked?

Obviously, when you're winning, you're in the news; so then you become of interest to people. He was winning. For a little country like Sweden, for somebody to play on such a big stage and be the best in the world, it was inspiring. I grew up in a little town, and you start visualizing, "Hey, if somebody from my country can do it, maybe I can do it. You know, it looks like fun to be playing in sports." I think it was just that. Then also, he was popular. He was—and still is—a good guy. He represented a lot of things that I think Sweden was all about, like his consistency. He worked hard. He had a lot of sportsmanship. So, I would say that those are the biggest reasons.

Did you ever meet him when you were a young girl?

No, I never met him as a kid. I have met him since, but not as a kid.

Do you remember the first time you met him? Did he live up to your hopes and expectations?

Well, some people you just read about and see on TV, and then you meet them. It was later in life when I had been able to have some success myself, so he wasn't the first famous person that I ever met. That was helpful. He could say things that he could relate to my perspective—as far as winning majors or Grand Slams or whatever sport it is. I think that made it a little easier because then we could chat a little bit and not just stand there and not know what to say. (Laughs)

Obviously, you were an idol for a lot of young kids during your playing career. Did you think about that at the time? Were you aware of it?

Well, I guess when it's *you*, you don't necessarily think about those things. But, when you go to tournaments and people ask for your autograph, then you start seeing that. People name their child after you; then it's more real. But, when it's you, it's hard to look at it that way. I take it as a big compliment, of course. I try to do as much as I can to live up to that and hopefully don't disappoint anybody.

In talking with many of today's LPGA players, your name often comes up when I ask who inspired them when they were younger. How does that make you feel?

Well, I mean, it's flattering. It certainly is. Then you just start thinking, "Well, did I do the right things?" You're glad that you inspire people.

Borg was my *famous* role model, but I've always looked at *people* and tried to learn from them. So, like I said, it's flattering. Hopefully, you have given them some inspiration so that they can do it themselves. It's nice to talk to them, for sure.

Yani Tseng talked about what you have meant to her, both while growing up in Taiwan and now that she is a professional player competing in the United States. She talked about purchasing your home in Florida and the fact that you now serve as her mentor. She was rather infatuated with you. I am joking when I ask this, but did you ever feel like she was stalking you?

No. That never crossed my mind. When she joined the Tour, I didn't really play with her that much. I didn't know her very well. I was into my game. This was at the end of my career when I was starting to focus on other things, and I had an injury in 2007. But afterwards, at the end of my career, then she became more—well—we started to communicate a little bit. I started to understand her interest and realized that I had inspired her and that she wanted to chat with me a little bit. I was like, "I'm flattered, and I want to help." I do talk to some of the players today. I don't know if you call it a mentor perspective, but just to share my stories and help them avoid making the mistakes I did. It is tough to turn professional, and it is tough to be on the road. I've been though some of this stuff, and I enjoy sharing that.

When she told me about buying your home, she said one of the reasons she wanted it was because she wanted to fill up your trophy case with her own trophies. Did you know that?

Oh, yeah. We were kidding early on because in the house I had built a custom-made trophy case in the office, and she said, "I want to buy the house 'as is'." I said, "Well, hang on. Not everything [goes with the house]. (Laughs) That stuff is mine, and I'm taking my trophies with me." So, we were kidding about that. Then, after maybe six months, she started to win, and I said, "Hey, I don't think this is going to be a problem for you to fill up the trophy case." And, it wasn't. She started filling it up pretty quickly. Maybe I was another inspiration for her to win trophies and say, "Yeah, this is my goal. This is what I want to do."

Lorena Ochoa talked with me about the influence you've had on women's golf. Everyone realizes that you've had a world-wide impact on the game. You must be proud of that.

Oh, yes. Absolutely. I mean, it's tough to single anybody out, but I was part of an era that was a fun era for women's golf. I had an amazing ride. I had a career that I'm very proud of. It was the rivalries that I enjoyed—with Carrie Webb, with Se Ri Pak and a little bit with Lorena. It was a fun time. It really was. I think the game itself the last 20 years has just gotten better and better. It's fun to see the evolution of the game even though this is a little window in the golf history. Women's sports have grown, and it's fun to see that.

As a result of your charitable work, USA Weekend Magazine named you (along with Eli Manning) the most caring athlete in 2008. Your foundation (The ANNIKA Foundation) teaches children the importance of living healthy, active lifestyles. When you were considering retirement a few years ago, you said you wanted to devote more time to your foundation because you wanted it to have greater impact on children. You must have an overwhelming sense of pride about the job your foundation is doing.

I am proud. Again, it's hard to look at yourself and see the impact you have, but I do know that I give it my all. I'm thankful for having the opportunity to pursue my dream. Golf is a global dream, so we travel a lot. There are tournaments everywhere, so we're seen in a lot of places. It was fun. We had a full year. It was go, go, go all the time, but I thoroughly enjoyed it.

Nancy Lopez was another player who had tremendous impact on women's golf, and she talked with me about the jealousy other

players had towards her when she was winning all the time her first two years on the LPGA Tour. You went through a stretch in your career where you were nearly as unbeatable. Did you ever notice any jealousy or resentment from the other players when you were winning all the tournaments?

Um, well, I did realize that it was tough at the top—for a lot of reasons. You are the person that people try to copy or try pull down or try to beat or *want* to beat. I mean, that's what we all do. In every sport, I think you see that. But, I had never been in that situation, and when you're number one there's a lot of—I wouldn't say *scrutiny*—but they analyze what you do, what you say, what you wear and what you get. You know what I mean? There's no doubt there's some jealousy out there. There were things that I had to learn to just not take personally because it affects you. I had my goals. I wanted to achieve certain things. I was just determined to get there. People's opinions and people's perspective is what I learned not to get involved with. It was enough to just handle my career. Players come and go, but I knew what I wanted to do. Like I'd say, "When I leave the game, these are the things I want to have achieved. To do that, I gotta focus on my career." It is lonely at the top—as a lot of people say. I think I experienced that throughout the years. But, hopefully, you build a nice little circle of friends and your family and a network of people you can talk to. That can help you through those things.

Career Notes: Annika Sorenstam recorded her first career victory in the 1995 U.S. Women's Open. Annika, who set numerous records during her career, won the LPGA Player of the Year Award eight times and had the lowest scoring average on the Tour six times. Sorenstam became one of the few players—male or female—to break 60 in an official event when she shot a 59 on March 16, 2001, at Moon Valley Country Club in Phoenix. In 2005, she tied Nancy Lopez's LPGA record by winning five straight tournaments. A model of consistency, Sorenstam was the first LPGA player to record 29 consecutive under-par rounds (Her record was tied by Lydia Ko in 2015). With more than $22.5-million dollars in LPGA Tour earnings, Annika is the only LPGA player to have crossed the $20-million mark.

*   *   *

Yani Tseng was the youngest player—male or female—to win five

major championships in golf. After beginning play on the LPGA Tour in 2008, she won her fifth major in 2011—at the age of 22 years, 6 months, and 8 days. A native of Taiwan, Tseng was the world's top-ranked women's player from February 14, 2011, to March 24, 2013. That span of 109 weeks is the second longest streak in history, bettered only by Lorena Ochoa's 157 consecutive weeks.

The last several years have been difficult for Tseng. As of October 27, 2015, she has not won a tournament since March of 2012. When Tseng captured the Kia Classic that year, she had won three of the first five 2012 LPGA tournaments and appeared to be on her way to winning Player of the Year honors for the third straight year. However, she has now gone without a victory for more than three years. Tseng turned to her childhood idol, Annika Sorenstam, for support and advice. Although she had a pair of second-place finishes in 2015, Tseng has been unable to regain her winning form.

I spoke with Yani Tseng on August 18, 2011, prior to the LPGA tournament at Pumpkin Ridge Golf Club. At that time, she was the top-ranked women's golfer in the world.

You have made it known that Annika Sorenstam was your childhood idol, and I understand you now have developed a relationship with her.

Yeah, she's my hero all the time. When I was young, I'd look at her and I'd say, "Oh, one day I want to play with her." That's kind of my motivation to get into the LPGA and play with all the best players on the Tour. It's all the younger players' dream to come here and then play in the tournament and enjoy it here and meet all the greatest players in the world.

What was it like to finally meet your childhood idol?

Actually, the first year I was really, really nervous. I didn't know, "What should I say?" I was just so nervous that I couldn't focus on golf. I just kept watching her play. It was so different. But, now, I kind of am used to it. And, then to be a friend with her, it's my honor. Even now when I see her, I am still nervous to talk to her.

Do you recall the very first time you saw Annika in person?

The very first time I saw her was at the U.S. Open when I was 13, so that was nine years ago. At that time, I'd just say, "Oh, wow! That's Annika!" I just knew she was number one in the world. I just told myself, "Oh, one day I want to play with number one in the world." After a couple days, I knew more about her, and then I just told myself, "This is my goal—to be an LPGA player. Then, I can play with her."

You eventually got to play in a tournament with her, didn't you?

Yeah, it was in her tournament in Sweden. That was the first time I played with her. We played a practice round for nine holes, and I was really nervous. All I remember—I was very nervous. I didn't know what I should say. It was like a dream. It was unbelievable. After nine holes, I was like, "I just played with Annika?" It was like a dream. It was unbelievable.

You even purchased Annika's house in Florida. That's incredible. How did that happen?

I don't know. I never thought that was going to happen. Two years ago, I didn't feel that I can afford that much money to buy that big house. Our family, we decided, "I mean this is *Annika's* house." And then, whoop! I want to travel in her footsteps, and I love the house, too. I just told myself and told my family, "I think I can do it. I just need to keep playing good, and I think I can afford this house." I returned back to the office. I saw the empty trophy case. I told myself I need to work hard to fill the trophy case.

The home you purchased is located very near the home Annika built for her family. You are now neighbors, and I understand she has become a mentor to you.

Yeah, sometimes I go to her house visiting her, and sometimes she visits me at my house. We're just like a hundred yards away. She's very nice. She always tells me, "If you have any questions, you know where I live. Just knock on my door, and ask me any questions." That's really, really sweet.

Obviously, with the number one ranking in the world and all of the success you have had at such a young age, there are many young girls that look up to you. What does that mean to you?

It's really different because I'm still 22. I still have a big idol I can look at. But, I wish I can be a good model for them. I want to play good, and I want to be a good person. It doesn't matter if its inside the rope or outside the rope, I wish I can help them out if I can tell them my experiences about everything. When I go back to Taiwan, I always have something I can tell them, so those are the things where I can help.

Career Notes: Yani Tseng was the LPGA's Player of the Year in 2010 and 2011. Through September, 2015, Tseng has won 15 LPGA tournaments, including five majors. She has earned more than $10-million on the LPGA Tour.

*   *   *

Lorena Ochoa is unquestionably the best golfer ever to come out of Mexico to compete on the LPGA Tour. A native of Guadalajara, Mexico, Ochoa replaced Annika Sorenstam as the world's top-ranked golfer on April 23, 2007, and she remained number one until May 2, 2010—a record span of 157 weeks. Ochoa announced her retirement from the LPGA Tour in April, 2010. She made the announcement while still ranked as the best female golfer in the world.

Count me among the many fans of Lorena Ochoa. A remarkable player during her relatively short time on the LPGA Tour, I found her to be quite similar in charm to a player from a previous generation, Nancy Lopez. Every single time I interviewed Ochoa, I found her to be absolutely delightful. She was engaging, funny, and—above all—the best player in the world. Yes, Ochoa was the complete package. I was among the many fans who were disappointed when she stunned the golf world by announcing she was leaving the LPGA Tour at age 28. Although Ochoa remains actively involved in women's golf, I believe the LPGA Tour has not quite been the same since Ochoa said goodbye.

In early 2011, I emailed my questions to one of Lorena Ochoa's representatives who asked Lorena the questions and recorded her responses. I received an mp3 file with Lorena Ochoa's responses in April, 2011.

Who was your first childhood idol?

It was Nancy Lopez. I remember when I used to practice, and on the weekend, we used to watch every bit of golf on TV. Every time, I see Nancy Lopez. I remember it. I see her playing. I see her winning tournaments. What I mostly admire about her—always—was how nice she was with all the fans and all the time she spent hanging out with us and being, you know, just nice with all the players as well as the fans.

You mention Nancy, but did you have others that you looked up to as you grew up?

In different occasions in my career, I admired different players—on the men's side, too. One of my favorites later on was Betsy King. I had the chance to become friends with her and spend time together. Another one is Annika Sorenstam. We all admired her as somebody that gave so much to the game and so much to all of the players. Annika has been—always—an inspiration to me.

You obviously met your childhood heroes since they were pro golfers.

I feel very blessed because I had the opportunity on different occasions to meet the three of them. Nancy Lopez, we got to play at her tournament in Atlanta. I was really honored to receive an award that she gave to me when I was a rookie player in the LPGA. Later on, I spent time with Betsy, and then at the end of my career, I was playing together with Annika. You can learn from everybody. You can learn from each one of them. It's been—for me—just wonderful to have the opportunity to spend time with them—to learn and to listen to their advice.

Somebody that we all admire—in my case, I always said that I wanted to be like her when I grow up—is Juli Inkster. She's one of my favorites. She's somebody that's been very instrumental in my profession. And, she is very nice, very kind, very competitive. Juli is still around here. She was playing very strong and was giving all she could to the game. So, I guess since Juli is out there, she's one of my favorites, and I have only nice things to say about her. She's an inspiration, and hopefully we are friends for many, many more years.

Career Notes: Lorena Ochoa first appeared on the LPGA Tour in 2002. She captured LPGA Rookie of the Year honors in 2003. She earned the Tour's Player of the Year Award in each of her last four full seasons. Ochoa won 27 LPGA tournaments, including a pair of majors. The leading money winner on the LPGA Tour in 2006, 2007 and 2008, Ochoa earned more than $14.8-million on the Tour. She serves as host of the annual Lorena Ochoa Invitational in Mexico City, which is considered one of the most significant sporting events in Mexico each year.

* * *

5

Just Be Yourself

Ken Griffey, Jr. was one of the best baseball players ever to don a major league uniform. A veteran of 22 big-league seasons with the Mariners, Reds and White Sox, "Junior" could do it all. He hit 630 home runs, which ranks sixth all-time. He was as stellar with the glove as he was with the bat. Griffey, Jr. won ten straight Gold Gloves for his play in the outfield in the 1990s. Following in the footsteps of his father, Ken Griffey (a star with the Big Red Machine in Cincinnati), Junior spent little time in the minors before advancing to the major leagues. He made his big league debut at age 19 in April of 1989. With his baby-faced looks, the teenager soon earned the nickname, "The Kid."

I think it is important for you to know that without Ken Griffey, Jr.'s contributions while wearing a Mariners' uniform, there would no longer be a Major League Baseball team in the Pacific Northwest. Without question, 1995 was the year baseball was saved in Seattle, and Griffey, Jr. played a significant role in making sure the team stayed in the Emerald City. The Mariners had been hemorrhaging money for years. It was believed that if they did not reach agreement with King County to replace the outdated and tomblike Kingdome, the team would be sold and moved out of the Northwest. While civic leaders and the club were trying to drum up support for construction of a new stadium, the Mariners were struggling on the field. In late May, Griffey suffered a broken wrist while running into the wall to make one another of his amazing circus catches. He was sidelined for eleven weeks and missed 73 games. In early August, the Mariners were 13 games behind the AL-Western Division-leading Angels and rarely drawing crowds of significant number.

But, in mid-August, Griffey returned to the lineup. Nine days after his return, he hammered his first career walk-off homer to give the Mariners a 9-7 win over the Yankees. Some say that blow was the catalyst for Seattle's remarkable end-of-season run. The Mariners and Angels ended the regular season in a tie. In a one-game, win-or-go-home playoff before more than 52,000 now-rabid Seattle fans, the Mariners beat the Angels 9-1 to advance to postseason play for the first time in franchise history.

In the best-of-five American League Division Series, the Mariners dropped the first two games to the Yankees in New York. However, Seattle came back to win three straight at home. In the deciding fifth game, Griffey slid home safely on an Edgar Martinez double in the bottom of the 11th to give the Mariners the ballgame 6-5 and the series three games to two. The photograph of Griffey—wearing a broad smile while peeking out from the bottom of the celebratory dogpile at home plate—is one of the most iconic in Seattle sports history. Griffey was clearly the hero of the series. He blasted five home runs in the five ALDS games against the Yankees.

While Seattle lost the ensuing American League Championship Series to Cleveland in six games, fan enthusiasm generated throughout the Northwest during the Mariners' incredible stretch drive led to an agreement to construct a new ballpark. Because of Griffey's contributions during the Mariners' remarkable run, Safeco Field is known today as "The House That Griffey Built."

I spoke with Ken Griffey, Jr. on June 12, 2011, in Beaverton, Oregon, at the Caddies 4 Cure charity event. I was also in attendance at Safeco Field in Seattle on August 10, 2013, when Griffey, Jr. was inducted into the Seattle Mariners Hall of Fame.

Ken, as you grew up, did you have a boyhood idol?

I didn't really have one. I grew up in a house where you would see stars day in and day out. From age eight, my dad was like, "Just be yourself. I don't want you to be Joe Morgan. I don't want you to be Pete Rose. I don't want you to be Johnny Bench. I just want you to be my son." That was the biggest thing. He was like, "It's hard enough just being yourself. You don't want to act like somebody else. Have your own sort of style and flair—if you have it. If you don't, you don't. But, I just want you to be George Kenneth Griffey, Jr." When he said that, it was like, "Okay. He doesn't want me to be him. He just wants me to be me."

My brother's a big Willie Randolph fan. Willie wanted to borrow a quarter because the pay phone was in the clubhouse, and he didn't have but a dollar bill. Willie said, "I need a quarter." My brother said, "I got one." Willie said, "Okay, but I only got a dollar." My brother said, "Okay. That'll work. (Laughs) My brother got a 75-cent increase, so he's always been a Willie fan. Rickey Henderson and Dave Winfield were always good. But, I didn't have anybody as a kid that wasn't nice to me, so I liked everybody. Everybody was so open and played with us kids. I'd be out there playing catch with Rickey Henderson.

Growing up, many of us imagined being some pro athlete in our backyards or in our driveways. So, you say that you didn't have that experience when you were a kid?

My dad just said to be myself. The greatest thing is the buzzer-beater for basketball and, for baseball, the walk-off home run like Joe Carter hit (to win the '93 World Series). We all dream about that. That's what baseball is and what sports is. It's going out there having fun playing. Nobody goes up there thinking, "I can make a whole lotta money, and I can be a Hall of Famer." No. As a little kid, you love baseball—or you love football—or you love basketball. There is no shoe (endorsement) deal. There is no glove deal. You just love the sport.

Parents have to understand that not everybody's gonna make it to the pros. I just want *my* son to go play. I coach baseball. They're seven, eight and nine. I have a nine-year-old (Tevin). I'm not the head coach, but they still ask me all the questions. The head coach will come to me and say, "Hey, Ken. What do you think?" I'm like, "You're the head coach." A parent will say, "What do you think? I think I need my son to do this." I say, "No. What you need your son to do is just go have fun." The greatest thing about baseball for that level is, "Who brings the snacks?" That's all they care about. They know the last out. They jump up and down no matter if they win or lose 'cause they know that it's time to get something to eat and drink. The Capri Suns come out, the Snickers, whatever. And, they're gone. They're happy. That's what sports is about. We take it so serious half the time. They get so involved in numbers. As a parent, 630 home runs don't mean anything. It's the smile on my kids' faces when they do something that means the most.

When I coach, I help everybody. There were some great coaches—not only on our team—but on a couple other teams. One of our kids made a great catch down the left field line, and this guy, Roger, he was the first base coach for the other team. He ran all the way over there, gave the kid a high five, and ran all the way back. I'm like, "That's a coach. That's a guy who coaches and enjoys what he does. He's not worried about winning or losing." Who cares about winning and losing at age five, six, seven, eight, nine, ten? I told my son, Trey (about to enter his senior year of high school), "I don't care about losing until you get to college. I want you to develop because there are 50 state champions for each level in high school, so you got like 300 state champions. There is *one* national championship in college. There is *one* World Series winner. That's when you worry about it. Right now, just go out and have fun, and be *you*."

A lot of kids in Seattle still wear your #24 jersey. Was there any sense of responsibility you felt knowing that kids looked up to you, or were you still just being yourself?

No, I was just bein' me. Like I said, it's tough enough to be you. You can't be anybody else, so just have fun. Like everybody else, there are good days and bad days to meet people. You might catch somebody at a bad time. It happens. There are times we're just trying to walk around and do things. Since day one, I've told my wife, "It's easier for you to go out and do what you need to do, than me. I've gotta *plan* when I'm going to the mall." I ask myself, "Do I really want to go to the mall? Do I *really* need that shirt? Nah!" (Laughs) But, now we have an understanding. For every three things that *she* buys, she has to buy me a shirt. (Laughs)

You have a daughter. How do you handle being a parent of a girl involved in sports when in their games it seems good sportsmanship is just as important as winning?

Having a daughter in sports makes you really appreciate sports because it's so tough to them. They're so *nice* to each other. My daughter (Taryn) is so nice. I'm like, "No! I need you to attack! I need you to embarrass her!" And, she's like, "Daaaddddd." I tell my boys that, and they're all like a pit bull. They're like, "All right!" I tell my girl, and she's lookin' at me like, "No. That's not gonna happen." I get so frustrated with her. I look at my wife and I go, "That is definitely *your* child." (Laughs)

Have you had major league players approach you to say you were their boyhood idol, and if so, can you name names?

Yeah, I get that all the time. It's fun. I played with Cecil Fielder, and now I've played against his son, Prince. To some of the guys, I say, "I played against your dad, Tony Gwynn, and now you, Tony Gwynn, Jr." So, they're looking at me. I'm looking at them. We all in the same boat. We know what it's like being the son of a major leaguer. It's a little alumni club, but everybody thinks that everybody's competing, like, "I need to be better than *this* son." But, we're just trying to go out there and play as hard as we can for our team and do what we need to do for our team to win. I still talk to Prince. I still talk to Tony Gwynn, Jr. Prince's son goes to school with my kids. We sit there, and I tell him, "There's no competition." I get more excited about what other people do than what I've done. I've done it. I lived through it, so I don't look at it that way.

People in sports have to be more relaxed. So many people are angry about their teams or about this guy. They're trying to go out there as an organization to be as productive as possible.

The following quote is from Ken Griffey, Jr. during a news conference held in Seattle on August 9, 2013, the day he was enshrined in the Seattle Mariners Hall of Fame. Griffey, a childhood hero for many children in the Pacific Northwest when he played for the Mariners, was asked by a reporter if athletes have any responsibility knowing that kids idolize them and if he ever thought about that when he was playing.

At 19, I just wanted to *survive.* (Laughs) I don't really look at it at that time as being a role model. I just wanted to go out and play baseball. At that time, I didn't have a family. It was just me, and I was trying to figure things out… And, having a responsibility? I understand it now more than I did at age 19. It's on the job training. You try to be the best player and try to be the best person. Sometimes, people misunderstood you. You're misunderstood day in and day out. But, for the most part, I just wanted to be me. I grew up in a household that my dad let me be me.

As you get older and start having kids, you understand a little more of what you mean to people. I found that out firsthand with my youngest, Tevin. His favorite player is Michael Vick. He got a chance to meet him, and I got to see his *look* when Michael Vick ran over to him. Having so many parents looking at their kids look at *me* that way, then, to have me look at *my* child look at somebody *else* that way—was pretty humbling. After the game, Mike gave him his jersey. Tevin wore it from Jacksonville all the way home. Like I said, I understand it now—having it happen to me—more than I did when I was 19.

At that same news conference, Griffey, Jr. revealed why he often wore his baseball cap backwards. It was because he desired to emulate his dad.

The only reason why I wore my hat backwards was my dad had a 'fro. I couldn't wear his hat because it would bounce and hit me in the face. So, I just turned it around and wore it backwards. From that point on, I just started wearing my hat backwards. It wasn't like I tried to have a fashion statement or anything else—even though it ended up being one. For the most part, I just wanted to be like every other kid—wear their dad's hat and pants and shoes and things like that. He had a size eight head, and I had like a five and three-quarters. It just wasn't gonna fit. (Laughs)

The following quote is from Ken Griffey, Jr. speaking during the on-field ceremony when he was inducted into the Seattle Mariners Hall of Fame on August 10, 2013. In front of a sellout crowd at Safeco Field, Griffey, Jr. paid tribute to his parents for raising him to be a good kid and good parent.

My mom and dad were unbelievable. They let me be a kid. Basketball season came around, I played basketball. Football [season, I played] football. They weren't concerned about me making it to the big leagues. They wanted me to be a kid and enjoy the things that kids do. He is the one player that I looked at and wanted to be like.

And, then I have my mom who—while my dad was playing—drove me and my little brother to all our sporting events. I didn't realize how much dedication that my mom had until I retired. I went home, and I sat on my couch for the first two days. My wife looked at me and said, "Well, we've gotta go to Tennessee, Atlanta, Chicago, back to Atlanta, Augusta, and then home." I looked at her and said, "How long we gonna be gone?" Then, she says, "That'll be for the next three weeks." I looked at her like, "I'm not goin'. (Brief pause)" I went.

Career Notes: Ken Griffey, Jr. was a 13-time All-Star and the MVP of the 1992 All-Star Game. Over his career, he batted .284 and drove in

1,836 runs, which ranks 15th all-time. Griffey, Jr. was voted the Most Valuable Player of the American League in 1997. He led the league in home runs four times, including 1997 and 1998 when he hit 56 homers in back-to-back seasons. From 1996 to 1999, he averaged 52.25 home runs per season. He also tied a major league record by slugging a home run in eight straight games. Griffey drove in an incredible *433* runs over a three year span (140 in '96, 147 in '97, and 146 in '98). It's no wonder Griffey, Jr. won seven Silver Slugger Awards in the 1990s. He was a three-time champion of the Home Run Derby at the All-Star Game. Named to MLB's All-Century team, Griffey, Jr. was enshrined in the Seattle Mariners Hall of Fame in 2013. He was inducted into the Cincinnati Reds Hall of Fame the following year. There is little doubt that he will be headed to Cooperstown in his first year of eligibility in 2016.

* * *

6

Make The Bread

Mario Andretti overcame long odds to become one of the very best—and most popular—drivers in racing. For several years after the end of World War II, Andretti lived with his family in a refugee camp in Lucca, Tuscany. While living there, he got a chance to see his first Grand Prix race. Then, when Mario was 15, his family came to the United States and settled in Nazareth, Pennsylvania. On a small nearby track, Mario began to seriously pursue his dream of becoming a race car driver. He ended up as one of the most successful drivers of all time.

Of the thousands of athletes I've spent time with in my four decades of covering sports, there are few I have enjoyed being around more than Mario Andretti. It might be because when I raced slot cars as a kid in the 1960s, I pretended that my car was being driven by Mario Andretti. Also, I still imagine myself to be "Mario" every time I stomp hard on the gas pedal when I'm driving. Simply put, Mario was a hero for most racing fans of my generation, and it's always special to meet one of your idols. However, Mario is more than just a man who graces the history books as one of racing's all-time greats. I see him as a man who exhibits total grace. A fiery competitor during his racing days, he is now is soft-spoken and mild-mannered. When he speaks, it comes across that he is proud of his heritage—both his family roots and his roots in racing. He understands where he's come from and how fortunate he is to have lived this amazing life. Mario also understands his place in racing history and could make the case that he is the best driver of all time. But, he doesn't toot his own horn in an attempt to promote himself. He speaks with humility. He shows respect for his peers—even long-time rival, A.J. Foyt, with whom he's had some notable disagreements over the years. Every time I had the opportunity to interview Mario, he was incredibly generous with his time. On each occasion, I determined that Mario is not only a great champion, but a wonderful man.

I have discussed many subjects with Mario Andretti through the years, but I spoke with him about his childhood heroes during a telephone conversation on December 8, 2011.

Mario, who was your first boyhood idol?

Clearly, it was Alberto Ascari. He was a very prominent champion in the early '50s. His career really came into prominence in the late '40s, and he was twice World Champion before the mid-'50s. He was killed in 1955. It was in Monza testing. It was ironic because he escaped death in the Monaco Grand Prix in Monte Carlo the week before. He flew into the harbor. Something happened, and he went through the chicane. He went through the hay bales, and the car went right into the harbor. He had to swim back to land to survive. Then, he's killed at Monza. As far as the individual that was really, truly 100% responsible for me creating a path for my life and my career, that was Alberto Ascari. He impressed me to the degree that I just wanted to emulate him. I'd say, "If I could just be like him." And, that stayed with me forever.

The ironic thing is that when he was inducted in the International Motorsports Hall of Fame, I had the privilege of presenting the plaque—posthumously—to his son, Antonio. I had never met Alberto Ascari. As a kid, I would dream about meeting him, but then I got to know his family a little bit including his wife, Mietta. Alberto Ascari was an incredibly strong influence on me, and I'm very thankful for him.

Ascari once won nine consecutive championship races. You would have been about twelve years old at that time. Reading about

Ascari's success in the newspapers and magazines, what did it mean to you to see him win all of those races?

Well, that's what drew me to him, you know, the way he was described—"ice in his veins." He was always very cool, very calm, while he was charging like mad. In 1954, near the refugee camp where we stayed, there was a garage where my brother and I used to hang out. And, they knew how passionate we were about racing. They took Aldo and me to Monza to watch the Italian Grand Prix. That's the very first time I saw the Grand Prix cars there. Ascari finished third, but the Ferrari was entirely outclassed by the Mercedes at that point. He fought so hard. He was the only one who had the car out of shape coming out of the corners—tail hanging out and all that. He showed so much heart. Every part of it was very inspiring—how successful he was and also how much of a fighter he was, even when he was with inferior cars. I loved his versatility in driving sports cars and wanting to interact with the media. You know, stuff like that.

You were 15 when Ascari was killed. How did you react when you heard the news?

It was like losing your closest family member. It was just an incredible void. I just could hardly believe that—a totally sad moment. But, it was happening all too often during this period. Fatalities were very common. This was his turn, I guess.

What did it mean to you to have the chance to meet the Ascari family?

Well, it was so special, not only because I felt that it was very precious for me. I saw an appreciation on the other side as well. Many times the champions of the '50s are somewhat forgotten. For them to see me as a contemporary so infatuated with his exploits and his career—how important it was for me to be inspired by him and to pursue racing—that was the best part of it. It seemed like it was a mutual admiration on both sides. Those are such special moments in anyone's life, certainly my life. So, that's the only way I can describe it.

You were an idol to many young racing fans in the 1960s and 1970s. Did you think about being a hero to that entire generation of fans?

Well, I don't know if I can really put it in that perspective. The only thing that was always forever present to me was the fact that when I came to America, I would go to races. I remember clearly being a very timid young man. In Trenton, New Jersey, there was an Indy Car race with all the champions—Eddie Sachs, Roger Ward, all the greats of the time. And, I was like maybe sixteen. I go to approach Eddie Sachs, and I walked up to him. I was so scared, and *he* actually started a conversation. He was so nice. I never forgot that. As the career progressed for me, I got to the point where people were approaching me. My entire life, I remembered that conversation with Sachs and how important that was to me. I figure if I'm in that position, I would definitely do the same. It affects different people in different ways, of course. But, at the same time, it's really a responsibility, and it's a privilege. I always feel today when people come up and want your autograph or they express something about your career, it's very flattering. It's the ultimate compliment. But, for me, it all stems from what I experienced as a young man with Eddie Sachs.

Sadly, Eddie Sachs died in a fiery crash at Indianapolis. It had to be difficult for fans to become closely attached to race drivers in that era because so many died tragically.

Well, yeah. That's very much so. But, to me, it also showed how courageous these drivers were by confronting something while driven by so much passion knowing that this has such an incredibly dangerous aspect on the other side. That was part of the allure and the challenge that I had in the sport. Maybe we can beat the odds. The ultimate aspect of how I justify myself being in the sport and facing the risk is to look at risk-reward. I felt that nowhere in life could I get back, from whatever effort—whatever job I would choose—the rewards that I would get out of race driving. So, I took the calculated risk with my eyes wide open. There was no Plan B for my career. When asked what would be my Plan B, I always said, "Well, maybe becoming a fighter pilot." But, being involved in the ultimate in performance and having the opportunity to engage and be in control of something that can be so violent, to me, that was the ultimate challenge. That's what I looked forward to every single day of my career.

Like father, like son. Your son Michael became a racing champion in his own right. Do you know if you were his boyhood idol, or were you just "dad"?

I think I was too close to him. I think I was just dad, really. I'm not even sure who his idols were. You'd almost have to ask him. He was so close to it. He was born into this environment.

(Laughs) When Michael was in elementary school, the teacher was asking the kids, "Okay, what does your dad do?" It came to Michael, and she said, "What does your dad do?" He said, "He goes to the airport and makes bread." (Laughs) That's because he used to ask me, "Dad, where you goin' now?" I'd say, "I'm going to the airport. Gotta make the bread." So, he says, "He goes to the airport and makes bread!" (Laughs) I'm sure that I was not his idol. I'm not his idol by going out and making bread. (Laughs)

Career Notes: Mario Andretti earned his first Indy Car victory in the 1965 Hoosier Grand Prix. Andretti finished third in the 1965 Indianapolis 500 to earn Rookie of the Year honors. That same year, he won his first United States Auto Club championship at age 25. Mario won two more USAC championships and later added a CART championship. His four championships are tied for second-most all-time in USAC/CART/IndyCar. When Andretti won the 1978 Formula One championship while driving for Team Lotus, he became the first driver to win championships in both USAC/Indy Car and F1. Mario

Andretti is the only driver to win the Daytona 500 (1967), Indy 500 (1969), and also win a Formula One World Championship (1978). Andretti still ranks second all-time in USAC/CART/IndyCar victories (52) behind only A.J. Foyt (67). The Associated Press named Mario and Foyt as the Co-Drivers of the 20th Century. Andretti was inducted into the Motorsports Hall of Fame of America in 1990 and the International Motorsports Hall of Fame in 2000.

*   *   *

Michael Andretti won more races than any other driver in the now-defunct Championship Auto Racing Teams series. Michael's 42 CART victories places him third all-time in USAC/CART/IndyCar wins behind A.J. Foyt (67) and his father, Mario Andretti (52).

I first interviewed Michael Andretti at Portland International Raceway in the 1980s when the Champ Cars made their annual visit to the Rose City. During his days as a driver, I always felt Michael seemed just a little less "media-friendly" than his father. In his dealings with the media (or at least with me), Michael only smiled occasionally. While he was always pleasant enough, I got the sense that he did not really enjoy having to talk with reporters and might have been doing so simply to fulfill his obligations to sponsors. I remember once thinking to myself that it had to be difficult for Michael to live up to the high standards set by his famous father. Michael did admit to me in interviews through the years that being an Andretti had its good points and bad points as far as racing was concerned. Sure, it had opened doors for him, but being an Andretti also came with very high expectations.

In the years Michael and Mario were teammates driving the K-Mart/ Havoline cars for Newman-Haas, I observed that reporters often preferred to interview Mario because he had the higher profile. I wondered if that bothered Michael or if he was actually happy that his dad garnered most of the attention, which —in turn—took the pressure off him. Several times I walked away after interviewing Michael thinking that racing in the shadow of his legendary father had to put a lot of pressure on him. I wondered if Michael was trying so hard to live up to the Andretti name that he wasn't enjoying himself. I now believe that—regardless of what I might have thought previously—he truly was having the time of his life. Michael was doing what he loved, and he was very good at it. Did he win as many races as his father? Not quite. Was he pretty darned successful? You better believe it.

Michael Andretti is now one of the most respected owners in auto racing. His team has won multiple championships. He has become one of the most powerful men in IndyCar racing. During my most recent conversation with him, it struck me that Michael seems quite satisfied with his place in auto racing history. I was also happy to see him smile several times. I spoke with Michael Andretti in the Honda Hospitality tent prior to the Grand Prix of St. Petersburg (Florida) on the morning of March 27, 2015.

Michael, I asked your father if he knew who you first idolized as a young boy. He said I would have to ask you, so here we go. Who was your very first boyhood idol?

It had to be my dad. It ended up being him my whole young life, for sure, because he was my hero at that time.

Your dad told me the story about you—as a kid—telling your teacher about what your father did for a living.

Oh yeah, I said, "He's a baker because he makes bread." He always used to say he was going out "to make bread", so I thought he was a baker, yeah. (Laughs)

Your dad means so much to racing fans. Heck, even *I* grew up wanting to be Mario Andretti. For you—his son—what was it like for you to be living in the same house with your boyhood idol?

You know, it depended how you looked at it. There was good and bad to it, you know. When you're the "son of Mario" and you're driving in the profession where he's a legend, it put more pressure on me. So, I had to deal with that. But, I learned to deal with it pretty early. I think it helped me when I got to the bigger points of racing where there's really a lot more pressure. That's one good thing. I always felt like I could always handle the pressure. I think maybe part of the reason I could handle pressure was because I grew up with it.

With the success you had as a driver and now as a successful IndyCar owner, people acknowledge your impact on the sport. What does it all mean to you?

I mean, I don't know. I'm the luckiest guy in the world. That's the way I feel. I feel like I had a great driving career. I loved every moment of it. I love the sport, and I love that I've been able to have the opportunity to stay involved with the sport at a high level beyond my driving years as an owner, a race promoter and all that. I'm very lucky to be doing what I love to do.

Career Notes: Michael Andretti was inducted into the Motorsports Hall of Fame of America in 2008. Andretti won the 1991 CART championship during one of the years he was a teammate of his father at Newman-Haas. As his days as a driver were winding down, Michael moved into ownership, forming a partnership with Kim Green and Kevin Savoree to create Andretti Green Racing. The team was restructured in 2009 and renamed Andretti Autosport.

As an owner, Michael Andretti has been affiliated with four IndyCar championships. Andretti Green Racing won the team championship in 2004 (Tony Kanaan), 2005 (Dan Wheldon) and 2007 (Dario Franchitti). Andretti Autosport won the 2012 IndyCar championship with Ryan Hunter-Reay behind the wheel. While Michael never won the Indy 500 as a driver, he has won "The Greatest Spectacle in Racing" three times as an owner. Andretti drivers that have parked in Victory Lane and taken the traditional drink from the winner's bottle of milk were Dan Wheldon (2005), Dario Franchitti (2007) and Ryan Hunter-Reay (2014).

*   *   *

Marco Andretti is the son of CART champion Michael Andretti and grandson of four-time USAC/CART champion and Indy 500 winner Mario Andretti. Marco drove the #27 Andretti Autosport IndyCar for his father in 2015. He finished ninth in the point standings.

I certainly haven't spent as much time talking with Marco Andretti as I have his father and grandfather, but I find him to be a chip off the old block—and that's saying something when you're talking about the Andretti family! He is well-spoken and extremely passionate about racing. I admire his ability to remain positive even though he has managed only two victories in his first 167 IndyCar races. I can hardly imagine the pressure Marco must feel—whether he admits it to anyone—to follow in the championship footsteps of the last two generations of Andretti race car drivers.

Marco has repeatedly come close to breaking through. He has Top 10 finishes in more than half of his career starts (85 times in 167 races). That indicates he is an outstanding driver, someone who can keep his car on the track and stay out of trouble, while working through traffic at 200 miles per hour. Marco has driven the wheels off his race cars, and I remain confident in his ability to win races on a more consistent basis.

I interviewed Marco Andretti by phone on April 24, 2014, while he was in Birmingham preparing for the Grand Prix of Alabama.

Let's go back to your early days as a child. Can you name your very first boyhood idol?

Oh, man. You're really gonna make me pick right now, aren't you? (Laughs) I don't know. I guess at the time I was really close to my father. I wasn't around for too long so that I was able to understand my grandfather's career. You know, I was very young. But, it's probably a close battle between my father and my grandfather. And, then there's obviously Ayrton Senna back in the day. He was hugely influential, and always has been—to *every* driver. You know, I think those are probably my top three.

Young boys like to be around race cars and also like to spend time with their parents. As a kid, you were around race cars and around your dad, who just happened to be one of the top drivers on the CART circuit. That had to be pretty cool for you growing up.

Oh, absolutely. I was definitely privileged to be able to be so close. I was even sitting in the debrief room and could really watch things firsthand. That was a cool part of it for me—having racing in the family. Obviously, really being able to see him away from the track was very important once I became a racing driver, you know, to see his natural approach to certain events.

Your dad was a champion. You got to see him win races. Even though you were young, you were able to see what it takes to be a champion. That had to be a good learning experience.

Yes, it's a learning experience that I better step my game up. That's what that is. But, obviously, it's big shoes to fill. Like I said, I was very lucky to have that in the family and have a lot of success with both my grandfather and my father. It was—and still is—cool. One of my favorite things to do is look back at their careers and different races and stuff like that. But, to be there and be able to witness it was definitely special.

You are now driving for your father at Andretti Autosport. Does that change things at all?

If there's anybody you'd want to be your boss, why not have it be your dad? Having an idol as your boss, you want to emulate a lot of what he does anyway. When he's literally the one in charge, then you have to do a lot of what he wants you to do. But, it's good to know that he's pointing you in the right direction.

Mario was a great champion, and everybody loves him. He's been an outstanding representative of the sport for many years. Are you able to separate Mario—your grandfather—from Mario—the racing legend?

Um, I don't know. I'm often reminded of it. Just being around him, there's always somebody there that really brings that home to me— what he is and what he's done. To be honest, I don't really need that person to tell me about Mario Andretti's history. I *know*. I know what he's done, and I listen to his advice. He probably doesn't think I listen to everything, but I definitely listen to everything that he's saying. I appreciate a lot of input.

There are many young racing fans who consider you their idol. What do you think of that?

Well, I'm honored. Being where I am right now in my career, I see that this is a very frustrating point in my career because of not having enough wins. But, I think when you look at me—and if you look at laps led—we have been competitive. We just haven't really capitalized. To have fan worship at such a young age, I'm just honored. I mean, there's nothing else I can say. I guess a lot of people still really believe in me and that we can achieve great things. Obviously, I need to have that believe in myself, and a lot is possible.

You watched your dad when he drove in the Indy 500 in 2003. Then, just three years later, you made your Indy Car debut. While at Indy in 2003, did you ever dream that you would become the youngest-ever Indy Car driver just three years later?

I don't think so, man. I'm actually sitting right now in exactly the same spot that I was in 2005 when we made the decision to do it. I remember team co-owners Kim Green, Kevin Savoree and my father all sitting me down right here in Hospitality at the race track and saying, "Are you ready? We think you're ready. Are you ready? Do you want to do it now, or do you want to do it next year? We want ya to drive for us." I was like, "Are you guys kidding me? I'm ready. I don't want to drive an Indy Lights car anymore." (Laughs) And, that was after only three Indy Lights wins. I was honored that they believed in me at a young age. I was like, "I want to do this. I'm ready." I signed the contract not too much later after we had that conversation.

Career Notes: In 2006, at age 19 years, 167 days, Marco Andretti became the youngest winner of a major open-wheel race when he won the IndyCar race at Infineon Raceway. (The record was later broken by Graham Rahal.) The same year, in his first Indianapolis 500 appearance, Marco finished second to Sam Hornish, Jr. by 0.0635 of a second and was Indy 500 Rookie of the Year. At the end of the 2006 season, Andretti was named the IndyCar Series Rookie of the Year. Marco had to wait five years before earning his second IndyCar victory. It came at Iowa in 2011. He hasn't won since (through the 2015 season). Marco has finished in the Top 5 in the Indy 500 five times. He finished sixth in the 2015 Indianapolis 500.

* * *

7

It Was Just Automatic

Stephen Curry was voted as the NBA's Most Valuable Player in 2014-15. He became the Warriors' first league MVP since center Wilt Chamberlain won the award as a rookie in 1960. Curry averaged 23.8 points and 7.7 assists during the regular season to lead Golden State to a franchise-best 67-15 record. Once in the playoffs, the 6-foot-3 point guard stepped up his game and averaged 28.3 points, 6.4 assists and 5.0 rebounds. In only one game in each of the four playoff series was Curry *not* Golden State's scoring leader. He scored at least 32 points nine times in the 2015 postseason. Stephen Curry, a son of former NBA player, Dell Curry, has earned his reputation as the best three-point shooter of his generation. He might be the best long-distance shooter in basketball history.

Curry's performance throughout the 2015 playoffs was one of the two or three best I have seen in my nearly 40 years covering the NBA. His three-point shooting was beyond compare. A remarkable shooter with outrageous range, Curry set NBA playoff records for three-pointers made in a four game playoff series (20 vs. New Orleans in the first round), in a five game playoff series (27 vs. Houston in the Western Conference Finals) and in a six game playoff series (26 vs. Memphis in the Western Semifinals). He made a total of 25 shots from beyond the arc during the NBA Finals which helped him shatter the record for three-point shots made in a single postseason (98). Curry also tied the NBA Finals' record for three-pointers made in a quarter when he sank five in the fourth quarter of Game 3. He was efficient, too.

Curry shot better than 42% from three-point range in the Warriors' 21 playoff games. He was just ridiculous! And, it was ridiculous that he was not named the NBA Finals MVP. With due respect to Andre Iguodala, it was Curry who led the way as the Warriors marched to their first NBA title in 40 years.

As you would expect, in addition to being named as the league's MVP, Curry was named All-NBA First Team in 2015. When the Warriors won the NBA championship, Curry became the first player to win an NBA title while eliminating the other four members of the All-NBA First Team in his team's four postseason series. In Curry's case, he and the Warriors eliminated Anthony Davis (New Orleans), Marc Gasol (Memphis), James Harden (Houston), and LeBron James (Cleveland). Simply amazing! There might have been doubts about Stephen Curry's abilities when he was in high school. When he was in college, there still might have been some who questioned how good he would become as a pro. But nobody is questioning his skills now. Stephen Curry is the league's M-V-P—and an NBA champion.

I interviewed Stephen Curry in Portland, Oregon, on March 16, 2014.

Who was your boyhood idol?

Well, uh—besides my dad—it was Reggie Miller. I loved watching him play the NBA on NBC. Coach (Mark) Jackson and him teaming up and playin' the Bulls and playin' the Knicks, I used to love that on Sunday afternoons. I just loved watching him play.

You mentioned your dad. He was such a solid pro and a great shooter. Was he actually your first idol?

Oh, yeah, for sure. He was the first guy I knew who played NBA basketball and what that meant. I was born his second year in the NBA, and he played 16 seasons. So, I remember a lot of his career. Not many NBA guys have the privilege of having their kids understand what they do for a living and watch the second half of their careers. I was fortunate enough to remember a lot—a lot of the travel, going to games, going to practices, and being around him and meeting his teammates.

When you first met Reggie Miller, was it kind of a special moment for you?

Oh, for sure. It was in Charlotte at the old "Hive." We were just walkin' through the tunnel after a game. I was kind of star-struck, for sure. He was nice enough to stop and say hi to my dad. My dad pointed me out to Reggie, and he gave me a high five. That was a big deal at that point of my life. I was about six or seven. I knew who he was. I knew all about him. I used to collect trading cards back in the day, and he was one of my prized collections.

Obviously, you are a hero for many young kids today. They collect your basketball cards just like you used to collect Reggie's when you were young. Do you ever think about that?

It's wild because in this age of social media, they get a chance to talk to us. You see what they say and how much they support you. I would have been one of those kids—trying to get Reggie's attention—if that was around back in the day. It's very, very surreal that that's kind of the situation. I don't take that for granted. You have a lot of power when it comes to that.

Career Notes: Curry made a combined 18-of-33 three-point shots in Games 3, 4 and 5 of the NBA Finals. In Game 5, Curry scored 37 points—17 in the fourth quarter—to help the Warriors overcome LeBron James' second triple-double (40 points, 14 rebounds, 11 assists) of the Finals. In the championship-clinching Game 6, Curry had 25 points, eight rebounds and six assists to help the Warriors finish off the Cavaliers. Curry set other marks during the Warriors' franchise-record 67-win regular season. He broke his own NBA record for three-pointers made in a season by sinking 286 shots from downtown. He and Klay Thompson—the "Splash Brothers"—teamed for a third straight year to set an NBA single-season record for triples made in a season by a pair of teammates as they drained 525 shots from beyond the arc. Curry won the NBA Three-Point Contest during the 2015 All-Star Weekend by beating his fellow "Splash Brother" and Kyrie Irving in the final round. In the final round, Curry made 13 straight shots before missing his final attempt. Curry has played in two All-Star Games. In 2015, he started for the Western Conference and contributed 15 points, 9 rebounds and 5 assists in a 161-158 win for the West.

Curry was lightly recruited while in high school. One of the few Division I schools to offer him scholarship was Davidson College, a small school in North Carolina. He quickly made a name for himself at Davidson by averaging 21.5 points as a freshman. As a sophomore, Curry averaged 25.9 points and led Davidson to NCAA Tournament upsets over Gonzaga, Georgetown and Wisconsin to reach the Elite Eight. In his junior season, Curry led the nation in scoring (28.6 points) and was a consensus First Team All-American. Curry played only three seasons at Davidson, but scored 2,635 points, establishing Davidson and Southern Conference career marks. The two-time Southern Conference Player of the Year was a first-round pick (#7 overall) of the Warriors in the 2009 NBA Draft.

* * *

Kevin Love is a three-time NBA All-Star (through October, 2015). Love carried the offensive load for the Minnesota Timberwolves for six seasons before joining the Cleveland Cavaliers in a trade in August, 2014. He might have helped LeBron James and the Cavs win the 2015 NBA title had he not suffered a serious shoulder injury in a first-round playoff series. The injury required surgery, and Love missed the remainder of the 2015 postseason.

Kevin Love is the son of former NBA first-round draft pick, Stan Love. Kevin is a nephew of one of the founders of The Beach Boys, Mike Love.

Kevin Love grew up in Lake Oswego, Oregon. During his basketball career at Lake Oswego High School, Love led his team to the 2006 Oregon large school state championship. Love also led his high school team into state championship games as a sophomore and as a senior. In his final high school game, Love scored 38 points in the state championship final, but he came away disappointed because the state crown went to Kyle Singler's South Medford High School.

The Love vs. Singler matchups in high school were so much fun to watch. Two of Oregon's all-time best prep players—both in the same graduating class—always put on a great show. They were different players. Singler was an athletic 6-foot-9 wing. Love was a thick, powerful 6-10 center—truly a man among boys on the court. Yet, the two players—and their high school teams—had tremendous battles. After his senior season, Love was named the Gatorade National Boys Basketball Player of the Year, the nation's Naismith Player of the Year, the Wooden Player of the Year, and a Parade and McDonald's All-American. In his senior season, Love averaged 33.6 points and 17 rebounds. He scored a state record 2,628 points in his prep career. It was a special time in Oregon high school basketball. I'm glad I was there to see it.

I talked with Kevin Love on March 1, 2013, in Portland, Oregon.

Who was your first boyhood idol?

For me, there are a lot of ways to answer this question, my dad being first and foremost. I lived under the same roof as him all those years growing up. Him having played in the NBA for a few seasons—and him being my dad and all—that was pretty easy for him to be my idol. I learned a lot from him, the success he had and also failures he had. He was a guy I always looked up to and was able to learn from.

Then, guys like Larry Bird and Charles Barkley and Shaquille O'Neal and those type of players were guys that I looked up to while growing up. Obviously, everybody has Michael Jordan up there on their list—and Magic Johnson, as well, from a basketball standpoint.

Then, as far as baseball, it would be a lot of guys that played on the Mariners and especially Ken Griffey, Jr. In his hey-day up in Seattle for the Mariners, it was a big deal to me. So, I'd say those guys are ones I look up to.

The first time you met them, for example, Larry Bird or Magic Johnson, what was that like? Were you star-struck, or because you've been around the NBA your whole life, was it sort of routine?

Well, Bird and Magic, yeah, definitely it was special. And, a guy like Griffey, when I met him for the first time, it was a surreal moment for me. But then, it just became somebody that I work with or somebody that I became pretty familiar with and even developed somewhat of a friendship with as well. That's been stuff that the NBA has afforded me, and it seems like the better I get, it opens up more doors for me to meet different people and to do different things in my life. But, especially with people that influenced me at an early age, it was definitely surreal to meet them. It kind of brought me back down to earth, and I said, "Hey, man. I used to look up to these guys when I was young."

You're an NBA All-Star. You do a lot of charity work, too. So, there are many kids looking up to you in the same manner that you used to look up to your boyhood heroes. Do you ever think about that?

Oh, sure. It's funny. Sometimes I have to keep that in my mind with every decision I make. It's different because I don't really look at myself in that way. I know that I'm a good basketball player, but, at the same time, I *have* to think that way. That is what I was getting at. I just continue to remain humble and get better. But, still at some points, I take a step back and realize I was in their shoes at one point, and it was very cool for me. That's the mindset that you have to have.

Career Notes: Kevin Love averaged 19.2 points and 12.2 rebounds during his six years in Minnesota. His numbers dropped (16.4 points, 9.7 rebounds) in his first season with Cleveland because he assumed a less prominent role on offense. However, Love re-signed with the Cavaliers in the summer of 2015. He is believed to have agreed to a five-year $110-million contract in order to pursue a championship ring with the Cavs.

In 2010-11, Love was named as the NBA's Most Improved Player after leading the league in rebounding (15.2 per game). Before leaving college to play in the NBA, Love played one season at UCLA. He averaged 17.5 points and 10.6 rebounds and led the Bruins to the 2008 Final Four. Love was named the Pac-10 Player of the Year and was a consensus First Team All-American. Love was selected by the Memphis Grizzlies in the first round (#5 overall) of the 2008 NBA Draft and was traded on draft night to the Timberwolves. Kevin Love was a member of the USA National Team that won gold medals in the 2010 FIBA World Championships and the 2012 Summer Olympics.

*   *   *

Kiki Vandeweghe played 13 years in the NBA and was a highly-productive offensive player. Kiki is the son of a former pro basketball player, Ernie Vandeweghe. Kiki's father played for the New York Knicks in the early 1950s while simultaneously starting a career as a physician. Following in the footsteps of his father, Kiki also played for the Knicks. He also played for three other NBA teams—the Nuggets, Trail Blazers and Clippers.

Kiki Vandeweghe later became general manager of the Nuggets. He also spent time as GM of the Nets and served as their interim head coach in 2009-10. More recently, Vandeweghe has worked as an executive in the league office. In August, 2015, Vandeweghe was promoted to NBA Executive Vice-President, Basketball Operations. He is now in charge of the league's Basketball Operations department.

Kiki Vandeweghe was one of the NBA's top offensive players when he was acquired by the Trail Blazers in June, 1984. However, it was a somewhat controversial deal in Portland. As good as Vandeweghe was offensively, there were many Trail Blazers' fans—and a few sports reporters—who thought Portland gave up far too much to get him. Denver received center Wayne Cooper, guard Fat Lever, forward Calvin Natt, and two draft picks—including a first rounder. Lever had shown potential and had been a part-time starter. Cooper had started more than half of Portland's games over the previous two seasons. Natt, one of the NBA's toughest players, had averaged 17.2 points and 6.8 rebounds in 4½ seasons in Portland. Making the deal even more difficult for some to accept was the fact that people remembered what the Trail Blazers gave the Nets to acquire Natt in early 1980. The Blazers sent the Nets All-Star power forward Maurice Lucas and two future first round draft picks. A few Portland fans continued to be unhappy for years after Vandeweghe's acquisition, and you might be able to understand why. Natt averaged 23.3 points and 7.8 rebounds in his first season in Denver and became an All-Star. Cooper averaged nearly 13 points and eight rebounds in his first two seasons in Denver. Lever became a two-time All-Star for the Nuggets. In six seasons in Denver, Lever averaged 17.0 points, 7.6 rebounds and 7.5 assists. Vandeweghe was a consistent scorer for the Blazers and saw his scoring averages increase in each of his first three seasons with Portland from 22.4 to 24.8 to 26.9. He was clearly one of the top offensive players in the game. But, his scoring average dropped the following season to 20.2. And, the next season, Vandeweghe was averaging only 13.9 points when he was dealt for a first round draft pick that was later used to select Byron Irvin.

Despite averaging 23.5 points while playing for the Trail Blazers, it seemed to me that some fans never totally accepted Vandeweghe. I'll admit I was one of the sports reporters that initially felt the Blazers gave up more assets than necessary to acquire Vandeweghe. However, I came to appreciate Kiki's offensive skills. I can still picture him rising up for a jumper while displaying perfect shooting form. Kiki also took advantage of his deceptively-quick first step and large hands to score at the basket. I have a mental image of him driving past the defender, extending his arm while palming the ball, *and then laying the ball softly off the glass. I appreciated the beauty of his offensive game.*

I always enjoyed interviewing Vandeweghe, and I was quite pleased when he agreed to be a part of this book project. I'm also very happy that he has moved up the ladder at the NBA and is now one of the men in charge. He deserves it.

I caught up with Kiki Vandeweghe in Portland, Oregon, on April 27, 2014.

I'd like to ask you about your first boyhood idol. Is there someone who immediately pops into your mind?

Yeah. The person that pops into my mind is my dad. It was just automatic. He was my boyhood idol. He could do no wrong. That's the way I looked at it. I saw it as he played basketball; he was the best basketball player who ever played the game. He was also a doctor, and he was also the best *doctor*. He knew everything. He always made the right decision. I wanted to be just like him. I tried to emulate what he did. He was my boyhood idol.

How cool was it for *him* to have a son who grew up and had the type of skills that you possessed when you were played in the NBA?

Well, (laughs) I hope it was okay for him. You know, he really encouraged me not to play basketball—not that he didn't show me how to play and drive me to games, and things like that. But, he thought it was a difficult road. He thought I would get a lot of pressure because he had played pro basketball. I was a very good swimmer. So, he said, "You should stay with swimming." But, he said, "Listen. Once you make your decision, I'll support you all the way."

You were an idol to a lot of young kids. Did it mean something to you? Did you even know?

I think you don't have the perspective when you're actually playing, but maybe you would have better perspective today. So many kids actually *do* know who you are if you're a professional player. They do look up to you and follow you. It's obviously different today because it's so transparent. Everything is chronicled. But, back when I was playing with Clyde Drexler and Terry Porter and Jerome Kersey, all the guys here in Portland, it was a little bit different day. You tried to do the right thing. You tried to help out where you could. We were very sensitive to the needs of the community. We did a lot of things for charity and a lot of things for kids. It was always a soft spot for us. But, I think—on some level—we knew that the kids looked up to us a little bit. If we could, we tried to guide them in the right way. We wanted to give back a little bit. To me, I think that's the important thing. You give back. Nobody's perfect. You're always gonna make mistakes, but you try to do your best for the right reasons and give back as much as you can. There's so much knowledge that we players have accumulated over the years. To not give back and help the next generation, that would really be a mistake. It's the right thing to do.

Career Notes: Kiki Vandeweghe was a Western Conference All-Star in his final two seasons in Denver (1983-84). Vandeweghe scored 15,980 career points and averaged 19.7 points a game during his 13 years in the NBA. Vandeweghe averaged more than 20 points per game seven straight seasons. His best season was 1983-84, when he averaged 29.4 points for the Nuggets.

* * *

Terry Kennedy was a catcher for 14 years in the major leagues with the Cardinals, Padres, Orioles and Giants. He was one of the better-hitting catchers in the 1980s, even winning a Silver Slugger award in 1983. Terry's father, Bob Kennedy, was a front office executive for several major league teams and also managed the Cubs and Athletics in the 1960s.

After his playing career ended, Terry Kennedy spent more than two decades in the minor leagues as a manager or instructor. As a field manager, he moved up the ladder and reached the Triple-A level. He last managed the Triple-A Tucson Padres in 2012. In 2015, Kennedy served in the position of Major League Scout for the Chicago Cubs.

I met Terry Kennedy when he was managing the Triple-A Portland Beavers in 2010. He was the epitome of a guy who has lived his entire life in baseball. Terry and I talked for 15 or 20 minutes about growing up around major league players, his life as a player and his struggles to make it back to the majors as a manager.

I talked with Terry Kennedy in his office prior to a Portland Beavers game on August 13, 2010.

My first boyhood idol was former St. Louis Cardinals great, Stan Musial. Who was your first boyhood idol?

That's hard to say. My father was in baseball. He was my first real idol. But, the player that I saw that I think was the ultimate professional was Tom Seaver.

Thanks to your father, you had a chance to meet many of the biggest names in the game. A lot of people would consider you a very lucky guy.

When my father was managing, he introduced me to all the great players. I met them all. When he was managing the Cubs, I met everybody in the National League. When he was managing the A's in '68, I met everyone in the American League—Frank Howard, Brooks Robinson and Frank Robinson. Mickey Mantle was still playing. I was around a lot of idols. It's hard to really pick one. I have such respect for all these guys that played. But, when you're older and you get to know them, your opinion might change. When they're an idol, they're perfect people. Then, when you get to know them, they're not so perfect. We realize that if the Hall of Fame was full of really good guys, there would probably be only two there in the Hall and your idol, Stan Musial, would be one of them.

That's another thing. I came up with the Cardinals, and I got to know Stan. He's one of *my* idols. He's a good man. I played for Red Schoendienst. I played with Lou Brock. I'm really fortunate. I don't know how anyone in my position can pick one guy. Some of my idols are guys that helped me get to the major leagues—like Dave Ricketts and George Kissell. Ricketts played quite a bit, but George Kissell never played, and still he's one of my idols. I think it depends on how you define idols.

You mentioned your dad. I know you never saw him play. Why was he one of your heroes? Was it because he was a manager or because he was your father?

It was because he was my dad. He had a cool job. He was a handsome guy. He had his [stuff] together. People liked him. People respected him. I thought this is a pretty good guy to copy. He had a lot of integrity, which I saw much more as I got older and understood what integrity meant. People would come up to me later and say, "Your dad was really good to me when I was a player." A guy would come to dad and say, "Hey, my wife's pregnant. I need more money." He'd give them another $100 a month. That's what he'd do.

You mentioned 1968 when your dad was managing the Athletics. You would go into the clubhouse and see all these players. One of the players was future Hall of Fame outfielder Reggie Jackson. What was that like for you as a 12-year-old kid?

The weirdest thing is that was Reggie's second year, and I ended up playing against Reggie in the big leagues, which I teased him about to no end. I played against Joe Rudi and Sal Bando. I played against Rick Monday. I played against Gene Tenace. I played against a lot of those guys. I hit against Vida Blue. It was strange. Even though I was 12 at the time, just ten years later I was playing against them. So, that was odd. They were still playing, which says a lot for them. I didn't really watch the games back then. I'd be out on the field and playing around before the games, but then I'd play around the stadium during the games. I was there for Catfish Hunter's perfect game and didn't really pay attention to it. Your priorities are different when you're a kid.

You and your dad were the first father-son combination to each get a run-batted-in in World Series competition. What does that mean to you?

I thought that was cool. I don't know if anybody's done that since— maybe the Boones. But, that was cool. We didn't have very many links as far as our playing styles because I was a catcher. It was nice that we both did that. I'd like to have the championship ring that he had, but I didn't get there. It was neat that we got that record. I did it on my first at bat against the Tigers in '84. I ended up getting that RBI, and I didn't really know about us being the first ones until later.

You were a four-time All-Star. You probably had young kids imitating your batting style while playing Wiffle-Ball in the backyard. Did you ever think about that when you were playing? Does anybody ever approach you to say you were their boyhood idol?

No. There's nobody like that. They don't know who Terry Kennedy is. These kids hardly know who Willie Mays is nowadays. But no, I really didn't think about it. I appreciate it when people say things to me now. It makes me feel like I didn't waste my time. But, I don't have a "dig-me" room. I don't have anything except those four All-Star pictures. I felt like, for a moment there, I was as good as they were. To play with Mike Schmidt, Gary Carter and Andre Dawson—they're all in the Hall of Fame now. I was part of that for a short while. That was pretty good.

You talked about what an odd sensation it was for you when you became peers with some of the players you had watched growing up. What went through your mind when you realized you were going north with the big league club the first time you made the "Show"?

I'd been around clubhouses so long, I was not afraid to talk to anybody—anywhere—because of growing up around it. On the field, I wasn't their equal yet. You have to prove yourself. Lou Brock was pretty good to me. There were some guys there with the Cardinals that weren't very good guys. That was not a very good time for the Cardinals in the late '70s. You're so busy trying to establish yourself that you don't sit back and say, "I'm one of these guys. I'm a big leaguer." I didn't think about that. I never played for the money. I wanted to do certain things. I set some goals, and longevity was one of them. So, I made that goal. I realized that there are a lot of things that are beyond your control even when you make it to the majors.

You are now a manager of a Triple-A team. Are you managing because you love the game and want to be part of it, or is part of the equation that you saw your dad manage and thought that it was a pretty cool job?

Yeah, I'd rather wear this uniform than go wear a suit and be stuck in an office. Guys that were in a position like I'm in right now gave me a lot—the guys in the Cardinal organization, the instructors, the coaches I had in the minors, the coaches in the big leagues. I figure if I can give back half of that to somebody here, then I've repaid my debt.

Career Notes: Terry Kennedy batted .264 in the majors. He hit 113 career home runs and drove in 628 runs. Kennedy had his greatest success playing in San Diego. In six years with the Padres, he batted .274 and hit 76 homers. Kennedy was a four-time All-Star, three times with San Diego (1981, 1983, 1985) and once with Baltimore (1987). Kennedy played in two World Series—1984 with the Padres and 1989 with the Orioles. He hit a home run in Game 4 of the '84 World Series off Detroit's Jack Morris.

*   *   *

Pete Ward played major league baseball for nine years from 1962 to 1970. He spent most of his career with the White Sox, but also had short stints with the Orioles and Yankees. Although he played a majority of his games at third base, he also played more than 100 games in the outfield and at first base. In January, 1963, Pete Ward was involved in a trade that featured a pair of future Hall of Famers—Hoyt Wilhelm and Luis Aparicio. Ward was traded from the Orioles, along with Wilhelm, Ron Hansen and Dave Nicholson, for Aparicio and Al Smith.

I first learned of Pete Ward when—as a 10-year-old boy—I opened a pack of 1964 Topps and pulled out a Pete Ward card. There was Pete in his White Sox uniform bending over at the waist in position to field a ground ball. There was a little trophy on the front of the card designating Ward as one of the "Topps 1963 All-Star Rookie" selections. Never did I dream that—many years later—I would get to know Pete on a personal basis.

Ward grew up in Portland, Oregon, and went to Jefferson High School. He attended Lewis and Clark College and played baseball for three years at the school. Baseball fans in Portland were proud of Ward's accomplishments in the '60s and enjoyed following his career. By the time I arrived in Portland in 1980, Ward had left baseball and was running a successful travel agency. Pete brought former major league stars to Portland each year to be part of his annual baseball clinic. Baseball fans looked forward to seeing ex-players like Mickey Mantle and Brooks Robinson come to town.

I talked with Pete Ward by phone on January 15, 2015.

Who was your very first boyhood idol?

It was probably my dad, Jimmy Ward, because of his hockey career. That's what brought us out to Portland is when he came out and coached the Portland Eagles and the Portland Penguins. He came out in 1944, and he coached in Portland until 1950. He spent 12 years playing up with the NHL's Montreal Maroons, and they won the Stanley Cup one year. So, I was kind of active in hockey. As a fan, in baseball, it probably would have been Ted Williams and Mickey Mantle.

What was it about them that you liked?

They could hit. (Laughs) Later on, I got the opportunity to meet them and play against them for a while. Actually, I didn't play Ted Williams. He managed the Washington Senators when I was playing. His career was done when I got to the majors. I saw him in spring training because I went to a few spring trainings before I actually played against the Senators. When I was growing up, Ted Williams was just an unbelievable hitter. I played against Mantle for a few years.

How was it playing against an idol?

Just going to spring training was really surreal—just to go out and be playing in games. Frank Robinson hits you a ground ball. You get it and throw him out. But, that star-struck feeling goes away pretty quick. You see they're just like we are.

Did you ever meet Williams or Mantle when you were a boy?

No, but Bobby Doerr introduced me to Ted Williams one day after I was playing in the big leagues. I left Chicago after the season, and there was a winter league in Sarasota. Bobby was there, and I was talking to him. He said, "Ted will be here tomorrow." I said I'd really like to meet him. So, I did. I got a chance to talk to him for about 40 minutes. That was one of the highlights of my life.

What did you talk about?

Well, *he* talked. I was really worried about what to say. Ted talked hitting. He asked me more questions than I could possibly even imagine, like, "Who's the toughest hitter in the league? Why is he tough? How come you aren't getting him out? What adjustment are you gonna make?" It reminds me of what Mickey Mantle said one time. (Laughs) One time he played in an All-Star Game. He went home and said, "Well, I'm not gonna locker next to Ted Williams at any more All-Star Games. By the time he got through talking, I was so screwed up with my hitting." (Laughs)

I remember that you brought Mantle out to Portland on occasion.

For 20 years, we did the Pete Ward Baseball Clinic. We brought in about a hundred former major leaguers. I brought Mantle out three times. I brought him here twice, and then one year I put on the clinic in Hawaii. He and Billy Martin and Maury Wills each came three different times.

Do you have any special memories of playing against Mantle when you were a rookie with the White Sox?

Well, it's funny because by that time, I'd kind of adjusted to playing major leaguers. I can remember playing in New York, and he hit a ball that almost killed Nellie Fox at second base. The ball hit Nellie in the chest. Nellie held on to it and threw him out. Another time, Mantle hit a ball off of pitcher Ray Herbert who was having a great year for us in Chicago. Mantle hit one, and he threw his bat. He was ticked off thinking he didn't hit the ball well. The ball went out—about 20 rows deep in right-center at Yankee Stadium. He hit it a little bit better than he thought. (Laughs)

There was just something about Mickey. For guys like me, if he ever said he would do something, he would do it. You didn't have to worry about it. Like, I got him to come out here, basically, with just a phone call. It was just, "Come on out." And, he says, "Yeah, sure. I'll be there." If he said he'll do it, he'll do it. I think he always kind of liked me. I think that's why he did a lot of that stuff for me.

Career Notes: Pete Ward batted .254 in 973 major league games. He hit 98 homers and drove in 427 runs. His most productive years were his first two seasons in Chicago. After batting only .143 in 21 at bats with Baltimore in 1962, Ward got 600 at bats with the White Sox in 1963, and he capitalized—batting .295, with 22 home runs and 84 runs-batted-in. The following season, Ward batted .282 and had career highs with 23 homers and 94 RBI.

*   *   *

8

The Logo

Jerry West was one of the premier basketball players of his generation. An All-American guard who led his West Virginia Mountaineers to the 1959 NCAA Championship game, West went on to play his entire 14-year Hall of Fame career with the Lakers. Like many great athletes, a list of West's basketball accomplishments could fill an entire book, but there is one thing that sets Jerry West apart from his contemporaries. His silhouette was incorporated into the NBA logo. As a result, one of West's nicknames is "The Logo."

I grew up watching Jerry West play for the Lakers in the 1960s and '70s. Far fewer games were televised during that era, but West was a huge star and the Lakers such a great team that we fans became accustomed to seeing Jerry West, Elgin Baylor and Wilt Chamberlain on the television sets in our homes. It was amazing how many times Jerry West delivered in key moments of games, which resulted in another West nickname, "Mr. Clutch."

Although I covered the NBA for many years while working in Portland, I never had a chance to talk with Jerry West until 2011, the year his memoir was published. In "West by West: My Charmed, Tormented Life," West revealed that, as a child, he was a victim of physical abuse from his father. Also, West revealed that he has suffered from depression for most of his life. It was a stunning revelation. Many of us asked ourselves, "What could Jerry West be depressed about? He's one of the greatest players and most respected athletes of all time. Why would he be depressed?" Clearly, people throughout

America became more educated about people living with depression once West came forward with his personal testimony.

While conducting a radio interview with West during the publicity tour for his book, I thought to myself how ironic it was that "The Logo"—one of his sport's all-time greats and a man worshipped by many fans—wasn't overjoyed with every facet of his life. I made a mental note to contact West later to discuss his thoughts on being an idol while living a secret life of torment. I called Jerry West on September 29, 2013.

Can you tell me who your boyhood idol was?

I can honestly say I probably didn't have one. Growing up in a small community in West Virginia, we didn't have much access to sports, except West Virginia basketball and football on the radio and in a local newspaper. There wasn't access to any of the professional sports teams or anything. It wasn't really until later that I would follow players a little bit. But, to be candid with you, growing up—early in my life—there was really no one.

Did you have favorite West Virginia players, or did you perhaps dream of playing for the Mountaineers?

No, not really. I don't know. I enjoyed the excitement of just listening to the game and hearing the crowds in the background. Also, I think at that point in my life, I just had so many little things I liked to do that most kids don't like to do. I loved the outdoors. I loved fishing. I loved going in the woods. And, when I was young, I picked up a basketball and I was able to sort of immerse myself in that. Basketball wasn't something that was really in vogue at that point in time. It was usually football and baseball that kind of dominated the world. I would say that I did follow the Cleveland Indians a little bit. I also followed the Cincinnati Reds a little bit, but it was really nothing other than wanting teams that were around you to win.

In your autobiography, you wrote that two of your sports heroes were boxers—Sugar Ray Robinson and Joe Louis—and that you liked football player Jim Brown. So, I guess they meant a little something to you along the way?

Well, they did. But, it wasn't until I was old enough to appreciate them. And again, we didn't have a TV. It was the early days of television. I had a great deal of interest in boxing because they used to have Wednesday night fights and Friday or Saturday night fights. I used to go to the neighbors to visit a friend of mine whose family had a TV, and I'd watch the fights.

Then, Jim Brown was someone who I had a great feeling about—as a player and, more importantly, as a person. He was out in front before most people were out in front about things that I think truly mattered in terms of the conscious of our country. Jim was—with regards to race—very outspoken in terms that a lot of athletes wouldn't dare to do, regardless of race or color. They just wouldn't do it, and Jim did. For some reason, I've always identified with people who have enough courage to say things that maybe in my whole life I would never have the courage to say because you just don't know who you're going to offend. I was always that kind of a person. I didn't want to offend anyone. I was one of those kids that wanted everyone to like me knowing full well that was never going to happen.

You wrote that Jamal Wilkes idolized you growing up. And, for this book, veteran NBA coaches Rick Adelman and Terry Stotts told me you were their idol. How does that make you feel?

First of all, it's flattering that someone would think enough of you to feel that you were maybe a little bit different than another athlete—and for *a lot* of different reasons. The one thing that I really never tried to do was attract attention. I wasn't a demonstrative player. I wasn't someone to try to call attention to myself because I didn't think it was important. That's not why I played. I played because I just loved the competition and the excitement of game days. Stuff like that was very, very important to me.

I've had a number of people who were basketball players that sort of patterned their shooting after me a little bit. Again, it's extremely flattering, but somewhere in this country today there are many players—in all sports—that young kids attain a huge liking for them. It's usually the way they play, and *how* they play, and how *hard* they play and how they *compete*. It's a great story to hear young kids come up and say, "I really thought this guy was someone that I wanted to emulate." It's really flattering, regardless of what an athlete's name is or whatever sport it might be.

You wrote in your book that you had mixed feelings about being idolized because you had some personal issues that people weren't aware of—depression, family problems with your dad and so forth. Yet, your silhouette is the NBA logo. Is that something you have mixed feelings about?

Well, I had a lot of mixed feelings about things in my life. As I say, I didn't play this game to be something special. I played this game because I just loved the competition. I loved the fact that I could sort of live my childhood fantasy. I never thought I would be anything but maybe a high school basketball player, and I got to be a good high school player. Then, I had an opportunity to be recruited by a lot of college teams. It makes you think a little bit differently about yourself; maybe someone else values you more than you value yourself. To get a chance to play at the collegiate level was another thrill—you know—to have the college education. If I hadn't been able to do something a little bit different than the average kid, that wasn't gonna happen. From there, obviously, it was like a kind of a storybook life. All the dreams I had as a kid—to play basketball at the highest level and being able to compete against the very best—little did I know was right ahead of me. I was able to do it. Frankly, I look back on it and see how fortunate I was—not only to play for so many years—but to be able to accomplish an awful lot as an individual and also for the most part to always play on really good teams.

Wilt Chamberlain and Kareem Abdul-Jabbar were legendary players. You played against both, were a teammate of Wilt's and coached the Lakers when Kareem was a star on the team. Outsiders have said the two of them could be a little standoffish. Based on your interactions with Wilt and Kareem, how were they to deal with?

Kareem was a consummate professional. He just played the game. He was an unbelievably gifted player. They talk about great players. I have no idea how he doesn't get mentioned more as possibly the *best* player. He was very bright. He was very studious in his approach to the game. He played the game at an unbelievably high level. And, he played the game so easily sometimes, I said to myself, "My gosh! Imagine if he played harder!" Then, at the end of the season, you'd look up and here he was with these incredible numbers. And, more importantly, he'd have incredible success—not only from an individual standpoint, but from a team standpoint.

Wilt was just one of those incredibly dominant players. I feel fortunate that I had a chance to play later in my career with him because he really helped me. After I had gone through a lot of my injuries, I wasn't the same physically. I just wasn't. Doctor care then was as good as it could get, but it certainly wasn't what it is today. I enjoyed playing with him. He was different. He could be very moody at times. But still, he was a player that was very prideful in what he did, and he played every night. I mean, he never missed a game because of injury. You look at some of the things he did as a player. No one will ever do that again.

You also co-captained the 1960 gold medal-winning U.S. Olympic men's basketball team with Oscar Robertson. He was your rival, but he was your Olympic teammate. How great was the Big O?

He was great. Period. He did everything well. He had an incredible command of the game. He was born with a computer mind. When I played against him, I realized that this was who I was going to have to compete against in the NBA and that I was gonna have to get better to be able to do it. I wasn't going to be able to do it in the same way. But, in my own way, I felt that I would be able to compete with him even though we played completely differently. When we were ready to play against his team, it was always the anticipation of playing against greatness. Early in my career, he was so far advanced of everybody else. I felt like I had a lot of catching up to do. It turned out to be a great rivalry—an individual rivalry and also a team rivalry.

Some players are mentioned time and again as basketball idols-- Jordan, Magic, Bird. Is it safe to say that if you're a great player who has had some success, somebody is going to idolize you?

Yes. It's surprising the number of kids out there who have someone that they have a great feeling about. But, more importantly, they want to kind of emulate, not only their success, but how they play. Every player plays different, okay? Some players play with a flair. A lot of kids want to play with flair. If that's not in your DNA, you shouldn't try to do it because you're not going to be very successful if you do. You should try to find your own niche in life—and particularly in sports—that allows you to excel in what you want to try to accomplish with your life and particularly as an athlete.

Career Notes: Jerry West holds the distinction of being named the 1959 NCAA Final Four Most Outstanding Player and the Most Valuable Player of the 1969 NBA Finals. Coincidentally, in both years, West played for teams that lost! In the NBA, West scored 25,192 career points and averaged 27.0 points, 6.7 assists and 5.8 rebounds per game. He was an All-Star in each of his 14 NBA seasons, and he was regularly named to the All-NBA and All-Defensive teams. Even though West played in the NBA Finals nine times, he won just one championship ring as a player (1972).

West spent 40 years with the Lakers as a player, scout, consultant, general manager and executive vice president for basketball operations. Although he won just the one championship as a player, he won six more as an executive and special consultant for the Lakers. He later became G.M. of the Memphis Grizzlies and helped them reach the NBA playoffs for the first time in franchise history. Since 2011, West has served as a consultant and Executive Board member of the Golden State Warriors—the 2015 NBA champions.

*   *   *

Terry Stotts, like Jerry West, played professional basketball before becoming a head coach in the NBA. Stotts, who begins his fourth season as head coach of the Portland Trail Blazers in 2015-16, previously spent two seasons coaching the Atlanta Hawks and two seasons as head coach of the Milwaukee Bucks.

I didn't know much about Terry Stotts when he was hired to coach the Trail Blazers, but it didn't take long for me to realize that Stotts is a fine coach and an even better person. Let me give you an example of why I believe that is the case. When the radio station for which I had worked for several decades laid me off in August, 2013, I sought out the Trail Blazers' players and coaches to tell them the news about my job status and to thank them for all they had done to make my job easier. I had been serving as host of the Blazers' Pregame and Postgame Shows and as the team's sideline reporter on the radio network. Coach Stotts and I weren't particularly close, but we enjoyed a good working relationship. I could tell Stotts was sympathetic when I told him about my job loss. He showed compassion and said he was sorry to hear that I suddenly found myself unemployed. His comments seemed genuine and helped ease the sting I felt after finding myself out of a job for the first time in my 37 years in broadcasting—33 of those years in the Portland market and more than 24 years at the radio station. I continued to see Stotts on Blazers' game nights when I picked up free-lance work with visiting teams' broadcast crews. Stotts asked how I was doing each time I saw him.

In November, 2013, I was hired to call play-by-play on the Trail Blazers' Radio Network when regular broadcaster Brian Wheeler fell ill. I caught up to the team in Brooklyn. Just before heading to the arena (Barclays Center), Coach Stotts saw me, walked over to where I was sitting and said, "I'm really glad to see you here. It's great to have you with us." That heartfelt welcome meant the world to me. It also showed the class of Terry Stotts.

Prior to all of that, I had talked with Terry Stotts at the Trail Blazers practice facility in Tualatin, Oregon, on February 27, 2013.

Who was your first boyhood idol?

Jerry West. There's no question. I was born in '57, and he came out of college in '60. So, when I was growing up, he was the epitome of the NBA. Obviously, he's the logo. Jerry West was six-three or six-four. Once I grew up and became six-seven or six-eight, I looked more towards Rick Barry as a person who I might be able to emulate. But, there's no question that as a boyhood idol, Jerry West was the man.

What was it that you liked about him?

Well, just everything. He was "Mr. Clutch." I was on Guam when the Lakers won the championship. We got all the Laker games, so I watched every one of their games during their NBA record 33-game win-streak. I really identified with that team and identified with him. He did everything. He embodied the NBA. He embodied what a pro basketball player should be.

I'm sure you've met Jerry West at some point. Do you remember where you met him for the first time?

Yeah, I do. It was at the L.A. Summer League. I think it was 1996 because Kobe had just gotten drafted. We happened to be walking out of the gym together. We were talking about Kobe Bryant and different things, and he called me by my name. As we left the building, he went to his car and I went to mine. I was giddy because Jerry West knew my name. That was the first time I'd met him and spoke with him. The fact that he knew my name was just a cherry on top.

His book, *West by West: My Charmed, Tormented Life* was kind of dark. None of us had known that West was physically abused by his father and had battled depression much of his life. Did Jerry's revelations change your opinion of him in any way?

No. It doesn't change what he accomplished as a basketball player and a general manager and just being involved in the NBA. Obviously, it helped me understand him a little bit more as a man. A lot of people have issues growing up that you don't know about. For him to be as honest as he was—and as open about some of the things that he faced—was pretty meaningful.

Coach, you have the respect of many Trail Blazer fans. Do you consider yourself a role model, in particular, for kids who might be dreaming of playing or coaching in the NBA?

I try to carry myself as one. I don't necessarily feel that I *am* one, but I'm sure that I am in some ways. No matter who you are, I think if you carry yourself in the right way—be a good person and do the right things—you'll end up being a role model to somebody.

Career Notes: Terry Stotts was a four-year starter at the University of Oklahoma. He was an Academic All-American as a junior and senior. Despite being drafted in the second round of the 1980 NBA Draft, Stotts never played in the NBA, choosing instead to play professionally overseas. He spent most of his playing career in France, Spain and Italy. He also played for Montana in the CBA under Coach George Karl. Stotts was disappointed in his first season as head coach in Portland when the Blazers lost their last 13 games to drop out of playoff contention. However, he guided the Blazers into the postseason each of the next two years, winning more than 50 games each season. The 2015-16 campaign will provide his biggest coaching challenge since moving to Portland as 80% of the starting lineup has to be replaced following the trade of Nicolas Batum and the free-agency defections of LaMarcus Aldridge, Wesley Matthews and Robin Lopez.

* * *

Rick Adelman is one of only nine coaches in NBA history to win 1,000 regular season games. He served as head coach for five NBA teams—Portland, Golden State, Sacramento, Houston and Minnesota. He guided his teams to 16 playoff appearances and four division titles. His Clyde Drexler-led Trail Blazer teams made two trips to the NBA Finals. Adelman teams played in four Western Conference Finals. Adelman was a head coach in the NBA All-Star Game three times. After spending 23 seasons as an NBA head coach, Adelman stepped down from the Timberwolves and retired from coaching on April 21, 2014.

I had the pleasure of meeting Rick Adelman many years ago when he was an assistant coach with the Trail Blazers. Believing that he was a character guy and a good coach, I was happy that he was named the team's interim head coach when Mike Schuler was fired in February of 1989. Having a good working relationship with Adelman, I was even more pleased when the "interim" label was later dropped. In Adelman's first full season as head coach of the Trail Blazers, the team won an impressive 59 regular season games but finished four games behind the Lakers in the Pacific Division. In the playoffs, however, they beat Dallas, San Antonio and Phoenix en route to an NBA Finals' matchup with Detroit. The Pistons won the Finals in five games. Portland won a franchise-record 63 games the following year, but lost to Magic Johnson and the Lakers in the Western Conference Finals. The Blazers won a second straight division title in 1991-92. They made it back to the NBA Finals, but lost in six games to the Bulls.

Those were amazing times in Portland, and as sports director of the radio station that carried their games—and hosting the 5th Quarter with Scott Lynn postgame show—I had the privilege of working closely with the coaches and players during one of the best NBA basketball eras in the Rose City. However, the Trail Blazers were unable to again reach those heights under Adelman, and he was fired after just two more seasons. I thought Adelman showed class when he met with the media at the Memorial Coliseum and thanked the organization for the opportunity he had been given. I'm very happy that he went on to become one of the NBA's winningest coaches. Interestingly, the Trail Blazers have won only two division titles since Adelman coached the team in the early 1990s. Portland has never been back to the NBA Finals.

I talked with Rick Adelman on March 5, 2012, in Portland, Oregon.

Who was your first boyhood idol?

I grew up in Los Angeles. It would be Jerry West. As far as basketball, it would be Jerry West. Again, I grew up in Los Angeles, so Sandy Koufax would be the other one for me.

Was it a little strange the first time you played against West in the NBA?

Yeah, it was because I watched him growing up my whole life. Then you end up getting a chance to meet him and play against him. It's just something you never think about happening. They were the big game in town for me basketball-wise. And, back then, you actually could go see them play; you could get tickets. So, I saw him play a lot and had a lot of opportunity to go see him play because they practiced at Loyola where I went to school. We got tickets to go to the Lakers games. I saw him play quite a bit.

Did you ever meet Koufax?

I never met him, but he's an idol for me. I saw him pitch the perfect game against the Cubs at Dodger Stadium. We were there. We were in college, and we went to the game. It was an amazing experience watching that game. I have that ticket stub somewhere, but I can't tell you where.

You played in the NBA. You were even the first captain of the Trail Blazers. Did you ever consider that you might have been an idol for young kids?

No. I never have considered myself an idol. I'm still amazed that I got into the league and played seven years. (Laughs)

Career Notes: Rick Adelman attended Loyola Marymount University in Los Angeles and was named the Most Valuable Player of the West Coast Athletic Conference as a senior in 1967-68. A seventh-round draft pick of the Rockets in the 1968 NBA Draft, the 6-foot-2 guard played seven seasons in the NBA with the San Diego Rockets, Portland Trail Blazers, Chicago Bulls, New Orleans Jazz and Kansas City-Omaha Kings. He averaged 7.7 points and 3.5 assists. Adelman went to Portland in the 1970 NBA Expansion Draft and was named the first team captain in Trail Blazers' history.

* * *

9

For The Next Generation

Jude Schimmel was a standout 5-foot-6 guard on the University of Louisville women's basketball team. A four-year letter winner, the Mission, Oregon, native played for the Cardinals from 2011-12 through 2014-15. She is the younger sister of former Cardinals' star Shoni Schimmel. While her older, taller sibling received more national attention and has become a WNBA All-Star, Jude Schimmel has shown that you don't have to be a star to have success. In fact, Jude was a key contributor for the Louisville recruiting class that recorded a school-record 112 victories over four seasons. Jude played in one Final Four, a pair of Elite Eights and three Sweet Sixteens. Jude and Shoni both played for Louisville in the 2013 NCAA Championship game.

Raised on the Umatilla Indian Reservation in eastern Oregon, Jude and Shoni are inspirations for thousands of Native Americans around the country. The Schimmels were featured in the 2011 documentary, *Off the Rez*. In 2015, Jude Schimmel authored a book, *Dreamcatcher*, about her life's journey from the reservation to becoming a major college basketball standout.

I reported on the Schimmel sisters after their parents moved the family to the Portland area so the girls could play against better high school basketball competition and improve as players in hopes of earning basketball scholarships. Being younger and less well-known to most basketball fans, it was a tall order for Jude to keep up with her renowned sister. There were some who questioned whether she was good enough to play at Louisville.

Some hinted that perhaps she only got a scholarship because Shoni was already a star for the Cardinals. However, Jude proved the doubters wrong. She had a fine collegiate career. After I interviewed Jude early in her college career, I watched with interest as her career unfolded. I was thrilled when Jude went on to have a significant impact for the Louisville women's basketball team. I talked with Jude Schimmel in Portland on December 16, 2011, when she was a freshman at the University of Louisville.

Who was your first childhood idol?

I remember when we were younger and our parents were our coaches on our AAU team, they would take us to the Portland Fire WNBA games and the Houston Comets games. I really liked (three-time WNBA MVP) Sheryl Swoopes and (2001 WNBA Rookie of the Year) Jackie Stiles. Those were two people I really looked up to. We watched their games all the time. Besides that, it would be my family.

Have you ever met Swoopes or Stiles?

No. I got Jackie Styles' autograph on a ball once, but, other than that, no.

You've been teammates with your sister in high school and now in college. What does that mean to you?

In high school, it was just kind of fun because it was a different level of competition. But, when we got into college, I just thought it was huge. It was a huge deal to me because there's not many sisters or siblings that make it D-I and play at the same college. I think it's a special opportunity. I'm really thankful.

There are kids on the reservation who look up to both you and Shoni. How important is that to you?

It's really important. I feel like that's one of the main things that keep me and my sister going. It's like we're doing this, not only for ourselves and our family, but we're doing it for the next generation—the younger kids that live on the reservation. We're people that they look up to, and we hope that they will follow in our footsteps.

So, you are very aware that those kids on the reservation idolize you and your sister?

Well, definitely. Most of the kids always yell, "Shoni! Shoni! Oh, my gosh!" And, then there will be the little, short ones shouting, "Jude! Jude!" So, I know that they're looking up to us because any time we see them, they're like, "Oh, my gosh! It's you and Shoni!" They give us hugs and say hi.

Shoni is such a remarkable player. Was she an idol to you, or was she just your sister?

She was my sister *and* my idol. When I was younger growing up, she was always the one that I looked up to. She was always the one on the court I could count on. I knew what she was doing. I felt I could rely on her. She was my idol both on and off the court.

I saw an article a couple years ago about the number of Native American women who were playing college basketball. I believe it said there were only 19 players. You must consider it a thrill and an honor to be one of the few Native Americans playing in women's college basketball.

Yeah, I was writing a paper the other day. The subject was "What's the most important thing about you?" I feel like one of the most important things is, I'm one of the one or two percent of Native Americans that get to go play college basketball. I owe most of the support to my family. Without my parents and my grandmas, I feel like it'd be way harder than what it is.

You mentioned that your parents were your idols and role models. They were critical to your success, weren't they?

Yeah, they were. They both had the chance to be successful, but then they got pregnant at a really young age. I feel like we're doing it both for them and ourselves. They're really, really supportive, and they know what's good for their kids. If it weren't for them, Shoni and me, we wouldn't be where we are.

Is there pressure because of that or is it just fun playing basketball and being in college?

I think there's both pressure and fun. Basketball is obviously fun. And, then there's pressure. We have to make it for ourselves, for the next generation and for our family.

Career Notes: Jude Schimmel scored in double-figures in all three of her NCAA Tournament games her senior season. She finished her career tied for the most NCAA Tournament games played in Louisville women's basketball history (15). Even though she did not start a game in her first two seasons and started only five games as a junior, Jude concluded her career ranked in the school's Top Ten in games played (135), assists (392) and steals (221). Her senior season, Jude started all 34 games and averaged 7.6 points, 3.4 rebounds, 3.8 assists and 2.2 steals.

*   *   *

Shoni Schimmel, a flashy guard for the WNBA's Atlanta Dream, is one of the most popular players in women's professional basketball. Schimmel has been voted as an All-Star starter in each of her first two WNBA seasons (2014, 2015) even though she has primarily played a reserve role for Atlanta since entering the league out of the University of Louisville. Shoni grew up on the Umatilla Indian Reservation in Mission, Oregon. In order for Shoni to play against better competition in hopes of landing a college scholarship, Schimmel's parents moved to Portland, Oregon, prior to her senior year of high school. The move paid dividends. In her final high school season, Shoni averaged 29.8 points, 9.0 rebounds, 7.3 assists and 5.5 steals. She was named a First Team

Parade All-American. Shoni's journey in pursuit of a college basketball scholarship was chronicled in the 2011 documentary, *Off the Rez.*

The Schimmel family story is truly remarkable. The odds are long for any Native American to leave the reservation and play major college basketball. That both Schimmel sisters ended up playing together for three years at a basketball powerhouse like Louisville, well, that's just about impossible to imagine. The entire family had to buy in to be able to make it happen. The girls put in the work to develop their skills on the basketball court. Their parents coached them in AAU basketball. Their mother, CeCilee Moses, coached them at Franklin High School in Portland. Their father, Rick Schimmel, did whatever was necessary to keep the family on track and the goal in sight. There were many doubters when they began their journey. Many didn't believe the girls would be able to step off the reservation and into the national spotlight. However, after the Schimmel sisters played for Louisville in the 2013 NCAA Championship game, you could say with conviction that Rick and CeCilee knew what they were doing.

I talked with Shoni Schimmel on December 16, 2011, in Portland, Oregon, during Shoni's sophomore season at the University of Louisville.

I know you started playing basketball when you were only four years old. Who was your first childhood idol?

Definitely my parents. They were there for me the whole time. They've always pushed me to be the best I can be. So, my parents.

Jude mentioned that your mom's early pregnancy changed your parents' lives because they had to put their own career goals on hold. She says that you two sisters are now playing sort of in tribute to your parents. Do you feel that way?

Oh yeah, definitely. They didn't get the opportunity to fulfill their dreams. So, we're kind of doing it, not just for ourselves and other Native American people, but for our parents as well.

You are an idol and inspiration for so many young kids on the reservation. What does that mean to you?

It means a lot to me. I'm out there playing basketball and doing what I like to do, but little kids are looking up to me. It kind of makes me do everything right and be the right kind of person. That's exactly what my parents have taught me.

In August, (of 2011) the entire Louisville women's basketball team joined you on the reservation to talk with the kids. What did those youngsters say to you when you were there with your teammates?

They were just all excited. They were all excited to see everybody with all of us being there. I don't think they quite understood it. They were just excited that we were all there. It was cool just to be able to have the team there and be on the reservation. It was like both of my worlds combined.

Portland used to have a WNBA franchise. Were you a Portland Fire fan?

Definitely. I can remember me and my sister and my cousin having my dad drive us to Portland to watch the games because we still lived in Pendleton at that time. Yeah, I remember the Portland Fire—Jackie Stiles and everyone.

Jackie Stiles was a great player, in fact, WNBA Rookie of the Year in her first pro season. Was she one of your idols?

She was. That was more Jude's player, though. She liked her *a lot*. I mean, I still liked her and what not. It's just I was a Cynthia Cooper fan.

Did you find yourself idolizing the women players—like Cynthia Cooper—more than the men's stars?

Yeah, definitely because it was more on the girl program, I was just kind of like looking at the girls. But, I mean, the greats like Michael Jordan are still there. I still look up to them.

The number of Native Americans playing Division I basketball is so small. How do you feel about that?

It's just different. I'm used to playing with Native Americans, and now you hardly ever see them out there playing basketball. So, it's different. But, the whole role model thing—I'm out there setting goals for everybody to be able to know that they can do it.

Jude told me that she looks up to you. Do you feel a responsibility to her, in addition to all those kids on the reservation?

Oh, definitely, just because she *is* my sister. I'm trying to be the best I can be, not only for me, but also for my sister. I know she can do it as well.

Career Notes: Shoni Schimmel averaged 8.3 points and 3.6 assists in her rookie season in the WNBA. She played in 34 games, starting only two. The 5-foot-9 guard was the MVP of the 2014 WNBA All-Star Game as she scored an All-Star Game record 29 points (since broken by the 30 point performance of Maya Moore in the 2015 All-Star Game). Schimmel led the Eastern Conference to an overtime victory over the West in 2014. In 2015, she was voted as an Eastern Conference starter for the second year in a row. A four-year letter-winner at the University of Louisville, Schimmel led the Cardinals into the NCAA Championship game in 2013 and to the Elite Eight in 2014. She became the first Louisville player to accumulate at least 2,000 points and 500 assists in a career. Shoni totaled 2,174 points and 600 assists. She led the Cardinals in points and assists in each of her last three seasons. Shoni sank 387 career three-pointers, one of the highest totals in the history of women's college basketball. She was recognized as an All-American her senior year after averaging 17.4 points, 4.5 rebounds and 3.8 assists per game.

*   *   *

Jacoby Ellsbury is a speedy outfielder who played on Boston's World Series championship teams in 2007 and 2013. He now plays centerfield for the New York Yankees. Ellsbury was originally drafted by Tampa Bay in the 23rd round of the 2002 draft. However, he chose to attend Oregon State University and play baseball for veteran coach Pat Casey. In his third season at Oregon State, he led the Beavers to their first Pac-10 title and was named 2005 Pac-10 Co-Player of the Year. He was also recognized as an All-American after batting .406, with 6 homers and 48 RBI. In the postseason, Ellsbury batted .351 while leading the Beavers to the 2005 College World Series—Oregon State's first trip to Omaha in 53 years.

My radio station was the "Home of the Beavers" when Ellsbury and Oregon State made the trip to Omaha in 2005. We broadcast their College World Series games and shared in the excitement as Oregon State pursued the national championship. Even though the Beavers didn't win the crown in 2005, Ellsbury's OSU teammates went on to win back-to-back NCAA championships the next two years. Ellsbury had helped set the table for a remarkable run of success for the OSU baseball team.

Here's something you might not know about Jacoby Ellsbury. He grew up in the small central Oregon town of Madras and spent the early years of his childhood on the Warm Springs Indian Reservation in central Oregon. Son of a Navajo mother, Ellsbury is believed to be the first player of Navajo descent to play in the major leagues.

I interviewed Jacoby Ellsbury by telephone on October 15, 2014.

Who was your first boyhood idol?

For baseball, it would be Ken Griffey, Jr. Being a kid from the Northwest and living in Oregon, the Mariners were the closest baseball team. Griffey played centerfield, batted left-handed, threw left. I just enjoyed watching him play.

I think, from just an all-around sport perspective, Michael Jordan—him with the Bulls and their run of championships. Around my time growing up, that was when Jordan was in his prime. I enjoyed just watching him play. I'd say those two guys were my boyhood idols.

Have you ever met Michael Jordan?

I have. I have. Yeah, actually I met him this year for the first time. It was for Derek Jeter's farewell. Jordan came in, and he was on the field at Yankee Stadium. I met him there. It was neat. You could just see everybody, you know, kind of stop and stare. Your eyes went to him, and so did everybody else's. It was a pretty neat experience, for sure.

How did the encounter go? Did Jordan live up to your expectations?

Well, I really don't get star-struck that much after playing with some of the players I've played with and being the competitor I am. But, seeing him, that was pretty special for me. I told him hello and just left it at that. He was there for Jeter, and he was getting a lot of people's attention. I just wanted to tell him hello and let him know I followed his career as a kid.

A lot of baseball players have mentioned Ken Griffey, Jr. as being one of their boyhood idols. You obviously saw Junior at the Kingdome in Seattle when you were young.

Yeah, I saw him maybe two or three times, but all the games were on TV. I just remember him and his style of play, his hat on backwards and the Home Run Derby at the All-Star Game. He was fun. It was fun for me to watch him play. Now I see him once a year. Nike does a vacation for some of their athletes. He's always there, so I see him for five or six days each off-season.

How bizarre was it to be on the same field as Griffey, Jr. when you first came up to the major leagues with the Red Sox?

Yeah, I played him when he was with the White Sox and then when he was with the Reds. It was neat. It was neat playing against someone that you looked up to. You collected his baseball card and wore the Mariners cap—all that neat stuff you do as a kid. So, to play with someone that you looked up to was pretty special.

When he was with the White Sox he personalized a bat to me. I saw him after the game and asked if he would sign a bat for me. That was pretty neat, pretty special. It's one of the things that I cherish in my memorabilia collection.

Do you think about being an idol to young fans? You obviously had many fans in Boston when you were with the Red Sox, and now that you are with the Yankees, you are worshipped by fans in New York. Do you consider yourself an idol?

I guess how I look at it is, I try to do the right thing on and off the field. When I play the game, I try to play it as hard as I can each and every play, you know, to give everything I have. That's how I go about it. I try to do everything the right way.

You donated $1-million to the Oregon State University baseball program. I know that OSU Coach Pat Casey and his players are very appreciative. Why did you feel you should donate to Beavers' baseball?

It was a special time in my life going to Oregon State, you know, having a great time while I was there and going to the College World Series. Pat Casey is still there, and he's obviously pretty much the main reason—or one of the big reasons—Oregon State is worth that. I just wanted to give back—to give those kids a great experience like I had. It was pretty much a no-brainer when they talked to me about some of the renovations that they're doing at the baseball stadium. It's been neat seeing how competitive they've been over the years. It's been fun to watch as an alumnus and going back there and seeing those kids.

Jacoby, I talked with Shoni Schimmel, the women's basketball star who grew up on the reservation in Umatilla. She talked about her parents being her role models because of their support while she pursued her dream of playing college and professional basketball. As Shoni pointed out, not many kids seem to be able to make their way off the reservation to pursue a better life for themselves. She's a huge role model for her people. With your mother being a full-blooded Navajo, do you hear from Native Americans who say they look at you as a role model?

Um, yeah, I live in Arizona now, and I put on clinics. It's a free baseball clinic for Native American youth. It's usually been about 300 kids the past three years, and it's continuing to grow. It's been fun just to hear their stories while they're wearing the Ellsbury jerseys—whether Boston Red Sox gear or the Yankee gear. It's been fun to see those kids faces light up knowing that, yeah, it is possible to have a great life beyond the reservation. Shoni Schimmel, she's obviously done a tremendous job of being a role model for those kids. Set a goal. Have a dream. Anything's possible. I think that's the biggest thing through the camp that I try to get through to kids. It's not necessarily about baseball. It's about having a dream, working hard and realizing you can accomplish anything through hard work.

Career Notes: After being drafted by Boston in the first round of the 2005 amateur draft, Jacoby Ellsbury made his major league debut in 2007. He batted .353 in 116 at bats to help the Red Sox win the American League pennant. He batted .438 in the four-game sweep of the Rockies in the 2007 World Series. In Game 3 against Colorado, Ellsbury had four hits, including three doubles. It was the first four-hit game for a World Series' rookie since Joe Garagiola accomplished the feat for the Cardinals in 1946. In 2008, Ellsbury's first full season in the majors, he hit .280 with 9 home runs and an American League-leading (and Red Sox rookie-record) 50 stolen bases. Ellsbury set a Red Sox record and led the major leagues with 70 stolen bases in 2009. Ellsbury spent most of 2010 on the disabled list, but bounced back in 2011. He was voted American League Comeback Player of the Year after batting .321, with 46 doubles, 5 triples, 32 home runs, 105 runs-batted-in and 39 steals. He finished runner-up to Detroit pitcher Justin Verlander in the American League MVP voting. Ellsbury led the majors with 52 stolen bases in 2013. He also set a Red Sox record with five steals in one game. After seven seasons in Boston, Ellsbury made the decision to leave via free agency. On December 7, 2013, he signed a 7-year, $153-million free-agent contract with the New York Yankees.

* * *

Notah Begay III was a three-time All-American golfer at Stanford University. Begay led Stanford to the 1994 national championship and fired a collegiate career-low 62 during the '94 NCAA Championships—one stroke off the school record held by teammate Tiger Woods. Begay was inducted into the Stanford Athletics Hall of Fame in October, 2014.

A Native American who grew up in Albuquerque, New Mexico, Begay formed the Notah Begay III Foundation in 2005. The NB3 Foundation seeks to reduce childhood obesity in Native American children.

On April 24, 2014, several years after I spoke with Notah Begay, he suffered a heart attack at age 41 while on the putting green at Dallas National Golf Club. Prompt action by medical personnel saved Begay's life. Among the first to wish him well was his former college teammate, Tiger Woods. Begay and Woods remain close friends.

I talked with Notah Begay on July 31, 2011, at the Pacific University Legends Golf Classic charity event in Beaverton, Oregon.

Who was your boyhood idol?

Of all the great idols I would have, it would be a hybrid of two people. Initially, because I'm a professional golfer, I would have to say Seve Ballesteros—who just passed away recently. And secondly—because of his Native-American roots and his ability to overcome adversity and win a gold medal for the United States—was Billy Mills.

If you met them at some point along the way, what was your first encounter with them like? Did they live up to your expectations?

Yes, certainly Seve was very charismatic and very straight forward and just sort of how everybody envisions him based on his appearances in the Ryder Cup and how he approached the game. I met him my rookie year on the PGA Tour. He was still an active player. I'm lucky. I'm one of the guys that actually got to compete against one of my boyhood idols. Golf presents that special opportunity, unlike most other sports where you retire when you're 25 or 30.

Billy Mills has been a great friend of mine for many years. I've watched his movie, and I've heard him talk about the race when he won the 10-thousand meters in Tokyo. It still gives me goose bumps when he tells me about it because I just can't imagine coming from out of nowhere to win a gold medal.

Notah, have you been able to process the fact that you are an idol for young golfers who followed you on the PGA Tour?

Yeah, it processes every day. Part of what golf has taught me—and with my Native American upbringing—is you always gotta think of the future generations. So, it's not just about me. It's what we leave behind and how we teach the game through sportsmanship, integrity and playing by the rules. I think those are good attributes and principles to teach young kids—kids that come out and learn from us on the PGA Tour.

NBA star Charles Barkley famously said in a 1993 commercial, and I'll paraphrase here, "I am not a role model just because I dunk a basketball."—in essence, suggesting that parents need to be the role models for their kids. Do you think athletes are role models whether they want to be or not?

Not by obligation. It's certainly an opportunity. It's just like philanthropy. Nobody is required to give back to charity or give their time or money to good causes that they feel are worthwhile contributions. But, that's what being a role model is. It's taking an opportunity to enlighten a young person to become a better citizen.

Career Notes: Notah Begay is one of the few professionals to shoot a 59 in competition. He did so while playing in the Dominion Open on the Nike Tour. During his years on the PGA Tour, Begay won four tournaments—two in 1999 and two in 2000—and earned more than $5.2-million. He was once ranked as one of the world's top 20 players, but a back injury limited his effectiveness and curtailed his career. Begay has remained close to the game he loves by becoming a golf commentator for NBC and the Golf Channel.

*　*　*

Grant Fuhr was part of five Stanley Cup champion Edmonton Oilers teams in the 1980s and early 1990s. His Oilers' teammate, the legendary Wayne Gretzky, once called Fuhr the greatest goaltender ever to play in the NHL. In 2003, Grant Fuhr became the first black to be inducted into the Hockey Hall of Fame.

Fuhr was suspended for the 1990-91 season after the NHL learned of his cocaine use during the 1980s. His suspension was eventually shortened, but he missed 59 games that season. Fuhr told the story of his remarkable career in his 2014 book, "Grant Fuhr: The Story of a Hockey Legend." An excellent golfer, Fuhr now serves as director of golf for Desert Dunes Golf Club in

Palm Springs, California. He also competes in many celebrity tournaments for the benefit of charitable causes.

I talked with Grant Fuhr on the phone on June 6, 2011, as he prepared to participate in the Caddies 4 Cure charity fundraiser in Portland, Oregon.

Who was your first boyhood idol?

I was fortunate to meet Glenn Hall when I was a kid. He lived in the next town over in Stony Plain. I got the opportunity to meet him. For me, it was a big thrill in the fact that he was a goalie and I wanted to be a goalie. It worked out great for me.

When you went out to play, did you pretend to be Glenn Hall?

I liked Glenn. I liked Tony Esposito—Tony more because we played the same hand. I think that was the biggest dream. But, the chance to meet Glenn and find out what a great person he was, I think that was one of the biggest thrills for me.

He lived up to your expectations?

He did, and we got to be good friends. That makes it even better.

Did you ever get a chance to play against either Glenn or Tony?

Actually, Glenn was a little before me. Tony Esposito I got to play against my first year in the NHL, which was a great thrill.

The first time you met those two guys that you looked up to. Did it seem a little strange?

It did a little bit. You get a chance to watch them as a kid. To actually meet them and find out they're super nice people, you just have more respect for them.

Grant, the story has been told many times. You were adopted by white parents when you were just a couple of weeks old. I know race was never a big deal with you, but you became the first black to be inducted into the Hockey Hall of Fame. You were very emotional that day during your acceptance speech. What did all that mean to you?

It was a great honor. Obviously, just getting elected to the Hall of Fame was a fantastic honor. The fact that I was able to become a non-traditional member, I guess you could put it, was a big thrill. I've met some great people, like Willie O'Ree—the first black player in the NHL. I got the chance—the honor—to meet Willie, and I became friends with Willie. The fact that I am in the Hall of Fame kind of honors the first black NHL players a little bit; I think that's a huge deal.

You had so much success as a player, there's no question that you were an idol for young hockey fans—black and white. Did you ever think about that during your playing days?

No, we were having too much fun playing. The biggest thing was we were having such a good time playing that we didn't really worry about winning. We were just having a good time with it.

You've spent some time in the NHL serving as a goaltending coach. Have you had any goaltenders come up to you and say, "Grant, you were my guy growing up?"

We've had a couple. Unfortunately, I was still playing when they said that, so it makes you feel old pretty quickly. (Laughs)

Career Notes: Grant Fuhr won four Stanley Cups over a five-year period while playing goaltender for the Edmonton Oilers in the 1980s. While Fuhr was in net for four Stanley Cup champions, he actually has five championship rings. He was a member of the 1989-90 Oilers when they won the Cup with Bill Ranford between the pipes. Fuhr was

Edmonton's first-round draft pick (#8 overall) in the 1981 NHL Draft. Before he retired in 2000, Fuhr won 403 regular season games for the Oilers, Maple Leafs, Sabres, Kings, Blues and Flames. The multiple-time NHL All-Star won the Vezina Trophy with Edmonton in 1988 and the William M. Jennings Trophy with Buffalo in 1994.

*   *   *

Erik Spoelstra became the first Asian-American head basketball coach in the NBA when he was promoted to the top job in Miami on April 28, 2008. He coached LeBron James, Dwyane Wade and the Heat to NBA championships in 2012 and 2013. But, the real story isn't that Spoelstra was able to slip two championship rings on his fingers. How he put himself in position to do so is such an incredible story, it seems perfect for the screenwriters in Hollywood.

I've been around so long that I covered Eric Spoelstra when he was playing high school basketball his senior year in 1988. I also closely followed his career at the University of Portland. But, I sort of lost track of Spoelstra after he headed overseas to play professionally right after college. Imagine my surprise when I later learned that he was working with Pat Riley in Miami. I was even more surprised when, a few years after that, Riley promoted Spoelstra to head coach of the Heat. Erik and I knew each other, but we hadn't really talked very often. I probably knew his dad, former NBA executive John Spoelstra, better than I knew Erik. However, I can't begin to tell you how much I enjoyed talking with the Heat coach about his basketball journey when we spent some time on the phone in early 2014. He had agreed to discuss his boyhood idol, but we talked about so much more. His inspirational story of rising from the basement to the penthouse is one that should give everyone the belief that hard work will pay off. I talked with Erik Spoelstra by phone on January 24, 2014.

Who was your first boyhood idol?

From a basketball sense, it was Isiah Thomas. He was my first idol in junior high school. I was such a big fan of Isiah and his game that I ended up wearing his number in sixth grade, seventh grade and eighth grade. I loved watching him play. He was small. It was somebody I thought I could relate to in that you could play a game and excel at it even if you're small. He was probably the first one. Then, as I got into high school, probably one of my biggest role models was Terry Porter. I actually changed my number to 30 my junior year in high school, and I wore that number all the way through college. I loved Terry's competitive spirit. I was a big fan of the Blazers at the time. He played the point guard position, but he was the heart and soul of the team. I really admired him as a player on and off the court. Those were probably my first two role models and idols.

Your two idols went from being players to head coaches in the NBA, as did you. It seems you followed their path.

You know what was interesting? I went to Isiah's basketball camp in Detroit when I was a kid. My dad's family is from Detroit, so I stayed with my cousin and my aunt. I hung out there for a week and went to Isiah's camp. That was one of the greatest gifts for a 12-year-old that you could have. It was an incredible experience and incredible summer. I still have the camp picture with Isiah. Then, later on when I began working for the Heat—around my third or fourth year—we signed Terry Porter. I was still a video coordinator working for Coach Riley. I'd already known him at that point, but I told him that I'd been such a big fan of his. And, just to keep his age in perspective, I said that I'd changed my number to 30 when I was in high school, which was *years* before that. (Laughs) But, I told him I admired him so much. We all sensed, even then, that he would get into coaching. He had that type of understanding and passion for the game to take the next step. So, those were my first basketball-playing idols. Immediately, I related to Isiah because of his electrifying play and because he was small. (Laughs) I thought it was so cool that a small player could dominate the league in such an exciting way.

Then, as I got to college, I started to think that coaching would be something I'd like to pursue whenever I was done playing. Whatever level, high school or college, that's really all I was thinking at that time. Outside of my high school coach and my college coaches, my next big role model was Rick Adelman. I've really respected Rick as a coach and his ability to teach and to coach and to manage personalities and motivate. But then, also the respect level for his integrity for the game and his character and integrity off the court—those things I admired and wanted to emulate. He's probably the biggest influence I had when I started to think about getting into coaching.

Does Rick know that?

I don't think I've ever really talked to him about it. I've mentioned it before to the media, but—to be quite honest—nobody really cared about that before I won NBA championships. (Laughs) The last three or four years since our profile has risen, I've told that story a few times. But, I don't think I've ever told him. I was such a big fan of the Blazers, obviously, because of my dad. My family got to know the Adelman family. Because of the character and integrity that Rick brought to that position and getting to know him, at some point in college I was like, "Wow! That would be a pretty cool profession to get into." I certainly—absolutely 100%—was not thinking about the professional level. Rick had come from Chemeketa Community College and was so successful there. He had talked about that he could possibly coach in college, and that's where he initially wanted to break through. I just wanted to get into coaching, and I really wanted to emulate what he did, but probably just at the high school or college level.

Let's go back to when you met Isiah at his camp. Was he everything you expected? How did he react to you as a kid?

He didn't know who I was. I was just one of 300 campers. But, he was phenomenal. He was there every single day at camp. I remember him being a presence at the camp. It wasn't just a camp with his name on it.

I remember one of the days I won the "hustle" award. I got to go up and shake his hand and receive the award. Every single one of us was able to take a picture with him. I still have it to this day. (Laughs) Actually, my parents have it hanging up.

Some people never get to meet their childhood heroes, yet you got to meet Isiah Thomas, Terry Porter and Rick Adelman—your idols—at different stages of your life.

I don't know. I've had so many "pinch yourself" moments, "Is this true? (Laughs) Is this actually happening right now?" I'm grateful for all of the mentors and role models that I've had in my life. You gotta be lucky at the same time. Growing up in an NBA family, at least I had some familiarity with that world. But, that certainly doesn't guarantee anything, and I was never thinking about working in the NBA. I wanted to coach. Actually, a year out of college, I initially accepted the varsity head basketball coaching position at Sherwood High School in the Portland area. I applied for it and ended up getting it. I accepted it, and a week later, I turned it down because I had decided that—at that age—I still wanted to play. It was one of the toughest decisions I ever made. I continued to play in Germany. I mean, if I never went back to Germany, who knows? Maybe I'd still be a high school basketball coach somewhere in Portland. I was only 23. I talked about it with my family. Basically, the decision came down to—I could eventually get into high school coaching, but I wouldn't always be able to play professionally. At that age, I said, "Okay. I want to experience something new—live in a foreign country and play basketball while I can while I'm young." I went to Germany for a couple of years. Then, from there, I had just a lot of great timing in the turn of events.

While I was in Germany, I applied for a video internship with the Heat. Chris Wallace was with the Miami Heat at the time as Director of Player Personnel. They had a new position coming up in the NBA, and it was called Video Coordinator. You were basically an assistant to the coaching staff. There had only been a handful in the league. Dan

Burke, a nephew to Rick Adelman, was one of the first for the Trail Blazers. He worked for Jack Ramsay as an intern. Coach Pat Riley had a similar type of intern position with the Lakers his last year. When he went to the Knicks, he started to develop that position even more. It was a little bit more similar to what you see today. But, this was a new position, and Chris Wallace said that Dave Wohl, the GM at the time, was thinking about starting something similar. It was very vague what the position was, but at least I had heard that there was an opening. I was in Germany, and I still was debating whether I was going to continue to play or not. I thought at the time that I wanted to get into college coaching. It was during the spring, and the summer before, I had applied for graduate assistant jobs with the University of Portland, Portland State and the University of Oregon. I got turned down on all of those, so I continued to play. So, now I thought, "Hey, this internship position actually sounds kind of interesting. Maybe I'll do it for a summer and, after that, maybe I can still hook on with a college somewhere." The job description was kind of vague. It was only really supposed to be for a summer and just help out through the draft. It was such a new position. They didn't have anybody else apply, so I got the job. (Laughs) We didn't have a coach. Dave Wohl was the GM. Chris Wallace was working under him. It was a very small front office.

Now there was a change of ownership. Micky Arison took control. When he took control after the draft, he ended up hiring Bobby Huggins. There was a press conference. He accepted the job. Then, three days later, it all blew up. If Huggins actually accepted and stayed in the job, I don't know what would have happened. It would have been his call whether he would have kept me in this new position in the NBA. I probably would have just gotten blown out of there. I have no idea what would've happened. For the rest of the summer, there wasn't a coach. Then, Micky ended up hiring Pat Riley. He hired him away from the Knicks. You remember—the infamous fax and that whole story. It was so late in the summer, and—because it was such a contentious hire from the Knicks—Pat couldn't bring anybody from

New York. He wanted to bring his whole staff. He wanted to bring Jeff Van Gundy. He wanted to bring Bob Salmi, who was one of the NBA's original video coordinators. He couldn't bring any of them. So, after a strong recommendation, he ended up hiring Stan Van Gundy—Jeff's brother—sight unseen. (Laughs) He was like, "Hey, if you're like Jeff, I'll hire you." And, he hired Bob McAdoo and Scotty Robertson. On one of his first days—since Pat was so committed to video for teaching and processing information for the coaching staff—he actually came down to the dungeon where I worked. He said, "Hey, who are you?" I introduced myself. I said, "I've been a video intern for the summer and helped out with the draft." I asked, "Do you need anything?" He said, "Well yeah. Actually, we do need a video coordinator. Here's the job. It's 18 hours a day. It's miserable. It's in this office. I'll work you like you've never been worked before. You'll never leave this room, and you'll never see the light of day. Can you do the job?" I really had absolutely *no* experience. I had no idea what he was talking about in terms of the technology. (Laughs) I didn't know anything about the *profession* at that point. I said, "Yeah, absolutely. I'm your guy." So, he ended up keeping me.

I never spoke to him again for probably another two years. All my communication was with assistant coach Stan Van Gundy. I joke about this today, but for at least the first year, Coach Riley didn't know my name. (Laughs) All I was was a guy in the dungeon. I would get them information and video, pick up the dry cleaning and pick up lunch. But, my only communication with the coaching staff was through Stan. After a couple years, I developed a really strong relationship with Stan that is strong to this day. He's one of my closest friends. After a couple years, Stan started to tell Coach Riley, "Hey, this kid actually is doing a really good job. He's pretty good. We got lucky that somebody was able to manage this kind of work."

There are undoubtedly people today who look at the path you've traveled and hope to make the same kind of journey themselves.

Do you ever think about the fact that you could be an idol of sorts for someone hoping to gain entry into the NBA family?

Yeah, I do. I mean, I wasn't even one of the first to make this type of journey. I mentioned Dan Burke. He's now on the bench of the Indiana Pacers as an assistant coach. He influenced me. When I played for the Portland Trail Blazers Summer League team way back when, he was one of the coaches. And, Mike Brown was one to do it before me. We played against each other in college. But, he broke in with the NBA through video and then became one of the first head coaches who started from video. Now that you're starting to see a few others, like Lawrence Frank and Frank Vogel, I think there's a sense of responsibility. For whatever reason, we are part of a movement where there are some more doors opened for people like us where there weren't those possibilities 15 or 20 years ago.

Let's take that another step since I do so much work in the Philippines. My mother is Filipino and I take great pride in that as well. Realistically, on first glance, I probably am not the stereotypically-looking NBA coach—because of my ethnicity, because of my age, and because of my background and the fact that I didn't play in the league. But, we can be an example that— through dedication, with integrity and a tremendous amount of luck and being in the right place at the right time—dreams and possibilities can come true. If that inspires other people, then I'm 100% all for it. Sometimes, I don't look at myself like a role model like that, but when you hear stories like mine, then there's an opportunity there to show people that if you dream hard enough, things can happen, regardless of your background, your ethnicity, where you're from or your experiences.

Career Notes: In his seven seasons as head coach of the Miami Heat, Erik Spoelstra has won 63% of his regular season games (351-207) and 64% of his NBA playoff games (63-36). Yes, his Miami teams have been loaded with talent, featuring stars such as LeBron James, Dwyane Wade and Chris Bosh. But, Spoelstra has done a good job of managing things—including some rather large egos—on the court and off. With the guy who once just wanted to be a high school or college coach leading the way, the Heat played in the NBA Finals four straight years (2011–14) and won back-to-back titles in 2012 and 2013.

*　　*　　*

10

His Posters Were On My Wall

Scott Brosius spent eleven years in the majors with the Oakland Athletics (1991–97) and New York Yankees (1998–2001). In each of his four seasons in New York, he starred in the World Series. He earned three championship rings. Brosius, the 1998 World Series MVP, retired soon after playing in the 2001 Fall Classic and returned home to Oregon to complete his degree from Linfield College. He became an assistant baseball coach at Linfield, where he had played three years of college baseball prior to turning pro. In 2007, he was promoted to head coach of the Linfield Wildcats. In eight seasons as Linfield's head baseball coach, Brosius guided the Wildcats to four NCAA Division III Regional championships and an overall record of 270-96. In 2013, Linfield went 42-8 and captured the NCAA D3 national championship. Brosius stunned his alma mater by stepping down as Linfield's baseball coach in May, 2015, to pursue opportunities in professional baseball.

When you talk with Scott Brosius, he says how fortunate he was to have been a part of those championship teams. He points out the Yankees were good before he got to New York. He says the Linfield baseball program was good before he became involved as a coach. I'll tell you this. If Scott Brosius is anything, he is humble. Here's the truth of the matter. The Yankees were desperate for a third baseman when they acquired Brosius. He delivered far more than expected and helped them reach the World Series four straight years. And, about the Linfield baseball team he coached—yes, the Wildcats had fielded excellent teams for years. But, only after Brosius became head

121

coach did they win their first NCAA Division III championship. Those things might have happened anyway, but I choose to believe it was the addition of Scott Brosius—with his wide assortment of skills, positive attitude and extreme likability—that made the difference and helped the guys in Yankee pinstripes and Wildcat caps win championships. Brosius is a class act in every way. It won't be long before he's back in pro baseball attempting to work his magic one more time.

I talked by phone with Scott Brosius on November 7, 2013.

Scott, who was your first boyhood idol?

My very first, for sure, was Johnny Bench. I guess I was somewhere between five and eight years old when I first started being able to really watch and pay attention to baseball. Back at that time, there was really only one game on a week, like the Saturday Game of the Week. The Big Red Machine at that time was kind of in its heyday, so they were on Saturday mornings quite a bit. They were one of the few teams that I got to see often. At that point, I wanted to be a catcher, so Johnny Bench was the natural guy for me to watch and emulate. For me growing up, that's who I wanted to be as a young kid—Johnny Bench.

A lot of young kids want to be a catcher because you get to wear the mask and all the gear. Was that part of the appeal for you?

(Laughs) I'm sure it probably was. I don't really remember now why I was dumb enough at that point to say I wanted to catch. It's a position where there's just so much more activity. You're catching every ball. You're in every play. So, as a little kid, I loved putting on the gear and using the special glove and all that kind of stuff. Yeah, that was who I wanted to be.

Was there anything specific about Bench that drew your attention to him?

I just think, honestly, because I was so young, he was who I *saw*. I heard amazing stories about what kind of player he was and how good he was.

I remember they talked about that as a kid he could hold—whatever it was—like seven baseballs in one hand because his hands were so big. They told these larger than life stories about how great he was. Yeah, that's who you wanted to be.

You didn't grow up in a major league city. That made it a little different for you than those lucky kids that grew up in big league towns.

Back when I was a kid, I didn't get to go to too many Portland Beavers games. But, the big league club would come in and play. So, whether it was the Pirates or the Phillies—or whoever it might have been at that point—that one time a year when the big leaguers came in to play the Triple-A team was really the only look that I ever got in person at major league baseball. I never saw a major league game in person until I was playing professionally.

When you were playing, you were undoubtedly an idol for some. Did you think about that?

You know, I *did*. I just remembered who I was as a kid. I mentioned the Beavers games, and I remember going down being next to the field and watching the guys play catch. I remember looking at my dad and just going, "Look at how far they can throw the ball, and they're not even lobbing it! It's staying straight on a line. They're throwing that hard that far." Then, when a player actually came over and talked to me and I had them sign a piece of paper, I remember just looking at them starry-eyed and not being able to speak. So, no question, when I was playing, those were the kids that I kind of looked for at the ballpark—the ones that were there just to see the players and were looking for an opportunity to meet a player. Honestly, I tried to stay away from the ones that had notebooks of cards to get signed. I was there looking for the kids who I felt were just more like I was—just huge fans of the games and of the players.

Scott, did you notice any difference in how people treated you once you started playing for the Yankees? It seems there has almost always been a Yankee mystique.

Oh, no question. All my years in Oakland, we didn't have a lot of good teams. You even watch now and see that up until the playoffs, they really don't draw a lot of fans. Ten thousand people a night at the game is about all they get. So, I could pretty much go anywhere that I wanted around Oakland, and nobody really knew who we were. Then, I came to New York, and it was a completely different story. I remember my wife Jennifer and me going with our kids to this little diner. This was before we played our first home game. We started the year on the road and came home to New York. We were trying to still get settled. We were still living out of a hotel. So, we went to this little diner to eat. We sat down and before we could even order, a waiter walks over with two or three different appetizers and drinks. And, a guy in the back is waving and says, "Go get'em tonight, Scotty!" We just kind of looked at each other and went, "Wow! Things are gonna be different here." You couldn't walk down the street. Everybody knew who you were. There was just so much more attention on the team and on the players.

You coached Linfield College to a national baseball championship. Do you think being a former major league player gave you an advantage and helped you recruit some of your Linfield players?

I don't know. What's crazy now is you look back and 2001 was my last year in the majors. You start doing the math and you realize these guys were like five years old or six years old at that time. We don't talk a ton about my career, but they certainly know. We'll have conversations a little bit about my playing career and things like that. I don't know whether that leads to more credibility or not in terms of the recruiting process. One thing that I really try to talk to the guys about is, "Hey, these are some of the experiences I've had and what I've learned from them. Hopefully, you guys can learn from them as well." It's interesting. I've talked to a number of players—kids coming in—and these are kids that truly had no clue that I even played. They're just looking at Linfield, and I'm the coach here.

One of the people I've interviewed for this book is your former New York Yankee manager, Joe Torre. That was a lot of fun for me because—having grown up as a Cardinals' fan—I remember his 1971 MVP season in which he batted .363. Did you enjoy playing for Torre in New York?

I didn't have the same background as you. I didn't really remember him as a player. It's probably because—as a player—he had never been to the World Series. He never had those opportunities. Again, it's a sign of the times. It's who you've seen on TV—just the winning teams. So, I really never remember seeing him play. Certainly I knew his credentials. I knew the type of career that he had, and I knew what he'd accomplished in the game as a player and as a manager. Obviously there was a lot of credibility when he had a conversation with you. I think I've taken a lot from him. A lot of times he'd just come over and have the ability to say the right thing like, "Hey, I remember a game where I did this." He's a guy that had a much better career than I did, and he says, "Yeah, I remember the struggles. I remember what this was like." I think that's important. I really loved playing for Joe. I thought he had a great perspective on the game, great knowledge of the game, but also understood the day-to-day grind and what a player goes through.

There are players—like Torre and Chicago Cubs Hall of Famer Ernie Banks—that never got to play in a World Series. Here you are, admittedly less talented, but a World Series MVP.

I feel incredibly fortunate. No question. I say that all the time. I hopped on the train at the right stop. That team was already a winning team and had won a World Series in '96. I came off just a brutal year in '97 wondering if and where I'm gonna have a job in '98, and I get traded to the Yankees and get to be a part of four World Series teams. I really understand how fortunate I was to be a part of those teams and get those opportunities to play—especially when you see guys that have played so many more years and accomplished so much within the game, but never got those opportunities.

Scott, I appreciate you spending time with me discussing your career and boyhood heroes because there were some very well-known, old-school athletes who declined interviews or asked for large financial payments to tell their stories for this book. It's understandable, I guess, but it was a little disheartening to find out that some sports idols would choose not be part of this project unless they were paid.

Well, they just grew up in such different times. Now, we're fortunate enough to be in a time where if you're smart and play long enough—and just pay attention to doing things in an intelligent way—you're going to leave the game in a pretty good place financially. These guys, who were really incredible players, played in a time where they've now had to go back to work, and some are without the skill set to be able to really do that. So, you're right. It's kind of sad, but I kind of see where guys like that might say, "This is how I make my living."

Before I go, I have to back up a little bit because the question you asked me in terms of my boyhood idol was specifically about the *first* guy I could remember. But, I have to tell you the guy that really shaped me or impacted me—or was really more truly my personal idol growing up—was Dale Murphy. As I got a little bit older and got towards junior high and high school, we were at a place in time where cable TV showed up. You could watch the Cubs on WGN, and you could watch the Braves on WTBS—pretty much on a daily basis. Of course, Murph was playing for the Braves, and he was having an incredible career. I also knew he was from Portland. But, more importantly for me, everything that I heard was just about what kind of person he was—how he treated teammates and how he treated fans. The quality of person that he was, I mean, he was really truly the guy where I said, "This is who I want to be when I grow up." I was never the type of player that he was, but he was my role model. I wanted to be known as somebody like Dale Murphy, in terms of how he went *about* it, not just what kind of career he had. Every time that I see him and talk to him, I'm still sort of like, "Wow! This is Dale Murphy!" Like I said, Johnny Bench was my idol as a kid, just because I was young and I thought I was going to be a catcher. But, Dale Murphy was really the guy that I would say was a role model for me. His posters were the ones that were on my wall in high school and in college. He was truly the guy who was a role model for me. When my wife and I started dating here at Linfield, we were talking about baseball, and she said, "My family and I used to go watch Dale Murphy at Wilson High School." I was like, "Oh boy! You just jumped up a notch in my book right there. You know who Dale Murphy is!" Yeah, he was the man.

Do you remember when and where you met Dale Murphy for the first time?

I don't remember specifically where we were the first time that we met. It might have been at the Active Oldtimer's Baseball Association of Portland Banquet. It might have been somewhere else. But, he knew who I was. (Laughs) I was starry-eyed. I'm like, "Murph, I gotta tell ya. You were my guy." Every time I see him now, it's the same thing. A couple years ago at the Oldtimer's Banquet, I bought his jersey. He brought it in to be auctioned off, and I bought it. He goes, "I would have given you a jersey." I'm like, "No! You're my guy!"

I made the greatest trade ever. I was playing in a fundraiser golf tournament. They had a bunch of autographed baseballs from different players that were raffle prizes. So, sure enough, I win a raffle, and I win my own signed baseball. So, I walked up to the lady—smiling—and showing her the baseball. I said, "Well, here's the deal. This is me, and I just won this." She says, "I'll tell you what. Why don't you just trade for one of the others that haven't been picked up? We'll just make a trade." I look down, and there's a "Dale Murphy MVP '82-'83" signed baseball, and I go, "I can trade this—*my* baseball—for *his*?" And she goes, "Absolutely." So, I made this trade and walked away. I'm going, "Man, some poor guy has no clue that he actually won Dale Murphy, but instead got Scott Brosius.

Career Notes: Scott Brosius made his major league debut on August 7, 1991, and he broke in with a double and a homer against the Mariners. In 1996, he hit a career-high 22 home runs and batted .304. However, the following season his average dropped more than 100 points to .203, and the Athletics dealt him to the Yankees. New York fans didn't have high expectations for Brosius in light of his anemic hitting in 1997. However, he anchored the third base position and helped the Yankees win American League pennants in each of his four seasons in the Bronx. They were World Series champions his first three years in New York. His first year in the Bronx, in 1998, Brosius raised his batting average 97 points to .300. Despite hitting in the bottom third of the Yankee lineup most of the time, he managed to drive home a career-best 98 runs to help New York win an American League record 114 games in the regular season. In the 1998 World Series—a four-game sweep of the Padres—he batted .471 with two home runs and six RBI. He hit both of those homers and drove in four runs in New York's 5-4 win in Game 3. He was named the 1998 World Series MVP. In 1999, Brosius earned the American League Gold Glove for his defensive play at third base, and he batted .375 in the World Series to help the Yankees sweep four straight from the Atlanta Braves. In 2000, he hit .308 in the World Series as the Yankees beat the New York Mets in five games. Brosius had only four hits in the 2001 World Series, but one of those was a game-tying 2-out, 2-run homer in the bottom of the ninth of Game 5—a game New York eventually won 3-2 in 12 innings over Arizona. Soon after the Yankees dropped the 2001 World Series in that thrilling seven game series, Brosius ended his playing career and headed home to Oregon.

*   *   *

Dale Murphy was another Oregon native that found success in the major leagues. A power-hitting outfielder, Murphy played 18 years with the Braves, Phillies and Rockies. A two-time National League MVP, Murphy hit 398 career homers. One of the most fan-friendly athletes of his time, Murphy was—and still is—almost always willing to sign autographs and take pictures with fans. He is even more accessible to his fans today via social media.

Dale Murphy was already in the major leagues by the time I began working as a local television sportscaster in Portland in 1980. Even so, I quickly learned about the home-grown product that was blossoming into a star for the Atlanta Braves. I showed highlights of Murphy hitting a home run or making a leaping catch on a routine basis on my 11 p.m. sports reports. There was no shortage of Murphy highlights, especially during his National League MVP years in 1982 and 1983.

I've enjoyed numerous conversations with Murph since getting to know him during his playing days. He is extremely likable—outgoing and friendly— the kind of person you would like to have as your next door neighbor. Always a giver, Murphy received several of baseball's top awards for his charity work during his playing days. He proudly continues to serve others today.

I talked by phone with Dale Murphy on January 8, 2013.

Thinking back to when you were a kid, who is the person you would consider your first boyhood idol?

I remember at a real young age going to Portland Beaver games with my dad and hearing these names—Sam McDowell, Luis Tiant and Chico Salmon. These are names that I'll never forget. Then, I started playing ball, and a lot of people don't realize that, yes, I was born and raised in Portland, but for two years, I actually lived in the Bay Area down in San Francisco. My dad got transferred down there with Westinghouse. So, if you were in the Bay Area in the '60s, you know who my hero was. (Laughs) It was Willie Mays. There's no question about it. I got to see him play at Candlestick Park and really got interested in the Giants.

Then as I got older and was in high school, I was catching. My favorite player became Johnny Bench.

Did you have a chance to play against any of these major leaguers that you followed when you were a kid?

Yeah, and it was a real strange feeling. In fact, I think it was the winter of 1974 and Johnny Bench was the guest speaker at the Hayward Awards Banquet. So, I'm there, and he's making these remarks. Someone had told him that I may get drafted and that I was a catcher. During his talk he goes, "Hey, I hear there's a prospect here in Portland. I wish him the best." So, I ended up getting drafted in June of 1974 by the Braves—as a catcher—and it wasn't two years later, in September of '76, that I got my first call-up to the big leagues with the Braves. I got to play against Johnny Bench. (Laughs) It just was a real surreal feeling to get in the box and dig in. There I am in the box facing Don Gullett—or someone who I'd just watched a few years earlier on TV—with Johnny Bench catching. All I can say is it was hard to concentrate on hitting. Just the feeling of being there that close to Bench on the field and playing against him—competing against him—was a strange feeling, for sure.

I know players back then didn't fraternize the way they do today, but when you got a chance to talk with Bench, was he everything you expected?

Oh, yeah. Johnny was always really nice to me. He remembers that I looked up to him, and he'd heard the stories. My retirement night in Atlanta, the Braves remembered that connection, and Johnny Bench was kind enough to do a really nice tribute video for me up on the big screen there in Atlanta Fulton County Stadium. We're not close or anything, but Johnny was very good to me. I always appreciated him during his career. It was fun to compete against him. He was always very kind to me and very complimentary to me. That was always a big thrill in my career.

In the 1980s, you were a baseball hero to many kids across the nation. Kids everywhere knew you because Braves games aired on SuperStation WTBS, which was carried on cable TV systems around the country. Were you aware that kids idolized you?

Yeah, you know it. You think about it a little bit when you go to the ballpark or you get fan mail. You think about it and you try to remember that when you're playing. But, where it really hits you is when you retire. In the social media networks, whether it's Twitter or Facebook—and during some of my appearances now since I've retired—people come up to me and talk to me about being a fan of mine. It's just a very humbling feeling. You hope you did something good. That's what I hope players and sports personalities remember. They can have such a positive impact. They don't have to sign every autograph and do everything, but you can have a great impact when you just respect people and try and be involved a little bit and remember that you can have a good impact on people. I tried to remember that, and I'm very thankful I got a lot of good memories.

Career Notes: Dale Murphy was named to the National League All-Star team seven times in the 1980s. He won four consecutive Silver Slugger awards for his hitting and five straight Gold Gloves for his defensive play in the Braves' outfield. Dale Murphy's jersey number (#3) was retired by the Atlanta Braves in 1994.

*   *   *

11

Not The Sport That I Play Now

Juli Inkster is one of the most successful women's golfers in history. Inkster has won 31 LPGA Tour titles and nearly $13.9-million in prize money (as of October 27, 2015) during her professional career. The ever-busy Inkster has also begun a broadcasting career. In the last few years, she has worked as a golf analyst for The Golf Channel and Fox Sports.

Portland, Oregon, holds a special place in Inkster's heart. In 1983, she won for the first time as a pro in Portland. Sixteen years later, she won again in Portland to earn her 22nd career victory, making her eligible for the LPGA Hall of Fame and the World Golf Hall of Fame. As soon as she sank her final putt to win the 1999 Portland tournament, she received a celebratory champagne shower from her fellow competitors. Highly respected and extremely well-liked, Juli Inkster deserved that special moment. After all, she has given golf fans many special moments during her career—all while being one of the friendliest pro athletes in any sport.

I talked with Juli Inkster about her childhood idol on August 18, 2011, when she was in Portland to play in the annual LPGA tournament in Oregon.

We all had somebody we looked up to when we were young. Please share with me who you considered your childhood idol growing up.

I didn't even start golf until I was 15. I was a huge baseball fan. I loved Juan Marichal. When I played Little League, I pitched like

Juan Marichal—the leg kick and all. Baseball was my whole family's passion, so I followed the Giants a lot. I was more baseball-oriented. When I was 15, I qualified for the U.S. Open. That was my first big (golf) tournament. When I was 18, it was in Indianapolis. I remember seeing Nancy Lopez in the locker room—and Patty Sheehan and Kathy Whitworth. I knew of them, but it wasn't like I was in awe of them. I just never really followed golf—men's or women's. I just kind of fell into golf. Baseball was the sport I really followed.

Did you ever meet Juan Marichal?

No, I never did.

Paula Creamer mentioned you as one of her childhood heroes. She said you're now very good friends and talked about how crazy it seems for one of her childhood idols to have become a friend.

She's one of my idols, too—(laughs)—a reverse-idol. Um, yeah, I think that's the whole cool thing about golf. Someone my age can still compete with someone her age. And, we have gotten to be good friends. There's a lot of things that she does that reminds me of me when I was her age—not the dressing in pink part, but the golf part. She's got a huge passion for the game. She loves the game. I think she's just a great kid.

Career Notes: Juli Inkster is one of the few players to win three consecutive U.S. Amateur titles (1980–82). She joined the LPGA Tour late in the 1983 season and won in just her fifth tournament as a professional. She was recognized as the 1984 LPGA Rookie of the Year after becoming the first Tour rookie to win a pair of majors (Nabisco Dinah Shore, du Maurier Classic). Inkster won another Nabisco Dinah Shore in 1989. Ten years later, she won the LPGA Championship and U.S. Women's Open to complete a career Grand Slam. Inkster then captured the 2000 LPGA Championship and the 2002 U.S. Women's Open, giving her a total of seven major championships. Along with her success on the LPGA Tour, Inkster represented the United States nine times as a player in Solheim Cup competition. In 2009, at the age of 49 years, one month, 28 days (on the day the event started), she broke Beth Daniel's record as the oldest Solheim Cup competitor. Two years later, she competed in her ninth Solheim Cup and became the first to play while also serving as an assistant captain. Inkster served as captain of the 2015 United States Solheim Cup Team. The 2015 U.S. team staged a record-setting comeback on the final day of competition to regain the Cup.

* * *

Hersey Hawkins played 13 seasons in the NBA with Philadelphia, Charlotte, Seattle and Chicago. Selected by the Clippers with the sixth overall pick in the 1988 NBA Draft, Hawkins was immediately traded to Philadelphia. Hawkins was named to the NBA All-Rookie Team his first season. Two years later, he was an NBA All-Star and ended the season with a career-high scoring average of 22.1 points a game. With the Sonics in 1995-96, he averaged 15.6 points to help Seattle reach the NBA Finals.

I was covering the 1996 NBA Finals in Seattle when Hawkins and the Sonics battled the Bulls in Key Arena. It was an extraordinary matchup. Chicago had won an NBA record 72 games in the regular season that year. Seattle had the second-best record in the league at 64-18. Chicago had future Hall of Famers Michael Jordan, Scottie Pippen and Dennis Rodman. Seattle had star-power in (future HOF) point guard Gary Payton and forward Shawn Kemp to go with solid complementary players in Hawkins and Detlef Schrempf. When Chicago won the first three games, the series looked to be over. But, Seattle avoided a sweep with a Game 4 victory, thanks to double-doubles from Kemp and Payton and an 18-point scoring effort from Hawkins. Then, Hawkins scored 21 as Seattle won Game 5 to send the series back to Chicago. The Bulls finally wrapped up the championship with a victory in Game 6.

Throughout his playing career and right up to the present day, Hersey Hawkins has handled himself with class. He now works for the Portland Trail Blazers as the Player Programs Director. His job is to serve as a resource to help with the players' professional, social and personal development. With the well-respected Hawkins involved, the players could not possibly be in better hands.

I spoke with Hersey Hawkins in Portland, Oregon, on April 21, 2011.

When I ask about your boyhood idol, is there someone that immediately comes to mind?

Yeah, there are actually a couple of people that come to mind when I think about my boyhood idols. I was a huge baseball fan. I loved Harold Baines of the White Sox. I really looked up to Harold Baines. I think that was one of the reasons why, as a baseball player when I was younger, I actually learned to switch-hit. I was right-handed, but he was left-handed. I just sort of admired the way he played and the way he carried himself. He just always seemed very professional. When I started getting involved in basketball and watching a lot more basketball, I was drawn to Doctor J. Of course you loved the way he played, but you always heard good, positive things about him off the court—just the way he treated fans. I admired things like that.

He had retired by the time you played in the NBA, correct?

Yeah, I missed him by a couple years. But, I can remember my wife and I sitting at home when I was drafted by Philly my rookie year. We got a call, "Hello. This is Doctor J." It was like, "Who's playing a joke on me?" But, it was really him. He said, "Just wanted to say welcome to town. We'd like to have you over for dinner next week." I'm like, "Oh, my!" This is one of my idols growing up and—all of a sudden—I'm going to his house to have dinner. You could imagine the excitement I felt being able to go over to his house. It was just a once in a lifetime opportunity. That was the first time I'd ever talked to him. I'd never met him. I had probably been in Philly for 2½ or 3 weeks, and—out of the blue—he called to reach out to me.

Were you nervous getting ready to go to his home that night? You had to be nervous on some level, weren't you?

Oh, of course I was nervous. (Laughs) You know, this is the Doc! You don't know exactly what to say or what the conversation's gonna be like at dinner. (Laughs) But, he was very nice, very cordial. He was like, "Dress casual. Wear some jeans or whatever. That's fine." We just went over and had a wonderful dinner with them. He talked to me a lot about Philly and his playing days and how wonderful the city was. He said if I ever needed anything to give him a call. I didn't because I was one of those guys that didn't want to bother him. I know he has tons of other people reaching out to him. I actually went on a couple of trips with him and sort of got to know him a little. He was every bit of what you had heard about and sort of anticipated in the way he handled himself.

When you played at Bradley University and when you played in the NBA, you were surely somebody's hero. Did you ever think about it?

I don't know. I guess I never really thought of it that way even though you used to hear it a lot—especially playing at a college like Bradley where basketball is so critical to the whole community. I never thought of it that way. I always just wanted to go out and represent myself and the university—or whatever professional team I played with—with the utmost respect. I never wanted anybody to say anything bad about me or them. Keeping that in mind, you don't disappoint the people who look up to you or the people who sort of idolize you. But, I never made it a focal point.

Former NBA player Charles Barkley might have been the first to say athletes should not be relied upon to be kids' role models. He pointed out that parents should be the role models for their

children. But, there is always going to be a certain amount of hero worship for our sports stars. Pro athletes understand that, don't they?

Yeah, of course they do. I think—in a perfect world—we would love for kids to have their parents as their idols and role models. But, we know that this is not a perfect world half the time. Now that I have kids, I know most of the time they hate you. (Laughs) They don't want to be around you. So, of course, they look for other role models outside the family. I think that's why athletes become idols. You get on that pedestal. So yeah, I think it's very important that we handle ourselves in a way that kids can look up to us and sort of want to be like us.

Career Notes: Hersey Hawkins averaged 14.7 points per game in his NBA career. A native of Chicago, Illinois, Hawkins played four years at Bradley University. He was the nation's leading scorer (36.3 points a game) his senior season. He was named as a First Team All-American and the 1987-88 College Basketball Player of the Year. Hawkins remains Bradley's all-time scoring leader with 3,008 points. His 63 points in a single game also remains a school record.

* * *

Jack Sikma is a great example of a small town boy who made good. A guy who grew up outside the tiny town of St. Anne, Illinois, and who attended an obscure Central Illinois college, Sikma played 14 years in the NBA. He won a championship with Seattle in 1979. Since retiring, Sikma has been with several teams as an assistant coach. He spent the 2014-15 season working for the Houston Rockets. One of his primary duties was to work with 2014 first-round draft pick Clint Capela—a 6-foot-10 center—to teach him the intricacies of the position. The pairing made sense considering Sikma was an outstanding center in high school, college and the pros.

The first time I saw Jack Sikma, he was a senior at St. Anne High School in Illinois. It was March, 1973, and Sikma had led his high school basketball team into the Illinois High School Association Class A quarterfinals in the second year of the Illinois small-school state tournament. With a mop of floppy blonde hair, Sikma somewhat resembled the "Dutch Boy" from the paint company's advertisements. As I watched the game on television, I was impressed with Sikma as he poured in 36 points and pulled down 24 rebounds in an 88-70 win over Cerro Gordo. St. Anne was 30-1 as it advanced to play in the state semifinals. Despite a pair of double-doubles from Sikma on the final day of the tournament, St. Anne lost in the afternoon semifinals and also lost in that evening's third place game. But, Sikma was suddenly a hot commodity. Several Division I schools offered him a scholarship. However, he chose to play at Illinois Wesleyan, a small liberal-arts university in Bloomington, Illinois. At Wesleyan, he was a four-year starter and ended up as the school's all-time leading scorer and rebounder. When Sikma was a college senior, I had become a television sportscaster and was working in nearby Decatur, Illinois. I covered several of his college games and showed Sikma highlights on my evening sportscasts. I assure you it was a big deal when this guy from a small university in a small Illinois town ended up being selected in the first round of the 1977 NBA Draft. I'm sure there were a lot of people around the country who didn't know a thing about the guy the SuperSonics drafted with the eighth overall pick. They would soon find out. In his rookie season, Sikma helped the Sonics reach the NBA Finals, and the following year, Sikma led Seattle to its only NBA championship.

I talked with Jack Sikma in Portland, Oregon, on January 30, 2012.

I'm interested in knowing who you consider your first boyhood idol. Who immediately pops into your mind?

Well, the first guy that comes to mind is Ernie Banks with the Cubs. I was a diehard Cub fan. WGN had all the games on, and I would watch it religiously—especially through my elementary and junior high days—before I had to go to work on the farm. Ernie was the guy. The

Cubs had a couple good runs. I remember in 1969 they lost to the Mets in the "Miracle Mets" year. Being a Cub Fan, I don't know if I ever recovered.

Basketball-wise, I always enjoyed the Sunday afternoon games in which it was Bill Russell vs. Wilt Chamberlain. I was always pulling for Chamberlain. It's hard to believe that we'd ever call him an underdog, but against those Celtic teams, they had a heck of a time. I think they got them once or twice, but I always looked forward to those matchups when the Celtics played the Sixers in the Sixties.

Did you ever get a chance to meet Ernie Banks?

I have never met Ernie. I was close a couple of times. I know he lives in Southern California and frequents a hotel that the team stays at once in a while. There were a couple times I heard that I missed him by a night or so. But, I continue to be a Cubs fan—maybe not as diehard. But, Ernie was always the best. His attitude was always, "Let's play two." I enjoyed watching him.

Did you ever have the opportunity to meet Russell or Chamberlain?

I have met Bill Russell numerous times. He lives in Seattle, and I've run across Bill. I never met Wilt, but I've had a chance to chat with Bill a few times. I came to Seattle the year after he had finished coaching. He was part of that organization, and we would see him routinely as part of the team. He's an interesting man who has accomplished so much. It's always a good time when I am able to spend a few minutes with him.

When you and your teammates won the NBA title in 1979, there were many kids in the Northwest pretending to be Jack Sikma when they played basketball. Did you ever think about these kids that were looking at you in the same manner that you looked at Wilt and Russell or Ernie Banks?

Well, yeah. You think about it. It became a reality pretty fast, especially when you come to a team that had great success my first two years in the league going to the NBA Finals. Seattle hadn't experienced a major league championship, so it was a big deal. I enjoyed that part of it. People were so nice, and the fans were so supportive. I remember young kids being there, so I tried to hold myself up to a high standard. It was important to go out there and work hard and play hard every night. I think that resonated with a lot of people.

Career Notes: Jack Sikma was a seven-time NBA All-Star. In his 14-year career, he averaged 15.6 points and 9.8 rebounds per game. One of the best-shooting centers in NBA history, Sikma made 203 career three-point shots and led the league in free-throw percentage in 1987-88 (.922).

* * *

Bob Grim was an NFL wide receiver for 11 seasons with the Vikings, Giants and Bears from 1967–77. Prior to the NFL, Grim lettered three years at Oregon State University. As a 19-year-old sophomore, he played in front of more than 100,000 fans in the 1965 Rose Bowl game against fourth-ranked Michigan. Grim's 1964 OSU team had gone 8-2 in the regular season and was rated eighth in the country. However, the powerful Wolverines beat the Beavers 34-7. That Rose Bowl more than 50 years ago remains Oregon State's last Rose Bowl appearance. As a matter of fact, it was another 35 seasons before Oregon State got to play in *any* Bowl. During one painful stretch between the Beavers' appearances in the '65 Rose Bowl and the '99 Oahu Bowl, there were 28 consecutive years in which Oregon State had a losing record. Grim had a bird's eye view of many of those losses. He was the color commentator on Beavers' radio from 1983–2002.

Bob Grim's first broadcasting experience was gained on KGW-TV telecasts of Oregon State football games in the 1980s. I called the action. Bob was the color commentator. He was a natural—eloquent and insightful.

However, he did have one minor slip during one of our telecasts. The Beavers were playing at Arizona, and one of the Wildcats' players was Jeff Hammerschmidt. As Grim analyzed one particular play, he suffered a slip of the tongue. He misidentified the Arizona player as Jeff Hammersh*t. As Bob tried to maintain his professionalism and continue with his analysis, I broke in and asked, "What's his name again?" At that point, we both just lost it. For the next 20 to 30 seconds, the only audio heard on the telecast was the sound of the two of us trying to suppress our laughter. The harder we attempted to stop and get back to business, the more we laughed. By the time I turned around in the broadcast booth and saw Oregon State Athletic Director Lynn Snyder literally falling down in a fit of laughter, I had tears running down my cheeks. It was a great moment in broadcasting—one that Bob and I talk about to this day.

Bob Grim was at his home in Bend, Oregon, when I talked with him on January 5, 2015.

Who was your first boyhood idol?

My very first boyhood sports idol was Bob Cousy because as a kid, I wasn't very big. So, football was not foremost in my mind at the time. But, I absolutely loved basketball. I totally admired Bob Cousy. That was back in the day of Wilt Chamberlain and Cousy. There were so many great players then. I think Cousy was my first idol because he was smaller and I knew I wasn't going to be very big. (Laughs) I loved the way he handled the ball. And, they didn't have three-pointers then, but he had a great three-point shot. He was my guy when I was a kid.

Did you ever meet Cousy?

I met him in North Palm Beach. I met a fellow in Bend about eight or nine years ago that had relocated from Florida. Ron Fishman was his name. He retired and moved here to Bend. He wanted me to go to North Palm Beach to see his house. He was going to sell his condominium. So, I flew down there and we went to his country club, where he loved to play golf. As it turns out, Bob Cousy and his wife were members there. We went to the club, and sure enough, Bob Cousy walks in with his wife. So, I had a chance to meet him.

How did that go?

We just chatted a little bit. I told him that he was actually a role model for me because I loved the way he played the game. I said, "I'm not trying to date you, Bob, but I was just a kid." He laughed and said, "You know, I was pretty much a kid at the time, too." (Laughs) It was really nice. It was just great.

But, beyond Cousy, I don't think I really had any childhood sports heroes because I grew up in the Midwest in kind of a rural area. We weren't really close to a college, and we weren't close to much of anything from a sports standpoint—unless it was rodeo or something like that. Back in 1955, '56, '57, we had a little black and white TV. Even as little TV as there was at the time, every Saturday—if the NBA was on—I was there; I was watching. And, at the time, it was Red Auerbach and the Celtics. They controlled most of the NBA or at least that was my impression.

I didn't realize you had grown up in the Midwest. Where exactly did you grow up?

I was a war baby. I was born in Oakland because my dad was in the service stationed there. Both of my parents were from South Dakota. They moved back there after I was born and after he was discharged from the service. So, I spent until I was a freshman in high school in the Dakotas. I spent my summers on a ranch. My mother's parents had a cattle ranch—the ranch is still in the family—and I'd go spend my summers there. At the time, we lived in the capitol of South Dakota, a little town called Pierre.

You go from living in South Dakota to catching touchdown passes for the Minnesota Vikings. I'm sure kids collected your football cards and looked up to you. Did you ever think about that?

Not really. To be honest, it was a different world then. With the technology world of today, there are no secrets. There is so much more exposure and so much more public relations going on all the time with players at all levels. It just wasn't something that you really thought a whole bunch about. We were busy trying to win football games. Kids would come up to you. They all wanted autographs. That was fun. It was always great to have the kids around because they're terrific. Obviously, I could remember when I was a kid and what it would have meant to me. So, I always tried to go out of my way to make sure that I took care of that and signed all the autographs and talked to the kids that wanted to talk to me. That was fun. But, in terms of putting myself in some elitist class or some different category, not really—I didn't do that.

Career Notes: Bob Grim's best year as a pro was with Minnesota in 1971. That season, he had 45 catches for 691 yards with seven touchdown receptions. He was named First Team All-Conference by UPI and The Sporting News. He was also was named to the Pro Bowl that season. Grim played in a pair of Super Bowls with the Vikings (Super Bowl IV vs. Kansas City and Super Bowl XI vs. Oakland).

*   *   *

Xavier McDaniel played 12 seasons in the NBA with the SuperSonics, Suns, Knicks, Celtics and Nets. An explosive offensive player, the man known since his college days simply as "X," averaged more than 20 points a game in four of his first five NBA seasons. He was an NBA All-Star in 1988.

I first learned of Xavier McDaniel when he was playing collegiately at Wichita State. He was a hard guy to miss. It was while he was at Wichita

State that McDaniel began to shave his head and eyebrows to create a more intimidating look. This was long before a shaved head became somewhat commonplace in our culture. "X" kept that clean-shaven look the rest of his basketball career. But, McDaniel was more than just a guy with an intimidating appearance. He could really play. He brought a combination of energy and athleticism to the court, and he was a relentless rebounder. His senior season at Wichita State, McDaniel led the nation in scoring (27.2 points per game) and rebounding (14.8 boards per game), thus becoming the first NCAA Division I player to do so in the same season. The fact that he could accomplish the feat despite standing only 6-foot-7 is a testament to his relentless effort at both ends of the court.

I talked with Xavier McDaniel by phone on January 5, 2015.

Who was your very first boyhood idol?

It would be hard to say which one was first; I can't quite remember. But, I know Roger Staubach was one. And, Julius Erving was one. Both of those guys were idols of mine growing up. As far as football, it would be Roger Staubach. For basketball, it would be Julius Erving.

What was it about them that made them special to you?

When I read their books as a kid, it just inspired me—like Roger Staubach going into the Navy and staying in the Navy. I think he had to stay there for four years before he could even go to the NFL. It was just inspiring. That's how I became a Dallas Cowboys' fan when I was about nine years old. I also read a book about Doctor J and how he grew up. I think that's what really got me interested in sports—reading books about those guys.

Did you have an opportunity to meet both of your boyhood idols?

I was never able to meet Roger Staubach, but he's one of the reasons I'm a Dallas Cowboys fan to this day. I met Doctor J. I played against him. I remember the first time we went to Philadelphia when I was with the

Sonics. It was the first time I was playing against him. I walked into the locker room and said, "Man, I got to have your autograph." That was a very, very big, historical moment for me. I was trippin'. My teammates asked, "Man, why you go in there and ask for an autograph?" I said, "That's my childhood idol, man!" I mean, who doesn't love Dr. J? Every move that he made was like right out of a dream. Doctor J, every move that he's probably made, I tried to do while I was growing up. When I was a high school player and Doc had made that move under the basket and flipped it up against Portland—man, everybody was doing that move! It was just an honor to be able to play against him and an honor to have a good game against him the first time, too. I'll never forget that. We're talking about almost 30 years ago in the 1985-86 season. Playing against him, I had like 24 points and 8 rebounds. You know that had to be special if I can still remember that.

When you played at Wichita State and later when you played in the NBA, you were idolized by a lot of young fans. Did you ever think about that?

Well, as I got a little older, yeah. When you're in high school or when you're in college, you don't really think about that. Man, I get people comin' up, "I remember when you were in high school. You were good. Man, I love you." And, then I get the same thing with college and then on to the pros. So, the older I got, I started realizing people were now starting to idolize me. I was like, "Wow!"

Career Notes: Xavier McDaniel averaged 15.6 points per game during his NBA career. Selected in the first round (4th overall) of the 1985 NBA Draft, McDaniel averaged 17.1 points in his first pro season. He made the league's All-Rookie Team and finished runner-up to Patrick Ewing in the NBA Rookie of the Year balloting. "X" averaged more than 20 points a game the next four seasons for Seattle, including the 1988-89 season when he his primary role was to come off the bench to provide an offensive spark.

*   *   *

Kyle Singler has played three seasons in the NBA after compiling a quality four-year career under Mike Krzyzewski at Duke University. Singler played his first 2½ years in the NBA with the Detroit Pistons, but was traded during the 2014-15 season to the Oklahoma City Thunder.

During the time I was working in Portland as a sportscaster, Kyle Singler made a name for himself at South Medford High School in southern Oregon. Singler was a four-year starter and scored 2,207 points while leading the Panthers to a 110-10 record over his four seasons. The 6-foot-9 forward was considered one of the nation's premier prep players at the very same time that future NBA All-Star Kevin Love was playing at Lake Oswego High School in the Portland area. Love and Singler had classic battles when their teams met on the hardwood. Love's L.O. Lakers won the 2006 Oregon large school state championship by beating South Medford 59-57. But, Singler's Panthers came back to take the 2007 crown in a rematch of the 2006 title game. South Medford prevailed over Love and Lake Oswego 58-54. Longtime observers consider Singler and Love as two of the greatest high school basketball players in Oregon history.

On Singler's website, it says his favorite athletes are the late Pete Maravich and NBA legend Larry Bird. So, imagine my surprise when he told me about his very <u>first</u> idol. I talked with Kyle Singler in Portland, Oregon, on November 11, 2013.

Who was your very first boyhood idol?

I would say Wayne Gretzky. I grew up playing hockey. I was big into that, and he was the best at that time. I think he was still playing but towards the end of his career. I loved the number 99 and loved him.

I wasn't aware that hockey was that popular in southern Oregon? Were you a fan of the (Western Hockey League's) Portland Winterhawks?

Well, I actually grew up in Salem, too. So, I was fairly close to Portland. I played roller hockey instead of ice hockey, but that's where it came from.

Have you ever met Gretzky?

I've never met him. Nope. But, he was a guy I just dreamed about and wanted to be like.

You were a huge basketball star at South Medford High School. You were a standout at Duke, and now you play in the NBA. Kids have your trading cards and look up to you. Do you ever think about that?

Yeah, a little bit. It's kind of weird because on a day to day basis, you don't view yourself as that. But, you are a role model to a lot of young kids—especially kids in your area that know you, that have grown up to be like you and want to pursue the same path that you went on. It's a pretty cool thing that I'm put in a position where I'm kind of that person. But, I don't really view myself as someone special. I just try and be myself.

I know you said Wayne Gretzky was your first idol. When did you start following basketball, and was there anybody in particular that you followed?

I didn't start playing basketball until I was older, maybe 10 or 11. I followed Larry Bird, but my dad was probably the only one that I grew up watching and playing against—learning how to play the game. I didn't really grow up watching too much basketball because by that time we were down in Medford. We hardly came up to Blazers' games. When we did, it was Arvydas Sabonis. It was "Sheed." Guys like that I thought about and kind of wanted to be like.

You mention Rasheed Wallace. He's now an assistant coach on the Pistons. How strange is that to have him as one of your coaches?

Yeah, it's a little weird. But, it's really cool because I've gotten to know him pretty well. He's a real cool guy. He's a no-agenda guy. He wants the best for the players. Even though he's a North Carolina guy and I'm a Duke guy, we still get along. He's just great for our team.

Career Notes: Singler played for Mike Krzyzewski at Duke for four seasons and averaged in double-figure scoring each year, with a collegiate best of 17.7 points per game his junior year. Singler played in Europe for one year before joining the Pistons in 2012-13. In his first three NBA seasons, Singler averaged 8.1 points and 3.4 rebounds per game. Singler re-signed with Oklahoma City in summer of 2015 and will be in position to contend for an NBA championship ring in 2015-16.

*   *   *

Jack Jewsbury has played Major League Soccer (MLS) for 13 years.

The former St. Louis University All-American began his MLS career with the Kansas City Wizards in 2003. He played eight years in Kansas City before being traded to the expansion Portland Timbers prior to the 2011 season. Because of his prior playing experience, Jewsbury was immediately named the team captain by Timbers' coach John Spencer. As the team's makeup changed through the years, Spencer chose to assign the captain's title to a different player. But, Jewsbury has remained a consummate pro, even while accepting a lesser role with the Timbers.

I first met Jack Jewsbury on the day the expansion Timbers were introduced to the Portland media. As the newly named team captain, Jewsbury was in demand that day. He patiently talked with all the members of the media that sought his comments on Portland's entry into MLS. Jewsbury was a professional that day and has been every day since. Forced to play different positions all over the field, stripped of his captaincy—even being relegated to the bench—Jewsbury has remained a class act. The Timbers should consider themselves lucky to have had such a quality individual as a representative of the club in its first five years in MLS.

I talked with Jack Jewsbury about his boyhood idol at the Oregon Sports Awards in Beaverton, Oregon, on March 9, 2014.

Can you tell me who you consider your very first boyhood idol?

Yeah, it was George Brett of the Kansas City Royals. Obviously, not the sport that I play now, but growing up, I played baseball, basketball, soccer and did about everything. It was a short drive to Kansas City from my home town of Springfield, Missouri. I went to a few Royals games, and he was definitely the one guy I liked. I think I had 150 of his individual baseball cards. I was definitely a big fan of his.

Did you ever get a chance to meet him?

I actually did. I played for the Kansas City Wizards for eight years before I got traded here to Portland. One preseason, we were down in Scottsdale. The Royals go down to Arizona, as well. George Brett still has a big influence with the Royals. I went down for a preseason game, and I got to meet him in person—just randomly. I picked up a ball and had him sign it right in front of me. I told him about my past and how I looked up to him when I was younger. It was a pretty cool moment.

You had all those George Brett baseball cards and then you get a chance to talk with him. What was that like?

Like you'd imagine, it was a bit surreal. But, I think if I would have met him when I was 10 or 12, it would have been a lot different than when I was 29. Still, it was a cool moment and one that I'll always remember, for sure.

Was he nice? Did he live up to your expectations?

Oh, yeah—very outgoing and pretty witty. He was a funny guy and had some stories to tell. He didn't just brush me off like some average Joe. He definitely sat there and had a good conversation with me, so it made it even more special. He knew that we were a part of MLS so maybe that gave me more credibility than if I wasn't a pro athlete. He definitely was attentive. Like I said, it was a good moment.

There are young soccer fans that wear Jack Jewsbury jerseys and look at you as their favorite player. What do you think of all that?

Yeah, it's hard to really even wrap your mind around it, but it is something that we all embrace. We all want to make sure that we're role models on the field and also off the field in the way we handle ourselves and the way we portray ourselves in the cities that we play in.

Career Notes: While with Kansas City, Jack Jewsbury played a key role as the Wizards won the 2004 Western Conference Championship. He was a starter in the 2004 MLS Cup, won by D.C. United, 3-2. Jewsbury's first season in Portland remains the best of his career. He set career marks in points (22), goals (7) and assists (8). He was the only player in MLS that year to have multiple four-game point streaks. Jewsbury was named as Portland's first MLS All-Star in 2011. In 2013, Jewsbury—playing primarily on the backline—participated in 13 of the club's 15 shutouts. He helped the Timbers set a new MLS single-season record with 11 shutouts at home. Portland, in just its third MLS season, reached the 2013 Western Conference Championship. Jewsbury started all four MLS Cup playoff games and had two assists.

*   *   *

Terry Porter was an NBA point guard for 17 years. He spent most of his playing career with the Portland Trail Blazers and also spent time with Minnesota, Miami and San Antonio. Porter has been an assistant coach and a head coach in the NBA. The Milwaukee, Wisconsin native played collegiately for Dick Bennett at (NAIA Division III) Wisconsin-Stevens Point before being selected by Portland in the first round of the 1985 NBA Draft.

I met Terry Porter a short time after he was drafted by the Trail Blazers. He was coming to the NBA out of a small, relatively-obscure school, and it seemed to me—at first—that he had a little bit of a chip on his shoulder. I soon determined that Porter was just a mentally-tough player—a guy extremely focused on doing whatever was necessary to succeed at basketball's highest level. Porter quickly became the starting point guard for the Trail Blazers. After assuming a leadership role, he played a huge part in helping the Blazers become one of the NBA's best teams in the early 1990s. With Porter sharing the backcourt with Clyde Drexler, Portland advanced to the 1990 NBA Finals before losing in five games to Isiah Thomas and the Pistons. The following season, the Trail Blazers had the best record in the NBA (63-19), but lost in the 1991 Western Conference Finals to Magic Johnson and the Lakers. The next year, Portland had the best record in the West (57-25). Porter and Drexler led the Blazers into the 1992 NBA Finals, but they lost in six games to Michael Jordan and the Chicago Bulls. Along the way, Porter became a real favorite of the Portland fans and media. He is now a Team Ambassador for the Trail Blazers and part of the Blazers' TV broadcast team.

I talked with Terry Porter in Portland, Oregon, on March 15, 2012.

Who was your first boyhood idol?

We played football in our neighborhood. Anybody that had the name Terry or Porter was my guy. So, my guy was Terry Metcalf of the St. Louis Cardinals. He was the first guy I thought of. Basketball-wise, it was Magic Johnson at Michigan State.

Did you ever meet Terry Metcalf?

No, I never got a chance to meet him. Obviously, I met Magic a couple of times. I didn't tell him was my idol, though. (Laughs) I didn't tell him that. I didn't go there. (Laughs) When I guarded him the first time, I was like, "Oh, my God!" because when I was in college, I had his poster on my wall and everything.

When you and the Blazers were having all that success in the early 1990s, there were a lot of little kids looking up to you. Did you ever think about that?

You don't think about it while you're playing. You just go out and you play. You try to play well. You know that there are a lot of young boys that look at you and idolize your game and like the way you play, but while you're doin' it, you don't really think that much about it. But, I've had so many situations where people have come up to me throughout the years and say, "You don't know me, but I just want to thank you for the great years. I watched you play, and I'd go out in my driveway and say, 'Terry Porter! Five, four, three, two, one'." I hear all that type of stuff."

Career Notes: Terry Porter played in two NBA All-Star Games (1991, 1993), two NBA Finals (1990, 1992) and participated in the NBA playoffs 16 of his 17 seasons in the league. In 1,274 career games, he averaged 12.2 points and 5.6 assists. He remains Portland's all-time assists leader with 5,319. His jersey (#30) has been retired by the Trail Blazers. Terry Porter has been head coach of the Milwaukee Bucks and the Phoenix Suns.

*   *   *

12

Say Hey Kid

Joe Torre has been part of the Major League Baseball family most of his life. The younger brother of a major league player, Joe eventually became a big league player, coach, manager, broadcaster and executive. Torre broke into the majors with the Milwaukee Braves in 1960 and was with the team when it moved to Atlanta in 1966. He also played for the St. Louis Cardinals and New York Mets. Torre never played in a World Series, but got there often as a manager. He guided the Yankees to six American League pennants and four World Series titles (1996, 1998–2000).

In 2011, Torre was hired as Major League Baseball's Executive Vice-President of Baseball Operations. He was named Chief Baseball Officer on December 4, 2014. He oversees areas that include Major League Operations, On-Field Operations, On-Field Discipline and Umpiring.

Torre and his wife, Ali, launched the Safe at Home Foundation in 2002.

While in high school, I rooted for Joe Torre because he was playing for the Cardinals. In 1971, he earned the National League MVP Award by batting .363, with 24 homers and a league-high 137 runs-batted-in. I first met Torre in 1979 or 1980 when he was managing the New York Mets. On an off-night during spring training, my broadcasting mentor Jay Randolph and I joined Torre for dinner at Derby Lane—the dog track in St. Petersburg. Randolph left the track early that night, so there I was sitting at a table with Torre —a guy for whom I had cheered just eight or nine years earlier when I was a teenager. It was a rather dreamlike evening for a young broadcaster still becoming accustomed to meeting famous people in the world of sports.

It is interesting to see how connected many of us are when it comes to our boyhood heroes. We earlier learned that Scott Brosius idolized Johnny Bench and Dale Murphy. Murphy, in turn, idolized Bench and Willie Mays. As you read early in the book, Rick Barry was also a Mays' fan. And, you'll see in this chapter, there are actually many athletes who considered Mays their first boyhood hero. Joe Torre is one of those.

I talked with Joe Torre by telephone on September 12, 2013.

Who was your first boyhood idol?

I was a New York Giants fan living in Brooklyn, which was very dangerous at that time. As a 10-year-old or 11-year-old, Willie Mays came on the scene, and he caught my fancy. It was easy to understand why. He was exciting. I was a Giants fan, and I had a number of players that I really enjoyed watching. Don Mueller was one. But, as far as for excitement and idolizing, I'd have to say Willie was my guy. Then, later on when my brother Frank played in the big leagues in 1956, the one guy I hooked onto over there with the Milwaukee Braves was Eddie Mathews. I just thought Eddie was a combination of rough and tough. He could hit the home run and yet he had speed. He played the game hard. That's probably what I also admired about Willie—how hard he played the game.

Did you ever meet either of those players when you were a kid, or was it later on?

No. I never met Willie until I played against him. Then, of course, I met Eddie as a teenager because my brother was a teammate of his. That was a big thrill. Of course, a bigger thrill was becoming his teammate when I played in the big leagues starting in 1960.

It had to be exciting to get to play against Mays and become a teammate of Mathews.

Oh, yeah, and I can tell you what really caught attention. My first spring training with the Milwaukee Braves, I was catching. I'm not about to mention that either one of those guys was special to me because Eddie was a now teammate. So, I'm catching, and who steps into the batter's box but Mickey Mantle. You talk about goose bumps. Here I am catching, and he's in there hitting. He's got this rubber jacket on, and he's got these wide, broad shoulders, and I'm the catcher calling the pitches. That *really* got my attention. I wasn't a Yankee fan, but I admired what Mickey was able to do. This was probably 1961. What made it interesting was, that particular day in Bradenton, I hit a home run off Whitey Ford, who was pitching for the Yankees. The thing that was riveting in my mind was looking out there in right-center field and seeing Mickey Mantle looking up at the ball going out of the ballpark. That was a *vision* for me. Now, fast-forward about ten years later. I'm sitting right next to Mickey Mantle on the dais at a baseball banquet, and he is the one that brought up what happened that day. It blew me away that he would remember a spring training game that some kid played. I'd have to believe that the reason that he remembered it was the fact that I was Frank Torre's brother. He had played against Frank in two World Series, '57 and '58. But, having been a big leaguer for ten years, it still caught me off guard and made me feel pretty darn good.

You've held a number of positions in baseball and obviously have had the chance to get to know your idols a little bit. Were they everything you thought they would be when you were younger?

Um, you idolize them, and in Mickey's case, I liked Mickey a lot. You sort of felt bad for Mickey because you've been in his company and—not that he partied a lot, but he drank a lot. He was rowdy a lot, but he was always a nice guy. I liked that part about him. Again—as a kid—baseball was all I ever wanted to do, and I just idolized just being in his company.

Willie Mays—being on a number of All-Star teams with him—he was always an idol for me at that point in time. I played with a pretty good player at that time named Hank Aaron, who could do every single thing as well as Willie could do it but just didn't have the same flair as Willie. That was the difference. They were equals as far as abilities. Henry could do everything—probably not play center field like Willie could, but he played right field better than anybody I'd ever seen.

We haven't talked about him much, but I know that your brother, Frank, was an idol for you growing up.

Yeah, my brother was. It was sort of a love-hate relationship. When you go back over it, any time I got a compliment from Frank, it was better than any seven or eight articles that were written about me in the papers. He threw around those compliments like manhole covers. It wasn't something that was necessarily easy for him to do. It was great when I finally did get a compliment. I remember winning the World Series in '96 with the Yankees. On top of the fact that he just got a heart transplant, it was great just having him make a special effort to tell me how special I was. You know, it's still a sensitive area, but a happy memory.

You have discussed publicly that your dad wasn't the kind of guy that you could look up to. He made things pretty rough for everyone in your home when you were growing up. Would it be correct to say that Frank was sort of a father-figure for you?

Well, I think my brother Rocco was more a father-figure. Frank was more an idol who I admired because he was a big league player and that was something I wanted to do. So, I looked up to him as an idol in that regard. There's no question. I had a baseball player living under the same roof who was a big leaguer. Early-on in his career, he played in two World Series against the Yankees. You fast-forward a number of years and the next time the Yankees and the Braves played in the World Series, I was managing the Yankees. That was pretty wild.

Joe, I'm aware that you played APBA as a kid. I've played Strat-O-Matic baseball since the '60s and briefly played APBA as an adult. How much do you think board games like APBA and Strat-O-Matic help create idols or heroes? I ask because—as a kid—I sort of had one-on-one relationships with my idols on a daily basis, rolling the dice and visualizing those guys playing for me.

Yeah, the APBA—for me—was great. You know, not many kids can pick up the player cards and decide to play their brother. My brother was a good hitter. He was a .300 hitter. Even though he didn't have the power, he had still the ability to get on base. I was a little prejudiced, obviously. In real life, Joe Adcock did most of the playing at first base.

So, playing APBA as a kid, did you bat Frank cleanup?

No, I didn't do that. I always felt that my brother Frank really thrived in hitting in the second spot because he was a good hit-and-run guy—a contact hitter. He could do a lot of things.

You had an outstanding career as a player and many fans idolized you. With the success you had managing the Yankees you probably became an idol for kids hoping to grow up to be a major league manager someday.

Yeah. You know, it's still a great experience for me going around the country and having people recognize me. Probably the thing that means more to me than anything is the fact that people will come up to me, and they'll say they're not necessarily baseball fans, but they admired the way I conducted myself. You don't realize—while you're doing what you're doing—how many people you sort of reach and touch. That continues to be something I'm a little baffled by, but certainly appreciative of.

Joe, I grew up as a third-generation Cardinal fan. My first boyhood idol was Stan Musial, who retired in 1963. The following year, Bob

Gibson became my idol as he pitched the Cards to the World Series championship. You spent time in St. Louis with both of them. They were both Hall of Fame players, but would it be correct to say they couldn't have been more different as people?

Well, I played with Gibson on several All-Star teams, and I didn't like him very much because he wouldn't talk to me. Even when I caught him, he wouldn't talk to me. (Laughs) When I got traded to the Cardinals, he welcomed me with open arms. We're very close friends now.

Stan Musial, when I went over there to St. Louis, we just seemed to bond. We had a great relationship. Stan was a very special individual. When my wife Ali and I were living in St. Louis when I was managing, he'd give me a call like at 4:30 in the afternoon, and he'd say, "You want to meet Lil and I for dinner in about an hour?" I'd say, "Sure." You always said sure. He was just fun to be around. I always sat on his right to be next to him at lunch or dinner. Being with me just seemed to spur his memories like, "Oh. You're from Brooklyn, aren't you?" I'd say, "Yeah." He'd start tellin' me how he used to mutilate the Brooklyn pitching in those days as a player. But, Stan was about as sweet a man as you can meet. I was very fortunate to have the relationship and have access to him even in his later years. It was great. It really was.

Career Notes: A catcher, first baseman and third baseman, Joe Torre was an All-Star nine times in the 18 years he played in the big leagues. He hit .297 in his career, with 252 home runs and 1,185 runs-batted-in. He was very good as a player, but even better as a manager. Torre ranks fifth all-time with 2,326 managerial wins. In 2015, he travelled to Cooperstown to be inducted into the Baseball Hall of Fame for his contributions as a manager.

* * *

Vida Blue was one of baseball's best pitchers in the 1970s. The left-handed Blue, one of the hardest throwers in the game, had a dream season in 1971. He won the American League Cy Young Award and was voted the league's Most Valuable Player after going 24-8, with a 1.82 earned run average. In the best season of his career, Blue threw eight shutouts, allowed only 209 hits in 312 innings and struck out a career-high 301 batters. In his 17-year career with the Athletics, Giants and Royals, he went 209-161, with a 3.27 ERA. In recent years, Vida Blue has represented the Giants in the community throughout the San Francisco Bay Area. He also talks Giants' baseball on CSN-Bay Area and KNBR Radio.

I have interviewed Vida Blue several times over the years, and I also had the pleasure of serving as the master of ceremonies of a fund-raising banquet at which Blue was the guest speaker. I learned that night that Vida is a good public speaker. The fans that evening thoroughly enjoyed listening to Blue as he talked baseball. I understood why the Giants had hired him to represent the club out in the community. He was almost as good when talking about his life in baseball as he was when he was on the mound blowing away American League batters in 1971.

I spoke with Vida Blue by phone on February 17, 2011.

Who was your boyhood idol?

Well, that guy named Willie Mays. I had five uncles, and all of my uncles were San Francisco Giants' fans because of Willie Mays. Believe it or not, my mother's dad—my grandfather—he was a Dodger fan because of Jackie Robinson. Lo-and-behold, I got a chance to meet Jackie Robinson during the World Series in 1972 when the A's played against the Cincinnati Reds. He came into town. I got a chance to shake his hand and tell him that my grandfather was a big fan, and he threw out the first pitch. But, Willie Mays was *my* guy. Willie Mays can do no wrong in my eyes. I get a chance to sit around and talk to him, and it's so cool to be in his presence. In my opinion, he's the greatest living player of all time. I'm very proud of the fact that I have this relationship with him that I do now.

Did you ever have the chance to pitch against Mays?

I pitched against Willie Mays in the 1971 All-Star Game in Detroit, Michigan. He was leading off. I threw him two fastballs, and then I threw him a change-up, and he hit a ground ball to shortstop. I think Luis Aparicio was playing shortstop at that time. And, of course, I got a chance to play against him in the '73 World Series. I'm not sure if I pitched against him or not. I don't remember. It was when the Mets played the A's in the '73 World Series in which we won our second of three World Series championships. But, hey, man, Willie Mays is a living legend. Like I said, I'm so fortunate that he's still in this area and still working for the Giants. I get to see him and talk to him. We talk baseball.

Did you tell Willie the first time you met him that he was your boyhood idol?

Oh, absolutely, and I'm sure he's heard that many a time. He was a great player when he played for the New York Giants, and when they moved west, he obviously was the central figure of the franchise. The Say Hey Kid! Willie Mays!

Willie Mays is in his 80s, and I still close my eyes and think of him as some young kid running to left field and catchin' that ball over his shoulder off of Vic Wertz's bat. He'll never grow old in my eyes or in my mind.

When you first met him, did it in any way reduce your idolization of him? Did you suddenly say, he's just a guy like me, just a ballplayer?

No. (Laughs) No. Not with Willie Mays. I had the same reaction when I met Mickey Mantle at a card show in New York. I kind of like stood there for a minute, and he was talking and everything was moving in slow motion. It was kind of like, "Vida! Vida! Do you hear me talking to you?" I had to snap out of it. I'm so lucky that Willie Mays will walk up to me and say, "Hey, kid! How ya' doin'? What's goin' on? You need anything?" He's just as common as a person could be. He doesn't act like he's a superstar or anything. He just goes around and is Willie Mays. How cool is that?

I had a similar experience when I got to meet one of my boyhood idols, Bob Gibson, at a celebrity golf tournament. I understood that he's just another human being, but there is really something very special about getting to talk with a guy who meant so much to you as a kid.

You see that they're just another person, but I can't separate that in the case of Willie Mays. I have to keep Willie Mays up on a pedestal above anyone else. That's just the way I have to do it. He has my respect. I get to sit with him in his luxury suite sometimes, and he doesn't say very much, but you know he's in tune with what's going on down on the ball field. He still loves baseball with the passion that he had forty years ago, and I still love Willie Mays. It's one of those things. I idolize Willie Mays.

Are you aware that there have been a lot of people that considered you a boyhood hero?

When you're born and raised in Mansfield, Louisiana, you never think that you're going to be one of those persons. I lived my childhood through television, and once I got a chance to become a major league player, I had to be careful what I did and said. I am surprised that people give us this larger-than-life thing. I think it's because we're on television. People see you on TV, and the announcers talk about us being superstars and give us this larger-than-life image.

Can you remember the first time that somebody told you that you were their boyhood idol?

Not so much, but when people start asking for your autograph, you go like, "Why do you want my autograph?" In my breakout season in 1971, being on the cover of all these magazines and being interviewed, and being on national TV with Johnny Carson, it still didn't hit me for a while of the impact that I was having on people's lives. But, I do get people that tell me that they attended a game and saw me pitch and what I meant to the Afro-American community. It's nice to know that I was something that they could grab onto as far as some hope—just by watching me throw a baseball. It's amazing how people can connect with that stuff, but it makes a difference in their lives sometimes, just to get away from the rigors of life to come out to see this young kid throw a baseball. People live their lives through us. It takes away some of the despair in their lives through the course of the day by coming to watch an athlete perform on the field, on the court or on the diamond. It's amazing how that works. I'm glad that I was able to do that and make a difference in people's lives, even just for a few hours.

What about the first time that a current or former major leaguer told you that you were his idol? Has that ever happened?

Yes, I played in a charity golf tournament with Randy Johnson. He grew up in Livermore, California, which is a little town outside of Oakland. He actually told me that, "Man, I wanted to be like you." Me being a couple years older than him, he obviously saw me pitch when I was with the A's and then with the Giants. That was the guy that initially said that to me while he was in the major leagues himself. That was Randy Johnson. I was very flattered that he was a big Vida Blue fan and that I was his idol growing up as a kid.

When you went through your off-the-field problems, the drug issues and everything, did it enter your mind that you were letting people down?

No, first of all, you feel as though you let *yourself* down. In this business, especially in today's media, everything is quick. Everything is spontaneous. If something happens out of the ordinary, your name is on the front page. You're the headline. You're the breaking story. You're the news now. Unfortunately, that does happen. That's a part of being a major leaguer and being a professional athlete. I might not have carried myself in the best way, but I do know that I have good character. I try to use better judgment these days. Good things are gonna happen, and bad things are gonna happen. But, you do feel as though you let yourself down first. The trickle-down effect is the people's lives that you have touched in a positive way, and you hope that they continue to believe in you. You feel the hurt that you've put on yourself and the hurt that they feel too.

Career Notes: Vida Blue helped the Athletics win three straight World Series championships (1972–74). He went 20-9 during the regular season in 1973 and won 22 games in 1975, the year the A's won their fifth consecutive AL West crown. Blue was a six-time All-Star. He was the starting—and winning—pitcher for the American League in the 1971 All-Star Game. He started on the mound for the National League in the 1978 All-Star Game, and he was the winning pitcher—in relief— in the 1981 All-Star Game. He became the first pitcher to record All-Star wins in both leagues. Blue hurled a no-hitter against the Minnesota Twins on September 21, 1970. He teamed with three Oakland pitchers to pitch a no-hitter against the Angels on September 28, 1975.

* * *

Dave Henderson played 14 years in the major leagues with the Mariners, Red Sox, Giants, Athletics and Royals. He was involved in one of the most exciting postseason games in MLB history.

I had a chance to visit with Dave Henderson during the second of his two stints as a broadcaster for the Seattle Mariners. A good guy, Henderson was quite willing to share his boyhood idol memories. But, while we talked, my mind drifted back to 1986 when Henderson was playing for Boston. In Game Five of the 1986 American League Championship Series, Henderson *provided the heroics as the Red Sox staved off elimination. Down three games to one in the best of seven ALCS—and with Boston down to its final strike—Henderson hit a 2-2 pitch for a game-tying home run off the Angels' Donnie Moore. He later plated the go-ahead run with an 11*th*-inning sacrifice fly off Moore. The Red Sox not only won the game, they rallied back to win the ALCS in seven games and advanced to face the Mets in the World Series.*

While I have vivid memories of Henderson's clutch hitting against the Angels, there are a few things about that game I had forgotten. Henderson would have been one of the last players anyone would have expected to be a hero for Boston that night. He had appeared in only 36 games for the Red Sox after being acquired from Seattle in an August trade. Henderson had just 10 hits in 51 regular season at bats (.196) in a Boston uniform. He was not even in the starting lineup that night. He entered the game in the bottom of the fifth as a defensive replacement for centerfielder Tony Armas. That strategy backfired with two outs in the bottom of the sixth when Bobby Grich hit a long drive to centerfield. Henderson ran back to the wall and leaped into the air with his left arm fully extended. The ball hit Henderson's glove and deflected over the fence for a two-run homer, giving the Angels a 3-2 lead. In the top of the seventh, with the tying run on base, Henderson struck out to end the inning. Henderson looked more like a goat than a hero. The Angels led 5-2 entering the top of the ninth, but Don Baylor hit a two-run homer to bring Boston back within one run. Then, with two outs, Rich Gedman was hit by a pitch thrown by lefty relief pitcher Gary Lucas. Angels' manager Gene Mauch called on right-handed closer Donnie Moore to face the right-handed-hitting Henderson. That's when Moore—just one strike away from closing out the game and sending the Angels to their first World Series—surrendered the two-run homer to Henderson. Boston went on to win Game Five and won the ALCS in seven games.

I talked with Dave Henderson in Seattle on April 8, 2011.

If I ask about your boyhood idol, who pops into your mind?

Mine is easy because I grew up in the Bay Area. It's Willie Mays all the way. I met him when I was seven years old. He came in one of those Giants Caravans to our town, and he saw a little, scrawny, tall kid. He taught me a few things. As I got older, my uncle—Joe Henderson—played in the major leagues for Cincinnati. I'd go to the games and watch him pitch. The Cincinnati lineup was pretty impressive. But, nobody compared to Willie Mays in those days. Actually, he's still my hero to this day. I still think he's the best baseball player ever to play the game because he could do it all, and he's such a great human being.

After you became a major league player, did you ever have a chance to tell Willie the story about your first encounter with him back when you were seven?

Oh yeah, of course. He remembered coming to our small town (Dos Palos, California). We kept in touch over the last 20 or 30 years. He watched my career, and I've done a couple tributes to him in the outfield. He always appreciated that. Of course, Rickey Henderson and myself, growing up in that area, we all wanted to wear number 24 because of Willie Mays. But, I found out that Jackie Robinson was also pretty important in the scheme of things, so I've been 42 my whole career. Rickey Henderson has been 24—for Willie Mays.

You mentioned tributes. What kinds of things are you talking about? Did you make a basket catch on a fly ball?

No. (Laughs) I didn't go that far. He always flipped the hat off when he ran, so I did the Willie Mays "flip-the-hat-off" and things like that. The guys in the dugout knew I was doing a Willie Mays tribute.

Willie Mays was a childhood idol of so many from our generation. There truly was something about him, wasn't there?

Well, I get a chance to see these guys. I've talked to Hank Aaron and Willie Mays. Sitting down in Cooperstown one time, we asked, "Who is the best player?" They have so much, you know, *humanity* that they would never say one was better than another. Hank Aaron explains it, "If you had enough money to go see three games, come see me. But, if you only had enough money to see one game, go see Willie because he's gonna do something spectacular." That explains why I was attracted to Willie as a kid. Willie would do something spectacular in the field, on the bases and with the bat. And, Hank Aaron was just Mr. Consistency.

When you became a major leaguer, there must have been a time when you thought to yourself that there were kids looking up to you the same way you had admired Willie.

Well yeah, of course. I was a football player and just turned to baseball. I let all the football players know that this game of baseball is pretty easy as compared to football. You can actually make a good living playing baseball and not get killed. I was more of an inspiration to all of the football players.

I've heard fans approach former players and say, "You were my guy—my idol." Do you still have people that come up to you and say things like that?

I hear more that I treated somebody with respect and gave them an autograph. I get a lot of mail every day from people that want an autograph. They say I smiled a lot on the field and they loved that part about me—that it was still a game to me and wasn't a business. I reminded everybody that you can have a good time playing baseball.

Dave, when I talked with Vida Blue, he spoke about being in awe of Willie Mays even though they work together with the Giants. Paraphrasing now, Vida says he again feels like the six-year-old kid that idolized Willie every time Mays enters the room.

Well, I was the same way at the Hall of Fame. When you step into that hallowed ground and you see Bob Gibson and Stan Musial and Willie

Mays and Hank Aaron, you feel like a little kid. You don't feel like you deserve to be in the same room or sit at the same table with them. The respect that we give those guys is tremendous. They've earned it. They were the best of all time.

Career Notes: Dave Henderson batted .258 with 197 lifetime home runs. He played in four World Series. He batted .400 against the Mets in the 1986 Fall Classic and played in three consecutive World Series for Oakland (1988–90). Henderson earned his only championship ring in 1989. That was the year he helped the Athletics sweep the San Francisco Giants in the "Bay Area Earthquake" World Series. Henderson hit seven home runs in 36 career postseason games. He hit three ALCS homers and slugged four homers in 20 career World Series games.

*   *   *

Joe Carter, one of baseball's most feared sluggers in the 1990s, hit a historic home run in the 1993 World Series. Carter cracked a stunning three-run walk-off homer in Game Six to give Toronto an 8-6 victory and a second straight World Series title. With that home run off Phillies' pitcher Mitch Williams, Carter became the first player to hit a *come-from-behind*, World Series-ending home run. It is true Bill Mazeroski of the Pirates ended the 1960 World Series with a home run, but that game was *tied* in the bottom of the ninth when Maz homered over the left field fence at Forbes Field in Pittsburgh. Toronto *trailed* prior to Carter's blast. Not surprisingly, Carter was named the 1993 World Series MVP. He hit two homers and drove in eight runs in the 1993 Fall Classic.

Joe Carter became a national hero in Canada when he hit the walk-off homer to give Toronto its second straight World Series championship. It is still the single most significant moment in the country's baseball history. But, that home run almost didn't happen. Carter told Blair Kerkhoff of the Kansas City Star in a 2013 interview that he came very close to signing with the Royals when he became a free agent after the 1992 season. The Royals offered a better contract than the Blue Jays. Plus, Carter's wife had grown up in Kansas City and the family home was in K. C. Carter was looking for some sort of sign to help him decide which team he should play for in 1993. He told Kerkhoff that one December night, he saw Blue Jays' teammate Devon White and the Skydome in a dream. When he woke up to the chirping of birds, he looked outside and saw blue jays in his back yard. That's the moment he decided to re-sign with Toronto.

I spoke with Joe Carter on June 13, 2011, when he was participating in the Caddies 4 Cure charity golf tournament at the Reserve Vineyards and Golf Club in Aloha, Oregon.

When I say "boyhood idol," who is the first person that jumps into your mind?

Well, two guys—Willie Mays and Johnny Bench. Me being from Oklahoma City, and Johnny Bench, an Oklahoma native from Binger, Oklahoma, he was the guy that all the Oklahomans could look up to—along with Mickey Mantle from Commerce, Oklahoma. Those were the guys that we kind of kept an eye on. For me, though, it was Johnny Bench and Willie Mays. The phenomenal athlete that Willie Mays was, he could arguably—still today—be *the* greatest player of all time. Talking with him, he says, "If I'd known "40-40"—40 homers and 40 steals—was going to be such a big deal, I'd have done it six or seven times." But, back then, it wasn't a big deal. He certainly had the ability to do that.

Do you remember the first time you met Willie?

Oh, yes! I'll never forget. We were in Texas, and they had an Old-Timers Game. My hitting coach with Cleveland was (Mays' godson) Bobby Bonds. We were sitting down outside talkin' about baseball, and he said, "C'mon. Let's go." I said, "Where we going?" He says, "Let's go." So, we go up to this guy's room, and he knocks on the door. The guy inside says, "Who is it?" Bonds says, "Buck, it's me. Open the door." I'm like, "Who the heck is Buck?" He opens the door, and there is Willie Mays in his pajamas. And, my mouth was just like (opens his mouth wide and gasps). We sat there for about six hours talkin' baseball. I think I said maybe three or four words because I was sitting there going like, "That's Willie Mays right there!" You know, I'm 23 years old—a snot-nose rookie—and to get that opportunity was a phenomenal thing that I'll never forget. Never.

Vida Blue told me he grew up a Mays' fan in the Bay Area. He now works with Mays with the Giants and sees him every day. Blue says he still thinks to himself, "That's Willie Mays!"

I know! Mays still has that great spirit. Guys like him and Ernie Banks, you know they still have a passion and a love of the game. They played it when it was *real* baseball, so you know they had a love for the game. Every time I see Willie, I'm still in awe. No matter what I've been through or who I am, to me, he's always at the top of the list.

When you got your first chance to meet Johnny Bench, did he live up to your expectations?

Yeah, he did. I was a big Cincinnati Reds fan, and my father was a Dodger fan. We had fights all the time. When the Reds were playing on the west coast against the Dodgers, I'd go to bed, and I'd have the radio next to my bed. With that two hour time difference, it's twelve o'clock and the game still hadn't gotten over with in Oklahoma City. I'm listening to the game, and if they beat the Dodgers, I'd make sure and say to my father the next morning, "Hey, your boys got beat, and Johnny did this and did that."

The first time I met Johnny was at one of the functions, but it wasn't quite the same as with Willie Mays. I didn't get a chance to sit down and talk with Johnny the way I had with Mays. Still, Johnny is still a huge idol for all of us in Oklahoma.

You played in several big league cities, so you undoubtedly had young kids across the nation who idolized you. Did you ever think about that?

No. When you're playin' the game, you're playin' the game for the *love* of the game. I played it and had fun. You don't think about those things until you're out of the game. When you're playin' the game, if you're thinking about all the extracurricular things going on—if you're gonna be a hero and all that—then you're in it for the wrong reasons. My wife will tell you that I'm still a big kid, but I played the game as if I was a little kid. That's the only way I knew how to do things.

Can you discuss your biggest thrill in baseball? I've read that you always dreamed of hitting a home run to win the World Series, so I'm pretty sure you're going to tell me it was your World Series-clinching home run? But, I have to ask.

You know, the home run was so special, you can't really top that. But, there was another thrilling moment for a guy coming out of Oklahoma City, a guy a lot of the scouts said, "Well, he'll just be a good Triple-A ballplayer." When I was traded to Cleveland, in my first game against the New York Yankees, I'm facing "Louisiana Lightning"—Ron Guidry. Bert Blyleven was pitching for us. We won the game 6-0. Bert threw a shutout. I hit a grand slam and a two-run homer off of Ron Guidry. I should have had *seven* RBIs, but Brook Jacoby got clipped at home when he missed the plate. It would have been 7-0, and I would have had all seven RBIs. When the game was over and I finished talking with the press, I got on the phone and told my father. That was one of the biggest moments—to have six RBIs against the Yankees and beat "Louisiana Lightning."

You played a long time. Did you ever have players come up to the major leagues and tell you that you were their boyhood idol?

Oh, yeah! Towards the end of your career, you get that. They'd say, "Man, I grew up watching you play in Cleveland." They're 21 years old, and they're like, "I used to watch you 15, 16 years ago." To me, that's a compliment because I'm still around and they got a chance to make it up to the big leagues. So, I get that a lot. You know, I had great teachers—teachers like Fergie Jenkins. When I came up as a rookie, he was my first big league roommate. He taught me the ropes. Hopefully, I passed down to the younger guys what I learned from Fergie, and hopefully they'll pass it down to the next group of young guys when they come around.

Career Notes: Joe Carter played a total of 16 years in the major leagues with the Cubs, Indians, Padres, Blue Jays, Orioles and Giants. He hit 396 career home runs and drove in 1,445 runs. Carter was a five-time All-Star. The years the Blue Jays won their back-to-back World Series' titles, Carter's presence in the lineup made the difference. Not only did he hit a pair of home runs in each World Series in which he played, he had consistently done the job all season long. In 1992, Carter led Toronto to its first American League pennant with 34 home runs and 119 RBI. In '93, Carter hammered 33 home runs and tied his career-high with 121 runs-batted-in. It's easy to understand why Carter was inducted into the Canadian Baseball Hall of Fame in 2003.

*   *   *

Dave Stewart grew up in the San Francisco Bay Area and later pitched for 16 years in the major leagues with the Dodgers, Rangers, Phillies, Athletics and Blue Jays. His most successful years were spent wearing the uniform of his hometown Oakland Athletics.

Make no mistake about it. Dave Stewart was a standout pitcher. However, something he did off the field made an even bigger impression on me. Following the earthquake that rocked the 1989 World Series and led to death and devastation throughout the Bay Area, Stewart went out into the streets to offer help and support. The graduate of Oakland's St. Elizabeth

High School was greatly affected by what he witnessed in the streets of his city. His actions in the days after the tragedy catapulted Stewart from baseball player to hero in the eyes of many people around the country.

I talked with Dave Stewart by phone on January 19, 2011.

Think back to when you a small kid growing up in Oakland. Who was your first boyhood idol?

My very first was Willie Mays. My dad was a Giant fan, and we grew up watching the Giants. My dad used to take me to Giants baseball games. Willie Mays was actually the first professional player I ever met as a small kid. I was so young. It would have been in 1963 or '64. I just remember that my dad said Willie Mays was a really, really nice man and if we waited here outside Candlestick Park, if I wanted an autograph signed, Willie would surely do it. He did exactly what my father said. We waited outside the stadium just outside the fence area. That was my first experience meeting a pro player. Then, as I got older and was into organized baseball, I had the opportunity to meet Reggie Jackson. I was 14 years old. I became friends with Reggie from that point until the time that I was drafted by the Dodgers.

When you were pitching, you stared in at the batter before every pitch. There was no question that Dave Stewart was all business. You were an intimidating figure when you were on the mound. Your intensity was a little reminiscent of one of my boyhood idols, Bob Gibson, the Cardinal Hall of Famer.

Well, when I was a kid, Bob Gibson was one of my all-time favorites—I mean *all-time* favorites. I watched Gibson across the Bay in San Francisco, where I also watched Juan Marichal. Here in Oakland, I had the advantage of watching Catfish Hunter and Blue Moon Odom. You watched the Giants' matchups and you see Juan Marichal against Gibson, or Marichal against Don Drysdale or Sandy Koufax. I came up in the game at a really, really good time. Those guys were guys that I really enjoyed watching.

Your career is a real testament to perseverance. You were drafted in 1975 by the Dodgers, and although you appeared in one game in a September call-up in 1978, you didn't reach the majors full-time until 1981. Then, in your first six full seasons in the big leagues, you won only 39 games and never won more than 10 games in a single year. But, starting with your first full season with Oakland in 1987, you won 20 or more games for four straight years. Overall, you went 84-45 from 1987–90. You seemed to prove that if you put in the work and keep believing, good things can happen.

That's pretty much what it is. If you go through this life expecting good things and you continue to work hard, something good is bound to happen. You've just gotta keep your faith and continue to believe in God. Great things will always turn up.

Finally, Dave, I remember you immediately going out into the community following the 1989 San Francisco earthquake that interrupted the Bay Area World Series between your Athletics and the Giants. How heartbreaking was it for you to see your hometown devastated?

Very! The things that you see in tragedy are things that you never expect to see in life. That was one of the saddest moments that I can remember. The *first* real sad moment I can remember was turning on the television when I was a young kid and hearing about President Kennedy being shot. Death is a tragedy in itself, and the death of one of the country's greatest leaders is a great tragedy. But, the earthquake tops that for me because it was directly connected to me in my community. It was unbelievable. The way I look at it now is—even through all of the sadness and the displacement of people and the rebuilding process in the Bay Area—the best thing that came from the earthquake was the connection that came between San Francisco and Oakland through that period of time. You found two different sides starting to lean on each other and trust in each other and believe in each other.

Career Notes: In Dave Stewart's major league career, he went 168-129, with a 3.95 ERA. The hard-throwing right-hander was the American League's starting pitcher in the 1989 All-Star Game. Pitching in five different American League Championship Series, Stewart was 8-0 with a 2.03 ERA. He was the 1990 ALCS MVP with Oakland after being named the World Series MVP in 1989. He was named the 1993 ALCS MVP while pitching for the Blue Jays. Dave Stewart is currently the general manager of the Arizona Diamondbacks.

*   *   *

Clyde Drexler is still regarded as the best player in Portland Trail Blazers history. Drexler held many franchise records when he was traded to Houston in 1995. He was—without a doubt—the club's best player during the most successful three-year run in Trail Blazers' history (1990–92). For a short time in 2007, Drexler was a contestant on the popular TV show, *Dancing with the Stars*. Clyde would probably admit he was much smoother on the basketball court than the dance floor.

Clyde Drexler was my son's favorite player. It was easy to understand because Drexler was a star. But, it was more than that. Drexler took time to write Adam a personal note urging him to hang in there after my young son broke a tooth playing baseball. Later, to show his support of Drexler, Adam had the barber carve Drexler's initials—CD—in his hair. Yes, Clyde Drexler almost felt like a part of our family. He was certainly an important member of the Trail Blazers' family for more than a decade.

You might not realize that it was partly because of Drexler that Portland drafted Sam Bowie—not Michael Jordan—in the 1984 NBA Draft. Heading into the draft, the Trail Blazers appeared to be set at the two-guard position. They had drafted Drexler in 1983, and the young shooting guard had shown great promise in his rookie season. The Blazers also had

Jim Paxson at the two-guard, and he was an NBA All-Star in both '83 and '84.

Portland's greatest need was for a center. Just how serious were the Blazers about drafting a center? In May of 1984, the NBA fined the Trail Blazers a then-record $250,000 for making illegal indirect contact with underclassmen Patrick Ewing of Georgetown and Akeem (no H at the start of his first name at that time) Olajuwon of the University of Houston. The Blazers were trying to determine whether both 7-foot centers were going to enter the NBA Draft. If both college stars headed to the NBA, Portland knew it would end up with either Ewing or Olajuwon. At that time, the two worst teams in the NBA flipped a coin to determine which would have the first pick in the draft and which would have to settle for the second pick. Indiana and Houston actually finished with the two worst records in 1984, but the Blazers owned Indiana's first-round pick because of a 1981 trade involving Tom Owens. So, Houston and Portland would flip the coin to decide which of the two teams would get the number one overall pick.

The Blazers hopes of landing a premier center were dashed when Ewing remained at Georgetown and Houston won the coin flip. On Draft Night, the Rockets selected Olajuwon number one. Portland—still believing its greatest need was a center—settled for the oft-injured Sam Bowie of the University of Kentucky. Bowie had a solid, but unspectacular career. The third pick in the 1984 draft—North Carolina's Michael Jordan—went on to have a Hall of Fame career with the Chicago Bulls. Drexler also had a Hall of Fame career, and in 1992—when the Blazers played the Bulls in the NBA Finals—many people considered Jordan and Drexler to be the two premier players in the league.

I spoke with Clyde Drexler in Portland on April 25, 2014.

I'm asking everyone about their boyhood idols. Can you tell me who you consider to be your first boyhood idol?

Probably Willie Mays. I loved baseball. Willie Mays was the best player at the time. Obviously, everyone wanted to be like Willie Mays.

What made him so special in your eyes?

Well, hey! He was the Say Hey Kid! C'mon! What else is there? He could hit. He had power. He could steal bases. He could catch like no one else. He was a phenomenal player.

Did you ever get a chance to meet him?

I met him a couple times. The first time we were at a card show. I went just to meet him. I sat right next to him for two hours—had a *great* time. We talked the whole time. He signed a couple autographs for me, and he sent me a letter when we got home. Nicest guy ever! He was just a great guy. I mean, he just confirmed what I thought about him all those years.

So, when they asked you to be in the card show, did you accept the invitation because Mays was going to be there?

I said, "Who else is gonna be there?" because I don't really like to do card shows. I don't do very many at all. So, when they said, "Willie Mays," I said, "Oh, I'm in. (Laughs) Put me right next to Willie—right at the same time—and I'll do it."

As you know, there were many kids in Houston and Portland that idolized you during your playing days. What does that mean to you?

It's a tremendous honor. I didn't think about it at all, but it's a tremendous honor. You know, you go out and do your job as well as you can, and if people think highly enough of what you've done to want to emulate you, that's the highest compliment *ever* for an athlete—and a human being.

Career Notes: Clyde "The Glide" Drexler grew up in Houston and played at the University of Houston. Drexler led the Cougars'

"Phi-Slamma-Jamma" fraternity to back-to-back NCAA Final Fours in 1982 and 1983. The high-flying Drexler played his first 11½ NBA seasons with the Trail Blazers and his final 3½ seasons with the Rockets. He was a 10-time NBA All-Star and a member of the 1992 gold medal-winning U.S.A. men's basketball "Dream Team." Drexler led Portland to the NBA Finals in 1990 and 1992, and a franchise-record and league-best 63 regular season victories in 1991. During the 1994-95 campaign, Drexler was traded to Houston, where he promptly won his only championship while teamed with his former college teammate, Hakeem Olajuwon. When he retired, Drexler was one of only three players in history (with Oscar Robertson and John Havlicek) to have totaled at least 20,000 points, 6,000 rebounds and 3,000 assists. Drexler finished with 22,195 points, 6,677 rebounds and 6,125 assists. He also had 2,207 steals. Drexler remains Portland's all-time scoring leader and was the franchise's leading rebounder until his record was broken by LaMarcus Aldridge in March, 2015. Clyde Drexler was inducted into the Naismith Basketball Hall of Fame as an individual player in 2004 and as a member of the 1992 Dream Team in 2010. Drexler was named one of the 50 Greatest Players in NBA History in 1996. His jersey (#22) has been retired by the University of Houston, the Portland Trail Blazers and the Houston Rockets.

*   *   *

Marshall Holman was one of the most successful players on the Professional Bowlers Association Tour from the mid-1970s through the 1980s. Only 5-foot-9 and 140 pounds, Holman won 22 PBA Tour titles. A fierce competitor, Holman won a pair of U.S. Open championships and two Tournament of Champions titles. His first TOC win came when he was just 21 years old, which made him the youngest-ever winner in the Tournament of Champions.

Born in San Francisco, Holman's family moved to Medford, Oregon, when he was only four. Because of his fiery demeanor and meteoric rise on the PBA Tour, Holman became known as the "Medford

Meteor." With his playing career winding down in the 1990s, Holman transitioned into broadcasting. He has worked as a bowling analyst for ESPN, CBS and other media outlets.

For several years, my son's favorite sport was bowling. He loved watching it on TV, and Marshall Holman was his favorite player. We watched every Saturday, hoping that Holman would be one of the five bowlers in the televised finals. Holman was often described as colorful, emotional and flamboyant. He was extremely passionate and wore his emotions on his sleeve. When Holman was on the lanes, it made for terrific theater. Some bowlers might subtly pump a fist to celebrate a crucial strike. Holman would add a heavy dose of personal flair. He would spin around, leap in the air and scream in exultation. He would pump both fists in wild celebration while yelling directly at the fans, some of whom might have been jeering him just moments before. No, Marshall Holman was not shy about letting the fans in the bowling alley—or those watching on television—see exactly how much he enjoyed playing the game. No question, he played it better than most. He was so much fun to watch. I urge you to check out some of the old videos now posted on the internet. You'll wish Holman was still in his prime playing with the passion few others have ever exhibited.

I spoke with Marshall Holman on June 12, 2011, at the Caddies 4 Cure charity event in Beaverton, Oregon.

Did you have a boyhood idol?

Before bowling, I was a great baseball fan. Willie Mays and the San Francisco Giants—they were my team. Once I started getting into bowling, I loved Carmine Salvino. And, I loved Harry Smith and Dick Weber because, not only were they great players, they were players that had that little added flair of excitement. I think they infused all that into me because I was quite the ballistic player when I was a younger man.

You mentioned Willie Mays. Did you ever have a chance to meet him?

I did. I met him at a celebrity golf event in Atlantic City. It was really cool meeting him. Certainly, growing up, he was my guy—100%. As a kid, I got to see him play. He was still a great player. Yeah, it was a thrill to meet him.

Did he live up to your expectations during that brief encounter?

Yeah, I suppose so. Yeah, I mean, it was *Willie Mays!* That was good enough for me. He was very gracious, and I really did enjoy getting a chance to meet him.

Dick Weber was one of the all-time greats in bowling. I know you had a chance to bowl against him early in your career. Was that exciting?

Oh, very much so. In my first couple years on the PBA Tour, he was at the end of his competitive career. My first major victory—the '76 Tournament of Champions—I was in sixth place. He was in fifth place. Whoever won that game between us would make it to the Finals' telecast. I beat Dick Weber when I was 21 years old to make it to the Finals, and I won the tournament. I really think that being young and dumb was a great asset because—had I really thought about it—there was no reason for me to be able to compete with him at that point. But, it was a great memory.

In your final years on the PBA Tour, did young bowlers approach you to say they had idolized you as they were growing up?

Well, to a certain extent, yes. But, it seemed when the guys were coming up after I was sort of on my way out, they were just looking to put me in my place. And, they did! (Laughs)

Career Notes: Marshall Holman was the first PBA Tour player to surpass $1.5-million in earnings. He was named the 1987 PBA Player of the Year and earned three George Young High Average Awards. Holman, considered one of the very best players ever to compete on the PBA Tour, was ranked 9th on the PBA's 2009 list of the 50 greatest players in the Tour's first 50 years. Holman was inducted into the PBA Hall of Fame in his first year of eligibility in 1990. He also was inducted into the Oregon Sports Hall of Fame in 2001 and the USBC Hall of Fame in 2010.

* * *

13

Girls Looking Up To Us

Alex Morgan is a one of the stars of the U.S. Women's National Soccer Team. In huge demand as a product endorser, Morgan is certainly much more than a pretty face. She is a savvy businesswoman, who has turned her name into a successful brand. She is a marketing icon with incredible social media presence. As of September, 2015, Morgan has more than 2-million followers on Twitter. Morgan has endorsed major corporations, such as Coca-Cola, Nike and McDonalds. She has made appearances on numerous network TV programs and has been featured in many magazines, including the Sports Illustrated swimsuit issue. In 2015, she became the first woman to be prominently featured on the cover of the EA Sports "FIFA" video games sold in America. She and Barcelona star Lionel Messi share the cover of the "FIFA 16" games being sold in the United States.

As I learned the very first time I talked with Alex Morgan, she is driven. A star player and an entrepreneur, she can pretty much accomplish anything she sets her mind on doing. As I began to tell her about my book project, she said that she was also about to become a published author. Yes, in addition to everything else Alex Morgan has done, she has authored best-selling books. Morgan began by writing a series of kids' books called, "The Kicks." The first book, "Saving the Team," was released the day after I interviewed her. She has since released three other books in the series—"Sabotage Season," "Win or Lose" and "Hat Trick." She also published her autobiography, "Breakaway: Beyond the Goal," just prior to the 2015 FIFA World Cup. As you might expect—with her popularity and successful marketing efforts—Alex has sold far more books than most of us could dream of selling. As successful as she has been on the pitch, she's perhaps even more successful away from it. This Olympic champion truly is golden.

I talked with Alex Morgan in Beaverton, Oregon, on May 8, 2013.

If I were to ask you to name your first childhood idol, is there someone who immediately pops into your mind?

There are a few people that pop into my mind. I loved the game so much when I was younger. Having soccer become my passion and remembering the '99 World Cup so vividly, Christine Lilly definitely popped into my mind. I actually got to meet her when I was younger. I was definitely like, "Yeah, I want to be just like her." When I met her, she was a big star. She came and said "Hi" to our team. That little gesture meant so much to me. It went really far.

Have you ever told her that she was your childhood idol?

Yeah. (Laughs) We sat down at the very end of her career when she came back from her pregnancy. U.S. Soccer sat us down, and I got to ask her some questions. She's very aware that I looked up to her when I was younger. I was actually able to play with her for six months on the National team. It was a little surreal. That was a dream come true being able to play with my childhood idol.

What kind of things did you talk about when you first sat down with Christine Lilly?

We just talked about the different times in her life—the different teams, the different roles she played and the big goals she scored. And, we talked about how it felt to have all these little girls look up to her. Now I feel like I'm feeling that effect. I see that reverse-effect on the little girls looking up to my teammates and me. It's really cool to see that go full circle.

I was just going to mention that you are surely an idol for a lot of young kids. How do you feel about it?

Thank you. I try to represent my team well and myself in a positive manner. I know that there's a lot of little girls looking up to us that want to be in our shoes. As much as I can be a role model and inspiration to them is what I want to put on the field—and off the field as well.

Career Notes: As of August, 31, 2015, Alex Morgan has 91 caps and has scored 52 international goals. Morgan has accomplished a great many things on the soccer field, but her statistics are not as stunning as they might be if she had not been forced to battle a number of ankle and knee injuries the last two years. A left knee bone bruise limited Morgan's availability leading into the 2015 FIFA Women's World Cup. She ended up playing in all seven of the U.S. team's World Cup matches, but was only inserted into the starting lineup for the final five matches. Morgan was often frustrated in front of the net and scored only one goal in the seven games (versus Colombia in a 2-0 win in the round of 16). Morgan had arthroscopic surgery on her right knee in July, 2015, shortly after helping the U.S. women win the World Cup.

In addition to helping the U.S. Women's National Team capture the 2015 FIFA World Cup, Morgan helped the U.S. squad win the gold medal at the 2012 Olympics. Morgan headed in the game-winner in the 123rd minute to beat Canada 4-3 in the London Olympic semifinals— the game in which her friend, Christine Sinclair, scored the hat-trick in a losing effort. Morgan has teamed with Sinclair to win professional championships in the WPS (Western New York Flash, 2011) and the NWSL (Portland Thorns, 2013).

*　　*　　*

Christine Sinclair is the pride of Canada when it comes to women's soccer. The captain of the Canadian National Team, Sinclair is a huge star in her country. A native of Burnaby, British Columbia, she has won numerous awards, including the Lou Marsh Trophy as the nation's top athlete. Sinclair is the only soccer player ever to receive the Lou Marsh Trophy, and it was first awarded in 1939. She has been inducted into Canada's Walk of Fame. She's on a Canadian postage stamp. And, in 2015, Sinclair became the first woman to be prominently featured on the cover of the EA Sports "FIFA" video games being sold in her country. She shares the Canadian cover of "FIFA 16" with Barcelona star Lionel Messi.

Although she had already begun to make a name for herself on the international stage, I wasn't aware of Christine Sinclair until she starred as a freshman for the University of Portland soccer team in 2001. A niece of former (NASL) Portland Timbers players Brian and Bruce Gant, Sinclair received All-America recognition after leading all NCAA Division I freshmen with 23 goals and eight assists. I watched with greater interest when Sinclair led the Pilots to the 2002 NCAA championship. In the title game, she scored both of her team's goals in a 2-1 double-overtime win over Santa Clara, which gave the Pilots' athletic program its first national championship. It marked the final game for the university's legendary head soccer coach Clive Charles, who died of cancer in August, 2003. Sinclair also led the Pilots to the 2005 NCAA title, scoring two goals in a 4-0 victory over UCLA in the championship match. Sinclair set an NCAA single-season record with 39 goals in 2005. She also received her second straight Honda Award as college soccer's top women's player. She was really something at the collegiate level.

I wasn't the only one in the Northwest that was captivated by Sinclair's play during her time at the University of Portland. Few players in the colleges or pros had the ability to score like Sinclair (110 goals in 94 collegiate games). But, reporters sometimes found themselves a little frustrated when interviewing her. As great as she was as a player, Sinclair did her most of her talking on the field. She didn't seem to enjoy talking about herself. Sinclair was shy—extremely shy. However, now—as one of the world's most successful players on the international stage—she has become accustomed to the limelight and wears her fame well.

When Sinclair was young, there were far fewer female role models in sports. These days, young girls have a multitude of women athletes to admire. Christine Sinclair is among those most worthy of admiration.

I spoke with Christine Sinclair in Beaverton, Oregon, on May 8, 2013.

Who was your first childhood idol?

This is going to sound funny. In sports, it was Roberto Alomar, a baseball player for the Toronto Blue Jays. That's why I wear number 12. I grew up playing baseball as well as soccer. I was a huge Blue Jays fan. He's just someone I looked up to. Back in the day when I thought I was going to play in the MLB, I thought I'd be like him. (Laughs)

You are laughing, but did you seriously think you might be able to play baseball in the major leagues when you got older? Did you say to yourself, "I could be the first woman to play in the majors?"

You know, when you're younger, you don't think about things like that. I just loved the sport. I just wanted to keep playing.

What was it about Alomar that made him your idol?

He played the position I played, and I was a huge Blue Jays fan. So, it just made sense.

Did you ever get a chance to talk with him and tell him he was your idol growing up?

Yes, I have met him. I got introduced to him at a Blue Jays game last year. Then, we actually got to exchange number 12 jerseys. I gave him one of my Olympic jerseys, and he gave me one of his Hall of Fame jerseys. Pretty cool.

It had to be rather amazing to get to meet your childhood hero for the first time. What was that like?

The first time I met him, it was a surprise. Some people that I was with at the game were like, "Oh. We're going to watch the last couple innings in the private box." I'm like, "Okay." We walk in, and he's standing right there. I was like, "Oh, my gosh!" I was like a little school kid! (Laughs) He was incredibly nice. He was the one that actually thought about exchanging jerseys. He said he followed our National team during the Olympics. He was very nice.

When you at the University of Portland and now that you are an international star, you have many young girls idolizing you. Do you ever think about that?

It's not something I spend a lot of time thinking about, but I understand that it's part of my role with where I am now in sports. It's something that I take seriously—especially in the NWSL—spending time with the kids after games and signing as many autographs as I can because you realize that these kids are looking up to you. These kids want to be playing on that same field one day. It's our job to keep the league going so they have that opportunity. It's just about us doing everything we can to let those kids know that there is a future in the sport and to urge them to keep working hard.

Career Notes: As of July 1, 2015, Christine Sinclair has 228 international caps and has scored 155 international goals for the Canadian National Team. She ranks third all-time in goals scored behind Americans Abby Wambach and Mia Hamm. Sinclair might be best remembered for her play in the semifinals of the 2012 London Olympics. In that match against the United States, she scored three goals. Although the Americans won 4-3 in extra time, Sinclair led the Olympic tournament with six goals and helped Canada win the bronze medal—its first-ever Olympic soccer medal. After her stellar performance, Sinclair was chosen to carry Canada's flag in the Closing Ceremony in London.

Sinclair has played for the Portland Thorns in the National Women's Soccer League since the professional league was formed. She teamed with United States National Team star Alex Morgan to help Portland win the first NWSL championship in 2013. Prior to demise of the Women's Professional Soccer league, Sinclair was also part of two WPS championship teams—FC Gold Pride in 2010 and Western New York Flash in 2011.

* * *

14

When Deaf Wasn't Cool

Mike Glenn played in the NBA with the Buffalo Braves, Atlanta Hawks, New York Knicks and Milwaukee Bucks. Glenn, a four-year starter at Southern Illinois University, was recognized his junior season as the 1976 Missouri Valley Conference Player of the Year. After graduating from SIU, Glenn was drafted by the Chicago Bulls with the 23rd pick in the 1977 NBA Draft. However, shortly thereafter, Glenn was involved in an automobile accident and fractured his third cervical vertebrae. Glenn was released by the Bulls, but signed with Buffalo (now the L.A. Clippers) and went on to have a 10-year NBA career. Glenn has been the recipient of numerous awards including the NBA Walter P. Kennedy Citizenship Award and the NBA Spirit of Love Award. He is a member of the Missouri Valley Conference Hall of Fame and was selected to the All-Century Team at Southern Illinois University.

I was a college teammate of Mike Glenn at Southern Illinois University in Carbondale. When Mike arrived on campus in 1973, he was promptly inserted into the starting lineup on the Salukis' varsity basketball team. Since we played the same position—shooting guard—and since he was substantially more talented, I realized right away that I was not going to get much of a chance to play at SIU. I soon transferred to SIU-Edwardsville, where I would have more opportunity to get on the court. I met my future wife the day I set foot on the Edwardsville campus, so I have always joked with Mike that he played a key role in helping me find a woman.

Here are a couple other things you might not know about Mike Glenn. He had perfect attendance throughout his 12 years of elementary, middle, and high school—a teacher's dream student! And, in 2013, the former NBA player debuted as an actor. He played himself in the award-winning movie, "The Spirit of Love: The Mike 'Stinger' Glenn Story." The movie won "Movie of the Year" at the Inspirational Country Music awards in Nashville—beating out the movie "42" (Jackie Robinson's story), which was a commercial success. "The Spirit of Love" was inspired by Glenn's All-Star Basketball Camp for the Deaf and the Hard of Hearing, the nation's first basketball camp for hearing-challenged athletes. The camp is offered every summer free of charge to as many as 120 deaf athletes from around the country.

I talked with Mike Glenn by phone on December 27, 2013.

Who was your first boyhood idol?

I had a very unique childhood idol. My first idol was a deaf female basketball player. Her name was Mildred Nelson. She played for my dad, Charles Glenn, who was the coach at the Georgia School for the Deaf in Cave Spring, Georgia. He started the sports program there. It was in the segregated South. There was not a lot of money and interest in that kind of thing. It was a time when deaf wasn't cool. But, she was the best player on his team. She was the best player in the history of Georgia School for the Deaf. Mildred was a beautiful girl. She had beautiful dark, smooth skin. She wore number 12. And, Mildred could shoot that jumper so well. They had a tremendous team. One year, they lost like one game. Everybody was always just talking about, "Mildred Nelson. Mildred Nelson." I grew up in that environment. I would go to games and clap for Mildred. She was nice to me. I was a little guy, and she was teaching me how to play ball. She was my first idol and hero growing up with and going to practices and games with my dad and seeing his best player. Her number is retired. She was this black deaf girl who was beautiful and could play really well. She was a good shooter, man. She was knockin' down shots. So, Mildred was my first idol.

You were a great shooter. Did she play a part in you becoming the kind of shooter you were as a player?

Absolutely! Because she was the first person I saw as a hero, and she was a shooter. She could always shoot the ball, and it was just going *in!* Every time she was shooting these 15-footers, it was nothing but net. I admired the way she shot the ball. I started learning about the guys later. But, she was the big star on the team. She was *the* star. Dad had some guys on the boys' team that could shoot, and later I started identifying with them. But, she was the first star. She could shoot it so well that I also wanted to shoot the ball and get it to go in.

She and some of the deaf girls were the first ones to kind of adopt me into the deaf culture. You know, when you are the coach's son—a little kid—girls would come up to me at practice and start playing with me. They were the first to kind of adopt me and get me to learn how to speak sign language.

I've had my camp for deaf kids for 34 consecutive years, and I tell the kids, "My first hero was Mildred Nelson." I've told this story for many years. One year, they surprised me. I had not seen Mildred in 25 years, and they brought her to the camp. We have an all-star game at the end of camp, and they just walked her out on the floor. I'd not seen Mildred probably since high school. It was just so wonderful! It felt like seeing a family member because I'd admired her for so long. I've told all my campers that Mildred was my hero and this special person in my life. Then, she told me how proud she was—so proud of me and also proud that she was the first person I had seen as a hero. She gave me a big hug. It felt like your aunt or a family member that you haven't seen in years, when you just feel like, "I'm home now. I'm with this person that is a part of me." It was great. We just hugged there at mid-court. Everybody noticed that it was a special moment. I was just so glad to see her, and she had similar sentiments. It was a real special thing—a special moment. It's one of those times that you just have tears in your eyes. She was the impetus that really got me to love basketball and wanting to shoot the ball.

Then, it went other places, obviously. There were guys that came along that were real good and could shoot well. They worked with me, and I played with the guys when I started growing up. I had NBA stars I admired later on, but at this time I didn't know about any NBA stars. We're going back to the early '60s here. It wasn't like it is now.

You say that as you grew older, you became aware of the NBA stars. Which pro players did you follow?

My first idol of NBA caliber was Oscar Robertson. Again, that was kind of through my dad. He would say, "Oscar Robertson was such a complete player. Oh, Oscar Robertson was so great." I'd never really seen him play because they were hardly ever on TV. It was just those Sunday games on ABC every now and then. The Celtics were *always* on. So, I never really got to see him play. But, he had this book on how to play basketball and how to shoot. It was a little paperback book. I remember I just read that thing over and over until the pages were all torn out and ripped and shredded. I'd get in the mirror and practice trying to shoot like Oscar. That's how I patterned my shot after Oscar Robertson. There was only one perfect basketball player—Oscar Robertson—and everybody else has been human. He was just the epitome of perfection. I tried to emulate him. My shot is a mediocre imitation of him. Your elbow was in. Your elbow was straight up. All those things that he talked about, I tried to pattern my shot after him. He was, absolutely, my first NBA idol.

Guys can have multiple heroes. Not long after Oscar, my idol was Walt Frazier. With Walt, it was his demeanor, his style and the way he carried himself on the court. He was always cool. He wasn't complaining. I tried to emulate that as a youngster and throughout my career. I never saw him get technical fouls or get mad. I never did that either. All through high school, college and the pros, I would just raise my hand.

I received much acknowledgement because of it—from citizenship to different things. Those were things that an idol can do for you—impact the way you play and the temperament you play with. Those players had a real big impact on me—my whole style and success. Interestingly enough, I've worn both of their jersey numbers.

Lou Hudson was also an idol. That completes the set, really. (Laughs) In high school, I had two numbers—23 and 14—and that was Oscar and Lou Hudson. Lou Hudson was my guy when the Hawks moved here to Atlanta. I got to see him play, and he could shoot so well, too. I thought it was just fabulous the way he shot the ball. So, I wore 14 and 23. Because of them, both of those numbers are retired at my high school, Coosa High School in Rome, Georgia. In college, I tried to get 14 because of Oscar, but I think Dennis Shidler or somebody had it there at SIU, so I could not get that number. Eventually, the last number I had in Milwaukee, I got 10, which was Frazier's number. So, I really had the opportunity to wear the number of my three big idols. It was Walt Frazier. It was Lou Hudson. And, it was Oscar Robertson. I did get a chance to wear their numbers.

Did the fact that Walt Frazier played at Southern Illinois University just a few years before you arrived in Carbondale impact you in any way?

It introduced me to Southern Illinois. It really made Southern Illinois an option for me to choose as a college. I came out as the number one player in the state of Georgia, and I was third in my class academically. So, I had opportunities to go everywhere. I was recruited very hard by North Carolina and by schools everywhere, but I knew of Southern Illinois because of Walt. He was a guy that I admired tremendously. When I visited the school, I loved the school. I loved the opportunities and the possibilities. The good center—Joe C. Meriwether—was there, and we had a chance to work to build something kind of special again. Walt was a part of that formula of why I chose Southern. He was a guy that I idolized even before I went to Southern Illinois. These idols were guys that I attempted to shoot like, and I played imaginary games against them in the gym by myself. I spent countless hours playing all of them—*being* them and playing *against* them—and everything I could *imagine.* (Laughs)

Imaginary play aside, did you ever play against any of your idols in real life?

Oh, man. It was so incredible. I played against Walt only one time that I remember. It was the very tail-end of his career. He'd been traded to Cleveland, and it would have been my first or second year in the NBA. It felt so difficult, you know, because this is somebody you had admired and emulated. You had no desire to hurt him or beat him or anything. You were just delighted to be there with him. I just kind of was going through the motions, man. (Laughs) It was like walking through a dream. Any kind of competitive energy was not there at all. It was just like being in a dream, and you're just kind of floating through.

Let's go back to your first idol, Mildred Nelson. Obviously, both of you were adults when you were surprised by her visit at your basketball camp. As you've indicated, she was a basketball star in high school. Has she done well in life?

I think she did okay. I think she had substantial employment. She said she was fine. She looked fine and was healthy. It looked like life was treating her reasonably well. I was just really happy for that. With deaf people, sometimes it can get hard after high school. At that time, all the deaf kids in the state went to one school. They had dormitories and were supplied with three meals. They were kind of protected and sheltered. It gets hard out there in the real world for you when you can't hear and you can't talk. You're trying to navigate through life. It's hard to find employment. Life is tough for them. You never know how they're doing or how they've come out. She came back one subsequent year, so she's come to a couple of my camps. We gave her a camp shirt and everything. As far as I know, she's still doing well.

193

You have undoubtedly been an important person in the lives of young people, whether they were fans of your basketball or because of your work with the hearing impaired. You are almost certainly an idol for them—maybe in part because you were proficient in sign-language. Have any kids you've worked with shared how they feel about you?

Oh, absolutely. I felt great. One in particular is this kid named Willie Brown that I worked with. He was like a 13- or 14-year-old little, skinny kid. He came and was MVP at my camp three years in a row. He's from Macon, Georgia, a little south of Atlanta. I worked with him one-on-one and counseled him. Willie was one of the first deaf people in America to play Division I basketball. He played two years at Hofstra University. I brought him up to New York where we were having the camps. They got to see him up there, and they did some publicity on him. He got scouted, and they offered him a scholarship to play at Hofstra University. He played two years at Hofstra and had a lot of success there. Then, his dad passed. He wanted to come close to Georgia. Georgia State offered him a scholarship and he played his final two years at Georgia State. Willie had a couple of little looks with NBA teams. Denver let him come in and work out with the Nuggets. He came in and worked out with some of the Hawks. And, check this out. He went to three CBA camps, one in Albany, New York, where Jerry Oliver was a very good coach. He also went to Fort Wayne, Indiana, where Terry Stotts was an assistant coach for Jerry Oliver. Willie Brown tried out for his team. Terry remembers that, too. He was helping Jerry out, and I was there signing for this deaf kid. It was a unique experience. They had never had that. Here I was signing for this six-eight kid that was trying out for the team. He came very close. This was before the disabilities' laws, and nobody had money for interpreters. This was before the advancement of deaf people and the recognition that they can do these kinds of things. So, he didn't have money for an interpreter and had trouble communicating, but he was like right there—one of the last cuts. He represented himself well. Willie is a referee now. I got him into refereeing here in Georgia. He refereed some of the state tournament.

The coaches like for him to referee their games. They say, "Willie's gonna referee the game. He's gonna give me good game. He's not going to be influenced. He's going to call the game he sees, and he knows the game." I'm very close to Willie. He's a wonderful man. He has a wife and three kids. So, I kind of served as an inspiration for Willie,

As a matter of fact, Willie helped arrange getting Mildred to camp the first time. Through the deaf network, he knew somebody that knew where she lived. She was down in the Augusta area, which I didn't know. He helped arrange that, and he was very proud of that, too. He was proud of me for signing, communicating and introducing all these pros to him—letting him work out with Dominique Wilkins, Dan Roundfield, Marvin Webster and all that. Then, at the same time, he was proud that it was deaf people that had taught me and that my hero was a deaf person. It was a very unique little circle there.

Career Notes: Primarily serving the role of mid-range jump-shooter off the bench throughout his career, the 6-foot-2 Glenn averaged 7.6 points per game while shooting better than 54% from the field. Nicknamed "Stinger" by his New York Knicks teammates because of his sharp-shooting ability, Glenn shot nearly 59% from the field for Atlanta in 1985—a remarkable percentage for a jump-shooter. Glenn has stayed close to the game by working as a broadcaster working for ESPN, Turner Sports and CNN/SI as an analyst. Glenn currently works for Fox Sports South, covering the Atlanta Hawks. Mike Glenn is an in-demand motivational speaker who delivers a highly-inspirational message.

* * *

15

More Than I Could Handle

Dan Fouts grew up with a keen interest in sports—no surprise since he is the son of Bay Area Hall of Fame sports broadcaster, Bob Fouts. Like his father, Dan Fouts established his reputation for excellence while working on the West Coast. The younger Fouts was an All-Pac-8 quarterback for the University of Oregon Ducks before he became an All-Pro quarterback in San Diego with the Chargers.

Dan Fouts was elected to the Pro Football Hall of Fame in 1993 in his first year of eligibility. He is also in the University of Oregon Hall of Fame and the State of Oregon Sports Hall of Fame. His jersey (#14) has been retired by the San Diego Chargers.

I had the opportunity to interview Dan Fouts several times while working in Portland television and radio. I always found him to be a fun guy. Fouts has always been generous with his time and is a great story-teller. I could understand why he was able to transition so easily into broadcasting. It should surprise no one that once Fouts wrapped up his playing career he followed in his father's footsteps and headed into sports broadcasting. Fouts covered NFL games on CBS and worked for several years as a sports anchor on KPIX-TV in his hometown of San Francisco. Many will remember when Fouts worked with Al Michaels and comedian Dennis Miller on ABC's Monday Night Football—a failed experiment that was certainly not the fault of Fouts or Michaels. Fouts is now again with CBS and is one of the network's most respected football commentators.

I spoke with Dan Fouts by telephone on February 2, 2015.

Who was your first boyhood idol?

You know, I was really lucky because my dad was a sportscaster in San Francisco. He was the "Voice of the 49ers" for twenty years when I was growing up. Also, in 1958, the Giants moved to town. And, a couple years after that, the Warriors moved to town. All of a sudden, we go from having just the 49ers to also having the Giants and the Warriors. And, my dad was involved in a lot of it. I got to know and meet—and idolize—the stars of those teams. You start with Willie Mays. Then, you go to the 49ers. There were so many great 49ers there at the time with Y.A. Tittle, John Brodie, Hugh McElhenny and Joe Perry. I could go on and on. And, then with the Warriors, there was Wilt Chamberlain, Nate Thurmond and Tom Meschery. I had more than I could handle as far as idols are concerned.

Yours is a little different story than most. You had access to your boyhood idols at a very young age. Did you actually meet all of your idols as a kid?

I met most of them, yeah, because I tagged along a lot of times. And, I would be a ball boy or keep numbers for my dad in the press box. Yeah, I'd go to as many games as he'd let me go to. You know, I could drive you right to where Willie Mays lives. He didn't live too far from where we lived in San Francisco. It was that type of situation.

A lot of times we put these stars on a pedestal and look at them as someone very special. Was Willie Mays special in your eyes, or was he just somebody that you came to know through his association with your dad?

Well, he was the best. He was absolutely the guy you checked the box score in the newspaper every day to see how Willie did. I guess he would be number one on my list. But, it was also seasonal. If it was football season, it was all about the Niners. If it was basketball season, it was all about the Warriors.

When you were playing football at Oregon and later in the NFL, there were kids looking at you the same way you looked at your boyhood idols. Did you ever think about that?

At times, but you don't dwell on that as an athlete. I think you're so concerned with just winning the next game and getting ready for the next season. But, when you're at a public event and you see the kids' faces, and you hear the whispers and notice the fingers pointing at you, it makes you feel good.

Did you like the autograph thing?

Do you mean signing them or getting them? (Laughs)

Let's go both ways. Were you an autograph collector as a kid, and if so, did that resonate with you when you were older?

Well, absolutely. I tried to get as many as I could. I don't have a single one anymore, which is a shame because I had some pretty good ones.

When people ask for your autograph, does it take you back to when you were a kid?

Oh, yeah. I never refuse one. It's become a business, and I get maybe twenty requests a day in the mail. They send them to the Chargers or to the Hall of Fame –or they even have my direct address now through the internet. It's a big business, but if someone wants to make a dollar off my name, that's fine with me.

Career Notes: Dan Fouts was voted by pro football fans in San Diego as the "Greatest Charger of All Time" for the NFL team's 50th anniversary year in 2009. Fouts had done plenty to earn that distinction. In 15 years in the NFL (1973–87)—all with the Chargers—the 6-foot-3 quarterback threw for 43,040 yards and 254 touchdowns. Although not particularly fast, Fouts also rushed for 476 rushing yards and 13 touchdowns. Fouts was selected for the Pro Bowl six times. He was First Team All-Pro in 1979 and 1982 and Second Team All-Pro in 1980 and 1985. The Pro Football Writers of America voted Fouts the NFL's Most Valuable Player in 1982. Fouts set numerous passing records during his professional career. In fact, when he broke the single-season NFL record with 4,802 passing yards in 1981, it was the third straight year Fouts had set a new league mark. He led the league in passing four straight years and was the first NFL QB to throw for more than 4,000 yards in three consecutive seasons. When Fouts retired, he had joined Johnny Unitas and Fran Tarkenton as the only NFL quarterbacks with more than 40,000 passing yards. Fouts never played in a Super Bowl, but did lead the Chargers to four straight playoff appearances (1979–82). He quarterbacked San Diego in two AFC Championship Games.

*   *   *

Mike Krzyzewski has won more games as a Division I men's college basketball coach than any else. Coach K, who started his head coaching career at Army before taking over as head coach at Duke University in 1980, is the only men's coach to win more than 1,000 D-I games (through September, 2015). A true model of success, Krzyzewski won his fifth NCAA Division I championship in April, 2015. Only the late John Wooden has won more (10). In 2015, Coach K also tied the legendary UCLA coach's record for most Final Four appearances with 12.

Having watched him coach at least 100 games on television—and having great respect for his many accomplishments—I was thrilled to learn that Mike Krzyzewski was coming to coach his Blue Devils in a game in Portland in late 2010. Knowing that I would one day be writing this book, I immediately made plans to interview him during his short time in the Rose City. I was truly curious who this legendary coach might have idolized when he was a young boy. Was it another coaching legend? Perhaps it was a former

NBA star? Was basketball even his favorite sport as a kid? I asked myself all those questions before I finally got the chance to ask him one-on-one just moments after he held a press conference at the Rose Garden Arena. I was aware Mike Krzyzewski had grown up in the Chicago area, so I guess I should not have been surprised when he began to tell me about his childhood heroes. I spoke with Mike Krzyzewski in Portland on November 27, 2010.

Who was your boyhood idol growing up?

I didn't have one boyhood idol. I had every sports person who played for a Chicago team—whether it be Ernie Banks, Rick Caseras, Willie Galamore, Bobby Hull in hockey, Glenn Beckert at second base, Kenny Hubbs. I would sit in Wrigley Field as a youngster and want to be like all those guys. Then, when I went to Blackhawks games, I'd wanna be Bobby Hull or Stan Mikita—or Glenn Hall in the net. I'd rather have a mask, though. (Laughs)

In your outstanding career in basketball, you have undoubtedly met some of these people along the way. What was it like? Were they everything you thought they'd be?

Yeah, and I think the older heroes were even better because they never got paid very much. They just played the game because they loved it. Although he's not that much older than me, I think the guy that I really idolized is John Havlicek. You know, Havlicek just played the game. They're all good guys because they always knew that the game was bigger than them. They loved the game that they played, not just because they were getting paid for it, but because they loved playing it.

Coach K, you are surely an idol to a lot of kids that are thinking they might want to coach someday. What would you say to them?

Well, first of all, that's an honor. The main thing I'd say is always be truthful—first to yourself and then to everybody you meet. I'd say to follow the passion that's in your heart in a truthful way. Surround yourself with good people. Good people will make you better.

Career Notes: After his team won the NCAA Championship in 2015, Coach K ranked first all-time with 1,018 NCAA Division I victories. With an overall record of 1,018 wins and only 310 losses, his winning percentage (.767) is among the best in history. He ranks number one in NCAA tournament victories (88). In addition, through 2015, Krzyzewski has had more players drafted in the NBA Draft Lottery (20) and in the first round of the draft (30) than any other coach. Mike Krzyzewski has also served as the head coach of the U.S.A. Basketball Men's Senior National Team since October, 2005. (Gregg Popovich will succeed him in that role in 2017.) He guided the U.S. to gold medals in the 2008 Beijing Olympics, the 2010 FIBA World Championship, the 2012 London Olympics and the 2014 FIBA World Cup. His coaching record is 75-1 since being named the USA Basketball men's coach.

*　　*　　*

Johnny Davis helped the Portland Trail Blazers win their only NBA championship in his rookie season (1976-77). The six-two guard played with four NBA teams over ten NBA seasons. Davis has remained close to the game, serving as an NBA assistant coach or a head coach for a majority of the last 25 years. Davis was the head coach of the 76ers for one season and the Orlando Magic for nearly two seasons. He also spent a brief time as the interim head coach of the Memphis Grizzlies.

I got to Portland a couple years after Davis had left town. Although Davis helped a couple other NBA teams reach the playoffs, he was never again fitted for a championship ring. Whenever Davis returned to play in Portland, fans made him feel welcome by giving him a nice ovation. They followed Johnny's career and always rooted for him to do well.

When Davis was promoted to interim head coach of the Grizzlies during the 2008-09 campaign, he only got to coach two games before Memphis hired a new fulltime head coach. It was one of Davis' teammates from the Trail Blazers' championship season, Lionel Hollins. Davis remained with the team as an assistant coach.

I talked with Johnny Davis on March 3, 2014, in Portland, Oregon.

Can you tell me who you consider your very first boyhood idol?

In basketball, my idol was Dave Bing. I'm from Detroit. He played for the Pistons. All of the kids on the playgrounds wanted to be Dave Bing. Every time he made a basket, the P.A. announcer would go, "Bingo!" So, every shot you'd make, you'd say, "Bingo!" I really liked his style of play. He jumped and was athletic. He was quick, fearless, smart, and he could shoot. I enjoyed watching him play as a kid. He was an idol for me.

Now, in baseball, you gotta remember back in 1968 when the Tigers won the World Series, it was Al Kaline! Oh, wow! I was watching the games on TV, and I had an opportunity to go to one of those games. And, wow! He was my boyhood idol. We all wanted to be Al Kaline during baseball season. He was a baseball idol of mine.

In hockey, it was Gordie Howe. I loved watching Gordie Howe play.

I wasn't much of a football fan, but I did like the Lions. Lem Barney, he was a great player. I liked watching him play, as well.

Dave Bing ended up being Detroit's mayor. I guess he had brains as well as athletic ability.

Yes, absolutely, and he owned a steel company called Bing Steel which did very, very well. So, he was more than just an athlete. He was also a businessman. He later got into politics and became the mayor of the city of Detroit. He just had a wonderful career, and he's still going strong.

Do you remember the first time you met Dave Bing and your other boyhood idols?

Yes. It was unbelievable because Dave Bing came to watch the city championships for high schools in Detroit, and I was one of the top players in the city at that time. All of the top players got a chance to meet him. That was special. That was surreal. But, what was *really* surreal was he was in the latter stages of his career when I started my professional career with the Trail Blazers. The very first time that Dave Bing and I played against one another was right here in Portland at Memorial Coliseum. Boy, did he show me how much I still had to learn! (Laughs) After all the adoration, all of the imitation of him, all of the recollections of his games and how he played, to finally meet him on the court was really, really special. He was at the tail end of his career, but he was still a pretty good player. At that time he was with the Celtics, but—to me—he was still Dave Bing of the Detroit Pistons.

I never got a chance to meet Kaline. I did not meet Gordie Howe. But, those guys were just special. When you said Gordie Howe, you knew it was Red Wings. When you said Dave Bing, you knew it was Pistons. When you said Al Kaline, you knew it was Tigers. Now, a guy will start with a team and who knows where he'll be in a year or so. The loyalty—and the relationship between fans and the talent—you know, that was a special time. It's not like that anymore, unfortunately.

Kids in Portland in '70s cheered for you when you helped the Trail Blazers win an NBA championship. Did you think that you might be an idol for those kids in much the same way Dave Bing was one of your idols?

That didn't cross my mind at that time. As you get older and you begin to evolve in your career, you begin to understand the magnitude of the impact that you have on younger kids. That's very valuable, and you should treasure that. But, at that time, I had left school early—was only 20 years old—and was kind of maturing myself. I didn't think about the fact that there were probably some eight, nine and ten-year-olds watching me and saying the same things that I said about Dave Bing. I do understand that now.

When you think about that Blazer team, all of the guys were good guys. They were just terrific personalities and warm human beings. Throughout the roster—from Bill Walton to Maurice Lucas to Lionel Hollins, Bobby Gross, Dave Twardzik, Corky Calhoun, Larry Steele, Herm Gilliam, Lloyd Neal—you can go on and on and on; they're all great guys, wonderful people. And, their basketball IQ was second to none. All of them went on to have very productive and meaningful jobs and post-basketball careers.

Career Notes: Johnny Davis averaged 12.9 points and 4.5 assists per game during his 10-year NBA career. In his rookie season, he averaged 8.0 points in the regular season—10.5 points and 3.3 assists in the postseason—to help the Trail Blazers win the 1977 NBA championship. While Davis never won another championship during his playing career, he enjoyed some fine seasons with Indiana. He averaged a career-high 18.3 points a game in his first season with the Pacers (1978-79) and averaged 20 points per game in the 1981 playoffs for Indiana. Davis helped Atlanta reach the postseason both years he played for the Hawks. He averaged 17 points and 9 assists in the 1983 playoffs.

* * *

16

That Extra Five Seconds

Karina LeBlanc was the longest serving player in Canadian women's soccer history. The veteran goalkeeper announced her retirement from international soccer after representing host Canada in the 2015 FIFA Women's World Cup. LeBlanc, who grew up in Maple Ridge, British Columbia, had been a member of the Canadian National Team for 17-plus years. She represented Canada in three Pan American Games, five Women's World Cups and two Olympic Games. As the goal keeper for the Canadian Women's National soccer team, she helped lead Canada to the bronze medal in the 2012 Olympics in London. It was Canada's first-ever women's soccer medal in Olympic competition.

I met Karina LeBlanc in 2013 when she was the goalkeeper for the Portland Thorns in the National Women's Soccer League. I knew she had grown up in B.C. and had played for years on the Canadian National team, so I thought she might have some interesting stories to tell. I am so happy I talked with her. She told me about meeting several of her childhood heroes. One of those interactions was extremely positive. Another broke her heart.

I spoke with Karina LeBlanc in Beaverton, Oregon, on May 8, 2013.

Who was your first childhood hero?

Well, it's a cliché answer, but my parents. They did such a great job in raising me and letting me see how they dealt with difficulty. I had a couple on the athletic side. Basketball was also one of my first sports, and I wanted to be like Michael Jordan. So, I'd stick out my tongue when I played. Going back here—I'm aging myself—Peter Schmeikel in soccer. He was such a brave goalkeeper. And, then there were idols that were within reach. I had a couple of them that I had a chance to meet like Ken Griffey, Jr. I wasn't even a baseball fan, but it was one of those things where you'd see him on ESPN, and then I had a chance to meet him. He gave me that extra five seconds. It made the world of difference to me. I didn't know every stat about him. I just knew that he was famous and he'd worked hard in his sport. He'd had some quotes that inspired me, and when I met him—and he gave me that extra five seconds—it changed me. As an athlete, that's who I strive to be like because that extra five seconds meant the world of difference to me. If, as an athlete, I can have that effect on somebody, I'll take that person and make sure to do that. I think it's part of my job.

Sadly, not all athletes give that extra five seconds, and it can leave an emotional scar if they don't try to make a connection with you.

I actually had an athlete who didn't give me the time of day. It was somebody that I thought was *amazing*. Again, I had the quotes. I had pictures up on my wall. I saw this person in the airport, and I'm like, "Oh, my God! I'm your biggest fan!" And, not getting that five seconds *crushed* me. I actually felt like I wasn't worth anything. When you look up to somebody, and you're like, "Oh, my God. I want to be like them," you actually feel like you know them. (Laughs) That is what makes you idolize someone. You feel like you can connect. It made me who I am today in the sense that I will stay hours and sign every autograph rather than say no to that one person because I'd never want a child to feel like they're not worth something.

You don't want to name this athlete who disappointed you?

No, I don't because I actually met that person later on and they were sweet. I think maybe it was just circumstances and situations. From having teammates who get swarmed—like Alex Morgan and Christine Sinclair—sometimes it's like they do want to have a couple minutes to themselves. I've been on that end of it. But—in that moment—it *killed* me. I think that's why—for me—I never want to have that moment where I've disappointed a young person.

Once it's done, it's done. You don't get a do-over.

No. I'll forever remember it. That's why I don't want to bring up the name because it could have just been one of those moments where she wanted to be left alone, but it also taught me a very valuable lesson.

Obviously, you're great with kids, and you're an outstanding player. You are an idol for a lot of young girls and boys. Do you think about that?

Absolutely. And, people tease me. They're like, "If you're gonna make plans with Karina after a game, give her an extra half an hour." But, it's important because I think that we're role models whether you choose to believe it or not. It's something you take with pride. After the Olympics, I remember meeting a group of girls, and somebody said that we saved their lives. They were thinking of taking their lives, and seeing us play gave them hope and kept them alive. I think that's where you have to honestly take it personally and understand that this sport is just the beginning for us. When you're a role model, you truly have the ability to inspire and motivate, not just little kids, but people. You can help them to know that things are possible. It will get better. For me, I've had highs and lows in my career. In working with UNICEF and traveling around the world, I finally start to understand that those lows were for a bigger reason. It's about doing something for somebody else. I'm a true believer that we all have a greater purpose. Even with soccer, there will be a greater purpose for me.

Career Notes: Karina LeBlanc made 110 appearances while representing Canada on the international stage. LeBlanc was the starting goalkeeper for the Portland Thorns when they won the inaugural championship of the National Women's Soccer League in 2013.

*   *   *

17

On A Line With Gretzky

Brian Bradley played 13 years in the National Hockey League with Calgary, Vancouver, Toronto and Tampa Bay. A native of Kitchener, Ontario, Bradley also represented his country by playing for the Canadian National team in 1987-88. Bradley scored 182 career NHL goals, a majority of those coming while he wore a Tampa Bay Lightning jersey.

In the first few years of Tampa Bay's NHL franchise, Brian Bradley was arguably the Lightning's most popular player. It's natural for fans to gravitate towards the star of their team. Bradley was a two-time Lightning All-Star and the team's leading scorer. He was "the man" in the early days of the franchise. It's always nice when a player remains connected to a team after his playing career ends, and hockey fans in Tampa certainly appreciate having Bradley around to discuss the early days of Lightning hockey.

In the first year of the franchise, Bradley was one of the players that helped educate new hockey fans in the region about the intricacies of the sport. Those new fans had to learn that icing is not just that sweet stuff you spread on top of a cake. Bradley also played for the first Tampa Bay team to qualify for the Stanley Cup Playoffs.

Brian Bradley and I talked by phone on February 12, 2015.

Who was your first boyhood idol?

Wayne Gretzky was someone that I always looked up to. He played minor hockey against my brother. He was four years older, so as I got old enough to really understand what was going on, I followed his career in junior hockey in Sault Ste. Marie, then on to Indianapolis in the WHA and when he went into the NHL with Edmonton. I always followed Wayne Gretzky like a boyhood hero. He put up huge, astronomical numbers growing up.

I was also a huge fan of the Boston Bruins growing up. I liked Phil Esposito. I used to watch Bobby Orr. My uncle was a scout for the Boston Bruins back in the day. I used to always follow them on TV. My uncle would take me to the Bruins games when they came to Toronto. I was always a big fan of the Boston Bruins. Those were the people I grew up watching, admiring and idolizing, you know, Phil Esposito and Bobby Orr and the Boston Bruins—and definitely Wayne Gretzky.

Did you ever skate against any of your boyhood idols?

Well, I never played against Phil Esposito, but I played against Wayne Gretzky for a long time. For me to sit there and watch him play his minor hockey in Brantford and play hockey against my brother, to watch him play in Sault Ste. Marie and a little bit in the World Hockey Association and then in the NHL, and to finally get a chance to play against Wayne was a thrill. It was just exciting for me. Coming to Tampa, Phil Esposito was the general manager. When I first came here in '92 and got picked up in the expansion draft by Phil and Tony Esposito, I was excited. I had always wanted to meet Phil. I had never ever met him before.

What was it like to meet your idols for the first time?

Well, Wayne Gretzky grew up playing against my brother, and one time I got to meet him. He came back to my house in Kitchener when I was about 12 years old. He was 16 or 17. So, it was really kind of fun to meet Wayne for the first time. I was excited. He was such a great player. Everybody knew who Wayne Gretzky was in the hockey world in Ontario. He went to Edmonton and played, and everybody knows what happened there. It was just fun for me to meet him. After watching him play on the ice for five or six years without ever really having the opportunity to meet him, it was great. It was fun to see how down to earth he was—and the same with Phil. Phil and Tony Esposito treated me first class here in Tampa. They've always been great to me.

When you first talked with Phil Esposito in Tampa, did you tell him that you were a fan of his when he was with Boston?

Well, I probably didn't bring it up the first conversation, but I definitely did say, "Phil, I grew up admiring you. I was a big fan of the Boston Bruins." He kind of laughed and just smiled. Phil still works for the Lightning. I work for the Lightning. He does the radio and different things like that. I work with community relations and corporate sponsors and do a lot with the fans. We see each other a lot, and Phil's a great guy. We've known each other for the last 22 or 23 years now. Same thing with his brother, Tony, I mean, Tony has always been great with me. Phil and Tony Esposito have been nothing but first class for me since I've been here in Tampa.

You had some success with Vancouver in the 1989 NHL Playoffs scoring seven points in seven games. Then, you came to the Lightning in the 1992 Expansion Draft, and you had career years for Tampa Bay. I'm sure there were young fans in Canada and the United States that said, "Brian Bradley is no Wayne Gretzky, but he's a pretty good hockey player. He's one of my guys." Did you ever think about that?

Oh yeah. In fact, we're doing a thing tonight at the Lightning game. I'm going to meet and greet about 40 or 50 minor hockey players. Did I come down here to Tampa thinking that was ever going to happen? No, not really. I came down here just to work hard. I finally got an opportunity to be a number one center, and you know what? I think

I went out there and proved people wrong, more or less. I got the opportunity in Tampa where some of the places I never did get the opportunity.

I think the highlight of my career—besides scoring my first goal or playing my first game—was playing in the two All-Star Games. I remember playing on a line with Wayne Gretzky and Brett Hull in the All-Star Game in Montreal. For me, that was a special time. To finally make it and play in an All-Star Game was truly an amazing thing. And, to get to play with my boyhood hero, Wayne Gretzky, on a line in an All-Star Game, that's just another great story.

Career Notes: After being selected by the Lightning in the 1992 Expansion Draft, Brian Bradley led the 1992-93 Tampa Bay team in scoring with career highs in goals (42) and points (86). He also led the Lightning in scoring the next three seasons. In 1995-96, Bradley recorded a personal-best 56 assists—along with 23 goals—to lead Tampa Bay into the Stanley Cup Playoffs for the first time. In 328 career games in a Lightning uniform, Bradley accumulated 300 points (111 goals, 189 assists) which ranked as the most in franchise history at the time of his retirement in 1998. As of August 31, 2015, he still ranks sixth in career points in Tampa Bay Lightning history. Bradley, an NHL All-Star in 1993 and 1994, remains affiliated with the Tampa Bay Lightning as a community representative.

*   *   *

18

My Dad Meant Everything

Steven Jackson has played 11 seasons in the NFL—the first nine with the St. Louis Rams, the last two with the Atlanta Falcons. As this book heads to print October 30, 2015, Jackson is a free agent who still hopes to sign with a contending team to play in 2015. He is the leading rusher among active NFL players.

Jackson played three seasons at Oregon State University before leaving after his junior season to enter the NFL Draft. Jackson was a part-time starter as a true freshman and became a star when he led the Pac-10 in rushing as a sophomore. His junior year, Jackson set a school record with 2,015 all-purpose yards (record since broken). He was drafted by the Rams in the first round of the 2004 NFL Draft. In his first pro season, the Las Vegas native started the Steven Jackson Foundation, which promotes education and healthy living among today's youth.

I still have vivid memories of calling play-by-play on television of Steven Jackson's first college game at Oregon State, so it's a little difficult for me to believe that 2014 might have been his last year as a player. As a true freshman at OSU, he battled for playing time with Ken Simonton, who had been a Heisman Trophy candidate the previous season. Simonton was good, in fact, the Beavers' all-time leading rusher. But, Jackson was just too talented to remain on the sidelines. When it came to be decision-time, there was no doubt he would leave Oregon State after his stellar junior campaign. It's hard to believe that so much time has passed since Jackson scored five touchdowns in a Las Vegas Bowl victory in his final college game.

I have no doubt that 2,743 body-punishing carries in the NFL has played a role in Jackson's diminishing skills. I just hope he is signed by a contender in 2015 so that one of the NFL's most solid citizens and outstanding representatives might have one last chance to play for a winner— something he's never done.

I talked with Steven Jackson by phone on January 13, 2015.

Who was your boyhood idol?

It was my father. I say that because he served in the Marines during Viet Nam. He and my mother had my sister, Rhonda, at a very young age. Two days before he took off for Viet Nam, he married my mom. Then, nine months later, Rhonda came into this world. I can only imagine the stress he was under as a young man, not only fighting the war, but hoping that he could make it back to see his family again. As a person now in my walk of life having the responsibility of taking care of other loved ones, I appreciate seeing him do it with dignity and grace and bring us up in the right way—having integrity and being faith-based—and always making sure that I'm a man of my word. I believe different genders have to play different roles in life, and me being his son, he taught me that men always do what they say and a handshake is just as good as writing your name on a piece of paper. Those certain qualities you just don't find everyday any more. When people do recognize those qualities in you, it means a lot. It means a lot, not only that my daddy instilled it in me, but for people to know that if I say I'm going to do something, I'm going to do it. If I'm going to commit to a team or if I'm going to commit to a cause, they know I'm gonna be there, and I'm gonna see it through.

At what age do you think you began to fully understand what he had gone through as a Marine in Viet Nam?

It wasn't until I was actually 20 years old. At that particular point, that's when I was getting ready to decide if I was going to be a professional or stay that last year at Oregon State. I mean, you start thinking about life's choices, and here I am. I think this is the biggest choice that I have to make in my life. When he and I sat down, we talked about him being in Viet Nam. He was on guard at 20 years old. You start thinking about the magnitude of the stress that he was under at such an early age. When you say you're like 31—or whatever age you are—kids and teenagers normally think you're such an old person. As you go through life and you actually hit that number—and have to make some decisions and life choices—then you realize how young a person is. Being influenced heavily by my father, I have a ton of respect for our troops because now I actually realize how young these young men and women are that are sacrificing their lives for our freedom.

Meeting you when you were a freshman player at Oregon State, and seeing how you represent yourself as a professional football player, I don't think you have changed much as a person. The character you continue to show is a real testament to your upbringing.

I think so. Opportunity comes, and you have to be able to take advantage of it. But, at the same time, when you're blessed with the talent and you're blessed with abundance, it shouldn't change you. It should only magnify who you already were. That's what I believe. Thank you for acknowledging that. I don't think I've changed much. I just try to use the platform that I am on to help influence others to do things in a positive manner and do things in the right way.

There are so many people who see you as a role model, whether it's for the work you do on the field, the work you do with your foundation or your other community service. Are your off-field contributions something you *want* to do, or are they things you almost feel like you *have* to do because you're an idol for so many?

It's kind of two parts. Originally, in 2004, I founded the foundation. I actually thought of it as something that I *should* do because from the Las Vegas area, there are not many people that make it out—especially to be an athlete. But, as I got more involved—as you put in the man hours and the sweat equity more than just writing a check to make a donation—you realize the lives you're that you're affecting. You actually are able to see their eyes and talk to the people, young and old, and see that a moment of your time really can change a life. Maybe they want to make bad decisions or basically they want to give up. You just encourage that person to keep fighting and keep striving toward their dream. I would say that I felt like I needed to do it because I just thought, "Here I am a professional athlete. This is the next step. You have a charity." But, as I began to actually put in the time and put in the effort and get to know the people in the community, I actually enjoy it now. I don't see it as something that I *have* to do, but something that I *want* to do.

Being a person of strong faith, which means more to you—your Hall of Fame-worthy career or what you've done for people that are less fortunate?

Absolutely, I think what I've done and the lives that I've affected so far in my 31 years. I cherish that more because as we all know records will be broken. The next generation will come, and they'll just view me as another old running back. Believe me. I hear it in the locker room already. (Laughs) But, being able to touch some of these young people's lives and encourage them to pursue whatever it is that they want to be, that actually is very much more rewarding than any amount of touchdowns or any amount of yards that I've rushed for.

Career Notes: Steven Jackson ranks 16th in NFL history with 11,388 rushing yards (through 2014). The 6-foot-2, 240-pound running back has scored a total of 68 rushing touchdowns. He also has 460 receptions for 3,663 yards and nine touchdowns. Jackson is the Rams' all-time leading rusher with 10,138 yards. For the Rams, he rushed for more than 1,000 yards eight straight seasons. His best season was 2006—his first of three Pro Bowl seasons—when he rushed for 1,528 yards on 346 carries, with 13 rushing touchdowns—all career highs. He received All-Pro recognition in 2006 and 2009.

*   *   *

Steve Grogan played his entire 16-year NFL career as a quarterback with the New England Patriots. He set franchise records for career passing yards and touchdowns (records since broken by Drew Bledsoe and Tom Brady). Grogan grew up in Ottawa, Kansas, about an hour southwest of Kansas City. He led his high school team to state titles in track and basketball, and a state runner-up finish in football. In 1986, Ottawa High School named its football stadium, Steve Grogan Stadium, in honor of its most famous football alumnus. After attending Kansas State University, Grogan was selected by New England in the fifth round of the 1975 NFL Draft. Midway through his rookie season, Grogan took the starting job from Jim Plunkett. Despite winning only three games that first season, Grogan led the Patriots to an 11-3 record the following year in 1976. It was clear he had found a home in New England.

Steve Grogan currently owns the Grogan Marciano Sporting Goods store in Mansfield, Massachusetts. The store was originally founded by Peter Marciano, brother of boxing champion Rocky Marciano. Peter owned the store for more than two decades before selling it to another party. After that person experienced some financial trouble, Grogan came to the rescue and bought the store. Grogan wasn't sure he would like being the owner of a sporting goods store but thought he would try it since he had been involved with sports his entire life. It appears to be a good fit. Grogan has owned the store for more than 20 years.

I spoke on the phone with Steve Grogan on April 8, 2015.

Who was your first boyhood idol?

I would probably have to say my dad, Jim Grogan. He played a lot of softball and basketball around town, and I'd go to the games with him and watch him play. I loved watching sports and being a part of it. Back in those days, we didn't have SportsCenter or have all the highlights on from all the teams and leagues around the world. He was somebody I was in contact with daily, and he just was a great example on how I needed to live my life.

I grew up in a small town. I'm aware that small-town sports, and community involvement in sports, is a pretty big deal in small towns.

Oh, it is. There is a small college there—Ottawa University—and I used to go to their football practices. I'd sneak into the gym and play on weekends. I'd go to track meets. The athletes that were participating there were guys I looked up to when I was a kid because they were college athletes. I don't know their names now, but a huge part of my growing up was watching those guys compete and play games. I just loved it.

As you got older and started playing, did you ever find athletes that you tried to emulate, perhaps patterning your game after them?

I don't really think so. There were guys I loved to watch playing. Terry Bradshaw comes to mind. He was with the Steelers when I was in late high school through college. I just loved the way he played the game. I liked a lot of the Kansas City Chiefs. As I was growing up, they had some great teams. They played in two of the first four Super Bowls. Those were guys that I enjoyed watching. But, there aren't a lot of names that I can say that I tried to be like.

You played for the Patriots from '75 to '90. You had success due to the play of offensive lineman like John Hannah and Pete Brock who helped you find room to run around and put up some numbers. While I know that you understood those linemen had a lot to do with your success, a quarterback is often the face of the franchise and gets all the attention. Most fans idolized you. Did that have an impact on you in terms of how you lived your life?

Oh, I think absolutely. Again, that's the way my parents brought me up. The role models that kids have that influence their lives are the people they're in contact with daily—not just the athletes. But, the athletes do have a responsibility to show kids what's right or wrong. That was always in the back of my mind.

Career Notes: Steve Grogan played for the Patriots from 1975–90. Despite playing through a multitude of painful injuries and having to undergo multiple surgeries, Grogan threw for 26,886 yards and rushed for 2,176. He threw 182 touchdown passes and scored 35 rushing touchdowns. His most production season was 1979, when he passed for 3,286 yards and 28 touchdowns and rushed for 368 yards and two TD.

*   *   *

Joey Harrington was one of the most successful quarterbacks in University of Oregon football history. As starting quarterback of the Ducks his final 2½ seasons in Eugene, Harrington compiled a win-loss record of 25-3. Oregon fans labeled Harrington "Captain Comeback" as he lifted the Ducks to 11 wins in 13 games in which they trailed or were tied in the fourth quarter. He led his team to a share of the Pac-10 title his junior season and an outright conference crown his senior year. In 2001, Harrington was recognized as the Pac-10 Offensive Player of the Year after leading Oregon to its first 11-win season and a season-ending number two national ranking.

Harrington formed the Harrington Family Foundation more than a decade ago, and the Foundation has raised more than $1-million for students in Oregon. A 2012 inductee into the State of Oregon Sports Hall of Fame and the Oregon Athletics Hall of Fame, Harrington currently works in local radio and television in Portland, Oregon.

It's important to note that Joey Harrington was a hugely important part of Oregon's rise as a college football power. As Harrington ended his starring run at quarterback for the Ducks, their home football facility, Autzen

Stadium, received a $90-million facelift. 12,000 seats and 32 luxury boxes were added on the south side of the stadium. The enthusiasm generated by Oregon's success with Harrington at quarterback undoubtedly played a role in the expansion of Autzen Stadium. Since the day Harrington became the starting QB as a sophomore late in the 1999 season, the Ducks have not played a home game without it being played in front of a sellout crowd. Entering the 2015 season, Oregon has sold out 103 consecutive games over 16 seasons.

Now that Oregon has been a college football power for more than a decade, it's difficult to believe there was a time not all that long ago that little was known about Ducks' football east of the Rockies. In 2001, the University of Oregon kicked off a Heisman Trophy campaign for Harrington. A huge 80-by-100-foot billboard showing a full-length photo of the quarterback—labeled JOEY HEISMAN"—was erected across from Madison Square Garden in New York. The $250,000 the school paid for the advertisement was money well spent. Not only did it give Harrington's Heisman hopes a boost, it made people outside the Northwest aware of the Oregon brand. Despite receiving 54 first-place votes (including one from this author), Harrington finished fourth in the 2001 Heisman voting behind winner Eric Crouch, Rex Grossman and Ken Dorsey. Harrington dominated Heisman voting in the western part of the country. The billboard helped Oregon establish its brand, but could not help Joey win the Heisman.

I spoke with Joey Harrington on June 12, 2011, at the Caddies 4 Cure charity fundraiser in Beaverton, Oregon.

Who was your first boyhood idol?

I can't really remember trying to emulate somebody until I was maybe in middle school or high school, and then it was my dad. I never really tried to be John Elway or be Joe Montana, but my dad was in public education. As I crossed paths with a lot of people, I heard a lot of great stories about not only what a great coach and administrator he was, but what a great *person* he is. I think everybody would say that it carries a little bit more weight when somebody else tells you how great your dad is versus him telling you. (Laughs) And, that was the case—*a lot*. I had a lot of people tell me how great my dad is.

Joey, I almost expected that answer from you. You have always been a pretty grounded guy, and I wondered if hero worship is even a part of your vocabulary.

Yeah—especially now—it just seems a little bit weird. It was always kind of an uncomfortable thing being in that position as someone's sports' idol. Looking back on it, I think I was lucky to be in the position I was and have such a great role model so close to home.

You had fans idolizing you when you played at the University of Oregon and when you played in the NFL for the Lions. Kids wore your jersey. That had to be sort of surreal.

Oh, yeah! That's exactly the word for it. It was surreal. I think everything really started with that billboard in New York's Times Square. That was the ultimate surreal moment—standing on the corner of Madison Square Garden with my dad and looking up at the billboard with a huge picture of me. None of us really know what to say. A kid from New York walks by, does a double-take, and says, "Hey, is that you?" I was like, "Yeah. It is." He says, "Cool," and he keeps on walking.

I think the key to that is not to get too wrapped up in it because it's gonna end. Those days are over. I would hope that the things I did off the field—not necessarily the superficial things that people are drawn to—would be enough to continue to have a following in the right way.

Knowing you and your family a little bit, I was pretty sure you were always going to do things in the right way because of the upbringing you received from your parents. But, did you think about the following that you had and think that you had to sign autographs and be nice to those kids wearing your jersey?

There's definitely a lot of pressure to that. No matter how great a family you come from, it's still up to you to make the right choices. It makes it that much tougher when there are thousands of little kids watching. You don't want to let down the people who are rooting so hard for you and looking at you in the same manner that I know a lot of my friends looked to athletes when we were growing up.

You walked in here tonight, and they announced your arrival over a loud-speaker. You almost looked embarrassed by that. A fan watching you walk the Red Carpet said you're the reason he's a Duck fan. The adulation apparently never ends.

You know what, though? That's the nice part—when somebody comes up and says, "You are the reason I'm a Duck fan, and I appreciate the work you did." That means something. That makes me feel good. To know that the work that I put in is still appreciated, yeah, it makes me feel that it was worth it.

Career Notes: His senior season at Oregon, Joey Harrington was a Second Team All-American and a First-Team Academic All-America selection. Harrington was the first Pac-10 quarterback to lead his school to three bowl victories (1999 Sun, 2000 Holiday, 2002 Fiesta). At Oregon, he passed for 6,911 yards and 59 touchdowns, with 23 interceptions. He also had 18 rushing TDs and one TD catch. Harrington went to Detroit with the third overall pick in the 2002 NFL Draft and played his first four pro seasons for the Lions. He later played one year for both Miami and Atlanta. During his pro career, Harrington completed 56% of his passes for nearly 15,000 yards. He threw 79 touchdown passes and 85 interceptions.

*   *   *

Quinn Buckner, a 2015 inductee into the National Collegiate Basketball Hall of Fame, is one of very few men who have won a high

school state championship, an NCAA Division I championship, an Olympic gold medal and an NBA championship ring.

While Buckner had a solid professional basketball career, he is best remembered for what he was able to accomplish as an amateur athlete. A native of Phoenix, Illinois, Buckner was recognized by Letterman Magazine his senior year at Thornridge High School (Dolton, Illinois) as the best high school athlete in the United States. He was a high school All-American in both football and basketball. Buckner was captain of the 1971-72 Thornridge basketball team considered by many to be the best high school team in Illinois history. Buckner's team went 33-0 his senior year and won the first Illinois Class AA (large school) state championship. That happened one year after Buckner had captained the 1970-71 Thornridge Falcons to a 31-1 record and the championship of the final single-class Illinois state tournament.

Buckner played two years of football at Indiana University while also playing basketball for legendary Hoosiers' coach Bob Knight. Buckner quit football in order to concentrate fulltime on basketball. Knight thought enough of Buckner's leadership ability and knowledge of the game to name the six-three guard a captain his final three seasons at IU. In Buckner's junior year, Indiana went undefeated in the regular season and finished 31-1. The next year, the Hoosiers won a national title with a perfect 32-0 record. Through 2015, Buckner's 1976 Hoosier team remains the most recent unbeaten NCAA Division I championship team. 1976 was a very good year for Buckner. Not only did he win an NCAA title, he was a captain on the U.S. Olympic men's basketball team that went undefeated and won the gold medal in the Montreal Summer Games.

Quinn Buckner was one of the best high school basketball players I've ever seen. A man among boys in the early '70s, Buckner had great physical tools. But, as Indiana coach Bob Knight told me when I wrote the book, THORNRIDGE: The Perfect Season in Black and White, it was Buckner's

*knowledge of the game and how he handled himself on the court that truly
made him a man among boys.*

I talked with Quinn Buckner by phone on December 20, 2013.

**You were telling me that you didn't necessarily have a true boyhood
idol?**

I didn't have them in that sense. There were a couple things that
transpired. When Thornton High School won the 1966 Illinois state
championship, I was in the sixth grade. There were two guys from my
home town that were great players—Hershel Lewis and Sam Hamilton.
They were people that—if you wanted to play—you had to aspire to
be like them. Those guys were considered the best players. Really, there
were a number of great players at Thornton. Harry Hall was a big-time
player. Lamarr Thomas was a two-sport guy—All-State in football and
basketball—that I looked up to as much as anybody once I realized
that that was really where I was headed. So, my idols kind of moved
as I started to evolve and find myself. Lamarr went to Michigan State
on a football scholarship. He was a two-sport guy and had had some
success. So, right there in my hometown, there was Sam Hamilton,
Hershel Lewis, Harry Hall and Lamarr Thomas. My sister was ahead
of me in school, and she used to talk a little bit about them. I was aware
of all those guys.

Then, as I moved up through school, it moves again. Lloyd Batts used
to take me around where we would play basketball all the time. We'd
end up going to the West Side of Chicago playing at the Martin Luther
King Center. Lloyd, who was having a stellar career at Thornton and
would be recognized as the Illinois High School Player of the Year as a
senior, was a guy who took me around to play. Frankly, he probably took
me around just a little bit more than he took his little brother, Boyd (a
teammate of Buckner's at Thornridge). For me, it was a great experience
being there on the West Side where it was really tough basketball. You

had to be really tough. That's where I got my sense of staying calm and playing through the nonsense that can happen in a game.

So, you spent time hanging out with Lloyd Batts, who you told me was one of the players you considered an idol of sorts. What about the other guys you mentioned? Did you ever get a chance to shake their hands and tell them that you followed their accomplishments when you were younger?

The truth is Lamarr and Harry I really didn't know that well. They had had great success, and *we* were having success. Our Thornridge teams had started to take off. I think there was kind of like, not mutual admiration, but there was some *respect* for our Thornridge teams, primarily because I was my sister's little brother. These guys were in school with my sister, and my sister knew that—from talking with my dad—that I could do what I could do; you know, that I could play. Again, Hershel and Sam Hamilton lived in my hometown. So, I just spoke to them, and they were very helpful. Again, most of these guys I grew up with, so I didn't necessarily look at them with the awestruck feeling. But, I respected a lot of the positive things they did.

Now, you have to understand. My dad was an athletic director, and he knew talent. He was at a different elementary school, East Chicago Heights, which is now Ford Heights. They had really good athletes. As he watched me compete with those East Chicago Heights kids, my dad knew I had something that I didn't know. It was always me listening to *him* as my driving force athletically, as much as I could listen to Hershel or Sam Hamilton. If I were to bring home any information that didn't sit well with my father, he would tell me or put it in context. His value was that he was a father, so he put it all in context for you. My dad's been gone some 30-plus years, but looking back on it he helped me stay grounded that way. So, if you hear people blowing your head up, and you bring that overinflated ego back home, he'd say, "You gotta watch that because here's what it can lead to." It kept my feet grounded. The thing that I'm trying to say is, in retrospect, what my father was trying to make me aware of was, while there are guys that you can look up to for what they *do*, you have to be very aware that they're just people—with all that comes with that. He would say, "Just keep it in context." Again, he was putting it in context for me, but also letting me know, "Don't get carried away. You're just another person. You got some skills, but if you don't develop them and don't do the right thing, then you can't make that work for you and the people you're working for." All of those guys that I mentioned were strong influences in my athletic career, but none of them were stronger than my dad. That's the fact.

That is not a surprise to me. As you discussed with me when I was doing research for the book on your Thornridge High School team, your parents were both educators. They were hugely influential in your life, even when you tried to decide whether to quit football after your freshman year at Indiana.

Yeah, absolutely. There's no question. Listen, as I said to you when you were doing the book, "I'm the proud son of William and Jessica Buckner, and, (laughs) I am the son of them, without a doubt. My mother kept me grounded academically, and my dad kept me grounded athletically if I got a little carried away like young people can get carried away.

My dad had really wanted me to play football in college the second year. My dad looked ahead. He was trying to leverage me when the two pro basketball leagues were about to merge so that I could tell the NBA guy who didn't want to pay me because the ABA was gone, "Well, I'll just go play football." My dad got *all* of that. Just take that, and drive it backwards. He understood the *business* of the game as well as he understood the *gamesmanship* of the game. So, I'm being tutored with that all the time. For example, if someone took a cheap shot and hit me in a game, my father said, "You can't back down, but be smart about it." So, if a guy hit me in a game—and you can ask Coach Knight about this—I never got him right back. But, I got him during the course of the game when the official wasn't looking. That was part of it. My dad said, "Find a time when the official's not looking and just make sure you get him back." If you don't do that, in sports, people tend to run over you. That's not mean. That's part of the gamesmanship of the game.

Quinn, you were idolized by a lot of young fans when you won state championships in high school, when you went undefeated and won a national championship at Indiana, when you won at the Olympics and when you won a championship with the Celtics. Did you ever think about all those kids that looked up to you?

No. Honestly, I didn't think of being an idol until you brought it up. I don't think of myself as an idol. That's part of what my dad helped manage at an early age. I almost think having won at every level is an out of body experience. I know that I've done it. I appreciate that I've done it. But, it's not something that I wear as a badge of honor. Consequently, I don't think about what comes with that, part of which is people idolizing you. That, I don't get. I really don't. I understand—particularly here in Indiana—the reverence they put on the game of basketball at IU. But, I attribute it a heck of a lot more to the *team* than I will ever attribute it to *me*—on every level that I've ever played on. It's more about the team. I just happened to be one of the guys that played on the team. Now, I understand the value that I brought to the team, but I was just one of the guys that played on the team. None of this happens if the team doesn't win. None of it. Nobody thinks that much of you if the teams you play on don't win. They think you got some good talent, but I think people put a bigger premium on the fact that your *teams* were successful than if *you* were successful. At least I do. I put more value on the team's success than the individual's success.

The 1975-76 Indiana men's basketball team is still the last undefeated NCAA Division I champion. Some younger fans today might not know that you were a captain on that squad. When people talk about great teams and great players in college basketball, do you think you might be overlooked?

No, I don't feel overlooked. It doesn't bother me. I won't say I don't care, but it doesn't bother me. It's a different time, a different generation. That's almost 40 years ago. That's really the issue. That's at least two generations ago. Some of the kids today, their parents may not have been born. (Laughs) That's just the reality of it.

My former IU teammate Scott May and I have this conversation periodically. We look at it as simply somebody else is due to have whatever that recognition's supposed to bring you of being the last undefeated team. I don't want this to come off wrong, but you look at the value of your life and the things that are important in your life. While *athletically*, it's as important as anything you've probably ever done, it really isn't that important because you don't live an athletic life. It's just a part of what got you to where you are now in life.

Career Notes: Quinn Buckner played 10 years in the NBA with the Bucks, Celtics and Pacers. He won a championship ring with Boston as a backup point guard on the Celtics' 1984 title team. Buckner was never called upon to be a big scorer in college or in the pros, but he was an outstanding defender. He received NBA All-Defensive Second Team recognition four times. Buckner briefly served as head coach of the NBA's Dallas Mavericks, but was unable to find the same level of success as a coach that he had experienced as a player. Buckner has worked as a basketball commentator for several national networks and currently works as an analyst on the Pacer telecasts. Buckner is Vice-President of Communications for Pacers Sports & Entertainment.

*   *   *

Earl Watson played 13 years in the NBA with a half-dozen different clubs. The six-one point guard played with the Sonics/Thunder, Grizzlies, Nuggets, Pacers, Jazz and Trail Blazers. After his final season in Portland in 2013-14, Watson moved into coaching. He is currently a full-time assistant coach with the Phoenix Suns.

I had an opportunity to call play-by-play of several of Earl Watson's games on television when he was playing for UCLA. It seemed like he played there forever! That's probably because he started four straight years for the Bruins. He was a very solid point guard and earned All-Pac-10 First Team recognition his senior year in 2001. He played some of his best basketball with the Sonics, so I got to see plenty of Earl Watson through the years. I interviewed Earl several times after he joined the Trail Blazers. I considered him an excellent interview, a person who offered great perspective on any number of topics. He's a sharp guy. I think you will see him become an NBA head coach at some point in the future.

I talked with Earl Watson in Portland, Oregon, on December 21, 2013.

Who was your first boyhood idol?

It was my dad. My father was in the U.S. Army. He was a military drill sergeant, so everything was, "Six o'clock in the morning. Wake up. Fold the bed. It's gotta be tucked just right." Everything had to be almost perfect. You could have bounced a quarter on the bed. You know what I'm saying? It's old school. But, as a kid, I always loved basketball. And, I always loved any U.S. Army picture that existed. Those were my two dreams—military—NBA. As a kid, you don't know which one is more real than the other. Half the day, you were playing like you are a soldier. The other half, you were playing like you are an NBA player.

The creativity came from my father, and he was my first boyhood idol. For any child, parents are the most critical part of your life. I've been fortunate that my dad instilled my work ethic early in life. That's why I've been in the NBA so long. I try to pride myself on working hard and doing things the right way. I try to do things only one way—the *right* way. If it's not right, I don't do it. It's kind of like the same mentality that my dad instilled in me from him just being in the Army. I tell people all the time, "A lot of times, it's never *you* that actually achieves the ultimate dream of being an NBA player or being whatever you want to be. Sometimes, it's your *kid*." You instill that by going through the hardships, and the routes you take in life end up being instilled through your kid. You get to live—through your kid—a greater dream than you ever could imagine.

What did that mean for you to be able to become an NBA player, in essence, for your dad after all he's done for you?

That's the thing about my dad. It's never for *him*. It's for *me*. That's how he would say it, "Live your life. I'll live mine." But, it's amazing because he instilled in me something I can also give to my kids. So, now the baton is passed at the same level—if not higher—and the dreams have become bigger.

When you were in college, and in the years you've been in the NBA, did you ever think about the kids who might be looking up to you as an idol?

Never because I always live with humility. I really don't take myself that seriously. I feel like what I do is an amazing gift, an amazing opportunity. But, at the same time, I stay in touch with reality. This is Utopia. The NBA is Utopia. Eventually, Utopia ends, and you have to live a regular life. The NBA is a childhood dream, and after the NBA, you have adult dreams. You continue to dream, so I don't take it that seriously.

Back to when you were a kid trying to figure out which path you would take—basketball or the military. Like many kids, I played soldier and had the little Army men figures.

Yeah—those little plastic soldiers—you'd get a little packet with a *thousand* of them for like a dollar-fifty. (Laughs)

So, when you finally decided basketball might be the route you would take, was there a player who caught your fancy?

Yeah. For me, it was Magic. Magic Johnson was my first basketball guy. At that time, there was no NBA TV, so the Lakers were the main people on TV—Lakers, Celtics, the Bad Boys (Detroit Pistons). I grew up in Kansas City, so we got a lot of the Chicago Bulls home games on WGN. I remember them saying that Michael Jordan was a selfish player and that he'd never win a championship. They said he just wanted to score points. So, I saw the evolution of him grow until, "Oh. He's a champion!" It was amazing to see that journey and to watch that. That was my first introduction to the NBA. *Inside Stuff* with Ahmad Rashad started coming on every Saturday morning. That was my *national* introduction. It was good. And, I grew up in Kansas, so KU basketball was always big, but I was never a KU fan.

Career Notes: Earl Watson averaged 6.4 points and 4.4 assists during his NBA career. His best full season was 2007-08—his only year as a full-time starter and the Sonics' final season in Seattle. Watson averaged 10.7 points and 6.8 assists that season. In four years at UCLA, Watson averaged 11.2 points and 4.7 assists. Earl Watson holds UCLA records for most consecutive starts (129), career steals (235) and assists in a game (16, vs. Maryland, 3/18/2000).

* * *

Craig Robinson is the older brother of First Lady Michelle (Robinson) Obama and the brother-in-law of President Barack Obama. Robinson, considered one of the best basketball players in Ivy League history, attended Princeton from 1979–83 and was Ivy League Player of the Year in 1982 and 1983.

Throughout the decade of the '90s, Robinson worked in the financial sector. But, the allure of basketball brought him back to the sport as an assistant coach at Northwestern University. He later served as head coach at Brown and at Oregon State, quickly improving the basketball programs at both universities.

During Craig Robinson's tenure at Oregon State University, I was given the opportunity to call several games on the Beavers Radio Network. One of those games was at Maryland, and for yours' truly, it was the experience of a lifetime. The day prior to the game, the entire OSU traveling party toured the White House and had the privilege of meeting the First Family in the West Wing. The First Family also attended the game and sat just a few feet from my broadcast position. I shook hands with the President in the West Wing one day and sitting courtside the next. It was an experience I'll never forget.

Robinson also wrote a successful book, "A Game of Character" in which he discussed the impact his mother and father had on his life. His father, Fraser Robinson, played a key role and, not surprisingly, was top of mind when I spoke with Craig Robinson on August 27, 2013, at Gill Coliseum in Corvallis.

Craig, who was your first boyhood idol?

Before I knew what an idol was, my first *hero* was my dad, Fraser Robinson, who I watched get up and go to work every day. He was working for the City of Chicago, handicapped (with multiple sclerosis), on crutches, going to work every day—and coming home and taking the time to play ball with me. Whether it would be football, softball, basketball, we played whatever was in season.

Then, when you know what the word idol means, my first hero—and he continues to be one of my favorite guys—was Ernie Banks. Growing up in Chicago, I played first base because Ernie Banks played first base. Even though his original position was shortstop, by the time I came along, he was a first baseman. I just appreciated his character along with his great baseball ability. He carried himself kind of like my dad did. He was very thoughtful in what he said. He was gregarious. He got along with all different types of folks. Being a South Sider—rooting for the Cubs in the White Sox part of town—that's a tough one. But, my bedtime was 7:30. The Sox played at night. The Cubs only played in the day. I could come home from school and watch the Cubs on TV, and I never got to watch the White Sox. So, I was a Cubs' fan, and Ernie Banks was just one of those guys who you wanted to emulate.

We'll talk more about Ernie in a moment, but in your book, *A Game of Character*, you wrote about the important role parents play in raising children. I'm finding out that parents have been hugely important in the upbringing of many of the athletes I'm talking with for this book.

It is almost indescribable the effect that my dad had on me. My dad died 22 years ago. Every time I do something like this interview, it makes me remember how much I miss him. I think about him all the time. Things come up during the day that make me think of him. I was just using one of his sayings today in the office with my assistant coaches. He literally imprinted himself on me such that I look at my 21-year-old son, Avery, and I see my father. And, I look at my three-year-old, and I see my father. It is amazing how genetics work. There was a lot of love there. There was a lot of caring. There was a lot of discipline. There was a lot of nurturing. I could go on and on with adjectives that helped me develop into the person I am.

You told me earlier that you've met Ernie Banks. Do you remember where and when it was that you met him for the first time?

The first time I met Ernie Banks, I couldn't have been more than ten years old. Now, this was back in the day when baseball players lived in neighborhoods. We lived two blocks away from Billy Williams, who played left field for the Cubs. One day we're out in the park playing baseball. My friends and I are out there just playing pickup baseball. We see Billy Williams out with his daughters playing catch with Ernie Banks and Fergie Jenkins in the park by my house on the South Side of Chicago. Ernie said hello to us and shook hands and went back to what he was doing. Then, I met him again about three or four years ago. I was working at Oregon State, and I had written *A Game of Character*, but it wasn't completely done. I was working on the (Obama) campaign. So, I walk into a hotel in Chicago, and Ernie is staying there. I went up to him, and I was like, "Ernie Banks!" He was like, "Hey, fella! How ya doin'?" And, I said, "I'm Craig Robinson." He said, "I know who you are. You're Michelle Obama's brother." And, I was like, "Do you know we met many years ago?" So, I told him that story, and he treated me like he remembered me from when I was ten years old. Just the class and character of the guy, it was great. He was just as happy and gregarious and caring and loving as he was when I was ten years old.

Whether from your playing days at Princeton, your coaching days at Brown or Oregon State, or because of your ties to the White House, people obviously look at you a little differently. I'm sure you're sort of a hero for some people. Do you think about that, and does it impact how you live your life?

Oh, yeah. I think about it. Fortunately, I don't have to change because Fraser and Marian Robinson had me prepared so that I could just be myself now that people know who I am. Before—when they didn't know who I was—I acted the same way. So now, I don't have to do anything differently, which is a very comforting feeling that I don't have to change. I wouldn't know how to act if I wasn't being myself anyway. So, yeah, I do feel that, and I know that. But, I don't have to qualify my statements or be guarded about the way I do things. When I sit here and talk to you reporters, I would sit here and talk to you guys like that even if you didn't have cameras and you were just asking me questions about the team. I just always try and be honest. I try and be thoughtful. I try and be truthful. I'm not as engaging or as funny as Charles Barkley, but I try and be a little bit entertaining. I know this is part of the business. When your values are rooted from your parents—and they're good values of hard work, integrity, character and all that kind of stuff—it's easy to just go from one area into another without having to worry about who you are.

You had to suspend several players this year because they did not live up to expectations off the court. Do you talk with your players about the fact that they are looked up to by young Beaver fans? Do you tell them that when they don't act responsibly, they will be disappointing those young fans?

Yeah, I do. It is a tough thing because I wouldn't wish celebrity on anyone. I mean that sincerely. If you look at young celebrities, they have a rough time going from being young celebrities to being older celebrities. A lot of them don't make it because when you're young, you're so inexperienced that you don't know how to be a celebrity. You don't know how to be a role model. So, I try and talk to our players about their position in the community, but they're still 18 to 23-year-olds. They're still trying to figure out who they are. I don't want to throw them out with the bath just because they make a couple of mistakes. I want them to know that I've made mistakes. It's just that— back in the day when I made my mistakes—the whole world doesn't know about it because there wasn't cable. There wasn't Twitter. There wasn't this big social media bubble that we live in.

Career Notes: As of September, 2015, Craig Robinson ranks sixth on Princeton's all-time scoring list with 1,441 points and sixth on the school's career blocked shots list (97). Robinson led Princeton to NCAA Tournament appearances in 1981 and 1983. As a major college coach, Robinson spent six years as an assistant at Northwestern University before he was named head basketball coach at Brown University in 2006. In his first season at Brown, the Bears improved to an 11-18 record, 6-8 in the Ivy League. Brown swept the two-game season series from Providence for just the second time in school history. The next season, his last at Brown, the Bears again showed dramatic improvement. They set a school-record with 19 wins and posted an 11-3 Ivy League mark, good for second in the conference. Robinson won more games in his first two years than any head coach in Brown University men's basketball history.

After helping Brown recharge its basketball program, Robinson was hired as head basketball coach at Oregon State University in 2008 and coached the Beavers for six years. He took over a moribund program that had won only six games (0-18 in the Pac-10) the previous season. The Beavers had posted losing records in 16 of the previous 17 seasons. Three times during those years, OSU had won only six games in a season. However, in his first year in Corvallis, Robinson guided the Beavers to an 18-18 record and the championship of the College Basketball Invitational postseason tournament. The 18 victories were the most for an Oregon State team in 19 years.

An excellent recruiter, Robinson improved the talent every year in Corvallis, and in his fourth season, his first with only players that he had recruited, Oregon State went 21-15, winning 20 games for the first time since 1989-90. The once down-trodden program posted just its second winning record in 22 years. Oregon State qualified for postseason play for the third time in Robinson's four years at the school. That same year, the Beavers upset top-seeded Washington in the quarterfinals of the Pac-12 Tournament. Oregon State led the conference in scoring for the first time in school history with a school-record 78.9 points per game and also led the Pac-12 in steals for the third straight season. Oregon State basketball was again relevant.

When Robinson and the Beavers parted company in 2014 after six seasons together, Craig Robinson ranked fourth in Oregon State career coaching victories with 94. While the immediate on-court improvement had been dramatic, Robinson's greatest successes at Oregon State might have been what he accomplished off the court. Robinson campaigned for and helped push through the construction of a new $15-million basketball practice facility next door to venerable Gill Coliseum. He reached out to two legendary Oregon State stars, Gary Payton and A.C. Green, who had distanced themselves from the Beaver basketball family during the down years. At Robinson's urging, both players reconnected with the OSU program and have become vocal supporters at Beavers' games. Payton's son, Gary Payton II, was recruited to Oregon State by

Robinson and developed into the 2015 Pac-12 Defensive Player of the Year.

Craig Robinson was hired by ESPN as a college basketball analyst in 2014.

*   *   *

Jeff Green is a professional basketball player with a very inspiring story. A 6-foot-9 forward currently playing for the Memphis Grizzlies, Green was a standout at Georgetown University before leaving school after his junior year to head to the pros. Just prior to his fifth NBA season, Green's career was temporarily halted when he had to undergo heart surgery. It turned out to be just a bump in the road for Green, who has come back strong to be a reliable NBA player.

Green missed the entire 2011-12 season after being diagnosed with an aortic root aneurysm in a preseason physical examination. He soon had surgery to repair his heart and then began the tedious rehab process. Initially unsure about his basketball future, Green took advantage of his down time to return to Georgetown and earn his degree. He became the first person in his family to graduate from college.

After returning to the NBA, Green has been a very productive player. In fact, he scored a career-high 43 points against Miami in March of 2013. After surviving his heart scare, Green now makes time to talk to children with cardiac issues. Green is, without a doubt, an inspiration to those kids—and to all of us.

I interviewed Jeff Green in Portland, Oregon, on January 11, 2014.

Who was your first boyhood idol?

First, I want to say my dad. My favorite *player* growing up was Magic Johnson—and Scottie Pippen. So, those three guys were important to me—especially my dad, who really helped me become the person I am. Basketball-wise, I would say Magic Johnson is number one because he was a player who everybody looked up to. I was growing up, getting taller, playing basketball and trying to play every position. That was *him*. You always want to be like guys who set the bar high, and he was definitely one of those guys.

What was it that your dad did for you growing up?

He set the rules. My parents were divorced at a young age for me. He stayed in my life, and he set the rules for me. He made sure I didn't travel down the wrong route to become somebody who I didn't want to be. He was a basketball player himself, and I think that helped. He went down the wrong route. He made sure I was in every good position to pursue my dreams of playing basketball. Without the guidance of him, who knows where I'd be?

Have you ever met Magic Johnson?

I have not. My rookie year, I missed him by five minutes. My rookie year, I was able to play in the Rookie-Sophomore Challenge in New Orleans. After the game, my family met me for dinner at Morton's Steak House in New Orleans. I was in a lot of traffic, and they were already there. They knew who my idol was, and I get there, and they said, "You just missed Magic!" He met my family. My pops and my mom, they got a chance to meet him. I had just missed him by like five or ten minutes. I was devastated. Hopefully, I'll get a chance to meet him one day.

Do you think about that, that there are kids looking up to you the same way you looked at Magic?

It's funny that you say that. During Christmas, I had a chance to meet a kid named Spencer who was having heart surgery. There were a lot of other kids at the hospital, and they all were fans of mine. You never think about that—being in the position I am—that people look up to you. It's humbling that you have kids who look up to you and want to be like you because you grew up the same way. You never would think it would happen to you. It's very humbling.

Career Notes: After winning a state championship at Northwestern High School in Hyattsville, Maryland, Jeff Green was a standout at Georgetown University. He shared the 2005 Big East Rookie of the Year award with Rudy Gay of U-Conn. In January of 2006, he scored 18 points to help Georgetown upset previously-undefeated and top-ranked Duke. It was the Hoyas first win over a number one team since 1985. In 2006-07, Green made clutch shots down the stretch in several games, including a game-winner with 2.5 seconds left against Vanderbilt in the NCAA Tournament's round of 16. The next game, Green scored a team-high 22 points to lead the Hoyas to an overtime win over top-seeded North Carolina. As a result of that victory, Georgetown was on its way to the Final Four. The 2007 Big East Player of the Year, an All-American, Green gave up his senior year at Georgetown to enter the NBA Draft. Boston made Green the fifth player selected in the 2007 NBA Draft, but he was traded to Seattle in the deal that brought Ray Allen to the Celtics. Green was named to the NBA All-Rookie Team after averaging 10.5 points in 2007-08. He played 3½ seasons with the Sonics/Thunder before being traded to Boston in early 2011. Green joined Memphis during the 2014-15 campaign. In his first seven NBA seasons, Green has averaged 14.3 points and 5.0 rebounds per game.

*　　*　　*

Greg Kelser teamed with Magic Johnson to lead Michigan State to the 1979 NCAA Division I basketball championship over Larry Bird and Indiana State. That same year, Kelser was selected fourth overall in the NBA Draft by the Pistons. Kelser played only six seasons in the NBA due to injuries. He has been on the broadcasting crew of the Pistons since 1988.

I was a young sportscaster working in local television in the Tampa-St. Petersburg market when Greg Kelser and Magic Johnson won the 1979

NCAA Championship. The game was the most-watched in college basketball history, and it was truly special. It was the first of dozens of showdowns between two of the all-time greats, Magic Johnson and Larry Bird. But, outside of Michigan, many people have forgotten how important Greg Kelser was to that Michigan State team. He was a fabulous player. It was Kelser that would often leap high above the basket to corral an alley-oop pass from the flashy Johnson and then throw the ball straight down through the hoop. In the Spartans' championship season, Kelser averaged nearly 19 points a game. And, he delivered when it mattered most. Kelser had a magnificent all-around game against Indiana State in the title game. The 6-foot-7 Kelser scored 19 points, pulled down a team-high 8 rebounds and had an MSU-high 9 assists. He might have had a triple-double, but played only 32 minutes because of foul trouble. Kelser was an All-American, on the court and in the classroom. Greg Kelser was known as "Special K"—not because he loved the breakfast cereal of that name, but because his basketball abilities were truly special and his last initial is "K".

I talked with Greg Kelser in Portland, Oregon, on November 11, 2013.

Who was your very first boyhood idol?

Do you mean *after* my dad – Walter Kelser? For me, it would probably be Bill Russell because he's the one that I remember watching earliest in my life who I was impressed with enough to want to be a basketball player.

Does he know that? Did you ever have a chance to meet him and tell him how you felt about him?

Oh yeah. He knows it now. The first chance that I got to meet him I was playing in the NBA. He was broadcasting at that time for CBS. He had some very kind things to say about me. It was only later on that I told him, "I watched you growing up." I don't know that he was all that happy to hear that. (Laughs)

I mentioned Bill Russell because he came to mind first and foremost. But, the one that I was just absolutely in *awe* of when I met him was Muhammad Ali. Again, I grew up watching him. I was a big fan of Muhammad. He was just as nice as he could possibly be to me. I was 22 years old when I met him. I had just finished my rookie year in the NBA with the Detroit Pistons, and he was in town for a welterweight championship fight between Thomas Hearns and Pipino Cuevas. I got a chance to spend like 30 minutes in his hotel room because a friend of mine knew him and took me there to meet him. Now, that was surreal. (Laughs)

Ali had many fans. For instance, Doc Rivers told me Muhammad Ali was his boyhood idol. And, you tell me you got to hang out in Muhammad's hotel room. That's so cool.

That's the thing. As a kid, you grow up watching and being inspired by all these great athletes and people. Then, when you grow up, you're in a forum that allows you to start meeting some of them in person. That's what being a part of the NBA provided me. I got a chance to meet people that I never would have met had it not been for that.

There are kids who looked up to you as a player and now look up to you as a broadcaster. Do you think about that?

Well, here's the thing. The impact that a lot of people had on me growing up—and then to meet them—it sort of validates the admiration that was once there. I'm very cognizant of that when I meet people now. I don't care how I feel. It's very important to be nice. It's very important to be approachable because they're going to take that away as a lifelong memory.

When we started, you mentioned your dad. What did your dad mean to you?

My dad meant *everything* to me, as did my mother. Thankfully, my mother is still living. My father has passed on. Because of my dad and his years in the Air Force, I was the son of a military man and got to travel the world and live in different places. I learned to understand and appreciate the differences between people and to celebrate those differences as opposed to allowing those differences to create division. My dad—being in the Air Force—taught me that at an early age.

Career Notes: Greg Kelser is still regarded as one of Michigan State's best players. He remains the only Michigan State player to score 2,000 points and grab 1,000 rebounds over the course of a career. Sadly, injuries prevented Kelser from having a long playing career in the pros. Over his six NBA seasons with the Pistons, Sonics, Clippers and Pacers, he averaged 9.7 points and 4.6 rebounds.

*   *   *

Peter Jacobsen has been a professional golfer since joining the PGA Tour in 1976. A colorful personality, Jacobsen has worked as a golf analyst on several networks including NBC and The Golf Channel. A man of many talents, Jacobsen has written a pair of books, *Buried Lies* and *Embedded Balls*, and he has co-designed a number of golf courses. He appeared as himself in Kevin Costner's 1996 movie *Tin Cup*. A music-lover, Jacobsen formed a rock and roll band—*Jake Trout and the Flounders*—with three fellow PGA players, (the late) Payne Stewart, Larry Rinker and Mark Lye. They put out a pair of albums and entertained guests at numerous golf events in the 1980s and 1990s. Jacobsen also owns his own event management company which has successfully staged a number of professional golf tournaments throughout the country.

From 1986 to 2002, Peter Jacobsen hosted the Fred Meyer Challenge at various sites in Portland, Oregon. The charity golf event included a Pro-Am that brought some of the biggest names in entertainment to the Northwest. Bob Hope, Jack Lemmon, Clint Eastwood, Huey Lewis and Glenn Frey were among the many stars from Hollywood and the music world that came to be a part of "Peter's Party." The golf pros who competed in the annual two-day event were a virtual "Who's Who" of the sport. Arnold Palmer was Jacobsen's playing partner each of the 17 years of the Challenge. Jack Nicklaus played in the Challenge. So did Tom Watson, Gary Player, Tom Kite, Greg Norman, Phil Mickelson, Lee Trevino, Raymond Floyd, Ben Crenshaw, Curtis Strange, Chi Chi Rodriguez, Payne Stewart, Johnny Miller, Sergio Garcia, Isao Aoki, Fuzzy Zoeller, Craig Stadler, Larry Mize—the list goes on and on. Many considered the morning golf clinics the highlight of each year's Challenge. Jacobsen, a few of his golfing buddies and a celebrity or two would put on an entertaining show for the fans. They would discuss proper shot-making technique, but would also hit a few trick shots and tell some jokes. Jacobsen would do hilarious spot-on impressions of other players, such as Palmer and Stadler. The Fred Meyer Challenge created many wonderful memories for golf fans in the Northwest.

I phoned Peter Jacobsen to talk about his boyhood idol on April 28, 2011.

Peter, who was your boyhood idol?

Well, I had two people. Obviously, I idolized my dad. My dad was a very important figure in my life. He was a stud. He was a serviceman. He was a Navy flier, a Navy pilot. I just admired him. I liked the way he was. I wanted to be like my dad. But, I think Arnold Palmer was my boyhood idol because when I started playing golf around the age of 12, my dad talked about Arnold like he was the King. Any time we watched golf, we watched Arnold on TV. I liked his swashbuckling style, the way he engaged with people and that he genuinely like people and liked golf. I was drawn to that.

Do you remember when you first met Arnold?

I remember exactly when it was. It was at the Oswego Lake Country Club on the driving range. Arnold and Dave Marr were in town doing an appearance. My mom had done a little bit of work with Jantzen, so I was invited to come out to the clinic they were doing. Actually, Dave Marr and Arnold asked me to hit a couple of balls, which I did. They went, "Hey, wow! It looks like you're a player." They encouraged me at 14 years old. I never forgot that. That's the type of encouragement that you need from your heroes. It's great when you meet your boyhood idol and he's everything and more that you'd hoped he would be.

You later started playing on the PGA Tour and suddenly you were competing against Arnold. What was that like?

It was very surreal to compete against people that I grew up watching like Palmer and Jack Nicklaus and Gary Player and Lee Trevino and Tom Watson. It was great to be able to tee it up in the tournament with these guys that just years before I'd *watched* compete in the tournaments. I remember when I was in college driving down to watch the Crosby down at Pebble Beach. I would drive down with Jeff Sanders and my brother, David. We were on the Oregon golf team together. We would just drive straight from Eugene. We would buy a ticket. We'd go watch Arnold and Jack and Bob Goalby and Doug Sanders and Lee Trevino compete with people like Jack Lemmon, Jackie Gleason, Bob Hope and Clint Eastwood—all the great Hollywood celebrities. To me, it was a dream. It was a dream come true. So, when I got my card and actually played in the Bob Hope *with* Bob Hope, and played in the AT&T—the Bing Crosby—with people like Eastwood and Lemmon, it was incredible.

There's no doubt that you were the idol for a lot of young players. Did you ever think about that?

Well, I never thought about me being an idol to kids, but I always remembered how important it was to treat the young people coming up in the game as people like Arnold Palmer, Trevino, Nicklaus, and Dave Marr treated me. They showed me the respect that I had hoped I would be shown. That's all we're looking for when we meet our idols. When you're at the Blazer game and you meet Brandon Roy or you meet LaMarcus Aldridge, you hope that they actually treat you as though you're friends. I don't ever think that I'm anybody's idol, but I want to make sure that I pass on the legacy of respect that I got from those great players in the game before me. I want to make sure that I pass that respect on back down. I think the game of golf is in great hands because we do connect our past and our futures together quite well. When you go to the Masters, you see a Nicklaus and a Palmer and a Player and a Doug Ford and Bob Goalby. Then you have a chance to meet the Ryo Ishikawas and the Rory McIlroys. You realize that there may be 40, 50, even 60 years of age difference there, but everybody knows everybody.

After leading the Masters for three rounds, Rory McIlroy talked about how he grew up idolizing Tiger Woods, and there he was playing against him and trying to hold him off on Sunday. Do you have players come up to you now and say, "Peter, you were my guy?"

Yeah, and that's really fun. It's very rewarding, but it's funny for me to think that kids grew up watching Tiger Woods because I remember when I first met Tiger when he was 12 or 13, defending his title out at Waverley Country Club at the U.S. Junior Amateur Championship. Now that he's 35 years old, it just goes to show you how quickly time passes, but how important it is to remember those who came before you. I remember when Tiger was looking up to the players. Now, obviously, there are players looking up to Tiger. That's why it's so important every day of your life to be you. Whether you're Scott Lynn, Peter Jacobsen, Arnold Palmer or Tiger Woods, it's important to retain that dignity because you never know who is watching. You never know who is taking notes. (Laughs)

Career Notes: Through September, 2015, Jacobsen has won seven PGA Tour events and two Champions Tour titles. Both of his Champions Tour victories came in majors (2004 U.S. Senior Open, 2005 Senior Players Championship). Jacobsen's last victory on the PGA Tour (2003 Greater Hartford Open) at age 49 made him one of the oldest players to win a PGA Tour event. He was voted the PGA Tour's Comeback Player of the Year in 2003. Jacobsen played in two Ryder Cups (1985, 1995). The Portland, Oregon, native played on the golf team at the University of Oregon. He was a three-time All-American and the winner of the 1974 Pac-8 Conference men's golf title. Jacobsen was inducted into his alma mater's Athletics Hall of Fame in 1993. He was a 2003 inductee into the State of Oregon Sports Hall of Fame.

*   *   *

Chris Chambliss is best remembered for his walk-off home run in the deciding fifth game of the 1976 American League Championship Series—a game-winning blast that propelled the Yankees into the World Series. Chambliss batted .524 (11 for 21, 2 HR) during the '76 ALCS. It was the start of some good times for the Yankees. Chambliss and his New York teammates went to the World Series three consecutive years (1976–78). In a championship-clinching Game 6 victory in 1977, Chambliss hit a home run off Dodger pitcher Burt Hooton for his only World Series homer. The following year, the Yankees again beat the Dodgers in six games in the World Series. Chambliss has served in several organizations as a major league coach and minor league manager. He was the Yankees' hitting coach when New York won World Series titles in 1996, 1998, 1999 and 2000. There can be no debating whether Chris Chambliss was a winner. He has a total of six World Series rings to prove it.

When Chris Chambliss won the 1976 American League Championship Series with his home run on the first pitch of the bottom of the ninth, it was only the second time a baseball postseason series ended on a home run. (Bill Mazeroski's homer to win the 1960 World Series was the first.) If you watch the video of the Chambliss homer, you'll notice that he had a difficult time rounding the bases because of the many fans that poured onto the field to celebrate. When he was in the clubhouse, his teammates asked him if he had touched home plate. Chambliss and two security men went back onto the field so that he could step on home plate—just to be safe. Home plate had been stolen by the fans, so Chambliss stomped on the ground where home plate had been, thus assuring New York's victory.

Chambliss also takes great pride in the home run he hit off Burt Hooton in Game 6 of the 1977 World Series. New York was trailing 2-0 when Chambliss hit a 2-run shot to tie the game. He also doubled off Elias Sosa a bit later. But, few people remember Chambliss' heroics in that game because that was the night Reggie Jackson hit three home runs to solidify his claim to the "Mr. October" label.

I talked with Chris Chambliss in Seattle on April 8, 2011, when he was working as the Mariners' hitting coach.

Chris, who was your very first boyhood idol?

My dad, I guess. My dad played a little bit of football. He taught us all the sports. We grew up playing ping pong and tennis. We played racquetball later. I learned a lot of sports. I played football, basketball and baseball for four years in high school. My dad really got us into sports, me and my three brothers.

When did baseball become the most important to you?

Well, I stopped playing football after my second year of junior college. I played two years of college football. Then, I got a scholarship to UCLA, and that's when baseball kind of took over. That's the only thing I was doing.

As far as baseball is concerned, was there a player whose baseball card you collected, or that you idolized?

No, there really wasn't. I did keep baseball cards. For some reason, I used to follow the Chicago White Sox. I don't know why. We lived in southern California. My mother loved the Dodgers so we paid attention to those guys, too. But, I really didn't have a player I idolized.

When you were a major league player, I'm sure there were young kids who saw you hit that momentous game-winning home run in

the ALCS and immediately started saying, "Chris Chambliss is my favorite player." Did you later hear from any of those youngsters?

Well, yeah. The people in New York keep reminding me of that home run. Really, everywhere I go, people remember me for that home run.

Career Notes: Chris Chambliss played 17 major league seasons with the Indians, Yankees and Braves. Over his career, Chambliss batted .279, with 185 home runs and 972 runs-batted-in. With Cleveland in 1971, he batted .275, with 9 HR and 48 RBI and was named the American League Rookie of the Year. Traded to New York on April 26, 1974, Chambliss became an important player for the Yankees. As the first baseman during the Yankees' "Bronx Zoo" years, he played for the incomparable—"You're hired. You're fired. You're hired again. You're fired again."—Billy Martin.

*   *   *

Dave Husted was a highly successful player on the Professional Bowlers Association Tour in the 1980s and 1990s. Husted was only 22 years old when he won his first U.S. Open title in 1982. Husted won two more U.S. Opens and won those back-to-back (1995-96). The right-hander became the only bowler in the modern era (since 1971) to accomplish the feat. Nobody has won consecutive U.S. Open titles since Husted turned the trick nearly 20 years ago. Only Pete Weber (with five) has won more modern-day U.S. Open titles than Husted.

Having spent most of my broadcasting career in Portland, Oregon, I got to know Dave Husted and his family many years ago when he was having a ton of success on the PBA Tour. In my entire 40-year career, Dave Husted is one of the nicest pro athletes I have ever met. He is humble, gracious and an outstanding family man. While Dave is mild-mannered, he was a ferocious competitor and a threat to win every week on the PBA Tour. Going back to his roots after leaving the PBA Tour, Husted has worked alongside his father as a bowling proprietor in his hometown of Milwaukie, Oregon.

I spoke with Dave Husted via the telephone on January 6, 2015.

Can I ask you to tell me who you consider your very first boyhood idol?

I would have to say my father. It was just the way he conducted himself and the way he taught me to look at things. He instilled the core values in me at a young age. He told me to always try to do the best you can. I always looked up to him and idolized him. I wanted to be like him growing up, and it's continued to this day. He's a very important part of my life.

I know you and your dad (PBA Charter member Champ Husted) have operated Milwaukie Bowl for many years. Did he ever spend time on the Pro Bowlers Tour?

He dabbled a little bit. He didn't really tour, but he did bowl some tournaments on the West Coast.

I'm not surprised to hear you say that your father was your boyhood idol. I'm aware that you come from an outstanding family, and parents have such a profound impact on their children.

Oh, absolutely. In today's world—where a lot of kids don't have both their mother and father—I'm very, very fortunate to have both of them and still in good health. They're always there to listen to you—always there with you for the ups and downs—always there providing a supporting word. They give you unconditional love. They teach you all those things that I can pass on to my kids, and their kids pass on to their kids, and so on and so forth. I'm just very fortunate to have two solid parents. I love them dearly.

You were a pretty good athlete when you were young. How did you end up deciding to bowl for a career?

I played a lot of basketball through high school, and my senior year we did have a really good team. We went to the state tournament. My first love really was basketball. I loved to play basketball. But, then I got to a point with the bowling that—I don't like to use the word *dominate* but—I was doing very well in my age group. I just thought, "You know, I think I want to give this a try and get serious about it." After I graduated high school, I went out and bowled a few tournaments— which I wasn't nearly ready to do—just kind of to get my feet wet. I had a discussion with my parents saying, "I'm gonna go out and try the summer tour. If I don't do very well, I'll just come back and go to school, and life goes on." But, I happened to have some moderate success. So, I stayed with it, and the rest is history, as they say.

Dave, your family has been in bowling for as long as I can remember. It seems bowling is in your DNA.

My dad and granddad built Milwaukie Bowl in 1957. They had a partner—a lumber man from down south in the Cottage Grove area—a family friend that sort of got them started. He was kind of the money man. They started in 1957. Then, we acquired Kellogg Bowl in the late '60s. We've been in bowling our whole lives. I kind of grew up in the bowling center.

Since you were always around bowling, did anybody on the PBA Tour capture your attention?

Oh, yeah. Growing up, it was Mark Roth. He was the first power player in bowling. He really cranked the ball and got the ball to hook a lot when the game was still played a little bit straighter. He was something different. I wouldn't say I patterned my game after him, but I liked his action. I liked his game. Then, there was Marshall Holman from Medford. He was the same way. He was extremely powerful in his game, as well, so that kind of caught my eye. Once I started bowling and went out on tour, I knew that that was something I really wanted to do. The fourth tournament I bowled in—at Tucson on the summer tour—I finished fourth. That was some validation that, "Hey! I could actually do this, I think." There again, I was not really ready. I didn't have a lot of experience bowling in tournaments, but I went out there and made myself competitive. It got better and better every year, and then I started having some pretty good success.

When you were winning the U.S. Opens and all those other tournaments, you must have known that there were young kids throughout Oregon that loved watching you and were inspired by you. You probably were the reason a lot of kids in the Portland area were begging their moms and dads to take them to their local bowling alleys.

Well, you know, that kind of comes with the success. Looking back on it, I'm sure that it might have inspired some people or helped them stay in the game. Or maybe they said, "If that guy can do it, why can't I?" Whatever it took to get people interested was fine. I think back to when I was young and how I felt bowling in tournaments. If I could help some kids—and even still today do that—then it's all worth it, definitely.

What was your biggest thrill in your pro bowling career?

The first U.S. Open way back in 1982 because my family was there. It was very special. It was my first title. I'd been close before but couldn't quite get over the hump. Being that it was a really big tournament—and winning with my mom and dad there—it was real special.

Since your dad was your boyhood idol, it had to be goose-bump time when you were able to share that U.S. Open trophy with him.

Oh, it definitely was. Since he bowled some, he knows how hard it was to bowl in tournaments and the grind of it all. It was very rewarding to have my parents there and basically have them share in that moment. All the hard work and the support that they had given me through the years, it was nice to give them something back with that victory.

Career Notes: Dave Husted's 1995 U.S. Open victory came in front of the largest crowd to witness a PBA men's event (7,212 at Joe Louis Arena in Detroit, Michigan). Husted won a total of 14 titles on the PBA Tour and was the ninth PBA player to accumulate $1-million in Tour earnings. The affable Husted was well-respected by the media, fans and his fellow competitors. He won back-to-back PBA Steve Nagy Sportsmanship Awards (1988-89). Husted was ranked #23 on the PBA's list of "50 Greatest Players" in the PBA's first 50 years. He was inducted into the PBA Hall of Fame in 1996 and the USBC Hall of Fame in 2012.

*   *   *

19

Mom Was Like A Rock

Bill Krueger pitched 13 years in the major leagues with the Athletics, Dodgers, Brewers, Mariners, Twins, Expos, Tigers and Padres. Krueger spent his early childhood in Illinois before moving to Oregon, where he attended McMinnville High School. He was a two-sport athlete at the University of Portland prior to starting his professional baseball career. Since 2000, Krueger has been the baseball analyst on Fox Sports Northwest / ROOT SPORTS Northwest—primarily focusing on the Seattle Mariners.

Bill Krueger was one of my broadcasting partners on Fox Sports Northwest. We worked dozens of games together. I called the action, and Bill served as a color commentator on our college basketball and college baseball broadcasts. Bill was uniquely qualified to offer expert analysis of both sports. He attended the University of Portland on a basketball scholarship and also played baseball for the Pilots. Unlike a few analysts I worked with, Bill always did his homework and was thoroughly prepared by the time we started our game broadcasts. As a play-by-play man, I appreciated that very much. I have also appreciated Bill's friendship through the years. He's a class act in every way. I'm very happy for the success he's had in broadcasting after his playing days ended.

I talked with Bill Krueger by phone on May 17, 2011.

Can you share with me the name of your first boyhood idol?

My boyhood idol was Billy Williams. I grew up in a suburb of Chicago in Waukegan, Illinois, on the far north side. I became a Cub fan—just like anybody that lives north of Chicago. We're all Cub fans. My mom was a huge baseball fan. She grew up in downstate Illinois, and she followed baseball because her father was a big baseball fan. She loved baseball. She's the one that really got me into baseball.

She knew that there was a special guest coming to Waukegan. I think I was six or seven years old, and Billy Williams was coming to our area. At the time, Billy Williams wasn't a big star. He was a good, young player for the Cubs. We rarely got a Cub to come as far north as Waukegan, which is 40-some-odd miles north of Chicago. So, he made this appearance, and my mother took me down there. Lo-and-behold, he's there as big as life. There was hardly anybody there at this store. Billy was just absolutely gracious. He spent time with me and talked to me. It became kind of a really major moment for me because after meeting Billy, I instantly wanted to know all about him. So, my mother taught me how to look at the box scores and how to figure out a batting average. When the Chicago Tribune came in, I was instantly diving into the sports page wanting that box score. That's where the love affair began. He ended up becoming a great player with the Cubs, a part of that Murderer's Row of Banks and Santo and Williams. I became a devotee, and he was my guy.

The story doesn't end there. I got a chance to play professional baseball and actually made it to the major leagues. That was a huge moment for me. Any player you ever ask can remember the day they got called up to the big leagues. I got called up in early April of 1983. I was in spring training with Tacoma. I had not actually played any Triple-A baseball at that point. I had been a Double-A player. I came to camp and had a real nice finish to camp. I threw six shutout innings against Cleveland right before the camp broke. Sure enough, there was an injury in the Oakland staff. Rick Langford goes down, and they need somebody, and it's me. They call me up, and I fly into Oakland. I get a cab over to the Oakland Hyatt where everybody stayed. I walk in the door, and the first person I meet is Billy Williams—now the hitting instructor for the Oakland A's. I think it's a huge irony that the first person that really drives me into baseball is this guy, Billy Williams, and then the first person I meet when I join my professional big league team is him again. He ends up being absolutely the same wonderful person that he was when I first met him. Now, I'd been to spring training. I'd been to camp, so it wasn't as if playing with big leaguers was new to me. And, it wasn't as if I hadn't seen Billy in the spring, but I thought it was kind of an interesting moment.

I know the American League has the designated hitter and that you were a pitcher so you normally didn't bat. But, did you ever work with Billy Williams on your hitting?

No, I was pretty real about where I belonged in the game and that was to pitch. Billy really supported me as a pitcher. It was just a really warm feeling to come in after a game and shake your hero's hand. I mean, can you imagine that? It didn't last for very long because he wasn't there for a long time. But, while he was there, he's slapping you on the back. It was pretty doggone cool. (Laughs)

Bill, did you ever tell Williams that you were that little six-year-old boy that saw him in that store in Waukegan? And, what do you recall from that day you met Williams at the store?

The store was the Waukegan Dry Goods, and I can remember being downstairs in this store. I can remember that, and I can remember that I sat on his lap. I remember that much. It was my first exposure to a big league player. I was pretty young and had my eyes wide open.

You said you thought he was a great guy when you met him as a kid. How was he when you were in the same clubhouse with him in Oakland? Was he pretty much the same guy, or had he changed as you looked at him through your now-adult eyes?

I don't think he changed. I think Billy was always kind of low-key—more on the quiet side. Coming from Alabama, he came out of the tough South when black players had to kowtow to "the man." He survived all that. Then, you remember with the Cubs—the big stars of the team—I think were Santo and Banks. Banks was the huge star. Initially, I don't think Billy really got his just due. It took him awhile to get his just due. He was real consistent and was sort of the "inside-the-game" guy. When you ask the great pitchers—the guys that could really throw hard—the guy they were scared of was Billy Williams. There was nobody's fastball that he couldn't hit. Whether it was Sandy Koufax or Don Drysdale or Bob Gibson or Tom Seaver, he was known for being a guy that you just couldn't throw it by. He was just one tough out. I think he got his due when he started that ironman march where, for a while there, he held the record in the National League for consecutive games. Then, you started looking at his numbers. He was putting up 30 home runs and 100 runs-batted-in, and he hit .300 a lot. Those were big numbers in the '60s. So, yeah, Williams—number 26, left field, the stance—he had a little hitch in his swing. When I was in the back yard working on my stroke, I was Billy Williams. Of course, I was everybody else, too. Remember, that's how we played in the backyard. We had everybody down, left-handed or right-handed. We imitated them all.

You became a major leaguer, and you had your own baseball card. Did you ever think there could be kids in their backyards pretending to be you?

I never really saw myself in the same stratosphere as my hero. I go out and meet kids. I talk to people. A lot of times the kids don't necessarily know me, but the parents might. And, they might know me for more than just being a broadcaster. I have people come up and say, "Oh yeah, I remember you as a Mariner in 1991. I remember you. I remember watching you pitch. I remember coming to the games." That always makes you feel good.

My feeling is that this is a great opportunity—when I'm in front of kids—to let them know that, "Hey, I was no different than you. I was a little kid with dreams, and I wasn't the best guy on my team." You know, I just had great parents that let me have it. They just let me dream. They didn't burst my bubble and tell me that I needed to quit playing these imaginary games in the backyard and doing all the crazy things I did as a kid. I just loved sports. I lived them. You have these amazing vicarious things that you carry around with you. You never think in a million years you're gonna be there, (laughs) and then you are. So, my responsibility to kids today is to be real and to let them know that there are all these possibilities out there. I tell them that you should never let your dreams die and you should never be sold short by anybody else. You *own* those dreams. They're yours. Nobody can take them from you. I'm real big on that.

We played all kinds of games that just never ended. We only probably played twelve Little League games. The rest of it we made up. Down at the school yard, or wherever, the myriad of places to play some kind of competition were endless. We had a fenced-in backyard with about a 5½ foot fence. There was a garage, and in the corners where the fence hit the garage, there were bushes. Those were imaginary fielders, so you had different places you could hit the ball. Over the garage, of course, that was a homer. The corners were a little bit tighter, so you had to hit the ball up the middle of the field to have success in the game. (Laughs) The school yard we played at was not fenced, but we had this bench that was out in left field. So, when we played home run derby, I always had to hit the ball the other way to try to homer over the bench. I was a position player through college, and when I played, I could really hit the ball to left field. I think a lot of that was because, in home run derby, I had to hit the ball toward the bench to get a home run because there was nothing to right. If you want to play the game, you can't hit the ball over there to right because it doesn't score. It's just an out. (Laughs) But that kind of stuff—the endless made-up games that we played that had different rules that we made up and we controlled—it's just much different than today where things are a lot more organized.

Bill, I guess those of us who enjoyed watching you play major league baseball have your mother to thank for getting you interested in the game. As you mentioned earlier, she was a huge influence on you.

I played a couple sports through high school, and then got recruited to be a basketball player at the University of Portland. To be a Division I basketball player was really my goal, and I made it. But, the conversations that I had with my mom in my freshmen year when I came home from the University of Portland to McMinnville were always the same. It was like a broken record. I would have the pile of laundry and an empty stomach, and she would say, "How ya doing? So, are you gonna play baseball this year?" And, I would say, "No, Mom. I'm on a basketball scholarship. I'm gonna play basketball." She would say, "Okay, but you really should play baseball." I'd say, "Well, I don't think I will, but I'm glad that you think I should play baseball." And, this would go on and on and on. Finally, it reached the point where she's like, "You know what? If you don't play baseball next year, maybe you shouldn't come home." I'm like, "So, you're kidding, right?" And, she wasn't kidding. So, the next year—my sophomore year—I turned out for baseball. The rest is history. I played both sports in college, signed after a baseball tryout, changed from being a first baseman to a pitcher and the whole nine yards. I think a lot of that was the idea that dreams never die. My mom loved baseball, and she thought that I could be a good ballplayer. She wanted to see me play baseball. Maybe deep down, she knew something that I didn't know. She kind of knew that I was good at it, that it came a little easier to me. The other side of it is she just enjoyed the game and she thought it would be good for me to continue to play. She saw me play as a high school player, and I guess she knew something. Moms are always right. We know that. They're always right. (Laughs)

What do you think it was like for her to watch you pitch in the majors?

I think it was a dream for her. I really do. The devotion of your mom to you—to kids—is an incredible thing. There's nothing that matches it.

She would be the one that would come to the game. She was organized. She would have her scorecard. She'd have the radio with the headset. She'd get her hot dog before the first pitch. She kept track, and she would sit there like she was in the game. My dad was the total opposite. He couldn't stop talking, couldn't sit still, up on the concourse, going for a cigarette, nervous as a cat. My mom was like a rock. (Laughs) My mom, that's just who she was. She wasn't messing around; that's for sure. (Laughs) They got to go and see me play, really, my whole career. They had time to come to games and share that whole experience with me. It was really great. It was really great to have that.

Career Notes: Bill Krueger began his career with the Athletics, who signed him as an amateur free agent in 1980. The left-handed pitcher made his major league debut April 10, 1983. Over his career, Krueger pitched in 301 major league games. He started 164 games and came out of the bullpen 137 times. Krueger's career win-loss record was 68-66. His career ERA was 4.35.

* * *

Seth Jones is a defenseman for the Nashville Predators in the National Hockey League. Seth was selected in the first round (#4 overall) of the 2013 NHL Entry Draft after he was named as the top-rated North American skater in Central Scouting's final 2013 ratings. He has been a key contributor for the Predators in his first two NHL seasons.

Seth Jones has been around pro sports his entire life. His father, Ronald "Popeye" Jones, played 11 seasons in the NBA with six different teams and is currently employed as an assistant coach with the Indiana Pacers. I covered many games in which "Popeye" Jones played against the Trail Blazers, and I can tell you the 6-foot-8 forward was a relentless rebounder. We all know that sons often follow in their father's footsteps, but Seth fell in love with hockey when the family lived in Denver at the time his dad was playing for the Nuggets. "Popeye" Jones, a hockey fan, took his sons to a few Colorado Avalanche games, and Seth immediately chose hockey over basketball. Seth Jones became infatuated with hockey when he was only five years old. "Popeye" could see that his sons were more interested in hockey than hoops, so he sought out the counsel of then-Avalanche star Joe Sakic when he bumped into him at the Pepsi Center (where both the Nuggets and Avalanche played). Jones asked the future Hockey Hall of Famer for any advice that might help his sons become better hockey players. Sakic, making the natural assumption that the young Jones kids would grow up to have size and athleticism, told "Popeye" to have his sons work on their skating. As a result, Seth took skating classes for a year before he began playing organized hockey at age six. There is no question that the success of the Avalanche in that era was one of the factors that helped sell young Seth Jones on the sport. Seth was a six-year-old fan sitting rink side when the Avalanche won Game 7 of the Stanley Cup Finals in 2001. When young Seth looked out on the ice and saw players from his favorite team hoisting the Cup, it was a life-changing moment. He became motivated to become a professional hockey player in hopes that he might be able to hold Lord Stanley's Cup high over his head someday.

I talked with Seth Jones by phone on July 15, 2013, when he was still in Portland—just a couple weeks after he was selected in the NHL Draft.

Who was your first boyhood idol?

I had a couple of people. Along the lines of hockey, it would probably be Nicklas Lidstrom. He was so great on and off the ice. He was a role model for a lot of young kids. A lot of people wanted to be—and play hockey—like him. On the other hand, away from hockey, my mom was my idol. I have an older brother and a younger brother, and she took care of us when my dad was always on the road playing basketball. I really respect her. She's strong and strong-willed. I really like Lidstrom on the ice and my mom off the ice.

I know that in interviews you are always asked about your father because he was the higher profile parent since he was a professional

athlete. But, you say it was your mom who was there most often for you and your brothers.

For sure and I give her a lot of props on every angle of my life. She took us to 6 a.m. practices, and not just me. Like I said, I have two brothers that both played hockey at the same time. You can imagine how much she was driving to and from the rink and to and from school to pick us up. I appreciate everything she's done. I wouldn't be where I am without her.

As far as Nicklas Lidstrom is concerned, have you ever had an opportunity to meet him?

I have not. I have not, though hopefully in the future, I will.

You were an idol for many young hockey fans when you played with the Portland Winterhawks. And, as you head into the NHL, there's no doubt that many kids will become your fans. Do you think about the fact that you're an idol for kids?

Yeah, it definitely comes into my mind. I can see kids walking down to me, whether it happens in a rink or anywhere else. They kind of look at me and smile. It is cool being a kid's idol. That's why you gotta pay more attention to being respectful and talk to people. And, you have to be a good player out on the ice, but also be a good person and good character guy off the ice.

Career Notes: Seth Jones made his NHL debut on his 19th birthday, October 3, 2013, at St. Louis. In his rookie season, Jones scored six goals and accumulated 19 assists (3rd most by a rookie in franchise history). In his second NHL season, Jones played in all 82 games and contributed eight goals and 19 assists. He also had four assists in Nashville's six playoff games. The 6-foot-4 defenseman tied his career high with a two point game (1 goal, 1 assist) in a 4-3 win over Washington on January 16, 2015. Prior to entering the NHL, Jones played one season of Junior

Hockey for the Portland Winterhawks. He had 42 assists and 56 points, and was named the Western Hockey League Rookie of the Year. Jones also was named the Canadian Hockey League Top Prospect of the Year. Jones appeared in 26 playoff games and totaled 7 goals and 19 points to help Portland win the WHL championship and reach the Memorial Cup Final. Jones has represented the United States in international competition since 2010. He was a member of the U.S. Men's National Team that captured the bronze medal in the 2015 World Championship in the Czech Republic.

*   *   *

20

Coolest Thing In Town

Greg Biffle drives a stock car in the NASCAR Sprint Cup series for Roush Fenway Racing—the racing team he joined in 1998. Biffle, who was born in Vancouver, Washington, and who grew up in Camas, Washington, earned his job in NASCAR's premier racing series by winning championships in the NASCAR Truck Series and in the Busch/Nationwide Series.

I first met Greg Biffle when he was driving in the NASCAR Truck Series. He was already making a name for himself in racing, and it was a great "local boy makes good" story for media in the Northwest. Biffle continued to climb the ladder in NASCAR, and when he won his first Cup race, it was the lead story on all the local sports segments. I've interviewed Greg at least a half-dozen times through the years and have always been impressed with his down-home, folksy charm. When you talk with Greg, it is pretty clear that he is proud of his Northwest roots. The Northwest is just as proud of him.

I talked on the telephone with Greg Biffle on January 20, 2015.

Can you tell me who you consider your very first boyhood idol?

When my brother and I were very young, my cousin, Michael Fowlks, was a teenager. He came to live with us. He was the coolest thing in town. That was probably who my brother and I looked up to. My brother and I—and him and my dad—would do stuff all the time. He was 15, 16, 17 or 18-years-old when he was with us. I'd say we thought he was pretty cool when we were growing up.

What were the circumstances that brought him to live with your family?

Well, like every teenager, he was getting in trouble at school and those type of things. His mother and father lived in Southern California, and that's where my parents grew up before we moved to the Northwest. He wanted to come live up there. They visited us all the time and our families did their family vacations together. So, he ended up moving up with us for a summer and working for my parents. My parents owned a small steel construction company. He ended up moving up and working for the summer, and then he decided to stay for a school year. That was how he ended up coming up to the Northwest, and he ended up really enjoying the area.

What was it about him that you liked? Was it just that he was a cool teenager?

Yeah, I mean, you know. You got my brother and me, the eight or ten-year-old guys. We're wrestling and playing with him, and we're doing stuff outside and outdoors. He's got a car, and he gives us rides to places. It's what every boy between six and ten or twelve-years-old would want around. There's a cool guy to do all that stuff with because your parents are working. He was just there for all that. It was really neat to be able to hang out with him.

Was there eventually a sports idol for you at some point?

I don't really recall any actual sports idols. We played a lot of sports and watched a lot of sports. My parents were Dodger fans because they grew up in L.A. So, we attended sporting events—my brother and I both. We played basketball and baseball and wrestled. Well, let me go back. I was on a motorcycle at five, six, seven, eight-years-old. I begged my dad for a go-kart all the time, but we lived kind of out in the country in the foothills of the mountain, so there was really no place to ride it. Then, I'm driving the tractor. I'm driving the forklift. I'm driving around when I'm ten, twelve and thirteen-years-old. Like, when I was thirteen, I could drive a car as good as I could when I was sixteen or seventeen. I'd go get my grandma's car all the time and tell her, "Dad needs this to jumpstart the tractor." And, I'd be just driving around because I wanted to drive. You know, I just loved cars. So, of course, cars led to my interest in racing.

My dad was a big boxing fan. My dad watched Muhammad Ali, Joe Frazier and all these different athletes boxing. Then, we started watching NASCAR and oval track racing. I guess that's more when I got interested in racing. I'd just become a teenager and started racing. I started racing Portland Speedway oval track Friday and Saturday nights when I was 15 or 16. I suppose that's when I really became infatuated with a sport. Ernie Irvin and Mark Martin were kind of my idols, so to speak. They were the first true athletes—sports figures, you could say—that were my idols.

What was it like when you first raced against Ernie and Mark?

Well, I'm trying to remember if I raced against Ernie Irvin. I believe I did. I was Mark's teammate. I'm door-to-door, banging wheels with Mark Martin coming to the checkered flag at Homestead, and I beat him by a fender for the win the final race of the season. Then, I become his teammate. It was a spectacular thing for me.

You raced at Portland Speedway, a track that no longer exists. You later became involved with Sunset Speedway, a quarter-mile dirt track in Banks, Oregon. Did you get involved because of a feeling that you should give something back to the sport?

That was what I wanted. I realize short track racing is dying all across the U.S. Jerry Stram runs that track out there. I wanted to try and help promote short track racing. I grew up out there in the Northwest, and Portland Speedway and others have shut down. That's why I became involved in that track. We promoted a lot, and I came out there and run races to do things to try and help short track racing in the Northwest.

You drive the #16 car and have fans all around the country. Do you ever stop to consider the fame that you have and that there are young racing fans who idolize you?

I do think about it, but I kind of get lost in the normalness of not really seeing myself in that light—especially this off-season. This off-season has been such a low-key off-season. No testing. No appearances. No this, that, and the other. I've sort of just lived the casual, normal, everyday life and just done normal things. You almost forget about the fame. And, then you'll meet people, and they'll be, "Oh, my God! You're Greg Biffle." I'm like, "Yeah. What's the big deal, ya know?" You sort of don't look at yourself like you're some big sports figure or athlete. Part of you wants to be normal. Part of you appreciates being looked up to and competing at the highest level you can every week. This last year was a tough season for us, and I think we're gonna be much better this year. We were definitely off-course as a company last year. It was rough. But, I think that we'll certainly win some races this year and make a challenge for the title.

Final thing, Greg. The legendary A.J. Foyt, who has driven stock cars, open wheel race cars, all *kinds* of cars during his incredible career, just celebrated his 80th birthday. You've undoubtedly bumped into A.J. at some point in your career. You've been out there rubbing elbows with the biggest names in racing. Are you ever star-struck when you find yourself in conversation with some of racing's true legends?

Yeah, absolutely. The thing is, when A.J. Foyt comes to the races—and he comes to a few of our races—he *knows* me. He recognizes me. It's just kind of odd, and sort of surreal, that a guy like that would know you when you've never really met him. He knows me from driving—from racing. He doesn't know me from us goin' fishin' together, you know? And, the same thing goes for Junior Johnson and all these guys that I know and have met and have got to spend time with. It's pretty neat. They're looking at us like guys looked at them. I'm sure when I retire I'm going to be looking at the new guys the same way as those guys are lookin' at me. It's a pretty neat thing to be involved in. You know, I got really lucky.

Career Notes: Greg Biffle picked up his first Sprint Cup victory at Daytona in 2003. He won two more Cup races the following year. Thus far, the best year of Biffle's Sprint Cup career has been 2005. He won five of the first 15 races on the schedule. However, he didn't win again until the season finale at Homestead. Even after his hot start and with *six* victories on the year, Biffle ended 2005 as the runner-up in the point standings behind champion Tony Stewart. He finished third in the point standings in 2008, sixth in 2010, and fifth in 2012. Now in his 14th year behind the wheel of a Sprint Cup car, Biffle has won a total of 19 Cup races (as of October 29, 2015).

* * *

Nate McMillan was known as "Mr. Sonic" because he spent his entire NBA playing career and the first seven years of his NBA head coaching career with the SuperSonics. As a player, McMillan wasn't much of a scorer. He played 12 years in the NBA and never averaged double figures in scoring. But, could he ever play defense. Whichever player McMillan was guarding knew he was going to be in for a long night. McMillan began his coaching career as an assistant with the Sonics. He was promoted in 2000 and spent five seasons as Seattle's head coach. Then, he moved to Portland, where he coached for 6½ seasons. McMillan is currently an assistant coach with the Indiana Pacers.

I got to know Nate McMillan after he became head coach of the Trail Blazers. He was introduced as the new coach in July of 2005, in an impressive ceremony in Portland's well-known Rose Garden. No, McMillan did not meet the fans and media at the Rose Garden Arena, the Blazers' home. He was introduced to the locals in the International Rose Test Garden in Washington Park on the outskirts of the city. It was a rather unusual location to announce the hiring of the team's new coach. But, it sort of fit because it was a somewhat unusual hire. McMillan had never been associated with any NBA franchise other than Portland's hated rival up the I-5 freeway. However, Trail Blazers' owner Paul Allen convinced "Mr. Sonic" to leave Seattle and move to Portland. It all just seemed a little bizarre.

McMillan had to rebuild the Blazers, and it took some time. Portland won only 21 games in McMillan's first season in the Rose City. The Blazers steadily increased their win totals the next three seasons, winning 32, 41 and 54. Portland won 50 and 48 games the next two seasons, but patience was running out. A lack of success in the playoffs put Nate on the hot seat. After starting the 2011-12 season with a 20-23 record, McMillan was fired.

I talked with Nate McMillan in Portland, Oregon, on March 19, 2011, when he was the head coach of the Trail Blazers.

Who was the first person you considered a boyhood idol?

Well, first is my older brother, Randolph. He would be the guy that I followed when I was a young kid. Wherever he went, I was probably a few blocks—or a block—behind him. We're five years apart as far as age, but I always wanted to just go wherever he went. He would go to different parks to play basketball, football and baseball. The older kids would be going, and little Nate would be somewhere hangin' behind. Occasionally, they would throw rocks at me to get me to go home, but most of the time I would end up where they were playing—watching him play. And, when they didn't have enough to play, they would let me play. So, my boyhood idol was my older brother. My brother did play college basketball at UNC-Wilmington. He played four years, but didn't make it to the pros. But, at the time we were growing up, we played whatever sport was in season. So, we played football, baseball and basketball. He was pretty good in all sports.

Other than your brother, did you eventually find somebody in the college ranks or pros that you watched with interest?

As far as college, David Thompson was my idol. Then, the pros, I liked Doctor J, but I was a Magic Johnson guy. Magic was a big guard who could pass the ball and would set up his teammates. I was a big guard and really wanted to play like Magic Johnson.

Did you ever meet those guys?

I didn't meet David until I made it to the NBA. The same with Magic, I had the opportunity to play against Magic. Those were the two guys. David was playing above the rim right there in Raleigh, which made me really want to go to North Carolina State. Then, Magic Johnson, being a big guard that would push the ball and look to set up his teammates, I just loved the way he played.

What was it like playing against Magic?

Well, with Magic, I had watched him play so much that I knew what would bother him. So, I would pressure him. I would really pick him up full court and make him turn because, as a big guard, those were the things that bothered me on the floor. I disliked a small guy just constantly up in me and making me turn and pressuring me. So, that was what I tried to do with Magic. I just didn't give him an inch to move. But, it didn't work. He just walked me down into the post, threw his sky-hook on me and walked out of the gym with a victory.

Career Notes: Nate McMillan averaged 5.9 points and 6.1 assists during his NBA career. When he retired, McMillan held Seattle's franchise record in assists and steals. He led the NBA in steals in 1994. McMillan played in the 1996 NBA Finals against Michael Jordan and the Chicago Bulls. "Mr. Sonic" appeared in more postseason games (98) than any other player in Sonics' history. McMillan's jersey (#10) was retired by the Sonics prior to their move to Oklahoma City.

*　　*　　*

John Hannah is one of the best—maybe *the* best—offensive linemen ever to play in the National Football League. Hannah played his entire 13-year career (1973–1985) with the New England Patriots after being selected in the first round (#4 overall) in the 1973 NFL Draft. He was a nine-time Pro Bowl selection and a ten-time NFL All-Pro.

Prior to his pro career, John Hannah was a two-time All-American under legendary Alabama coach Paul "Bear" Bryant. Bryant once stated that John Hannah was the best offensive lineman he ever coached. John Hannah grew up in a football-playing family. He was neither the first nor the last Hannah to play college football at Alabama. After John starred for the Crimson Tide, his younger brother, Charley, played at Alabama before joining John in the NFL. Their father, Herb Hannah (a former NFL player), and uncle, Bill Hannah, both played football for the Crimson Tide as well.

I talked about John Hannah's childhood heroes when I spoke with him by phone on April 7, 2015.

Who was your first boyhood idol?

There were two, my dad and my uncle. When I was growing up as a kid, we didn't get a lot of pro football down south. My dad, Herb Hannah, played at the University of Alabama and then played with the New York Giants. I kinda felt that was a big deal. At the time when I was a kid and started developing heroes, my uncle, Bill Hannah, was at the University of Alabama playin' football. He was kind of my hero. That's kinda how I grew up.

When I started watching pro football, the Green Bay Packers was my first favorite team, primarily because of Bart Starr. And, I watched

Fuzzy Thurston, Jerry Kramer, Jim Ringo and Forrest Gregg—that offensive line. I watched them.

A lot of times, kids never get to meet their idols, but you had your idols right there in the family. Did you ever consider yourself fortunate that your heroes were right there in your house when you were having a holiday dinner with the family?

I didn't think that much of it. I just wanted to be like them and accomplish the things that they accomplished. You never think of them as heroes. They're just your role models where you want to become like them. You pattern yourself after them.

Your former teammate Pete Brock told me that even as a young boy, he realized that he was never going to be a quarterback because of his large size. He always aspired to be an offensive lineman. How about you? Did you always want to be an O-lineman?

Yep, I always did. I always knew I was going to be an offensive lineman— never wanted to play anything else.

So, when you watched the Packers, were you more interested in watching Jerry Kramer and the guys on the offensive line or the quarterback, Bart Starr?

I really wanted to watch the offensive line. I didn't have one guy that I kinda watched. It wasn't like Kramer, per say. I watched the whole offensive line. I thought those guys were great. I loved to watch them play.

You played 13 years in the NFL and then later find yourself in both the College and Pro Football Halls (of Fame). Did you ever think about the kids who might be looking at you in the same manner you enjoyed watching your dad, your uncle, and that great Green Bay offensive line?

Well, yes and no. I knew there would be kids that would be watching me, but I always felt that the next generation is always bigger, better and stronger. Ya know what I mean? I always wanted to set a good example when I was on the field. I know that. It was on my mind.

Some of the athletes I've talked with have said they believe having a sports idol or role model can inspire kids to reach for and achieve their dreams. Do you believe that emulating a sports idol can inspire greatness and help kids realize their dreams?

Perhaps a little bit. But, I think it has to be something inside of you. There are a lot of people that look up to people that have accomplished a lot. But, there's a difference between looking up to somebody and being willing to pay the price to do it. I think you could *not* have a role model—and be willing to pay the price—and be a lot better off than a guy that has a role model but is not willing to pay the price. Having a role model is good, but I don't think that's the most important thing.

Career Notes: John Hannah was named to the NFL All-Decade Teams of the 1970s and 1980s. He was also selected to the NFL 75th Anniversary All-Time Team. Sports Illustrated once called Hannah the top offensive lineman in NFL history. Hannah's final game was Super Bowl XX, a 46-10 loss to the Chicago Bears. In 1991, Hannah became the first Patriots' player to be elected to the Pro Football Hall of Fame. He was inducted into the College Football Hall of Fame in 1999. Hanna is also a member of the New England Patriots' Hall of Fame. His jersey (#73) has been retired by the Patriots.

*　　*　　*

Beth Daniel was one of the most successful women's golfers in the 1970s and '80s. With 33 tournament wins and millions in career earnings, it's easy to understand how she ended up in the Hall of Fame.

I was a weekend TV sports anchor early in my sports career, and in 1978 and 1979, I was working in the Tampa-St. Petersburg market. As you probably know, there is tremendous interest in golf in Florida. Therefore, I made sure to include highlights of the men's and women's pro golf tournaments in my sports segments every weekend. It seemed like every Sunday—the final day of each week's tournament—I showed highlights of Nancy Lopez because she was winning so often. In 1978, she was Rookie of the Year and LPGA Player of the Year. Lopez won nine tournaments in 1978 and followed that up with eight more wins in 1979. She was the 1979 LPGA Player of the Year. Many considered Lopez invincible. However, there was one big difference starting in 1979. Beth Daniel arrived on the scene. Daniel was the LPGA Rookie of the Year in '79. The 1980 LPGA Player of the Year, Daniel won 11 tournaments from 1980–82. Lopez won eight events during that period. With both players being highly competitive in nature, their rivalry was one of the best in sports.

I talked with Beth Daniel by phone on September 9, 2011.

Who was your first childhood idol?

I'd probably have to say it was my brother. I have an older brother, Tony. He's six years older than me. We grew up in Charleston, South Carolina. I think one of the reasons I got into all the sports that I got into was because he was into them. He played all kinds of sports including golf. I just remember as a kid going to his Little League baseball games, his basketball games, and following him around at the golf course watching him play junior tournaments. When he was playing with his buddies, he would let me tag along, which was kind of nice for an older brother. A lot of brothers who are six years older than you—especially me being a girl in the '60s and '70s—wouldn't let you tag along and follow him around with his friends and everything. Tony did that. I think I realized what a bit of a sacrifice that was for him when he was around his friends. We're kind of a little bit of opposite personalities. He's real low-key, and it takes a lot to make him mad. He does not wear his emotions on his sleeve, and I do. So, I think I kind of appreciated that in him and wished that I could be a little bit more like that.

When you became a professional golfer, there were undoubtedly young girls interested in the game that started to look at you as an idol. Did you think of yourself as a role model for young kids?

I don't know if I thought about that so much early on. I think later in my career I thought more about that. Early on, I think I was just so into getting my career off the ground that I thought pretty much mostly about myself. (Laughs) It is a very selfish thing to be a professional athlete because you have to put pretty much 100% of your attention into yourself, into your sport and into your training. So, when I was first starting out on Tour, I didn't so much look at myself as a role model. But, definitely, later on I did.

Many LPGA players I've spoken with have mentioned Nancy Lopez as a person who was a childhood idol for them. Nancy was so dominant early in her career. She had to go through so much in her first couple years. It seemed as though she was carrying the weight of the LPGA Tour's success on her shoulders—at least until you showed up.

I think some people are just made to be able to handle things like that better than others. Nancy certainly had the makeup to handle that, and she did a great job of that. Nancy and I have a bit of a funny relationship. Our relationship now is fantastic, but we were always rivals. In junior golf, in college, and when we first came out on Tour, we were always rivals. We were always pitted against each other, and Nancy was always the one to beat. So, we really weren't friends until, I would say, after the Solheim Cup at Crooked Stick in 2005, when she was the captain of the U.S. team. She made me a captain's pick. I saw a whole 'nother side of Nancy that I'd never seen before. Now, I'm happy to say that we're very good friends.

273

Career Notes: Beth Daniel was the U.S. Women's Amateur champion in 1975 and 1977. Daniel attended Furman University and helped the school win the 1976 AIAW women's golf national championship. She joined the LPGA Tour in 1979 and was recognized as the LPGA Rookie of the Year. The following year, she won four tournaments and was named the LPGA Player of the Year. She became only the second player—joining Nancy Lopez—to win Rookie of the Year and Player of the Year in back-to-back seasons. Daniel also earned LPGA Player of the Year honors in 1990 and 1994. She won the Vare Trophy for having the lowest scoring average on the LPGA Tour in 1989, 1990 and 1994.

During her pro career, Beth Daniel won 33 LPGA tournaments, seven of those in 1990 when she set a single-season earnings record (since broken) and won her only major, the LPGA Championship. Daniel's last LPGA win came at the Canadian Women's Open in 2003. At 46 years, 8 months, and 29 days, she became the oldest winner in LPGA Tour history. Daniel had career earnings of nearly $8.8-million on the LPGA Tour. She qualified for the LPGA Hall of Fame in 1999 and was inducted into the World Golf Hall of Fame in 2000. Beth Daniel played in eight Solheim Cups and was the captain of the U.S. team that won the Solheim Cup in 2009.

*   *   *

Steve Yeager caught for the Los Angeles Dodgers for 14 years prior to playing his final major league season with the Seattle Mariners. A light-hitting catcher, Yeager was outstanding defensively. Would-be base-stealers were hesitant to run when the strong-armed Yeager was behind the plate. Yeager played on four pennant winners for the Dodgers and earned a World Series championship ring in 1981. That year, he shared the MVP award with teammates Pedro Guerrero and Ron Cey.

When you watch a baseball game today, you see catchers geared-up like NFL players. They're covered from head to toe with protective devices. Their shin guards extend down and cover the feet and ankles. Their chest protectors are designed to take the sting out of any foul tip. Catchers wear helmets that make them look like hockey goalies. They're about as safe as they can be while working in a very dangerous location on the field.

Catchers did not always have that much protective gear when they went to work behind the plate. For a time, they wore no real protection on their head. Then, catchers began wearing batting helmets, turning them around backwards to keep the bill of the helmet out of the way while they squatted behind the plate. Also, catchers' masks were primitive, far different from those in use today. One area that was left unprotected was the catcher's throat. That changed after Steve Yeager experienced a brush with death in a game in 1976. Yeager was in the on-deck circle when a pitch shattered Bill Russell's bat. Part of the broken bat hit Yeager in the neck, piercing his esophagus. Yeager underwent life-saving surgery, but his baseball future was in question because he could not risk suffering another injury to his throat. Dodger trainer Bill Buhler worked with Yeager to design a plastic shield that would hang down from the catcher's mask, which allowed Yeager to continue his playing career. The throat guard is a crucial piece of protection worn by today's catchers.

I talked with Steve Yeager by phone on February 11, 2015.

Who was your very first boyhood idol?

I think when you talk about your first boyhood idol, your father is always there. That goes without saying. But, a lot of kids that I ran with at a young age would always have something about their uncle, or their cousin, or their dad being a doctor or a lawyer, or that they've done *something*. I always say, "Well, that's nothing. My uncle was the first man to fly faster than the speed of sound—Chuck Yeager." So, I have to look back and say that the first name I ever dropped on anybody as my idol was Chuck Yeager.

What was the reaction of your friends when you would tell them your uncle had made history by flying the speed of sound?

I think their mouth would drop in disbelief. Of course, at my age, they didn't know what the speed of sound was. (Laughs) Most of the kids, when they're eight, nine or ten years old, they have no clue who Chuck Yeager was. They go look him up, and they say, "Oh, really? Yeah, okay. Now I understand. That's cool."

Can you remember the first time you met Chuck Yeager? Was it at a family function of some kind?

No. I was in the big leagues. He and Glennis, his wife, came to L.A., and I think he threw out the first pitch one night at the ballpark. I got to catch the first pitch. It was a treat. There were a lot of people that didn't know who he was at that point in time. As far as I'm concerned, he's one of the heroes in American history for doing what he accomplished. So, it was a big moment for me just to be a part of it.

Many of the athletes I've talked with have mentioned a sports idol, but you're talking about an entirely different kind of hero when you're talking about Chuck Yeager.

Probably most of the guys you've talked to have had some type of hero they've somehow looked up to. Back in West Virginia and Ohio— because of the weather—you played three sports. You didn't have a hero. You had guys that you knew. If you're playin' baseball, you might be Mickey Mantle in your pickup games in your backyard. You might be Hank Aaron or Eddie Mathews— some of the old greats that were around. As far as a hero or an idol, it was Chuck for me.

I'm sure when you were catching for the Dodgers that there were kids in Los Angeles that looked up to you. Did you ever think about that?

Well, the organization taught us a lot of things about not only how to play the game correctly, but also how to get along in society and how to conduct ourselves outside the ballpark. I think that was one of the things growing up in the Dodger organization that we were expected to do, and we did that. Even though a lot of athletes are idols for young kids, we make mistakes from time to time. Some of us get in trouble from time to time. But, you're still an idol for some kid for whatever reason. I think you have to conduct yourself in that manner, and say, "You know what? You're coming to the ballgame. You're gonna come watch us play, and I'm gonna give you a good performance. I'm gonna try not to embarrass myself or my teammates or the organization or the fans—especially you because you like me. I'm gonna play the best I can play." I think you owe that to these kids. The other factor is you acknowledge their presence. You say hello to them, and you try to be nice to everybody.

Spring training is just about to start, and it's a favorite time of year for fans. Is it also a fun time for the players since they can have a lot more interaction with the fans?

You can, and fans are a lot closer to you in spring training because you're walking from one field to the other, and they've got some roped-off areas where some fans will get close to you. They all want autographs. You'd love to stop and sign them all, but if you did that, some coach or some manager is gonna get mad at ya because you're supposed to be somewhere else. The guys do a pretty good job of signing a few in-between practices, after practice, before practice—whenever they get the opportunity. There are times that you can't sign an autograph, but there's never a time that you can't acknowledge the presence of a fan. There are little kids, and you just say, "Hi. I'm sorry I can't sign right now, but thanks for comin'. I hope you have a good time. I hope you enjoy yourself." At least you've acknowledged their presence instead of just blowing them off, and that means a whole lot.

Career Notes: Steve Yeager hit .228 with 102 homers and 410 runs-batted-in during his major league career. While he didn't hit much in the regular season, Yeager could provide some pop when performing on the brightest stage. In three of the four World Series in which he played, Yeager batted far above his career average. He hit .364 against Oakland in 1974, .316 against the Yankees in 1977, and .286 against the Yankees in the 1981 Fall Classic. In 21 World Series games, Yeager batted .298 with 4 home runs and 10 RBI.

*   *   *

Stacy Lewis is one of the very best women's golfers in the world. In fact, she was ranked number one in the world for several weeks in 2013 and 2014. What she has accomplished in golf is truly remarkable considering she has played through incredible back pain for much of her career.

If you play golf, you know the game places a huge amount of stress on your back. That's why I can't fathom how Stacy Lewis has managed to emerge as the best American player in women's golf. At age 11, Lewis was diagnosed with scoliosis (curvature of the spine). She wore a back brace for more than seven years. She wore the brace 18 hours a day and only removed it to play golf. (Just the thought of playing golf with scoliosis makes me wince in pain!)

At 18, Lewis had surgery to place a titanium rod and five screws in her back. Her golf future was in doubt. But, after redshirting for a year to slowly rehabilitate her back, Lewis became a star at the University of Arkansas. She became a four-time All-American and won an NCAA championship. She has since risen to the very top of women's professional golf—all while playing with a rod and five screws in her back. Amazing! Lewis' story is sure to inspire any young person living with scoliosis.

Stacy Lewis talked with me about overcoming her back issues during a news conference at the LPGA tournament in Portland, Oregon, on August 28, 2013. I also spoke with her about her childhood heroes after the news conference ended.

Do you sometimes feel that you're lucky to have had such a successful career after going what you went through with your back as a teenager?

Yeah. Ten years ago was when I had surgery. Coming out of surgery not knowing if I was gonna be able to play golf—but not even knowing how—I mean, I could barely *sit up* by myself. So, the surgery and my back, it just puts everything in perspective. At the end of the day, a bad shot, pulling out of the tournament or a bad round is really not that big of a deal. I get to do what I love every day. I get to play golf. I don't know how I get to do it. It's amazing what doctors are able to do now. To think that I have a rod and five screws attached to my spine and I bend and I twist every single day. It doesn't make any sense, but it just makes you so much more thankful for everything I get to do.

Who was your very first childhood idol?

Probably my parents. With everything I went through with my back—the perspective that they had on it and just their attitude towards dealing with it. My mom was just, "We're gonna do this. We're gonna do this. And, this is the way it's gonna be." She never really saw it as a horrible thing. She never gave me a chance to feel sorry for myself. She was just kind of matter-of-fact about it.

In the LPGA media guide, it says your dream foursome is actually a *twosome* with you and your dad.

Yeah. My dad was how I got started playing golf. My favorite days on the course are when we can get away from everybody and everything going on, and just play golf—just the two of us.

Obviously, you're an idol now for a lot of young kids, particularly kids with back problems. Do you think about those kids that are looking up to you for inspiration?

Yeah, I've realized it more throughout my career. Early on, I didn't want to be known as the person with the "back." I wanted people to just write about my golf. I started to realize that that's not the way it's gonna be and just me teeing it up every week—whether I win or whether I finish last—just me teeing it up inspires kids. I get so many letters from the kids, from parents, from coaches asking for words of encouragement or just saying thank you. That's what it's about.

Aside from your parents, were there any players that you followed that you tried to pattern your game after?

No, I didn't watch that much golf growing up 'cause I didn't really plan on doing this. But now, I like watching players. I liked watching Tiger Woods when he was at his best and he was dominating. I want to know what he's doing. I want to learn from that. I want to figure out what he's doing at the end of those tournaments to win. That's kind of why I watch it now.

Career Notes: Stacy Lewis was a four-time All-American at Arkansas before turning pro in 2008. She joined the LPGA Tour in 2009 and has since has won 11 LPGA Tour events and has career earnings of more than $10.2-million (as of October 30, 2015). Of her 11 tournament victories, two were majors (2011 Kraft-Nabisco Championship, 2013 Women's British Open). In 2014, Lewis became the first American— since Betsy King 21 years earlier—to win the LPGA "triple crown." Lewis won the Rolex Player of the Year award for the second time in three years. She won the Vare Trophy for lowest scoring average for the second straight year, and she finished first on the Money List with more than $2.5-million in earnings. Lewis represented the United States in the 2011, 2013 and 2015 Solheim Cup.

*   *   *

Brian Grant played 12 seasons in the NBA for the Kings, Trail Blazers, Heat, Lakers and Suns. Often considered the heart and soul of the teams on which he played, Grant was tenacious. The rugged 6-foot-9 power forward fought for every rebound and never backed down from any opponent. He was strong and physical, an intimidating presence on the court. However, Brian Grant was a gentle giant when he stepped off the floor. Unlike many who give lip service to community service, Grant became personally involved in the communities in which he played. In Portland, for example, Grant served as a spokesman for the Ronald McDonald House Charities. He started a foundation—the Brian Grant Foundation—to assist seriously ill children, their families and under-privileged young people. He has provided Thanksgiving dinners, adopted families at Christmas, begun a scholastic attendance program, and organized a bone marrow drive to try to save the life of a 16-year-old Portland boy. His contributions were recognized by the NBA when he was named the recipient of the J. Walter Kennedy Citizenship Award in 1999.

Sadly, in one life-altering moment, Brian Grant was diagnosed with young-onset Parkinson's disease in 2008. Only 36 years of age, Grant experienced some pretty dark times while trying to come to grips with his newly-diagnosed medical condition. He eventually made a choice to try to live a full and meaningful life rather than wallow in self-pity. Grant's neurologist was able to arrange a call from actor Michael J. Fox, who has been living with Parkinson's since his 1991 diagnosis. After speaking with Fox, Grant soon organized a fund-raising event, "Shake It Till We Make It," and raised $350,000 that was donated to the Michael J. Fox Foundation for Parkinson's Research. The annual "Shake It Till We Make It" Celebrity Gala and Golf Tournament continues to be a major fund-raiser for the fight against Parkinson's.

Brian Grant, a father of five boys and two girls, has refocused the mission of his foundation to empower people with Parkinson's to live active and fulfilling lives. He is living proof that it can be done. He is an inspiration to us all.

I talked with Brian Grant at the Oregon Sports Awards in Beaverton, Oregon, on March 9, 2014.

Who was your first boyhood idol, the first person you looked up to?

My grandfather. My grandpa, Tom Bennett—my mom's dad. He was my idol because he was a hard worker. He would come all the way to North Carolina to pick me up and take me back to Ohio. He would teach me how to fish and let me go hunting with him. He was my idol. He was my true idol. I wasn't really into sports or anything like that at the time, so I didn't have anyone like that to look up to. He wasn't just *my* idol. He was the idol of all my cousins. He was just a great man.

One thing I know about you is that you've been a fisherman pretty much your whole life. Was he the first to take you fishing?

Yes he was. We'd start off at little crappie ponds, and then we'd go to the river and get catfish. That man would catch and eat anything. (Laughs) He'd go rabbit hunting and not get a rabbit. So, he'd shoot a couple robins and come home pluckin' one. (Laughs) We'd be like, "What are you *doing?*"

It's nice that your boyhood idol was a big part of your life, a person close to you—family, in fact.

Well, he was my family, and I lost him six years ago. He led a really good life. He passed on a lot of knowledge to myself and was able to spend some time with my kids as well. So, that was really nice.

You were a fan favorite during your playing days. Now, you inspire us all with the way you continue to live life while dealing with Parkinson's.

Hey, I try to do the right thing. I don't always do the right thing, but I try. I try to help as many as I can.

Do you realize that people look at you in amazement for all that you are doing?

It feels good to go out in this Portland community and be recognized. When you're playing, you think it's gonna last forever. Sometimes, you want to shrug the attention off. It's when you're done—four or five years after retiring—that people don't remember you. That's where it really messes with you. Fortunately, I live in a community where they really appreciated a lot of the things I did here.

Career Notes: Brian Grant was a two-time Midwestern Collegiate Conference Player of the Year at Xavier University. The Kings selected Grant in the first round (#8 overall) of the 1994 NBA Draft. Never a team's first option on offense, Grant still managed to average 10.5 points and 7.4 rebounds over his pro career.

*   *   *

21

Superman In Spiked Shoes

Lawrence "Yogi" Berra was a Hall of Fame baseball player who played his entire career in New York—18 years with the Yankees (1946–63) and four games with the Mets (1965). A native of Saint Louis, Missouri, the popular Berra was a catcher and outfielder for the Yankees and helped them win 10 World Series titles during his playing career. No other baseball player has won as many championship rings as Yogi Berra, and no player has played in more World Series games than Yogi.

I never had the opportunity to speak with Yogi Berra, but would love to have had the chance. One of my earliest memories as a child is sitting in front of my family's black and white TV set watching Yankees' games during the home run chase of 1961. That was the year Yankee teammates Mickey Mantle and Roger Maris were both in pursuit of Babe Ruth's record of 60 home runs in a season. (Maris set the record with 61. Mantle finished with 54.) One thing that always stuck with me was the fact that the Yankees' best players that year wore single digits on their jerseys. Mantle wore number 7. Yogi Berra was number 8. Maris wore the number 9.

Books have been written by—or about—Berra, and most feature his many "Yogi-isms," pithy quotes and witticisms that have been attributed to Yogi—at least <u>some</u> of which he might have actually said. Former major league player and broadcaster, Joe Garagiola—who grew up across the street from Yogi in "The Hill" neighborhood in St. Louis—made a career out of telling humorous stories about his childhood friend.

Yogi turned 90 in May of 2015, but he passed away just four months later on September 22, 2015. The world was a better place with Yogi Berra in it. He was not just a sports icon. He was an American icon. Thanks, Yogi—for everything.

David Kaplan, Director of the Yogi Berra Museum & Learning Center on the campus of Montclair State University, asked Yogi the following questions on my behalf and emailed Yogi's responses to me on October 10, 2011.

Who was your boyhood idol and why?

Joe Medwick. He was my newspaper customer. He used to stop at my corner and give me a nickel for the paper, which was three cents. He'd chat with us—which was great—then go on his way to the ballpark. As a kid, I followed the Cardinals, and he was a great player. He was a bad-ball hitter. I became one, too.

Did you ever get to know your childhood idol?

Yes, I played golf with him and a couple of guys in St. Louis during the offseason. When he came to camp with the Yankees in my rookie year, he was at the end of his career. He was pretty helpful to me and some younger guys.

What was he like? Was he everything you expected?

He was always good to me. Some people thought he was unfriendly; not to me, he wasn't.

When you were playing, you were obviously a hero to a lot of kids. Did you ever think about that?

Well, the Yankees were pretty popular. I know we had a lot of fans. Sure, we knew kids looked up to us.

Did it affect the way you lived your life—knowing that little kids were watching you?

Being in the public eye, you know people watch you. You always try to treat people like you'd want to be treated.

Career Notes: Yogi Berra had a lifetime batting average of .285. He hit 358 career home runs and drove in 1,430 runs. In 14 trips to the Fall Classic, he hit a dozen homers and drove in 39 runs. Berra was behind the plate in 1956 when Don Larsen threw the only perfect game in World Series history against the Brooklyn Dodgers. The left-handed-hitting Berra had magnificent bat control. Remarkably, in five different seasons, he had more home runs than strikeouts. He was an American League All-Star for 15 consecutive years (1948–62), and he was a three-time American League MVP (1951, 1954, 1955). After his playing days ended, the much-beloved Berra remained in baseball as a coach and manager. He managed the Yankees (1964, 1984-85) and the Mets (1972–75). Yogi Berra was inducted into the Baseball Hall of Fame in 1972. His Yankee jersey (#8) has been retired.

*   *   *

Joe Garagiola played baseball in the 1940s and '50s before launching a long and distinguished career in broadcasting. Just a mediocre big league catcher, Garagiola parlayed his humor and quick wit into radio and television stardom. As a baseball broadcaster, he worked with St. Louis Cardinal play-by-play legends Harry Caray and Jack Buck. He worked with Red Barber on New York Yankees' broadcasts. During his nearly three decades with NBC, he worked with greats such as Vin Scully, Curt Gowdy and Tony Kubek on the network's Saturday Game of the Week—at a time there was only one game nationally-televised each week. Equally adept serving as the play-by-play announcer or the color commentator, the master story-teller spent years in the booth describing the action and spinning yarns about his days as a player, often in a self-deprecating manner.

As his fame as a broadcaster grew, Garagiola became a regular on NBC's *Today* show. He also worked as the host of several different game shows through the years. Garagiola occasionally filled in for Johnny Carson as host of the Tonight Show, and he guest-hosted the night two former Beatles, Paul McCartney and John Lennon, were guests on program. More recently, Garagiola achieved notoriety for his work on the Westminster Kennel Club dog show.

Garagiola grew up in St. Louis across the street from future Hall of Famer Yogi Berra in an Italian-American neighborhood known as "The Hill." Garagiola once told me, "Not only was I not the best catcher to play in the big leagues, I wasn't even the best catcher on my street." The two friends had a special bond which began during their childhood. Garagiola told me was the best man at Yogi's wedding and Yogi, in turn, was Joe's best man.

Having interviewed Garagiola numerous times throughout my career, I can tell you that of his many accomplishments, he seems most proud of his work on behalf of others. One of the leading advocates of the Baseball Assistance Team (B.A.T.), he has worked behind the scenes helping countless people associated with baseball who needed some form of help but were too proud to ask. Garagiola served as B.A.T. President for 14 years and received the organization's first Lifetime Achievement Award in 2011. He has testified before Congress several times to warn of the dangers of chewing tobacco and has pushed for a ban on spit-tobacco throughout baseball. And, Joe made sure the St. Peter Indian Mission School in Gila River Township, Arizona, got the help it needed to build a library for the Native-American children. Yes, Joe Garagiola is a rather special guy. I'm happy to have been able to visit with him many times through the years. I always came away feeling like I had just visited with an old friend.

I talked by phone with Joe Garagiola on October 12, 2011.

Who was your very first boyhood idol?

Joe Medwick. He was a left-fielder with the Cardinals—a triple-crown winner. He could do it all.

Yogi Berra told me that Medwick was his first boyhood idol. I know you lived right across the street from Yogi, but did Medwick live in your neighborhood as well?

No. The first time we ever really saw him close up was when Yogi was selling papers on Kingshighway. Medwick was one of his customers. We were maybe 12 or 13 years old.

What was it about Medwick that made him stand out in your mind?

First of all, he was the closest Cardinal to us. We couldn't afford to buy a ticket, so we would go with the Knothole Gang. There was a widow who would take a couple of kids every Saturday when the Cardinals were at home because we ran errands for her during the week. Medwick was the left-fielder, and that's where we sat. We sat in left-field, and he was the closest. It was just kind of natural that you became a fan of the guy closest to ya. It seemed like he did the most. I didn't get to talk to him until I got on the club with him. He went to Brooklyn, and he played with the Giants a little bit. But, he came back to the Cardinals; I think it was in 1948. That's when I was on the same team with him.

Was it strange to be on the same team as your boyhood hero?

Seeing Medwick the first time I saw him in the clubhouse, I just looked at him and remembered watching him play—hitting home runs and driving in runs. He had a funny walk. Ducky-Wucky Medwick from Cadaret, New Jersey, is what announcer France Laux called him. I have a sequence of pictures of him hitting—swinging and following through and all that. He pretty much did it on his own because he does a lot of things wrong in the picture, except the most important which was *hit the ball*. He had a hitch in his swing. He landed on his back foot. But, he was strong. He took a powerful swing, and he was consistently hitting the ball. So, when I first saw him in the clubhouse, all those flashbacks came, and I thought, "My God! What a great world this is. Here's a guy that I thought was Superman in spiked shoes, and now I'm a teammate." It was quite an experience. I've always said he was my hero as far as baseball players. I'd always find a way to sit next to him or talk to him. It was a thrill for me to be on the same team with him.

What was he like? Was he everything you expected as a kid?

Oh, yeah. He was everything I thought he'd be. He was patient then. Of course, his career was coming to an end, but he'd talk about hitting. I remember one time he gave me a lighter bat. It was great. He loved to laugh. Joe loved to laugh. He was a very handsome guy who always dressed nicely. When I became a broadcaster, I got to know his family. That was a real thrill because baseball players—that's as close as we came to having heroes. We listened to the radio all the time and listened to the baseball broadcasts. Those guys that did the job were *our* guys, and Medwick was number one in my book and number one in Yogi's book.

Joe, you were an idol for a lot of young kids as a player and later as a broadcaster. Did you ever think about that?

Not really. I can't say that I sat down one day and said, "You know, a lot of people are looking up to me." No, I did not do that. All I ever wanted to do was to do a good job and to have people say, "Hey, he's just like *we* are." And, I *am*. And, I *was* on television. I don't think I was any different on television than I was off. I didn't change my voice. I had help from a man named Al Fleischman who was the P.R. man for Anheuser-Busch. He sent me to a voice doctor because my voice was very high. Al sent me to a professor who helped me considerably in getting my voice down and helped me become a broadcaster. He had a great line that he used. He said, "We can use the time that you're on the air now to improve because people are really listening to *what* you say as opposed to *how* you say it—because I had just retired as a player.

You've done so many things to support charitable causes. Your support of B.A.T., your efforts to get a library built for the St. Peter Indian Mission School—a library that now bears your name. What do you feel your true legacy will be?

Well, (laughs) I can't say that I set out a plan to say, "Well, I'm gonna play baseball. Then, I'm going to be a broadcaster. Then, I'm going to be Saint Joe." No, things just happened. There's a prayer—not a church prayer by any means—but a prayer I heard from a fella named Fred Bauer. I always give him credit because I think that that's really the motivation behind some of the things that I get involved in. Fred had a prayer that said, "Lord, teach me to know that every day, down every street, come chances to be your hands and feet." If I had a flag that I had to carry, I would have that on the flag because that's what it's all about.

When I had my surgery in 2009—a six-hour surgery—I was under all kinds of medication and was knocked out. My dear wife of 61 years was there the whole time. She's the one that suffered. It was nip and tuck there for a while. But, when I got out and it looked like I was gonna be okay, I would pray to God, "Let me be your hands and feet, and let it be a long-time job." I tell my friends who get sick, "Just ask God for another job. He's got one for you. Maybe he'll give you an extra job and give you an extra couple of years."

Down at the Mission, we made big changes—everybody—not just me. I'm the front guy. You know, a guy would ask me to make a speech. I'd ask him for a donation, and they were willing to do that. There are a lot of good people in this world. The building itself is over 5,000 square feet, and it was donated. Donated! Jim Uhl, who was the President of Agate, Incorporated, called me and said, "Is there anything I can do? I'd be glad to try to do it." I told him what I was hoping to get was a library because we didn't have a library. We were using a regular school room. Ann Curry from *The Today Show* sent a truckload of books down there. We got so crowded that we could only allow three kids in the room to get their books and get out so that three more kids could get in. So, building a library was really a big dream of mine. Then, all of a sudden, things started to happen. David Dick called me. He was the architect. He did it pro bono. I had a list of the people who donated money. No, it was not easy. You were always asking for money. I'd have fun and say, "Well, I'm calling again." People would come up and give me a check. I'd look at it, and I couldn't believe it. I could not believe the number of zeroes that would be on it. You know maybe $10,000 or $15,000. I got a $500 bonus for signing a baseball contract! (Laughs) But, it was not a plan. I had no plan.

In the B.A.T. situation, Peter Ueberroth—who was then commissioner—called a couple of us in and told us what he wanted to do and made suggestions. I told him that I thought the real tragedy was what happened to the Negro League players. Guys who should have been in the big leagues even before Jackie Robinson, you know, those guys never had a chance. Now their careers were over, and some of them were really hurting. That gave me the force to keep going, keep pushing and keep getting people upset. We fought, and the Negro Leaguers are in it now being helped by the Baseball Assistance Team. I can remember sitting with my good friend, Joe Black, who died way too soon. In Los Angeles, we sat on the couch with a widow of one of the players, and the three of us were just holding hands. Joe was trying to give her confidence because she thought she was going to lose her house. I'll never forget the look on her face or the tears streaming from her eyes when Joe said, "Don't worry about it. We will see that you do not lose your house." This lady was in her eighties. I thought she was going to break Joe's neck and I thought she was going to break my back hugging us. That's the joy of it. It's not what you got. It's what you give. It's nice that people say the things that they do about me, but what can I say? You thank them and all that. But, I've had a real good ride, I'll tell ya. It was a tremendous thrill to see that library go up.

Career Notes: Joe Garagiola played nine major league seasons with the Cardinals, Pirates, Cubs and Giants. In 1946, his rookie season, Garagiola helped his hometown Cardinals win the World Series.

Although just an average hitter, the 20-year-old Garagiola went 4-for-5 and drove in three runs in a 12-3 Game 4 victory over the Red Sox. Although he often joked about his baseball career, Garagiola was no joke that day at Fenway Park.

*　　*　　*

Don Larsen gained fame by pitching a perfect game in the 1956 World Series against the Brooklyn Dodgers while a member of the New York Yankees. Larsen is the only pitcher to throw a perfect game (or no-hitter) in the Fall Classic.

I interviewed Don Larsen three or four times during my career and always enjoyed talking with him. A journeyman pitcher for most of his career, Larsen has profited for decades because of his one magical game in the '56 World Series. He has made appearances at minor league baseball stadiums where he has signed autographs and offered fans the opportunity to buy autographed 8x10" photos of him pitching in the perfect game. Prior to one of his appearances in Keizer, Oregon, I ran to an ATM so I could have enough cash to buy several of the photos. I have purchased very few autographs in my lifetime, but I wanted Larsen's autograph. After all, there has only been one perfect game pitched in the World Series.

I talked by phone with Don Larsen about his childhood hero on August 6, 2011.

Who was your first boyhood idol?

As a kid, I watched and followed baseball—especially the World Series. I was born in Indiana, but raised in San Diego, and Ted Williams was raised in San Diego, too. He was born and raised there. So, I would have to go with Ted as the most popular person in my life. I tried to follow his career a little bit, but it was a little difficult.

I understand what you're saying. There was no TV, and it was pretty much just the radio and newspapers. That was much different than the wide range of media covering baseball today.

You got everything today. You got the cell phones, and you can take pictures. You got all the memorabilia. You can play it at will. But, that's good, I guess. It keeps everybody happy.

Did you ever meet Ted Williams when you were a kid?

Not when I was a kid, but I met him a lot later on when I was playing against the Red Sox. Then, we were together a lot in San Diego. I really enjoyed his company because he was pretty tough, and I liked the way he handled himself.

When you say he was pretty tough, do you mean tough as a person or tough as a hitter?

Hitter! Pitching against him, the worst thing about it was he umpired his own game. Shoot. That was a little difficult. The umpire wouldn't call it a strike unless he swung at it.

What were you feeling the first time you faced Ted in a major league game?

It was wonderful, the competition and stuff. I didn't care if he hit home runs or not. I just wanted to have the challenge and be able to have a chance to pitch against him 'cause he was one of the greatest.

When you were playing, particularly after you threw your World Series perfect game, there were undoubtedly kids that looked up to you. Did you ever think about that?

No, that never come across my mind. But, even today I sign a lot of stuff that comes in the mail, I still get some wonderful letters from kids and adults commenting about the game and the way we handled ourselves in those days. I enjoy reading those letters.

I have to assume your biggest thrill in baseball was pitching the perfect game in the World Series since nobody else has ever done that. But, what about the day you first played in the major leagues? Was that a similar type of thrill for you?

Well, it was hard work to get there. I got with the St. Louis Browns and then they moved to Baltimore. We didn't have such good clubs at the time. So, when I got traded to the Yankees, it was a welcome experience knowing that you're with a better ball club and better players. I enjoyed those moments—especially playing in Yankee Stadium. It's awesome when you first walk in there.

Career Notes: Don Larsen spent parts of 14 seasons in the major leagues and went 81-91, with a 3.78 earned run average. He made his big league debut with the St. Louis Browns in 1953 and was with the team when the franchise moved to Baltimore and became the Orioles in 1954. He later pitched for the Yankees, Athletics, White Sox, Giants, Colts/Astros and Cubs.

*   *   *

Mickey Lolich pitched 16 years in the major leagues—13 with the Tigers, one with the Mets and two with the Padres. He was named MVP of the 1968 World Series after winning three games for Detroit against St. Louis.

Fans in Detroit love Mickey Lolich because of his many successful years with the Tigers. However, Northwest baseball fans know that Lolich was born and raised in Portland, Oregon, and that he had a long string of success as an amateur before he became a professional baseball player. He pitched in the 1955 Babe Ruth World Series and also led Lincoln High School to the 1956 state baseball championship—striking out 18 Medford batters in the title game. Lolich pitched in the 1956 Babe Ruth World Series and led his American Junior Legion team to second place in the 1957 World Tournament. It's easy to understand why baseball fans in Portland like to claim Lolich as "Portland's own."

I first met Mickey Lolich in the 1980s when I was the sports director of Portland's NBC television affiliate. I learned that Mickey was going to visit his father, who still lived in the family home in Portland. I made arrangements to go to his dad's house to interview Mickey for the TV station. It probably wasn't the best way to introduce myself to Mickey, but while shaking his hand, I said, "I hate you." Understandably, Mickey peered at me with a strange look on his face. I went on to explain, "I grew up a Cardinals' fan, and you broke my heart in '68." Thankfully, he laughed. Then he said he had only been doing his job and pointed out that he sure made a lot of Tigers' fans happy when he won those three games in the '68 World Series. For the record, I never really hated Mickey. Then again, I've never forgiven him for beating my Cardinals.

I talked by phone with Mickey Lolich on July 17, 2013.

You broke in with the Tigers, but you tell me you liked a different major league team when you were growing up in Portland.

Yes, I was a Yankee fan because back in those days—back in the '50s—they were really trying to promote Major League Baseball. Every Saturday, we had the Game of the Week with Buddy Blattner and Dizzy Dean. They seemed to always have the Yankees on. I swear that the Yankees used to save Whitey Ford to pitch those games. It just seemed like it. So, I became a Whitey Ford fan because he was a left-handed pitcher like me. When I played all my amateur days in Portland, I wore number 16—Whitey's number. So, I was a Yankee fan. Actually, when it came down for me to sign as a professional, I was going with the Yankees. I really planned on going with the Yankees. But, my uncle, Frank Lolich, was an avid baseball fan, and he was a very good friend of Johnny Pesky from Portland. He happened to call Johnny

Pesky. He says, "It looks like Mickey's going with the Yankees, but Detroit is after him, too. In your opinion, what do you think will be better for Mickey?" Pesky gave him the advice that the Tigers did not really have much in the minor leagues as far as left-handed pitching. Plus, Al Downing had signed with the Yankees the day before. So, Al Downing and myself would be battling through the Yankee farm system to come to the big leagues as left-handed pitchers. We were both starting pitchers in our careers. A lot of teams don't have room for two left-handed starters. Pesky said, "He should go with Detroit. He has a better chance if he goes with Detroit." So, I picked Detroit. That's how I ended up as a Tiger.

You talk about growing up as a fan of Whitey Ford. You eventually found yourself pitching against him in the major leagues.

When I did come to Detroit, I was a spot starter my rookie year. I pitched out of the bullpen, but I did make starts with the Tigers. Every time we played the Yankees and White Ford was pitching against the Tigers, the Tigers had a lot of trouble beating Whitey Ford. So, guys like Jim Bunning, Phil Regan, Frank Lary—a lot of those guys—sort of bowed out of pitching against Whitey. I bet you can guess who they told, "You're starting today." I caught Whitey a lot my rookie year. I lost nine games that year, and Whitey Ford beat me four times. (Laughs) But, my sophomore year, I became a full-time starter. I was pitching more regularly in the starting rotation, and I got my stuff together that year as far as getting into a regular routine. I beat Whitey a couple times. Eventually we evened out somewhere along the line as far as wins and losses.

Did you ever have an opportunity to talk with Whitey?

I met him on the field one day during batting practice. I walk over to him, and I say, "Hi Whitey. I'm Mickey Lolich. I'm a rookie with the Tigers." He says, "Well, good for you. I heard the Tigers had a new lefthander in their organization. I wish you success in your career." I said, "Thank you very much, *Sir*. I appreciate that." And, I walked away as a very happy young pitcher. (Laughs)

Do you still get recognized by a lot of Tigers' fans?

In Detroit, or in the Michigan area, I still am a pretty well-known name because of the 1968 World Series. That's all anybody ever talks to me about. Sometimes I remind them that I did pitch 16 years in the big leagues, not just that ten day period during '68. They just remember winning the World Series.

Career Notes: In his major league career, Mickey Lolich had 217 wins, 191 losses and an ERA of 3.44. In 1964, his first full season with the Tigers, he was 18-9. Even though the 1968 World Series featured both Cy Young Award winners from that season—the Tigers' 31-game winner Dennis McLain and the Cardinals' Bob Gibson (NL record 1.12 ERA)—Lolich was the difference as the Tigers stunned the Cardinals after trailing three games to one. Lolich pitched three complete game victories, including the deciding Game 7. The lefty pitcher, who had gone 17-9 in the regular season, was named the World Series MVP. His ERA in the three complete game wins was 1.67. In 1971, Lolich led American League pitchers with 45 games started (still the most for a Tiger lefty in a season), 29 complete games and 376 innings pitched (still a team record for a LHP). He led the league with 308 strikeouts, which remains a franchise record. Lolich won an American League best 25 games in 1971. He is the most recent Detroit pitcher to win 25 games in a season. He also won 22 games in 1972. Lolich pitched in the All-Star Game in 1971 and 1972. Mickey Lolich had 2,379 career strikeouts, the most of any American League pitcher.

*   *   *

Bobby Doerr is a Hall of Fame second baseman who played all 14 of his major league seasons with the Boston Red Sox. The California native is one of the few players in major league history to play the same position for the same team his entire career. Doerr played in the majors from 1937 to 1951, but missed the 1945 season because of military service during World War II. Doerr moved to Oregon in 1936 and spent much of his adult life as an Oregon resident. He beecame close friends with Red Sox teammates Johnny Pesky, Dom DiMaggio and Ted Williams. The story of their friendship is detailed in David Halberstam's outstanding book, *The Teammates: A Portrait of a Friendship*. Doerr was inducted into the Baseball Hall of Fame in 1986. His jersey (#1) was retired by the Boston Red Sox in 1988.

As this book goes to print in late October of 2015, Bobby Doerr is 97 years of age—the oldest living member of the Baseball Hall of Fame. On June 18, 2015, he became the oldest living Hall of Famer ever at 97 years, 72 days, surpassing the late Al Lopez who died at 97 years, 71 days in 2005.

In September, 2010, I had the privilege of visiting Bobby Doerr in Junction City, Oregon. Al Bell, a good friend, joined me, and we discussed baseball with the Red Sox legend in the comfort of his home. Even at 92, Doerr's mind was incredibly sharp. He could remember names and places. It was nirvana to spend time talking with a man who had played with Ted Williams and against legends like Joe DiMaggio, Bill Dickey and Bob Feller.

Before we left Doerr's home, he took us on a tour of his memorabilia room. Doerr had been collecting autographed bats, photos and other items for decades. Most of the items had been given to Doerr personally by his contemporaries—all legends of the game. He also showed us dozens of scrapbooks containing articles and box scores from his entire career. He said his parents had cut things out of the newspaper every day and put them in the scrapbooks to chronicle his career. I can tell you with absolute certainty that Doerr had more significant baseball memorabilia in his home than many sports museums. The man has lived a remarkable life and has the evidence to prove it.

I visited Bobby Doerr at his home in Junction City, Oregon, on September 14, 2010.

Who was your boyhood idol?

Charlie Gehringer was my favorite second baseman. He was, I thought, one of the real great ones, and I still do. Charlie Gehringer and Billy Herman were my favorite ballplayers back in those days. Billy Herman and the Cubs trained out there in the Los Angeles area. They trained on the coast there at Catalina Island. I remember going down and watching the ballgames. I admired the way Herman played second base, and I liked his hitting stance.

What was it that made them special?

Well, I think because they were second basemen—and because they were good. I liked their style. At that time, I knew I wanted to be a second baseman. That's all I ever played. But, in high school, I did play third base because they already had a regular second baseman. They had me play third. I didn't like third at all. At second base, you had a lot of action covering first on bunts and turning double-plays. I just liked second base.

I remember in my bedroom I had all the walls plastered with pictures of baseball players. Baseball Magazine used to have a big colored picture every month, and I would pin one of those pictures up on the wall. I didn't have any more space. There was no more room in my bedroom for any more pictures.

Do you remember the first time you met Charlie Gehringer?

I didn't meet Charlie Gehringer until I went to the major leagues. I remember he'd be standing there talking to some guys, and we'd all go over there and listen to him. He didn't say much, but what he said all made good sense. I thought so much of him. He was so good. I remember our players would try to take him out at second base to break up double-plays, but they never could get to him to take him out of double-plays.

You were undoubtedly a boyhood idol for young baseball fans in Boston during your playing days. Did you think about that at all?

Well, not too much. I remember going over to Bunker Hill. When we had friends over, we'd take them to Bunker Hill and other places. There was a little boy who run up to me and said Bunker Hill is so high in elevation and this and that. He seemed to know I was a ballplayer, and I got to visit a little bit with him. And, my gosh—years and years later—he came up to me at a game and said, "You probably don't remember me, but I'm the boy that was at Bunker Hill telling you all about Bunker Hill." I said, "Oh, I remember very plainly about you telling me all about Bunker Hill." It made you feel good to think that he was still around and enjoying baseball.

The first game you played against Charlie Gehringer in the big leagues, he's suddenly your peer. Was that a weird feeling?

No. Playing against him was always a great thrill. I just admired him so much. He was such a fine man. He was quiet. At Cooperstown, I enjoyed talking with him. Still, he was real quiet. You had to bring up the conversation pretty much. But, he was one of the real fine guys.

Before I go, let me ask you about my boyhood idol, Stan Musial. In your opinion, was Musial deserving of my adoration?

Oh, you bet. Stan was a real fine wonderful man. He's a humble guy—always a fun guy. I remember when we were at the Hall of Fame. We'd be up on the stage. He always had his harmonica, and he'd pull his harmonica out and play it. A fun guy—a *nice* guy. I think he's one of the class guys. He was like a Charlie Gehringer. There's a lot of nice guys, but for *class*, Gehringer and Musial would be two real top guys.

Career Notes: Bobby Doerr made his major league debut at age 19 in 1937. An excellent defensive second baseman, Doerr could also hit. He batted .288 lifetime. He hit 223 home runs and drove in 1,247 runs. He drove in more than 100 runs in a season six times. He hit at least 12 home runs in 12 straight seasons. In 1946, Doerr drove in 116 runs to help Boston win the American League pennant. Against the St. Louis Cardinals in the 1946 World Series—Doerr's only postseason appearance—he batted .409 with a homer and 3 runs-batted-in. Doerr was an All-Star nine times in the 1940s and '50s. His best All-Star performance came in 1943 when he went 2-for-4 and hit a 3-run homer to help the American League post a 5-3 win over the National League.

*　　*　　*

Tommy John pitched 26 years in the major leagues with the Indians, White Sox, Dodgers, Yankees, Angels and Athletics. He made his major league debut in 1963 and pitched in the majors until 1989. John was 46 years old when he appeared in his last major league game. He did not pitch during the 1975 season after undergoing surgery on his pitching elbow.

John is perhaps best-known for the medical procedure that now bears his name. "Tommy John surgery" (ulnar collateral ligament reconstruction) is a procedure that reconstructs an injured elbow ligament by using a tendon taken from another part of the body. The procedure was first performed by orthopedic surgeon Dr. Frank Jobe—then a team physician for the Dodgers. The surgery soon became identified with John, the first baseball player to undergo the procedure. Prior to the operation, most were skeptical about John's ability to come back and pitch in the major leagues. Even Dr. Jobe put John's chance to return as a mere 1-in-100. But, John did come back, and he pitched at a high level for 14 more years. He made the All-Star Game three times following his surgery. Of John's 288 career victories, 164 came after the surgery that extended his career and made him famous in medical circles. Many professional athletes have since undergone Tommy John surgery, and most have been able to return to their sport. In fact, a

2013 study found that nearly one-third of the active pitchers in the major leagues had undergone Tommy John surgery at some point during their careers. Before Dr. Jobe operated on Tommy John in 1974, that type of injury was almost certain to end a pitcher's career. A lot of pitchers owe their careers to Tommy John.

I talked with Tommy John via the telephone on August 7, 2013.

Tommy, can you tell me, who was your first boyhood idol?

Yeah. Hank Sauer—a left fielder for the Chicago Cubs. I also liked Dee Fondy, who was a slick-fielding first baseman. I was a Cub fan growing up in Terre Haute, Indiana, but I used to fall asleep at night listening to Harry Caray, Jack Buck and Joe Garagiola doing Cardinals games on KMOX from Busch Stadium.

Why were Sauer and Fondy your guys? What made them special?

Hank Sauer was a slugger. He'd hit home runs, and the Cubs didn't have a particularly good team. I think their best pitcher at that time might have been a guy named Bob Rush. I liked the Cubs because my mom and dad were Cub fans. Hank Sauer used to hit 30 or 40 home runs almost every year.

It was funny. There was a newspaper writer going around asking all the Yankee players about their favorite big-league players growing up. I was older than most of those guys. I said Hank Sauer, and the next day Jack Clark came up to me. He said, "I read your comments. Hank Sauer was your favorite?" I said, "Oh, I loved him. He had a big bulbous nose and these huge arms." He said, "I talk to Hank every day. He's the best hitting instructor I ever had in my life. I talk to him every day about hitting. I'm gonna tell him that Tommy John said that Hank was his favorite ball player." I was just a Chicago Cub fan.

Did you ever get a chance to meet Hank Sauer or Dee Fondy?

I met Hank Sauer at a Chinese restaurant in San Francisco. I was with the Dodgers. Friends of mine, we all went into this restaurant. I looked over and I said, "Whoa! That's Hank Sauer." So, I went over and said, "Mister Sauer." He said, "Yeah?" I said, "I'm Tommy John. I grew up in Terre Haute, Indiana, and I idolized you as a young man." And, he says, "Oh, how's everything?" and things like that. I got to meet him that one time. He was a very nice man.

Dee Fondy used to come and play in my golf tournaments every year in Southern California. We would reminisce about all those old Cub days.

I collected your baseball cards back in the day. You were undoubtedly a sports hero for a lot of youngsters in my generation. Did you ever consider that fact?

Well, yes, I did. But, no, I didn't. People asked me, "Who did you look up to or what athlete was your hero?" I'd say, "I didn't have an athlete as a hero. My dad was my hero. I want to be like my dad." My dad was everything to me. He was my best friend and my coach—a disciplinarian and all this stuff. That's why—when your name goes out there and you're on a bubble-gum card—there are about a hundred-jillion eyes on you all the time. They expect good things out of you. That's why the pressure is on you to behave. That's why Derek Jeter is loved. You never hear of Derek doing bad things.

Which do you think has gotten you more notoriety—your 26-year major league career or the surgery that bears your name?

The surgery, by far! And, it will be out there forever. I'm proud of all those wins in 26 years and 700 starts, but I'll be known for "Tommy John surgery." A lot of guys that play the game now think that I'm a doctor and performed the surgery.

Career Notes: Tommy John pitched in five postseasons with the Dodgers, Yankees and Angels, with a cumulative record of 6-3 and an

ERA of 2.65. He went 1-1 in three World Series starts with the Dodgers in 1977-78, and 1-0 in three World Series games (2 starts) for the 1981 Yankees. He was particularly effective in League Championship Series games (4-1 in seven starts). John was named as an All Star four times—once with the White Sox, once as a Dodger and twice while with the Yankees. In 760 regular season games—700 of those as a starter—Tommy John had a record of 288-231, with an ERA of 3.34. He struck out 2,245 batters and walked 1,259. He pitched a whopping 4,710 innings (plus 88 more in the postseason).

*   *   *

Ron Fairly, a first baseman and outfielder, played 21 years in the majors, with the Dodgers, Expos, Cardinals, Athletics, Blue Jays and Angels. Fairly played in four World Series with the Dodgers and won three championship rings (1959, 1963, 1965).

Fairly played a key role in the Dodgers' 1965 World Series victory over the Minnesota Twins. He batted .379 (11-for-29), with three doubles, two homers and six runs-batted-in. He also scored seven runs in the seven game series.

After his playing career ended, Fairly became a broadcaster and spent many years working in the booth for the Angels, Giants and Mariners.

I first heard of Ron Fairly when I was a young boy. I was just learning about baseball when Fairly was helping the Dodgers win those World Series in the Sixties. Also, in the mid-'60s, I began playing Strat-O-Matic baseball, and Fairly was on one of the teams. I remember him (from his Strat-O-Matic card) as being a pretty slick-fielding first baseman. Much later in my life, I got a chance to meet Fairly a few times in the press box in Seattle when I would see the Mariners play. He was always cordial and a very good talker. I always enjoyed him on the Mariners' broadcasts because he often talked about his playing days and the guys he competed against in the '50s and

'60s. He was fun, and I was disappointed when he was no longer part of the Mariners' broadcast crew.

I spoke with Ron Fairly in Seattle on April 8, 2011.

When I ask you to discuss your first boyhood idol, who is the person that immediately comes to mind?

Well, I think, when you're as old as I am, the first guy has to be like Babe Ruth or Lou Gehrig or somebody like that. (Laughs) But really, the guys that were playing at that particular time; Joe DiMaggio was one. Mickey Mantle was another. Stan Musial was one. I followed all the great players during that time. And, then, lo-and-behold, I end up signing a contract and one of the guys that I always liked to watch, Duke Snider, ended up being my roommate.

What was it like to room with a guy you'd been following as a fan?

First of all, he's a first-class individual. When I joined the Dodgers, they were playing in Philadelphia. They were at Connie Mack Stadium in a little dinky old clubhouse. I go into the clubhouse and look around, and here is Sandy Koufax, Don Drysdale, Duke Snider, Pee Wee Reese, Gil Hodges, Carl Furillo, Clem Labine, Don Newcombe, Don Bessent, and it goes on and on and on and on. I'm looking around there and say to myself, "Holy cow! I'm wearing the same uniform *they're* wearing! Show some class, and don't ask for any autographs." (Laughs)

You earlier mentioned Stan Musial. He was my first boyhood idol.

I'll tell you a cute story about Stan. I was told that he was going to take extra batting practice one day. We're in St. Louis, and I went out to the ballpark just to watch him take batting practice. I was behind the cage just watching him. He was struggling a little bit. He hit a couple of balls in the cage. He hit a ground ball. He didn't quite hit the ball the way he wanted to. He turned around and looked at me, and he said, "Ron, what am I doing wrong?" I said, "What are you doing wrong? Stan, the only thing I can see is it's not 8 o'clock yet. That night, he had a single and two doubles, and he drove in three runs. It just wasn't game time yet, that's all.

When you met DiMaggio and Mays and the other big stars for the first time, did you become a six-year-old again?

I'll tell ya what I did. You hold back, and you wait for an opening for someone to introduce you to them. Then you can say, "Hi Joe. Hi Willie." How often do you get to do that?

Did they live up to your expectations when you met them?

Yes. Yes. Yeah, they did. There isn't any question about that. Willie always had that smile on his face. Stan Musial would say, "Are you a left-hand or right-hand hitter?" I'd say, "Left-hand hitter." Stan, a lefty-hitter, would say, "All right. You'll be all right." They'd say little things like that to welcome you. They're Hall of Fame guys off the field, as well as on.

You played on some great Dodger teams and played in the World Series. Did it ever dawn on you that you were a sports hero for a lot of kids during your playing days, sort of like DiMaggio and Musial were for you?

Not to the extent that they were. When you're in the major leagues for a number of years and you play in some World Series, there are a lot of people that know about you. They watch you and all that stuff, but not to the degree that those guys are idolized. They're on a different plane. They're at a different level. I know when I roomed with Koufax for a while that we had a rough time going out to have dinner anywhere because people would always interrupt. They'd always say the same thing, "Gee. I don't want to bother you—*but.*" And, they *were* bothering us. We started having more room service with Sandy.

Sandy was big on room service. Sandy was very private but very classy. He shies away from publicity, but Sandy was very much a team player.

Talking about Sandy, we were broadcasting a game from Kansas City one time. We look up and they're showing the 1965 World Series and Sandy is pitching. One of the players on the team said, "Who is that?" I said, "It's Sandy Koufax." He said, "Never heard of him. Was he any good?" (Laughs) That kind of took me back a little. I said, "Let me ask you something. If you strike out 200 batters in a season, is that pretty good?" The player said, "Yeah, that's good." I said, "What happens if you strike out *300* batters in a season?" He said, "Oh, that's *really* good." I said, "Well, the guy you're looking at *struck out* 311 more batters than he *walked*." The player's eyes kind of got big, and he said, "Wow. He must have been pretty good." I said, "Yeah. He was something else."

Career Notes: Ron Fairly played in 2,442 major league games. He hit 215 career home runs and had a lifetime batting average of .266. He hit a career-high 19 home runs with Toronto in 1977 at age 39. Fairly was a National League All-Star in 1973 with Montreal and an American League All-Star in 1977 with Toronto. He is the only player to have represented both Canadian teams in All-Star competition.

*　　*　　*

Rick Wise pitched in the majors for 18 years with the Phillies, Cardinals, Red Sox, Indians and Padres. Wise is another Portland, Oregon, product who had plenty of success before turning pro. Wise led his Rose City Little League team to the 1958 Little League World Series, and he pitched Portland's Madison High School to a state title in 1963.

Wise picked up his first major league win on June 21, 1964, in the second game of a doubleheader against the Mets. While an important day for Wise, it was even more significant for future Hall of Fame Phillies' pitcher Jim Bunning. Bunning tossed a *perfect game* in the first game of the twin bill. Seven years later, on June 23, 1971, Wise pitched a no-hitter against the Reds at Cincinnati's Riverfront Stadium. Not only was he the pitching star that day, Wise hit two home runs in the game. Always a good-hitting pitcher, he also blasted a pair of homers in a game against the Giants later that season. Wise hammered six home runs during the 1971 season and finished his career with 15 homers, including two grand slams.

I was a high school senior on February 25, 1972, the day the Cardinals acquired Wise from the Phillies in exchange for pitcher Steve Carlton, who was coming off a 20-win season. I did not understand why the Cardinals would trade their promising left-hander. I later learned that both players were dealt because each was seeking a pay raise and their respective clubs weren't willing to give in to their salary demands. Despite all of Carlton's potential, Cardinals' owner, "Gussie" Busch, chose to trade Carlton. As a Cardinals' fan, I didn't like the deal. To make matters worse for St. Louis fans, in his first season in Philadelphia, Carlton won 27 games for the last-place Phillies and earned the National League Cy Young Award. Wise, who had been a 1971 All-Star in Philadelphia, was a very solid pitcher for the Cardinals, winning 16 games in each of his two seasons in St. Louis. The trade looked a little better from the St. Louis perspective in 1973. Wise was the starting—and winning—pitcher in that year's All-Star Game, while Carlton lost 20 games for the Phillies in his second season in Philadelphia. Truthfully, I wasn't too disappointed to see that. But, for the record, Carlton ended up with 329 career victories and a plaque in the Baseball Hall of Fame. Wise was traded to Boston after just two seasons in St. Louis.

I met Rick Wise at a baseball banquet many years later and found him to be delightful. The many times I've talked with him since, he has always been very generous with his time and a great conversationalist. Not all pro athletes are as personable as Rick Wise. Thinking back to how I felt about that 1972 trade, I think it a tad ironic that Wise became a friend, while Steve Carlton never gave me the time of day. (Carlton did not speak to the press for a majority of his career.)

I talked with Rick Wise by phone on January 15, 2015.

Who was your very first boyhood idol?

Well, first of all, you did not get the coverage of sports back then like we do now. Growing up in the '50s, we didn't have a major league team here in Portland. We had the (Portland) Beavers, of course. Television had basically three channels, and the lines (interference) were going through it all the time. (Laughs) That's why we were outside as soon as the sun came up playing whatever sport was in season at the time. So, I didn't really follow, uh, well, I followed the Tigers because I was born in Michigan and my dad went to the University of Michigan. But, I didn't have any major league team nearby, and sports did not get the exposure at that time. So, it was hard to really latch on to someone because we didn't have them here locally.

Did you ever start to pay attention to the happenings in the major leagues before you pitched for the Phillies at age 18, or were you just wrapped up in everything you were doing with your friends in Oregon?

Well, even at an amateur level, we had a lot of success. We had a lot of success with Rose City Little League. Then, it was on to Madison High School, where we won the school's first state championship with the '63 baseball team. I don't know. I really didn't have a true childhood hero or someone that I looked up to in sports. I did look up to my father. He's the one who guided me in my formative years. But, going back to what I said before, we just didn't have the sports coverage, either print media or through television. It just wasn't the way it is now where it's 24 hours a day.

Those athletes I've talked with who grew up in major league cities did have sports idols they looked up to. I'm curious if you feel like you were cheated since you grew up far from any major league franchises. Do you feel like you missed out on something in your childhood or were you just doing your own thing?

I was busy doing my own thing. You know, I just concentrated on the present and what was available to us. You can't miss what you don't have. I mean, I had a wonderful growing-up period, just a wonderful time. All three sports, we played whatever came along and what season it was. That was our main focus. We didn't have video games and electronics. We were outside playing sports and enjoying life.

When you reached the big leagues, was there any player you found yourself a little star-struck to be playing with or against?

First of all, I was only 18 my rookie year in '64. Jim Bunning was on the team, but they were all major leaguers and I was only 18. Just the year before, I was in high school competing for a state championship. But, that's nothing because the next year, my first major league start was against the San Francisco Giants. Willie Mays and Willie McCovey both hit home runs off me. (Laughs) I mean, here I am facing them at 18, when the year before I was facing high schoolers. Being in that situation—being in the National League and being in Major League Baseball—was pretty profound.

When you began playing for the Phillies, there were young fans in Philadelphia that collected your baseball cards and wanted your autograph. Were you aware that you had young fans looking up to you?

Sure. Every player has his fans. You certainly have to appreciate that. We're playing a game for a business, for our livelihood. But, the fans don't see it that way. For whatever reason, they attach themselves to players and personalities that they gravitate towards. They follow them and pull for them. And, that's a good feeling for a player. You have to appreciate that and make sure you commit yourself to your fans and to the game that you're playing, in my case, major league baseball. You gotta respect it and appreciate it very much.

Career Notes: Rick Wise had his best individual season in 1971. He went 17-14, with a 2.88 ERA for a Philadelphia team that lost 95 games. That was the year he pitched a no-hitter and was named an All-Star for the first time. That 1971 season, he hit six home runs, including a grand slam. And, on September 18, 1971, Wise retired 32 consecutive batters and pitched a 12-inning complete game in a win over the Cubs. He had three hits and drove in the winning run with a single in the bottom of the 12th. Yes, he batted for himself in the bottom of the 12th! Wise also had a great season in 1975, when he went 19-12 for Boston and helped the Red Sox win the American League Eastern Division title. He also won two games in the postseason (one over Oakland in the American League Championship Series and one over the Reds in the World Series). He was the winning pitcher in Game Six of the 1975 World Series, perhaps the greatest game in baseball history. Wise had pitched a scoreless top of the 12th and became the winner when Carlton Fisk waived his home run fair in the bottom of the 12th—a blast that sent Boston fans into delirium and propelled the Red Sox into Game Seven against the Reds the following night. In his 18-year career, Wise had a 188-181 record with a 3.69 ERA. The two-time All-Star coached in the minor leagues for nearly 25 years. Before calling it a career, Wise spent close to 45 years in professional baseball. Rick Wise was inducted into the State of Oregon Sports Hall of Fame in 1987.

* * *

Dick Groat was a two-sport professional athlete in the 1950s. This was a generation before Deion Sanders went "Prime Time," playing in Major League Baseball and the NFL, and it was decades before Nike launched a "Bo Knows" campaign to showcase Bo Jackson's pro football and baseball abilities. In Groat's case, it was baseball and basketball that he played at the highest level. Groat starred in both sports at Duke University before playing in the pros for the NBA's Pistons and the MLB's Pirates. Groat eventually chose to make his living playing baseball, and he became a five-time National League All-Star. Today,

Groat continues to display passion for his first love—basketball. In 2015-16, Groat will be working his 37th season as a color commentator on broadcasts of University of Pittsburgh men's basketball games.

Like many kids, I collected baseball cards. I can remember, as an eight-year-old child, looking on the back of Dick Groat's 1962 Topps baseball card and reading that Groat had been a basketball star at Duke. I thought it interesting that Groat had been a good basketball player but had become a baseball star. I didn't know that Groat actually played both sports professionally until he was forced to choose one over the other.

As a young Cardinals' fan, I loved Dick Groat. He came to St. Louis in 1963 and was an All-Star for the Cardinals. Obviously, as the Cardinals' starting shortstop, he was a hugely important part of the team during the 1964 championship season. When I talked with Groat in 2012, I was considering the possibility of writing a book to celebrate the 50th anniversary of the Cardinals' 1964 World Series championship. Because of that, I asked Groat several questions about the 1964 season. The book never materialized, but I know baseball fans will enjoy reading what Groat shared with me about the '64 Cardinals.

I spoke with Dick Groat via telephone on February 15, 2012.

I'd like you to think back and recall your very first boyhood. Who would that be?

I guess it would be Ralph Kiner. He was the big gun on the Pirates in those days. We didn't have too many great teams in Pittsburgh back then, but Ralph led the National League in home runs seven consecutive years. He was not just a home run hitter. He hit over .300 a number of times. He was a great hitter. I looked up to him when I was a high school kid, and then I went to Duke. Then, I signed with the Pirates in June of 1952, and they were terrible. We had the most losses in the history of the National League. We had 112 losses that year!

As a rookie, I'm struggling, trying to make it, and Mr. Branch Rickey, Senior was the Pirates' general manager. We were shipping people back and forth to the minor leagues constantly. We were traveling by train in those days. I think it was early September, and we were walking to the train after playing a doubleheader in Busch Stadium in St. Louis. The Pittsburgh Press beat-writer with the Pirates, Les Biederman, said, "Dick, how does it feel to be leading the Pirates in hitting as a rookie?" I said, "I didn't realize I was." He said, "You had a great series here, and you're now leading the Pirates in hitting." That was obviously a tremendous thrill for me. So, we get on the train and get into Chicago. You had to pay your own cab fare from the train station to the hotel. We got to the hotel, and everybody's asking for this room and that room. I couldn't find my name on the rooming list. I said, "Holy mackerel! Don't tell me they sent me back to the minors." Pretty soon, I was the only one in the lobby. The traveling secretary was gone. I said, "I *have* to have a room here." The guy at the hotel finally turned and said, "Oh yeah. Dick Groat?" I said, "Yes." He said, "The room list says 'Kiner and Groat. Air-conditioned, if possible'." I'll never forget that as long as I live. I was in awe of Kiner. Now, I want to go up and go to bed because I don't sleep well on a train. Ralph went out for breakfast, and I didn't know which bed to take. I just sat around until he came in. He couldn't have been more wonderful and more friendly, just a first class gentleman in every way. But, I was really intimidated that first morning. I roomed with him the rest of the season. Having looked up to him in high school, rooming with him my rookie year was really special.

It's like I've told so many people that have kidded me about how bad that 1952 team was, "You don't understand. The only difference between you people and me is the fact that I was lucky enough to live the dream that we all had growing up. Every kid wanted to be a major league baseball player back in those days. As bad as we were, to be able to room with Ralph Kiner my rookie year, every day going to the ballpark was like Christmas morning to me.

When you were starring in the major leagues with the Pirates and Cardinals, you were idolized by many young fans. Did you ever think about that?

Really, I never did. Somebody mentioned this to me when I was in Durham the last time I was there. I had a knee that was cut from diving on the floor for the ball, so I wore a knee pad my junior year. I never realized it at the time, but they told me that half the guards in North Carolina high schools started wearing one knee guard.

My first love was always basketball. Bob Cousy was the guy I looked up to because he was the premier guard in all of basketball. I was a much better basketball player than I ever was a baseball player. I've always considered myself a retired basketball player. I loved the NBA back then. I hate it now. Trying to watch it, it's just not a pure type of basketball. Today, it's all strength and muscle. Players can carry the ball and walk with it. To me, they're the greatest athletes in sports. But, as great a talent as the NBA athlete is, I'd much rather watch a college basketball game than a pro game.

People didn't know, but I wanted to go back to play in the NBA. People don't realize this, but I was making twice as much money in basketball as I was in baseball. I didn't go to baseball for the money. It was for the longevity. Plus, I had signed a bonus contract with the Pirates in 1952 that was spread over five years. When I came back from Philadelphia in 1955 after coming out of the service, I had my contract to go back to the Pistons, again for more money than I was making in baseball. I said, "I can't sign this until I talk to Mr. Rickey." He had treated me extremely well, and I owed him to at least tell him I wanted to go back to basketball for another year or two. Mr. Rickey had no sense of humor about my going back to basketball. He just said, "The human body can't take that kind of beating." He was all prepared for this discussion because I said to him, "Gene Conley does it." He said, "That's not even a fair comparison, Dick. You're playing 150 games at shortstop, and you're a starting point guard. He's a pitcher and a backup center." He had all the cards in his deck. And, of course, my father would not allow me to break a contract.

In 1963, you played with my first sports hero, Stan Musial. It was your first season with the Cardinals and Stan's last season as a player. Tell me. Did I have a good guy as my idol?

You had the *best*. Stan Musial was the class of baseball players in every possible way. I was thrilled to death to have the honor of hitting in front of him the entire season in 1963. It dawned on me many, many years later why I had 200 hits—the best year I ever had in baseball. Who was going to walk me to get to Stan Musial? I got the best balls to hit all year long. I had 201 hits. It was the only time in my career I had 200 hits in a season. He's not only one of the great, great hitters of all time, but one of the great people ever to play the game of baseball.

You were the starting shortstop on the 1964 Cardinal team that stormed from behind in the final weeks of the season to win the National League pennant, and eventually, the World Series. One of the chief reasons the Cardinals were able to come back and edge the Phillies and Reds on the final day of the season was the June 15 acquisition of the Cubs' Lou Brock—another of my boyhood idols. One of the Cardinals' top pitchers, Ernie Broglio, was sent to Chicago for Brock. Dick, I've heard that some of the Cardinals' players didn't like that trade because Broglio had won 18 games for St. Louis in '63 and 21 games three years before that. It was a controversial trade at the time, wasn't it?

Very much so. When they made the deal, we players thought it was a bad deal. But, Lou did a magnificent job for us.

Brock caught fire. He had 33 steals and batted .348 after joining the Cardinals. You guys needed that because you were 11 games out on August 23rd and still 6½ games behind the Phillies on September

20ᵗʰ with only 12 to play. Did you think you still had a shot at the pennant?

Very much so, believe it or not. Bing Devine—who I just think the world of—was the general manager and made the trade for me. Then, I was able to convince him to buy Bob Skinner from Cincinnati. Skinner and I roomed together, and, of course, we'd been together with the Pirates, too. I can remember "Skins" and I livin' and dyin' coming down the stretch of the season. We were in New York to play the Mets two games. We figured we'd sweep the Mets, and then we had to go into Pittsburgh. Bob and I were convinced that we would win four out of five there and then play the Phillies at home with only six games remaining. Well, a guy by the name of Galen Cisco beat us in New York the second game of that two-game series, two to one. He really pitched a fine game. I remember getting on the bus and sitting down next to my roommate. Bob Skinner leaned over very quietly, and he said, "We need *five* in Pittsburgh now." (Laughs) And, we got all five!

After the Cardinals swept five from the Pirates, the team returned to St. Louis and won three straight from the Phillies to extend Philadelphia's losing streak to 10 games. The Cards moved into first place, 1 game ahead of Cincinnati and 2½ games ahead of Philadelphia. The Cardinals had only three games left—all against the Mets, who lost 109 games that year. But, New York won the first two games of the series to make it very interesting. The Cardinals, though, beat the Mets 11-5 in the regular season finale to avoid a three-way tie with the Phillies and Reds. St. Louis finished one game ahead of both Philadelphia and Cincinnati. What an amazing pennant race that was in 1964!

The Phillies kept stumbling and stumbling and stumbling. On Friday night the last weekend of the season, the Mets' little Alvin Jackson beat us in a very, very good ballgame. It was a one-nothing ballgame, and he beat Bob Gibson. I remember this so vividly. Joe Christopher was a teammate of mine on the 1960 Pirates. I came up with the bases loaded, and he's playing right-field for the Mets. I hit a line drive that would have been a double any other time because it was right on the line. But, Joe Christopher was standing there and made the catch. He was quoted in the newspapers the next day, "I played with Dick Groat. I know he goes to right field when he needs a big hit." It wasn't funny to me then, but it is now.

I never knew until years later that they had already set it up that if it worked out that way—in a three-way tie—we were going to have to fly that night to Cincinnati and play the Reds the next day. The winner would then play Philadelphia the *following* day. I never knew it. None of us were packed. We had no thoughts of going to Cincinnati or Philadelphia.

So, you won the pennant on the final day of the season, and then beat the Yankees in a seven-game World Series. The Yankees were an aging team, but they still had Mickey Mantle, Roger Maris, Whitey Ford and several other stars. Were the 1964 Cardinals as special to you as your 1960 Pirates?

The '60 Pirates had pretty much grown up together through the years where we finished last for three or four years. We *grew* together. The Cardinals just *meshed* very, very well. Part of the deal when I flew to St. Louis to sign my first contract was for me to make Julian Javier a better second baseman. He and I spent an awful lot of time at Al Lang Field where the Cardinals trained. There was an infield way out in left field, and every day we spent a half-hour to an hour working together. I was forcing him to go further toward first base when the double-play was in order—convincing him how quickly he could get to second base. He used to cheat toward second, and I kept saying, "Hoolie, you can't open that hole any wider with a man on first base. You have to plug that hole." In my opinion, he became as good a second baseman as there was—except for Bill Mazeroski, who was in a world all his own.

You played with a couple of outstanding second basemen, didn't you?

I was lucky. I had Javier and Mazeroski at second and Ken Boyer and Don Hoak at third. I had people surrounding me that could really play.

Do you stay in touch with your 1964 Cardinals' teammates?

It actually started in '63 and carried over into '64. Once you go through a pennant race with a team, those friendships last forever. There's a bond, especially when you go on and win it. Like the '60 Pirate team, all of us were very close. We still are. And, every time I've gone back to a reunion with the '64 Cardinal team, I have the same feeling about the guys like Curt Simmons, Bob Skinner and Ken Boyer—until Ken passed away. We have always remained very, very good friends. There's a closeness that never goes away once you fight for a pennant and win it. You're livin' under tension. You're livin' on coffee, and you can't even light cigarettes and the whole bit during the tension of a pennant race.

Dick, I was a 10-year-old fan of the Cardinals when St. Louis won the 1964 World Series. I'd like to thank you for all the memories.

I appreciate it. It's kind of a special day for me in realizing how old I am today. I became a great-grandfather for the first time today. It's a big day. Thank God both the mother and the daughter are doing fine.

Career Notes: Dick Groat still ranks in the top 20 on Duke's career scoring list and still holds the Cameron Indoor Stadium record for most points in a game (48). At Duke University in the early 1950s, the five-eleven point guard was twice named Outstanding Athlete of the Year in the Southern Conference. In 1951-52, after Groat averaged 26 points per game, he was named the National College Player of the Year by both United Press International and the Helms Athletic Foundation. On May 1, 1952, Groat's number 10 was the first basketball jersey to be retired by Duke. On Duke's diamond, Groat earned All-Southern Conference honors in 1951 and 1952. The 1952 Blue Devils went 31-7, the first 30 win season in school history. Duke would not have another 30 win season for 40 years. Groat led the Blue Devils to the

1952 College World Series, the first of only three trips the school has ever made to Omaha. While at Duke, Groat was twice recognized as an All-American in both basketball and baseball. He later became the first player to be inducted into *both* the College Basketball Hall of Fame and the College Baseball Hall of Fame.

Groat was the third overall pick in the 1952 NBA Draft. He played one season for the Fort Wayne Pistons, but—after spending two years in the military—was then forced by his baseball boss, Branch Rickey, to choose between a career in basketball or baseball. Committing fulltime to baseball, Groat played a total of 14 years in the majors with the Pirates, Cardinals, Phillies and Giants. He had a lifetime batting average of .286. Groat had his best years with the Pirates and Cardinals. With Pittsburgh, he was voted the 1960 Most Valuable Player in the National League after leading the league with a .325 batting average. That year, Groat's hometown Pirates beat the Yankees in the World Series when Bill Mazeroski hit a walk-off home run in the bottom of the ninth in Game 7. In 1963, after being traded to St. Louis, Groat led the National League in doubles (42) and batted .315. He finished second to the Dodgers' Sandy Koufax in that year's National League MVP voting. In 1964, Groat batted .292 during the regular season to help the Cardinals win their first pennant in 18 years. Groat earned his second World Series championship ring that year as the Cardinals beat the Yankees in seven games.

*   *   *

22

No One Was Ever As Good

Stan Brock played on the offensive line for 16 years in the National Football League after being picked by the Saints in the first round (#12 overall) of the 1980 NFL Draft. In Brock's rookie season in New Orleans, the Saints' quarterback was Archie Manning—father of current NFL quarterbacks Peyton and Eli.

Born and raised in Portland, Oregon, Brock followed in the footsteps of his older brother, Pete, by attending Jesuit High School and the University of Colorado before moving on to the NFL.

Stan Brock was my broadcasting partner during the Portland Forest Dragons' first season in the Arena Football League. We were having a great time working the games on television, but six games into the season, Stan told me he couldn't work with me anymore. He had sounded so knowledgeable working as a TV analyst that the team owner decided to make a coaching change. Head coach/GM Don Frease would no longer coach the team. Stan Brock was moved from the TV booth down to the field to be the new head coach. I mourned the loss of my partner because, frankly, Stan was very enthusiastic and a darned good analyst. Also, he was fun to be around. Stan Brock loves to tell a great story, and as you'll soon see, he didn't disappoint when I asked him about his childhood heroes. I talked by phone with Stan Brock on January 20, 2014.

Who was your first boyhood idol? Do you recall?

Yeah, I have a great recollection. Jerry Kramer. I knew he was from this area, and he played for the Green Bay Packers. Remember, back then you didn't have a thousand channels to watch football. But, Jerry Kramer would be the guy that would be my first idol.

You always thought you were going to be an offensive lineman? That's why Kramer was your guy?

I told my eighth-grade teacher that I was going to play in the NFL. What a stupid statement. But, it's just one of those deals where that's kind of what you think you're going to do. But, I never got to see Jerry Kramer. I never got to be around him. It was just that my dad and my brothers would talk about him. I didn't really know him. So, my true idols—who I thought were *the* greatest football players that ever played the game—were the guys that played at Jesuit High School in '67 and '68. I remember going to the games. I remember the players' names. Brian Doherty one time shot me a wrist band after a state championship game, and I put it in my scrapbook. I still have it.

There were guys like Joe McDonnell and his brother Chris McDonnell. I remember Joe McDonnell in the state championship game against Marshfield in 1968. I remember him kicking a field goal attempt. He got hit on the knee and broke his leg. I remember that. I remember I thought those guys were *the* greatest football players there have ever been because I was only 10 years old.

Then, my older brother, Pete, who is four years older than me, goes to Jesuit High School, and now he's playing at Jesuit. I'm like, "Oh, my God!" To me, it was like he was in the NFL. He was playing with the very best people in the world. Then, I got to meet and shake hands with Greg Bauer and Kevin Doherty and the guys in Pete's class. Honestly, those guys were my idols. Those were my heroes. In fact, even when I got to Jesuit, I never felt like I was as good as those guys. Those guys *had* to be so much better than me because there's no way they were playing the same game that I'm playing.

I get to see them today, and I have told them. I talk about it; I talked about it when we went to the Super Bowl. Somebody called and asked, you know, "Who were your idols?" *Those* guys truly were. I idolized them. I followed them. I made posters. I stayed around so I could see them after games. It's incredible. If they played with Jerry Kramer and the Green Bay Packers, they wouldn't have made any bigger of an impression on me.

You mentioned several Jesuit High School players. Did one or two stand out, or was it the whole group that you idolized?

It was the whole team. It was Jesuit High School and that group of guys and those players. The uncle of one of my very best grade school friends was Steve Barsotti. Barsotti was one of the Jesuit players. Sometimes I would get to see him and be close to him when he walked by. They were all *huge* in my book.

You are now all adults, and you've told them how you felt about them when you were 10 years old. How did they react?

It's kind of cool because they are honored. I've gone through now and played in the NFL, and then you talk to these guys. I told Brian Doherty that I still have his sweatband. They make me feel really good in that they're honored to have had that kind of an influence on a little kid.

Was Pete one of your idols, or did you just consider him an older brother?

As I said, he's four years older than I am, so when I was in eighth grade, he was a senior. He was an All-American as a senior. But, let's back up. So, I'm in sixth or seventh grade when he is starting on the Jesuit varsity team. He's starting on the same team—on the same field—that these guys who were my ultra-idols were playing. I'm like, "Oh, my God! My brother must be just the freakin' best thing in the world." I would go and watch practice. I would go during two-a-days and watch them practice and sit on the hill at Jesuit just so that I could see these guys and so that they could see me. And, once in a while, they would say hello to me. So, yes, my brother Pete was definitely in that same group.

Did it ever dawn on you when you were at Jesuit that you might have been an idol for little kids just like Pete and his teammates were for you?

No. Never. Never crossed my mind. Never ever. I always felt like those guys were so much better than we were, you know, better than *I* was. I can figure it out now, but I didn't have it figured out then. The same thing was true even when it came to the NFL. Again, my brother was four years older, so when I was a freshman in college, he was a rookie in the NFL. I was like, "Man, that guy's gotta be awesome." Then, by the time I'm a rookie in the NFL, I'm like, "Huh? *I'm* playing. It must not be that hard." (Laughs) That really wasn't my thought, but you get things built up in your mind—especially as a younger kid—and I just was absolutely enamored by those guys.

You broke into the NFL with the Saints. The first quarterback you're trying to protect is Archie Manning.

Yeah, and I'm lining up and playing against Jack Youngblood. I remember watching Jack Youngblood play when I was in grade school and high school, and I'm gonna line up and play against this guy! Then there's Archie Manning. I remember getting drafted and calling him *Mister* Manning and saying, "Yes sir. No sir." To me, he'd already been there and done that. So, those guys, now, that's a *different* group of idols once I got up to the NFL and played.

When I got in there with the Saints, they just automatically made me the starter my rookie year. I didn't earn it. They just made me the starter. There were older guys that played for the Saints. A bunch of them had played eight, nine, ten years. I thought those guys were just incredible football players to have played that long and be that disciplined. But, it still was not like my childhood idols. I really believed that if Steve Barsotti, Joe McDonnell, Chris McDonnell and those Jesuit guys played against these NFL guys, they would have killed them because to me they were Superman. You know, when you're little, your *dad* is Superman? No one can beat him up. That's how I felt about those guys. No one was ever as good as those guys.

You and Pete went into the Oregon Sports Hall of Fame together in 2009. I know the whole Brock family attended the induction ceremony. That had to be special for your entire family.

Yeah, that was awesome. To get to go in with my older brother was very, very special. I lost my dad last year, so for both Mom and Dad to be there was great. At the time, you don't really appreciate everything, but it was very special. I have two other brothers, Willie and Ray, who played—or went to training camp—in the National Football League. They were there that night. And, one of our brothers, Joe, was born with a mental handicap and is probably the most special of all of us. He's overcome things every day in his life that you and I take for granted, and he does it with a smile on his face and strength in his heart. So, that was very cool to have him there. My sisters were all there. It's fun being around them. We have a very cool, unique family dynamic in that we're all still very, very close. We talk all the time, and we share our ups and downs.

We talked earlier about Archie Manning. Did the Manning children spend a lot of time around the Saints when you were there?

Now, they were little. Eli wasn't even born when I first got there, but Cooper and Peyton were young boys. Archie didn't fish a lot, and he asked me if I would take his boys to go fishing. We were at this pond in Louisiana, and we weren't catching any fish. I had an old beat-up Chevy Blazer. I took the boys, Cooper and Peyton, and put them in my truck and pushed the seat all the way forward. I put some jackets and stuff behind them. I showed them, "This is forward. This is reverse.

That's the brake pedal. That's the gas pedal. Don't leave the property. Don't go through any gates." We're on this big ranch. This is 6,000 acres of a fenced-in place. They take off and go have some fun. They were probably 10 or 12 at the time—if they're even that old. They bring it back, and it's full of mud. They found the mud hole and just had a great time. So, I've always told people that I taught Peyton how to drive. I never talked to Peyton about it or anything. Then, just a few years ago when I was at West Point, a friend of mine was playing at a golf tournament in Florida, and Peyton was standing there in front of him. And, from behind Peyton, my friend said, "I know the guy who taught you how to drive." Peyton turned around and said, "Well, you gotta be talkin' about Stan Brock." That just kind of verified my story. Now I tell it a lot more often with greater confidence than I ever did before. I didn't know if he really remembered it or not.

But, you know, Archie took me under his wing my rookie year. Like I said, they just made me the starting right tackle the first day of training camp. I started and played every game after that. Archie really took me under his wing and taught me to go to the stadium early. He taught me how to get ready for a game and really took care of me. I have a great deal of respect for him and his family.

Career Notes: During Stan Brock's 13 years (1980–92) in New Orleans, the Saints reached the NFL playoffs four times (1987, 1990–92). He is a member of the Saints' Hall of Fame. Brock played for the Chargers from 1993–95 and helped San Diego reach the Super Bowl for the first time following the 1994 season. Brock was San Diego's team captain and called the coin toss for the Chargers in Super Bowl 29 in Miami. Since his playing days ended, Brock has dabbled in broadcasting and has coached football in college and the pros. He was head coach of the Arena Football League's Portland Forest Dragons for 2½ seasons (1997–99) and the AFL's Los Angeles Avengers for a year and a half (2000-01). Brock served as offensive line coach at the United States Military Academy for four years. Then, in January of 2007, he was promoted to head coach at West Point following the resignation of

Bobby Ross. Brock's Army teams struggled, going 3-9 in each of his two seasons, and he was dismissed as head coach in December, 2008.

*   *   *

Pete Brock played all 12 years of his NFL career with the New England Patriots. After a standout career at Jesuit High School in Portland, Oregon, Brock played at the University of Colorado and was recognized as a college football All-American in 1975. Soon thereafter, he became the first of three Brock brothers to play in the National Football League. The Patriots selected him 12th overall in the 1976 NFL Draft.

When I arrived in Portland as a television sportscaster in 1980, I quickly learned that the Brock boys from Jesuit were somebody that I needed to talk about on the air whenever they did something notable in their NFL games. They were well-known throughout the area. Now, both Pete and Stan were offensive linemen, so it wasn't easy finding highlights of either of them to air on my local sportscasts. When the Patriots were televised, I made sure to record the game in hopes of seeing a great block by Pete Brock that would spring Grogan for a touchdown. When that happened, I would show highlights of the Patriots' score and point out the blocking of "Portland's Pete Brock" as one of the reasons the play worked. Hey, I was just doing what I learned in journalism school—localize the story! In this example, it wasn't so much that Grogan had scored a touchdown, but our local guy, Pete Brock, had thrown the key block. I hope Pete appreciated my efforts. I interviewed Pete Brock by phone on April 7, 2015.

Thinking back to your earliest days, can you name your first boyhood idol?

I'd have to say Jerry Kramer was my first boyhood idol. It was in the late Sixties, like '66 or '67. The Lombardi Packers had won another World Championship, and he wrote that book, *Instant Replay*. I was in the sixth or seventh grade, and I wanted to play professional football. I was a huge Packer fan when they won the championship. Then, I had a chance to read his book and discovered that he was from Pocatello, Idaho. I thought, "Boy, if somebody else from the Northwest can make it to that level, maybe I can too."

Did you know that you wanted to be an offensive lineman at that point of your life?

Well, I wasn't gonna be a quarterback or a running back. I was pretty large at that age. In fact, the first step towards my NFL career was to go out for football for Beaverton Pop Warner. In the seventh grade, I was told I was too big to play. I weighed 175 pounds, and they had a 150 pound weight limit. So, I couldn't play football until I was a freshman at Jesuit.

I believe Jerry Kramer was retired by the time you reached the NFL, so you never got a chance to play against him, did you?

No, he had retired. I did have an opportunity to tell him he was my boyhood idol. There was an NBA versus the NFL Golf Tournament in Portland. They played it one year at the Oregon Country Club and another year at Lake Oswego Country Club. It was former NFL players against former NBA players. I pulled into the parking lot. There was a Suburban with Idaho plates on it. As I was getting my clubs out, I looked over. It was Jerry Kramer. I told him that story, and he got a big kick out of it.

At that point, you were both adults, so what was it like for you to have the opportunity to tell him how you felt about him?

Oh, it was absolutely thrilling to meet a guy who had played at that level. People still mystify that whole Lombardi era with the Packers and what they were able to accomplish. So, yeah, it was a thrill to meet him.

The Patriots became a successful NFL team shortly after your arrival. They had an outstanding offensive line anchored by you

and Hall of Famer John Hannah. What did it mean to you to be part of that group?

Well, it was terrific. Actually, when I broke in with the Patriots in 1976, I didn't have a starting spot waiting for me, but I played all the positions up and down the line of scrimmage, including tight end and wing-back in goal line and short yardage situations. In '76, we set an NFL team rushing record that existed until '78—when we broke it again. We averaged nearly 200 rushing yards a game over the course of 16 weeks and rushed for a single season team rushing record. We only had Sam Cunningham as a thousand-yard rusher, but we had a handful of them at six- and seven-hundred yards, including Steve Grogan. It was a tribute to the offensive line that I played on '76 through '78—and a dedication to the running game—that really made us a spectacular football team. You had Grogan throwing touchdown passes quite steadily to Stanley Morgan and guys like that. We had a pretty prolific offense, and it was all set up with the running game. That was a lot of fun to be part of.

When you played at Jesuit High School, the University of Colorado, and for the Patriots, you had many young boys watching you and aspiring to be like you. Did it ever dawn on you that roles had been reversed and now *you* were the person being idolized the way you once idolized Jerry Kramer?

No, not to the extent that I put myself up on a pedestal. But, knowing that maybe I was a role model for a kid, I wanted to make sure that I worked hard. If somebody wanted to say, "Okay, I want to be like that," then I wanted to make sure that my performance on Sunday—and the way that I acted during the week—was something that they could look at as a model. It wasn't something I thought of, "Okay, now you've attained this success. You're somebody's role model." That never really crossed my mind, other than the fact that I had a responsibility to my profession, myself, my family and everybody watching me, to do it the right way.

You mentioned your family. Younger brother, Stan, told me that you and your Jesuit High School teammates were his some of his boyhood heroes. Did you realize that?

Yeah, I knew. He was around all the time. Stan and I were always four years apart. When I went to Jesuit, he was playing Pop Warner football. Then, when he went to Jesuit, I was playing in college. Then, when he was in college, I was in the pros. There was always that four year gap between us. I knew he looked up to us. We had a terrific high school football team. Stan was our ball boy. He came out at practice and watched us do all kinds of things. He saw Greg Bauer and Kevin Doherty and Tom Wynne and those guys that were on those teams with me. Greg Bauer was the running back. He went on to have a great college career at the University of Oregon as a wide receiver. Greg rushed for almost 2,000 yards our senior year at Jesuit. He was a terrific football player and a great basketball player. Kevin Doherty was our quarterback. Tom Wynne was the tight end on my team.

Now, Jerry Kramer is one thing, but, quite honestly, the guys on the '67 and '68 football teams that won those two state championships were very special to me. Seeing Mike McMenamin, Gary Geiger, and Joe McDonnell and those guys playing offensive line, and then being state champions walking around with the yellow "state-championship" footballs sewn on their Jesuit letterman coats, you know, *those* are the guys I could see day to day and look up to. So, I understand why Stan says the same thing about *my* class that was four years earlier than his entry to Jesuit. That was a terrific football team that won state in '68. Because of those guys, there was no way I was going anywhere other than Jesuit, so it doesn't surprise me that Stan says the same thing about the team that was going to Jesuit four years ahead of him.

Career Notes: A standout offensive lineman, Pete Brock helped the Patriots reach the Super Bowl after the 1985 season but was disappointed when the Pats lost to the Bears 46-10 in Super Bowl 20. Brock was the Pats' starting center most of his career. Quarterback Steve Grogan set a number of Patriots' offensive records during that period of time, thanks to the protection he received from New England's O-line. Although primarily a center, the versatile Brock played every position on the offensive line at some point in his career. Pete Brock is currently the president of the New England Patriots Alumni Association. A member of the Patriots' Hall of Fame, he has also been involved in Patriots' game-day broadcasts.

* * *

23

Clyde

Walt "Clyde" Frazier was one of the NBA's biggest stars in the 1960s and '70s. The 6-foot-4 guard played ten years with the Knicks and parts of three seasons with the Cavaliers. The seven-time All-Star led New York to a pair of NBA championships (1970, 1973). Frazier began working as an analyst on Knicks broadcasts in 1989. He continues to work as a color commentator on Knicks' telecasts.

While Frazier had many memorable performances, perhaps his best came in Game 7 of the 1970 NBA Finals against the Lakers. The game is best-remembered for the heroic effort of center Willis Reed, who limped onto the court at Madison Square Garden and scored the first two New York baskets of the game after he had been injured in Game 5 and sat out Game 6. Facing a Lakers' team that featured Hall of Famers Wilt Chamberlain, Jerry West and Elgin Baylor, the inspired Knicks would win the game—and the championship—thanks to the play of Frazier. In one of the great Game 7 performances in NBA Finals history, Frazier had 36 points, 19 assists, 7 rebounds and 5 steals.

Nicknamed "Clyde" shortly after the release of the movie, Bonnie and Clyde (for reasons to be explained shortly), Frazier has earned a reputation for wearing stylish clothes, which often features fancy hats and fur coats. Frazier was one of the first athletes to be paid to wear a basketball shoe—a suede Puma sneaker.

I spoke with Walt Frazier by telephone on December 19, 2014.

Who was your first boyhood idol?

Growing up in the South, my first idols were guys in the high school—not necessarily professional players—because when I was growing up we didn't have professional players in my town. We didn't have ESPN and all that type of stuff. (Laughs)

We probably all felt that way, didn't we? When we were in grade school, those high school athletes meant a lot to us.

Yeah. My uncle was a few years older than me, so I used to follow him around to the football and basketball games. The different players on his team and my team were arch-rivals, so I used to be so perplexed. When they played, I didn't want either team to lose. I hoped they'd tie. (Laughs) I used to hang out with his players because he was like the trainer. Certain guys I admired. Some of them were defensive backs or running backs.

I was always a big football fan. I used to watch the Baltimore Colts with Johnny Unitas, Lenny Moore and Raymond Berry. I guess Johnny U. was my idol because I was a quarterback in high school. I used to try to play like him and throw the bomb. I was a good passer. So, other than the high school guys, Johnny Unitas was probably the first guy I really emulated.

Did you ever get a chance to meet Johnny Unitas?

Yeah! Yeah, I did. I actually got an autograph on a football from him. A very funny guy—he was real funny in person. I was in my 40s—maybe 45. I told him that I used to follow him and that I used to idolize him. I told him that I followed him and Lenny Moore and Big Daddy Lipscomb and that whole team. They were like our hometown team in Atlanta. So, those were the guys we kind of idolized growing up because we saw them on TV.

Even though you were an adult, were you star-struck when you met Unitas?

I grew up quiet and shy, so I kind of admired people from a distance. Even when I was around celebrities, I never would just go up and approach them. I'd kind of stand back and admire them. Maybe somebody would introduce us. I was always kind of that way even when I was in the NBA. When I made the All-Star teams, I'd do the same thing in the locker room. I'd watch Wilt Chamberlain. I'd watch Oscar Robertson and Bill Russell. I wouldn't be saying anything. I'd just be all eyes and ears, you know, watching them and listening to them. If they said something to me, I'd say something. But, other than that, I didn't really say anything.

Clyde, several former NBA players have told me you were their boyhood idol. Derek Harper says he patterned his game after you. Doug Collins and Mike Glenn told me they idolized you. When these players, who were outstanding players in their own right, say that you inspired them, how does that make you feel?

It's very humbling, man. I just saw Harp the other day because we played Dallas, and he was saying all of that. It was surprising because he actually played with the Knicks but he never articulated that to me. I guess it was because guys are sometimes overwhelmed when they meet their idols. But, now that he's out of the game, he's speaking freely like that, you know, how he bought a fur coat because of me when he got some money. It's really phenomenal when you hear that guys that are stupendous players in their own right have patterned their game after me. Like Doug Collins—I never knew early on that he grew up in Illinois. He saw me in college when I was playing at Southern Illinois because he's *from* southern Illinois.

Mike Glenn enrolled at Southern Illinois six years after you left Carbondale. He indicated that knowing you had been a Saluki star played a part in his decision to attend SIU.

I never realized that until I read about Mike and he was saying how he saw me play. He was from Atlanta. I was from Atlanta. So, he was happy to be going to SIU. Then, he happened to come to New York to play for the Knicks. It was really funny that he followed me to SIU, then to New York, and then also into broadcasting.

Mike also told me he wore the number 10 jersey at one point in his career because of you, your style and the way you carried yourself on and off the court. Did you ever consider that you were influencing a lot of young people?

Yeah because I used to see guys with the sideburns like me. Remember? I had the mutton chops. I'd see guys with that, and, of course, the "Clyde" hat. When guys were out and about, they tried to be wearing the "Clyde", and stylin' and profilin'. (Laughs) I remember Randy Smith. He was the first Russell Westbrook, man. That guy was so athletic—could run and jump. He bought the Rolls-Royce. He used to idolize me, so he bought a Rolls-Royce. I was pretty cognizant of it because everywhere I went there were a lot of people trying to emulate me—especially in high school. Kids would say, "Oh, they call me 'Clyde'. That's my name, man. My teammates call me Clyde'." They were wearing the Puma sneakers. That was pretty enlightening.

Your off-court style and sense of fashion drew so much attention. Were you always a fancy dresser?

No. In college, I wore the penny loafers and a button-down collar shirt just like everybody else. I used to idolize our coach, Jack Hartman. Hartman was a sharp dresser. Our assistant coach, a guy named Jim Smeltzer, he always wore a fancy tie and stuff like that. But, in college, I never had the money to afford sharp clothes. Now, coming to New York, back in those days everybody wore suits to the game. We used to always try to out-dress each other. We'd wear a shirt and tie because our idols were The Four Tops, The Temptations, Smokey Robinson. Whenever these guys performed, they were dressed up. Like today, the guys idolize the rappers. That's why they dress sort of like the rappers. But, we were all dressed up.

Dick Barnett was one of my idols. I had known about him growing up, when he was at Tennessee State. He was a sharp dresser, so I used to go where he had his suits made. He got his shirts made. So, I used to copy from the other guys. What set me apart was the *hat*. When I was a rookie, I wasn't playing good. In order to pacify myself, I would always go shopping. I'd dress up and go out. Then, I'd go back to my room and say, "Hey, I ain't playing good, but I still *look* good." (Laughs) I was always dressing good, but I wasn't playing good. Then, once I started to play good, they focused on my dress.

I never considered the fact that your stylish wardrobe evolved from a love and respect for what the musicians of the day were wearing.

Basketball has always been synonymous with music. It's cool. You could talk trash. That's what the companies have capitalized on. You see the NBA, you think of rappers now. They've got all the rappers and music. Whenever they play the highlights in the NBA, it's some type of rap music to it. We kind of used more jazz back in the day when we played—Ramsey Lewis, that type of jazz. Soft jazz was the music. Even when Dr. J and Earl the Pearl (Monroe) were doin' their thing, I remember a lot of the stuff they had with them was more like jazz they would have in the background. Today, all the ballplayers want to be rappers. The rappers want to be ballplayers. Most of the time, they don't want to be baseball players or football players. They want to be basketball players 'cause that's the cool thing on the playground. That's kind of how they grew up. That's the embodiment of the game today—how all the kids are into basketball. Look at baseball. Baseball is dying. Black guys rarely play baseball now because of the glamour in the NBA. You can go one-and-done. You can go right from college to the pros, make money and be creative, you know, the style of it all. That's the thing with basketball. You can be very creative. You can be yourself. You can be unorthodox. Whatever type shot you put up, as long as it goes in, that's the only thing that matters.

It's interesting that you earlier mentioned Dick Barnett. Gregg Popovich told me Barnett was one of his idols growing up.

Yeah, man. He was a character. When I came to the Knicks he was maybe eight or nine years older than me. He didn't smoke, didn't drink. He had superb conditioning. He really had an impact on me even to this day. These guys would just take vitamins. They didn't eat red meat. So, the discipline that Dick Barnett had really rubbed off on me. I'm maybe 10 pounds, 12 pounds heavier than when I played, and I haven't played in 35 years. That's pretty incredible.

Willis Reed is another guy who had an impact on me as far as professionalism. I admired the way Willis dealt with the fans. He was always cordial to the fans. Willis Reed has excellent handwriting. If you look at my handwriting, I copied his handwriting. I copied a lot of things from him—especially tenacity on the court, the way he prepared for the game. We had Bill Bradley on the Knicks. I had Bradley to idolize and watch the way he did things. We had guys like Emmette Bryant and Freddie Crawford. Freddie Crawford was a New Yorker. He went to St. Bonaventure. He kind of guided me off the court in New York—where to go, what people to talk to and what people to stay away from. It was a real experience for me being the youngest player at that time to come to the Knicks and having these guys take me under their wing and teach me the ropes of New York City.

When you came into the NBA, you were simply known as Walt Frazier. When did you become "Clyde"?

I was window shopping in Baltimore, and I was looking around at a hat store. I see this Borsalino hat—brown, velour, and it had a wide brim. In those days, like today, everyone was wearing a narrow brim. I put the hat on. Man, I go, "Wow! I look good in this hat." First time

I wore that, everybody laughed at me—my teammates and guys on the other team. So, I go, "Man, they just jealous. I'm gonna keep this hat on." As fate would have it, two weeks later the movie, *Bonnie and Clyde,* comes out. Then, when I wore the hat in the locker room, Knicks trainer Danny Whelan goes, "Hey, everybody! Look at Clyde!" That's how the nickname Clyde developed, you know, from that hat. (Laughs)

Most of my endorsements were dealing with Clyde and the fashion and being *cool*. That became synonymous with me. My alter ego was like, "The Clyde", and then the fur coats, then the Rolls-Royce. So, I was kind of the first guy with bling in the NBA.

When I was in college, I purchased a full-length leather coat with rabbit's fur on the sleeves and collar. Here I was a skinny, white guy wearing a blue leather coat with white fur. Your fashion style had really taken America by storm.

Yeah, I remember some of my friends who were white saying that they were trying to wear the hats. They wore the Pumas. They were nicknamed Clyde and all that stuff. It was really funny because in those days we didn't have the exposure that the guys have today.

You know, we were like the Egyptians, man. We didn't have a model to follow. We were just doin' our thing. I was 25 years old. I was in the greatest city in the world, New York City, and I was just havin' fun. I didn't have a bunch of advisors to sit me down in a room and say, "Hey, man. Go buy a Rolls-Royce. Go buy a fur coat. Go out. Have fun. You know, put on the hat." Nobody told me that. I'd just go shoppin'. Then, I'd go out. I was just doin' my thing and bein' myself. That's how the whole brand started. I created a brand without even trying—or even knowing what that was at the time.

Career Notes: Born and raised in Atlanta, Georgia, Walt Frazier played basketball at Southern Illinois University. He led the Salukis to the 1967 National Invitation Tournament championship. An All-American his senior season at SIU, Frazier was selected by the Knicks with the fifth overall pick in the 1967 NBA Draft. He remained with New York through the 1976-77 campaign and averaged 19.3 points and 6.3 assists as a Knick. While playing for New York, Frazier was named All-NBA First Team four times and NBA All-Defensive First Team seven times. When he left the Big Apple, Frazier was the Knicks' franchise leader in games (759), points (14,617) and assists (4,791). "Clyde" averaged 20.7 points in 93 career playoff games. He was named MVP of the 1975 All-Star Game after scoring 30 points—tops for either team. Frazier was a 1987 inductee into the Naismith Memorial Basketball Hall of Fame. The Knicks retired his jersey (#10) in 1989. His Southern Illinois jersey (#52) has been retired, and he is a member of the Saluki Hall of Fame.

* * *

Derek Harper played 16 years in the NBA, a majority of the time with the Dallas Mavericks. A first-round draft pick out of the University of Illinois in 1983, Harper played his first 10½ seasons with the Mavericks before moving on to play for the Knicks for 2½ seasons. He returned to Dallas before rounding out his career with single seasons in Orlando and with the L.A. Lakers.

I find it a little surprising that the Mavericks have not yet retired Derek Harper's (#12) jersey. He averaged 14.4 points and 5.9 assists in his 12 seasons in Dallas. He was a full-time starter for the Mavs for eight straight seasons. And, in his early years with the team, the Mavericks were pretty good. They made the playoffs six times in Harper's dozen seasons in Dallas. Not long ago, it appeared the Mavericks were making plans to retire Harper's number. In 2013, team owner Mark Cuban said the franchise would be retiring Derek Harper's jersey before the end of the 2013-14 season. However, in March of 2014, word came from the Mavericks that Harper's jersey would not be retired that season. As of August, 2015, Brad Davis and Rolando Blackman remain the only two players to have had their numbers retired by the organization. Even though Harper's number has not been retired, he remains a loyal Mav. He currently works as a color commentator on the Dallas Mavericks' TV broadcasts.

I talked with Derek Harper in Portland, Oregon, on December 7, 2013.

Many of us pretended to be someone when we were kids shooting hoops on the playground on in the driveway. Who was your first boyhood idol?

That's easy for me. It was Walt "Clyde" Frazier, a guy that I've idolized for a long time. As a high school kid, I played in an All-American game that Walt Frazier was at. I shared with him the same sentiments that I'm sharing with you. He's always been a guy that's done it with class. The beauty of what Walt Frazier was as a player is he played both ends of the floor. He's a guy whom after I patterned how I approached the game. I just liked the way he went about his business. He was so cool. You know what I mean?

How was it to meet him for the first time?

I was numb. It was very surreal. He thought I was crazy because here I am an All-American and being honored at an All-American basketball game. I was getting a lot of attention myself. However—when you start talking about watching basketball on CBS on Sundays—I'd watch the Knicks and then run out of the house wearing number 10 on my jersey with "FRAZIER" written on the back. Again, I shared all of those things with him, and he got a kick out of it. But, I was numb—and flabbergasted—about meeting Walt Frazier. I spent a lot of time with him while I was in New York playing for the Knicks for three years. After that, I just felt like I knew the guy. Clyde is so real and down to earth. It was just a lot of fun to be around him. And, the Knicks haven't seen a championship since those days when Frazier played for them.

For you, personally, it had to be pretty cool to be able to spend time with Frazier when you were playing in New York and he was broadcasting the Knicks.

Yeah, it was. It was. I had my whole family up there at the time. My brothers knew the love that I had for him. They really couldn't believe it. When I was in New York, it was Fantasy Island.

Derek, you were a star in the NBA. Did you ever think about the fact that kids were idolizing you the same way you had idolized Walt Frazier?

Oh, no doubt about that. To me, that's the giddiest thing about being a professional. I was fortunate enough to play 16 years in the league. I've never turned down people that asked for my autograph because I'm still honored by that.

You talked about being in the drive, being on the playground and those type things. You dream, and you dream of one day being there. When it actually happens, it's a blessing, something that you carry with you for the rest of your life.

And, I know that for a time, you emulated the way "Clyde" Frazier dressed and sported a nice wardrobe. Do you still wear stylish clothes?

You know what? Yeah, I do. Not quite like Clyde, but I do my own version of what Clyde is because nobody does it the way Clyde does it. I think the way that he does it really lets you know how comfortable he is in his skin. He's very comfortable in his skin. He can do it. He can pull it off. I can't. I have to keep it basic and be dressed like I am tonight.

Career Notes: In his pro career, Derek Harper averaged 13.3 points and 5.5 assists in 1,199 games. The six-four guard scored 16,006 career points and averaged at least 9.9 points in each of his 16 years in the NBA. An outstanding defender, Harper twice was named to the NBA's

All-Defensive Second Team. Only a handful of NBA players have recorded more career steals than Harper. One of the best players never to have been selected as an All-Star, Harper did play in ten NBA postseasons. In the 1994 NBA Finals, he averaged 11.4 points for the Knicks in a series that New York lost to Houston in seven games.

* * *

24

On The Top Of Pikes Peak

Bobby Unser won the Indianapolis 500 three times and did so in three different decades (1968, 1975, 1981). Bobby is the older brother of four-time Indy 500 winner Al Unser and the uncle of two-time Indy 500 champion Al Unser, Jr. The Unser family's nine Indy 500 victories are the most of any racing family. Bobby, Al, and Al Junior have each been inducted into various racing Halls of Fame.

Bobby Unser was a racing commentator on ABC television for many years and was part of the network's award-winning coverage of Indy Car racing.

I knew Bobby Unser loved to talk. I watched him for years when he was working on TV as a racing commentator. Bobby always seemed to have the gift of gab. Oh, yes, Bobby can talk. A great majority of the interviews I conducted for this book were completed in ten minutes or less. Even though I would have loved to talk longer with each of the athletes, I wanted to be respectful of their time. When I connected with Bobby, the interview lasted an hour. I didn't ask Bobby that many more questions. He just enjoyed talking about racing and about the people involved in racing. Several times, I told him we could end the interview because I knew I had taken far more of his time than we had originally planned. He said, "No, I don't mind. It's just racin'. Let's just keep goin'." Can you imagine being in my position? I was in heaven! I remember Bobby winning those three Indy 500s and later watching him broadcast races. I wouldn't have run out of things to talk about with him if I spent a week with him in Albuquerque. I talked with

Bobby just a few days before I connected with Al and three months before I caught up with "Little Al." I telephoned Bobby Unser on October 2, 2013.

Can you remember your boyhood idol?

Oh, for sure. But, I wouldn't have just one or two. When I was really young, I wanted to be a race driver. So, I used to get the cards from Indianapolis drivers and Pikes Peak drivers. They were my heroes. We used to get little cards. Today you would call them baseball cards. They were just pictures of Indianapolis cars and drivers. Somehow or another we got them when we were young kids. You'd pick out a car that you liked—like the Blue Crown Special—and you'd see what drivers drove it. Maybe you'd like the driver—Maury Rose or Bill Holland. Of course, when I was really young, I didn't meet hardly any of them. I didn't meet them until later on in life. But, the drivers that became the guys that I worshipped in a lot of ways were the ones I met. My Uncle Louie (nine-time winner of the Pikes Peak International Hill Climb, Louis Unser, Jr.) was a big hero of mine. He was the reason I decided when I was very young that I was gonna win Pikes Peak more than he did. It wasn't because I disliked him. Lord only knows, he was my *hero*. He was a hero for all four of us kids. He was bigger than life itself. My dad had raced Pikes Peak a number of times, and, of course, my Uncle Joe did, also. Uncle Joe got killed in a race car preparing to go to Indianapolis. We never knew him, and our parents just never talked much about Uncle Joe.

I know you started racing at a young age, and I've heard that you got to meet some of the drivers of that era as they passed through town. Tell me about that.

I started racing when I was awfully young—15 years of age. I was racing against grown men. We didn't have go-karts to learn by. You'd drive your shop-trucks or whatever. That's good training. But, I started racing at 15. At 16, I won a whole Southwestern championship for the Supermodifieds. In those days, drivers didn't fly around the United

States. Flying wasn't that easy to do, and airlines didn't go into that many places. So, they all drove from race to race.

Every year, Tony Bettenhausen would buy a new Cadillac He lived in California, and whenever he'd go back East to race—or when he'd head home to California—he would always stop by. We had a gas station and a garage repair station in Albuquerque on Highway 66. All the racers went by here at one time or another. You *had* to because you couldn't fly. The racetracks were not where they had commercial airlines in those days. We were on Highway 66. That was the only road that went across the United States—California to Chicago. They would all stop by and gas up here because they knew my dad from racing. They knew the Unsers—like Uncle Louie—from Pikes Peak. They knew that we were a racing family and that we were on Highway 66 on the outskirts of Albuquerque, New Mexico. It turned out that went on for many years. As long as I raced, we used to house drivers here. They could stop and get a little sleep and a shower and things like that. So, they all went by car from race to race.

Tony Bettenhausen was the one that took the most interest in me. He would always make sure that he stayed the night in Albuquerque. You gotta remember, for that day and time, he was a very successful human being and known throughout the world for automobile racing. I was maybe 13 or 14, so to me it was a big deal. He'd pull up and buy gasoline for his Cadillac and then ask if I wanted to go to dinner with him that night. I mean, that's a *big* freakin' deal. Besides that, he was one of the fastest drivers going in those days. So, he became very much a hero without me knowing all that much about him and without me being very old. Why Tony Bettenhausen selected me, I have no idea. Somehow, that man knew that Bobby Unser was going to be a real race driver someday. He saw something in me that I didn't see.

I have to think it was pretty amazing to get the chance to go to dinner with Tony Bettenhausen.

Oh, absolutely. I mean, God—to go to dinner with Tony and his wife—I would always just wonder, "Why is he doing this? I'm as much of a *nothing* as I could ever believe." I thought to myself, "You haven't accomplished anything in life except pump gas and grease cars and fix flat tires." (Laughs) The thing about Tony was Tony got the ink. Tony was a fast race driver. Tony, of course, later got himself killed at Indianapolis. I just couldn't believe that.

I was going to ask how you handled his tragic death in 1961 at Indy.

You know, really hard. But, how would a young kid take it? If something bad is going to happen in your life, better it happens when you're young because you're bulletproof. You can absorb anything, do anything. Nobody can hurt you. You never get sick, you know? All those good things happen to young kids. But, I was very sad and, for sure, read a lot of newspapers about it. It was just sad.

Bobby, did you have any other drivers that you looked up to?

If you had to rate them, there was a guy after Tony named Troy Ruttman. I was a little older then, but Troy took me under his wing. To this day, I don't know why, except he and my brother were extremely close friends. Both of them drove for Ford Motor Company at the same time in the stock cars. Troy became a giant hero of mine. Troy kind of inherited me for a little while. He did a lot of nice things for me. He found race cars for me to drive, and if I didn't have enough money to get there to the next race, he'd help me with it. He did things like that. He always paid the bills because I didn't have any money. We went to eat and he'd always pay the bill. I couldn't understand why he would do so much to help me out, but he did. It lasted years.

You were an idol for a lot of young racing fans when you were driving. Did you ever think about that?

Oh, I damn sure did. (Laughs) I raced professionally for 35 years to make a living. That's a long time. Basically, I'd guess about 80 to 90 percent of the charities that I do work for today have to be for kids. If somebody calls and offers me something for pay, money doesn't make that much difference to me. I'd rather do something for kids. We do a fair amount each year, and it's all because of Tony Bettenhausen and the drivers who used to come through Albuquerque.

I hear that you found another way to give back to racing for all the kindness you had received from people like Bettenhausen and Ruttman.

When I got a little older and built my first house, I built another room on it—a big room. I opened my house to a lot of race drivers—more for the ones that couldn't afford a hotel or a motel. I had a couch in there that made into a queen-sized bed. It always had clean sheets and clean pillowcases on it, so a lot of the drivers—midget drivers, sprint car drivers, a lot of those guys during that era—if they traveled Highway 66, they had to go by our house. I never had locks on the doors. A guy hauling through with midgets, he's not making much money at all. He knew that he could go through Albuquerque, and if the room was vacant, they could stay at our house. They wouldn't wake me up. They'd just get some rest and take a shower. We asked, "Leave the place clean. We'll change the sheets and the pillowcases. You just truck on down the road." Often, we wouldn't even know who it was that had stayed at our house.

In a racing family like yours, were there any rivalries? What was it like growing up as an Unser?

We got along extremely good. We all started racing really young, I mean, *really* young. My dad didn't have any money, but Supermodifieds had started racing in town. Daddy had driven races most of his life. My dad and his two brothers put the first motorcycle and sidecar on the top of Pikes Peak. They always taught us that we had to get along. There ended up being four of us brothers. The four of us ended up being into racing. The four of us always got along. That was really good. Louie ended up with Multiple Sclerosis and couldn't keep driving. Jerry got killed in '59 at Indianapolis. So, it was just Al and I. We won a *lot* of races, and we had a *lot* of fans.

Bobby, two of my boyhood idols were Mario Andretti and A.J. Foyt. You raced against them numerous times. Tell me about Mario and A.J.

First, you'd have to go A.J. I don't care how you look at it. He won Indy four times. And, I don't care how you look at that man. He's a grouchy old man today; that's exactly what he is. But, people don't realize that when he was in his prime of his racing—a young man, like when he was hooked up with George Bignotti—this guy was untouchable. He was good. He was good with the fans. The fans loved him. You couldn't find much wrong with A.J. You could say he was a bully. For sure, he was a bully. You can say he had a terrible temper. For sure, he had a terrible temper. But, he never hurt anybody. I saw almost all the races that Foyt did, and I never saw him hurt another driver. In other words, if Foyt got mad at you, you didn't have to worry about him doing something bad to you on the racetrack. Now, in a midget or sprint car race, he might just spin you out and park you, but it wouldn't be anything real bad. The guy was so good. He could work a race car like people do violins. He just never hurt people—never ever, *ever*. And, he wouldn't. It just wasn't his way. He was a good race driver. The young generation today—and it aggravates me—they don't realize how good he was. They see this old man now. He's still got the same temperament that he always had, but he can't do much anymore. The new guys, they just don't have any *idea* how good he was. He could drive a midget to perfection. He could drive a sprint car or a stock car, whether it was in NASCAR or a USAC stock car. It didn't make any difference. Foyt could drive it. And, he loved it. He did such a good job. Naturally, he became very famous, so he must have been doing a good job. He must have won a lot of races.

Now, Mario came in quite a bit later. Foyt wasn't finished, by any means, but he had definitely hit his peak and was going down the back side of the mountain. No question about that. Mario had natural talent. Good at anything. He could drive any kind of a race car that there was. During the early days, he and I used to be the closest of friends. He only weighed 135 pounds. I mean, that's nothing for a race car driver. You take a sprint car. None of them had power-steering in those days, but he'd never get tired. He wouldn't get any more tired than I would. He wouldn't get any more tired than Foyt or Parnelli Jones or Jim Hurtubise, you know, the guys that were legends. They were really tough. Mario could do it at 135 pounds. The guy just had so much natural talent. The only guys I've seen that had the super, super, super natural talent was like Ruttman, like Mario, like "Little Al" and like Parnelli. Those guys were born with the talent. If they'd never seen a race car, they could have gotten into one and in a short time done fairly good. They were just so naturally talented. "Little Al" didn't have to work at racing. He could just fall out of his bed and jump in a race car. It was just so easy for him. Mario was the same way. He didn't have to work that hard at it. He just really, really, really went fast and did it. The people learned to like him. And, during that era, Parnelli was probably the best in the world. There wasn't anything he couldn't drive. You talk about winning. Every race that he'd run, he'd damn near win. All the guys that I remember that were really good race drivers ended up with a big fan base.

People still like Foyt. And, yes, he's still one of the most memorable race drivers that ever lived. But, a lot of people didn't like the fact that he changed. He became old and grouchy. Foyt raced too long. Brother Al raced too long. Mario raced too long. They should have retired years before they did. Naturally, some of them went down in popularity a little ways. But, as soon as they retired, their popularity went right back up again because now the fans know that they aren't going to see an Al Unser running again. They're not going to see a Mario Andretti or a Foyt.

Do you still hear from fans who say that you were their idol?

Oh, absolutely. You ought to see the fan mail. It's amazing! What that shows me is that the new guys are not doing their jobs. (Laugh) Why are the fans still going to a Bobby Unser or an Al Unser or Mario? We still have the biggest amount of fans of all the race drivers.

Why do you think these people still want to connect with you? What was it about you that made them fans of Bobby Unser?

They always liked me because I went fast. Remember, you can be a slow guy and be the nicest guy in the world, but nobody will know you. You have to go fast. I say this to all the young drivers that I talk to. First, you must practice fast. Secondly, you must qualify fast. Third, you must lead the races. Now, the fourth is *winning*, but that's gonna take care of itself. If a person does the first three things that I say, he *will* win some races.

One last thing, Bobby. I'm curious as to how you ended up on TV after you retired as a driver. Is there a story behind that?

I'm at Indianapolis one time, and you do autographs by the hundreds. You do it for the kids that are outside the fence. They can't get in, so I go sign autographs for the kids. That was always a special deal. Now, there was an outfit called the Wide World of Sports. The man that was the head of all of that, Dennis Swanson, he later became the big boss. Well, one year, he was at the Speedway. They weren't doing the television, but he was there, and he had his kid with him. His kid was around 10 years old. The kid was on the fence—hanging there wanting an autograph. I'd just come off the track and had a lot to do. But, I went over to the fence, got the kid and had a little talk with him, did his autograph and gave it back to him. So, then, here comes Dennis years later, and he needs somebody to do his television. Now, ABC is gonna do live Indy Car TV. Wide World of Sports was still there. I'd retired from Indy Cars, so Dennis told his worker-bees, "You just get hold of that Bobby Unser, and see if he wants the job." Now, *I* wasn't a TV personality. I had done a little bit for CBS and a little bit for NBC, and these were always voice-overs—not on-camera. But, Dennis gives me a call and says, "Would you like to do it?" He saw something in me that I never saw.

Dennis didn't tell me this story until many years later. This just shows that if you like kids and you're good to them, that's how good things happen. It shows ya that you never know who's lookin' at ya. You never know what they're thinkin'. And, if you're not nice to them, Lord only knows what you might miss. I wasn't bein' nice to kids because I knew Dennis Swanson was there. First of all, his name wouldn't have meant anything to me. I signed his kid's autograph because that was my way of doing things. Kids were always very, very important.

Career Notes: Bobby Unser, his brother Al, and nephew Al Junior combined to win a total of 108 races in the USAC/CART/IRL/IndyCar series. The 108 victories are the most for any family in open-wheel racing history. Bobby won 35 Indy Car races, which ranks sixth all-time. He won two USAC national championships (1968, 1974). In 1956, at age 22, Bobby Unser won his first Pikes Peak International Hill Climb. He won six straight at Pikes Peak from '58 to '63. Thirty years after his first win, Unser won Pikes Peak for a record tenth time to break a tie he previously shared with his uncle, Louis. Bobby also had two stock car class victories and a single sports car class win, bringing his total number of Pikes Peak wins to 13. Bobby Unser was the winner of the International Race of Champions (IROC) in 1975.

*   *   *

Al Unser shares the record for most Indianapolis 500 victories (4) with A.J. Foyt and Rick Mears. Unser won "The Greatest Spectacle in Racing" in 1970, 1971, 1978 and 1987. "Big Al," the father of Al Unser, Jr. and younger brother of Bobby Unser, is the oldest driver to win the

Indy 500. He was just a few days shy of his 48th birthday when he won at the Brickyard in 1987.

Al Unser was considered one of the smartest drivers of his generation. He rarely made a mistake and earned respect from all of his fellow drivers.

Al Unser only raced twice in the CART races at Portland International Raceway. He finished next to last in the first Portland race in 1984. Even so, the Unser family celebrated because Al Junior earned his first CART win that day. 1985 was "Big Al's" last race in Portland, and he finished 4th, two spots behind "Little Al."

I had become a fan of Al Unser when he won the 1970 Indy 500. I had just received my driver's license, and I can tell you that I dreamed of how cool it would be to drive Unser's Indy-winning "Johnny Lightning Special."

I think the most amazing moment of "Big Al's" career came in 1987 when he won the 500 after going to Indianapolis without a car to drive. Penske Racing had ended its relationship with Unser. But, when Danny Ongais crashed during practice and was not cleared to drive, Penske summoned Unser to drive a year-old backup car. Unser hopped in the car and— on race day—drove into Victory Lane for the fourth time in his career. Unbelievable!

Al and his wife, Susan, created and operate a racing museum in their home city of Albuquerque, New Mexico. I intend to visit the next time I'm in that part of the country.

I talked with Al Unser by phone on October 4, 2013.

Who was your boyhood idol?

Well, that's a very broad question because different drivers started coming on the scene in different years. Just like we did, we finally got our success racing and people then started recognizing us. For me, you go back to Parnelli Jones, A.J. Foyt, Jim Hurtubise, Jim McElreath. There are just so many drivers that I looked at and idolized and said, "Boy. I wish I could be like him or race against him." Then, one day I *was* racing against them, and—it seemed like the next day—I was beating them. It's hard to believe that you looked at them at one time as an idol and would give your left arm just to walk beside them and be able to talk to them. Then, all of a sudden, you're racing them and equalizing them and beating them. That just happens in life.

Were you young when you met Parnelli Jones for the first time?

Oh yeah. He used to come through Albuquerque towing a race car or just traveling. The drivers didn't own airplanes like they do today. There is a different class of traveling today for the drivers. They brag, "Well, I own this Lear Jet or that jet or whatever." That just didn't happen back then, so they drove. Parnelli would come through, and I used stand back and look at him and say, "Man, I wish I could be like him." He was a man that just stood out. Then, when I started driving for him when he was a car owner, I was just amazed. At one time, I looked at him as an idol. Then, I raced against him, and, all of a sudden, he's my car owner. He's my boss. It was really a good feeling.

It's a rather unique situation to have your idol eventually become your boss. Was he a good car owner?

Yeah. He was a very good car owner. He would analyze everything. He used to tell me, "I only wish that when I was racing that I had your patience." I never understood that until years later. Parnelli didn't have any patience. He was like my brother, Bobby. My brother had no patience for a long time. He finally learned what patience was about, and then he started winning races. Parnelli won races, but he broke down or crashed more times than he won. That's why he retired. Firestone and his partner, Vel Miletich, said he was taking too big a chance. He had too much of a future in business. Parnelli decided to retire, and I think—deep down—he was fine that he did. He's never said, but he retired awful young.

Do you think that patience Parnelli talked about is why you won four Indy 500s?

Well, it's one of those deals that you really don't know. You're askin' a question that I've had a lot of time to think about over the years. During the time, I didn't know I had patience. I knew that I wanted to finish the race. It was very important for me to finish—whether it was second, third, fourth, fifth, sixth or whatever. You didn't learn anything by sittin' in the pits and not racing. And, you didn't make a living by sittin' in the pits lookin' at other drivers. So, it was very important for me to always try to finish a race. Maybe that was my patience. I don't know. It probably had a lot to do with it. I can look back and say that now.

Tell me about A.J. Foyt. I know he let you drive his backup car the first time you raced at Indy. But, he has the reputation of being a little grouchy at times.

Nah. That's Foyt's put-on act. Foyt has a heart that you just can't imagine. But, if you disturb him—if you raced against him and stepped on him—you better look out because when he steps back, he has a big foot. Foyt's not the bad guy he acts like he is. He's *not*. He really is a well-behaved race car driver or he wouldn't have been able to win the races that he did.

You and Bobby have mentioned the drivers would come through Albuquerque and stop by the Unser filling station. That was right on Route 66, wasn't it?

Yes. My dad owned it—a gas station, a repair shop, a towing service and all that.

That was a prime location considering Route 66 was the main drive across the country at that time. It sounds like when all the drivers

would come through town, they would stop by to see the Unser family.

You know, not all of them stopped. But, I would guess probably 75% or better did. It was really neat. We'd be sittin' there, and the driver would come up towing a race car on an open trailer. That's just not heard of today. The drivers—(laughs)—they ain't never sittin' with the dang semi (racing transporter)! But, back in those days, they used to tow their own cars. They would tow them for the car owners—anything to get across country because the money just wasn't there.

Al, many racing fans of my generation grew up idolizing Mario Andretti. He was one of your peers. Tell me what you thought of him as a racer and as a person?

Well, he was a teammate, and I got along with Mario very, very well. I mean, when he raced ya, he *raced* ya. He was always one of those type drivers that you had to be careful around. Even as a teammate, you had to be careful. He drove the car. If there was room for him to take, instead of an inch, he'd take a mile. But, as a person, he's a fine, fine gentleman. The man is very well-rounded as a person. I loved bein' a teammate with him. I'd do it again tomorrow. Even lookin' back at our good times and bad times, he was still a teammate that I could race with, learn from, laugh with and enjoy life with.

You were an idol for a lot of young kids when you were driving, especially when you drove the "Johnny Lightning Special" for Parnelli Jones. Did you ever think about all of the fans you had back then?

I don't think that you do. It's just one of those deals that, I think you look at and say, "Boy! This is neat, and I hope the winning continues. I hope next week I can do the same thing." Well, next week comes along, and you don't 'cause there are 35 to 40 guys tryin' to kick your tail. And, they do! There are so many people that are capable of winning if everything just clicks right. Well, you gotta make it click for yourself. It's hard. It's not easy. But, it's one of those deals that when you finally start being recognized as a top driver, you can be very proud of.

Speaking of being proud, you have to be very proud of your son's career. Al Unser, Jr. fashioned quite a successful career for himself. When I talked to your brother, Bobby, he said Al Junior could step into any kind of race car and have a chance to win.

Well, he could. He could jump into the IROC cars and win—and Bobby could, too—and I could. We won IROC races. I never did win any NASCAR races, but I run lots of them and run up towards the front. Al did, too. So did Bobby. Guys like Parnelli, Foyt, Mario, I mean, *all* of us were able to do that round circle of all the race cars. You name the race car—midgets, stock cars, *anything*—if it was a good car and a good day for us, we could win.

In closing, I'd like to ask if you think all you Unsers were simply born to drive race cars?

I loved it. Very few people in the world get to do what they really enjoy and win at it. We did. Bobby did. I did. Al did. My brother, Jerry—who died in a crash—would have been a winner. My brother, Louie, would have been, but he got MS (multiple sclerosis). Whether we were *meant* to do it or not, I'm saying that we *wanted* to do it. And, we worked hard at it. We actually just strapped it on and said, "Lord. Let's get with the program. I know I can do it."

Career Notes: With 39 career USAC-CART victories, Al Unser ranks fourth all-time behind only A.J. Foyt, Mario Andretti and Michael Andretti. Unser won three Indy Car championships. In 1970, he won ten races to tie A.J. Foyt's single-season record and earn the USAC national championship. He won CART championships in 1983 and 1985 while driving for Penske Racing. When Unser won the 1970 Indy 500 two years after Bobby had won for the first time at Indianapolis, they became the first brothers to win at the Brickyard. When "Big Al's" son "Little Al" won at Indy in 1992, Al and Al Junior became the first father-son duo to win the Indy 500. Al Unser drove nine years in the International Race of Championships series and was the 1978 IROC champion. He won the Pikes Peak International Hill Climb in 1964 and 1965.

*   *   *

Al Unser, Jr. had to wait awhile before he won his first Indy 500. But, once he won his first, it didn't take him long to win a second. Al Junior won the Indianapolis 500 in 1992 and 1994. "Little Al" is the son of four-time Indy 500 winner Al Unser and the nephew of three-time Indy 500 champion Bobby Unser. Boy, those Unser guys knew how to win in Indianapolis.

Yes, Al Junior did well at Indy. But, he truly excelled at Portland International Raceway during the annual race in Oregon. In 1984, the first year CART brought the champ cars to Portland, "Little Al" served as Grand Marshal of the Rose Parade—a major event during the annual Rose Festival in the city. Then, a week later, Al Junior won the inaugural Portland race. He won again in Portland in 1994 and yet again in 1995. Al Junior raced in Portland 18 times in the '80s and '90s and finished on the podium seven times. He had a total of 12 finishes in the top five in the Rose City.

I talked with Al Unser, Jr. by telephone on January 6, 2015.

Who was your very first boyhood idol?

Well, of course my dad was my idol. If you remove my father from it, I got to hang out at the race track a lot, so it was A.J. Foyt. It was Johnny Rutherford. It was Gordon Johncock. It was Mario Andretti. Then, once I started racing in the Indy Cars, Mario won the championship in '84. My dad won in '83, my rookie year. Then, I think Mario won in

'84. Mario and my dad—along with Rick Mears and Bobby Rahal—once I started racing, I started paying attention to what they were doing. (Laughs) The one who really stood out was Mario. I watched him dominate Long Beach, and I wanted to do that.

What was it like to be racing against all these guys you had been watching while you were growing up?

It was very surreal, okay? (Laughs) Imagine growing up and going to the races and being with A.J., dad, Uncle Bobby, Rutherford, Mario—all these guys. To me, they were super-heroes, you know, just immortal. Then, I raced in my first Indy Car race in '82 at Riverside. I qualified tenth. I finished fifth, and I was passing A.J. I was passing Gordon and Rutherford. I passed my dad, and he comes and passes me right back. (Laughs) It was pretty funny. But, after the race, I went, "Wow! These guys are men just like me." It was one of the highest highs of my life at that time to be able to race with these guys. Then, when I went and I outrun them, honestly, it was a little bit depressing because they weren't superhuman—because I knew I wasn't. (Laughs) The best way to put it, honestly, is it was surreal. It was a dream come true, and I could race with them. It was great.

You mentioned your dad first. Was he your idol because he was an outstanding race car driver, because he was your dad, or a little bit of both?

It was definitely both. Dad was—and still is—my idol. I go to him all the time for advice. I started racing sprint cars. I went from go-karts into a sprint car when I was 16. When I started racing on the dirt, dad had so much knowledge of the dirt. He full-on gave me the direction that I needed.

The Unser family has an unbelievable racing heritage. It wasn't just you, your father, and Uncle Bobby. There were also your uncles, Jerry, Jr.—who died practicing at Indy—and his twin, Louie, one

of the great mechanics and car builders of all time. I mean, the Unsers won the Pikes Peak Hill Climb so many times that many refer to Pikes Peak as "Unser Mountain." It's clear that racing is in the Unser DNA. With pretty much all of the Unsers involved in racing, did you feel pressure to succeed?

Sure. Absolutely, there was pressure. My dad really helped me out in this, and it's probably a good example of him being a good father. When I started racing sprint cars here locally in Albuquerque, that was the beginning of my professional career. He was noticing the questions that the press was askin' me about comparing my father and myself. They were comparing us. So, my dad pulled me aside one day and said, "I don't care what you do for a living. You can do whatever you want to do for a living. The only thing I care about is that you try your best. If you do that, then the best will come to you." When he told me that when I was 16, it took all the pressure off of me—just instantly took all the pressure off of me. Then the pressure was self-imposed by myself. (Laughs) The Indy 500, yeah, I wanted to win it really bad.

Your first Champ Car win came in 1984 in Portland. It was Portland's first Champ Car race. You had been the Grand Marshall of the Rose Festival Parade. Racing fans in the Northwest fell in love with you. Everything really came together for you that weekend.

It did. It absolutely did. The only down side to that whole thing was my father had a mechanical issue on the parade lap. His car quit runnin' on the back of the track somewhere, so he didn't even get to start the race. No one knows this, but for years later, my dad thought he was a bad luck charm to me. (Laughs) He thought if he was *in* the race, then I wasn't gonna win. (Laughs) It was just so silly, you know? But, yeah, it was a great weekend.

The fact that you were now racing Champ Cars put you in the public eye. Did you ever consider that there were probably little

kids looking at you in the same way you had looked up to your dad, A.J. and Mario?

Absolutely, I did. You betcha. That was one of the things that, as I went through my career, I paid attention to quite a bit. With me, it was just like common sense. When I was out there racin', I needed to be conscious of who I was racing against. Be careful with the guys you're not too sure about. And, the guys that you *are* sure about, you can run wheel to wheel with them and know that they're gonna hold their line and that sort of thing. The conduct on the race track was very, very important.

Career Notes: Al Unser, Jr. won 34 races in the USAC/CART/IndyCar series. Al Junior won CART championships in 1990 and 1994. When "Little Al" won his first Indy 500 in 1992, he became the first second-generation winner at Indianapolis. When he drove in his first Indy 500 in 1983, Al Junior became the first son to race against his father at the Brickyard. Al Unser, Jr. won the IROC championship in 1986 and 1988.

* * *

25

Far Ahead Of His Time

Galen Rupp is one of America's premier distance runners. A seven-time USA Track and Field (USATF) Outdoor champion in the 10,000 meters, Rupp is the U.S. record-holder at that distance. At the 2012 London Olympic Games, Rupp captured the silver medal in the 10,000 meters, the first American to medal in the event since Billy Mills won gold in 1964. Rupp hopes to return to the Olympics and win more hardware in 2016. Rupp trains as part of the Portland-based Nike Oregon Project under legendary U.S. distance runner Alberto Salazar.

I first started hearing about Galen Rupp when he was a teenager at Central Catholic High School in Portland, Oregon. He was winning and breaking records on a regular basis. High school cross-country runners usually don't get a lot of media attention, but it was clear right away that this Rupp kid was something special. As a result, he was featured on local television sports segments and in the local newspapers. When legendary U.S. runner Alberto Salazar began to serve as his mentor, it was a perfect fit. The winning and the record-breaking has continued in the years that followed. Although the challenge will be great, don't be surprised if Rupp brings home another medal for the United States in the 2016 Summer Olympics in Rio de Janeiro, Brazil.

I talked with Galen Rupp by phone on May 5, 2011.

Did you have a boyhood idol?

Being from Oregon, Steve Prefontaine was always someone that I think everybody looks up to since he grew up in the same state. I was able to hear so many great stories about him and see what a great competitor he was. He was someone I looked up to.

And, also, I'd say Michael Jordan. My dad was from Chicago, so I loved watching Jordan play—just the fire and fight that he had in him and how much he was able to get it done in clutch moments. I thought that was always really cool.

Since you're a Nike guy, I'm curious if you've ever had the chance to meet Michael?

No, I haven't yet, but hopefully someday. That would be pretty cool. (Laughs)

You're being coached by Alberto Salazar, one of the greatest distance runners in U.S. history. Was he someone you looked up to?

I feel real lucky to have him as my coach. He never really talked a lot about his accomplishments or his races when I first met him. Over time, as we got closer and got to know each other better, I'd get bits and pieces of different things. I'd hear stories about him from different people, too. The more I'd hear about him, he definitely is an inspiration to me too—just how tough he was mentally and his whole mindset. I think a lot of the things that he was able to do, he's instilled in me. So, yeah, I'd definitely say he's an idol, too. But, I guess it took a little longer for me to really know him—and understand and really recognize what a great athlete he was.

As your coach, he offers tips and advice. Do you always take his advice, or are there times you say, "No, that's not for me."

I'd say 99% of the time I take his advice. I think he knows running a lot better than I do. He definitely made some mistakes in his running career with the way he trained, and he's really learned from those mistakes.

One of the great things about him is he's humble enough to know where he made mistakes and correct those with me and the rest of his athletes. He's also not scared to go and ask for advice from everybody else. He's constantly looking for new information, new training methods and different workouts. He's really open to all that stuff, which I think is really important in a coach.

Young runners around the country know all about you and the success you've experienced, and I'm sure you're an idol for some of those kids. Do you ever think about how roles have changed and that you're now the guy kids are looking up to?

Uh, yeah, but it's still a little weird when people ask for my autograph or want me to come talk to a team or the school. I still look at myself as just a regular guy. But, if I can be a role model to other kids, that's something that would be great. I try to do things the right way in everything I do. Hopefully, kids can look up to that.

Career Notes: Galen Rupp was named the 2004 National High School Athlete of the Year while attending Central Catholic High School in Portland, Oregon. Rupp has set numerous American distance-running records at the high school, collegiate, and senior levels. While running for the University of Oregon, Rupp won an assortment of national championships. Among his many accomplishments, he was the 2008 NCAA cross country champion, the 2009 NCAA Indoor champion in the 3,000 meters and the 5,000 meters, and the 2009 Outdoor champion in the 5K and 10K. His senior year, he won five national titles and the inaugural Bowerman Award, which is given to the men's and women's national track and field athlete of the year.

*   *   *

Alberto Salazar ran for the U.S. Olympic team in 1984 after being denied the opportunity to compete in the 1980 Games when the United States boycotted the Moscow Olympics. Salazar won the New York

City Marathon three consecutive years (1980–82). He won the Boston Marathon in 1982. Salazar now serves as a coach for the Nike Oregon Project. Included in his stable of athletes are the reigning Olympic and World 10K champion, Mo Farah, and U.S. 10K champion Galen Rupp.

Salazar has had a couple brushes with death. In fact, he was clinically dead for 14 minutes after suffering a heart attack in 2007. He wrote about the ordeal in his memoir, *"14 Minutes: A Running Legend's Life and Death and Life."*

I had been working as a television sportscaster in Portland for only two months when Alberto Salazar won his first New York City Marathon in October, 1980. I was still trying to learn which local athletes and teams were important, and I learned almost from the get-go that Alberto was an important figure in Oregon sports. He was a 22-year-old senior at the University of Oregon when he won his first New York City Marathon. He had never previously run a marathon, but he came to learn he was really, really good at that distance. Salazar had won numerous national championships as a collegiate runner for the Ducks, but soon he would be recognized as America's best in the marathon. When Salazar won again in New York City in 1981 and 1982, and when he won the Boston Marathon in '82, he was without a doubt, America's premier distance runner. I remember being surprised when Salazar did not win the 1984 Olympic marathon. I was more than surprised—stunned actually—that he didn't even medal, finishing a disappointing 15th.

In the years since, I have become better acquainted with Alberto. I have interviewed him numerous times, and he has always treated me with respect and in a professional manner. I find him to be a wonderful talker and a man who truly loves his sport. For a time, Alberto Salazar was the best distance runner in America. He now coaches the best distance runners in America. It's perfect symmetry.

I spoke with Alberto Salazar by phone on January 15, 2015.

Who was your very first boyhood idol?

I would say that it was Ron Clarke. He was this famous Australian distance runner that held all the distance records in the world through the late '60s and maybe early '70s. He was really far ahead of his time. He was beating people by a half lap. He was my first one. Then, Steve Prefontaine was shortly thereafter. I would say Pre probably was my first true idol. I knew who Ron Clark was and thought he was cool and considered him kind of an idol. But, the first one that I really knew a lot about and was a real idol was Prefontaine.

Did you ever meet Ron Clarke?

Yes, I did. Many years later, probably in the '80s, I met him.

What was it like to meet someone you'd heard a lot about?

It was a really good impression. He was a guy that had done all these great things but was very friendly, very outgoing, very engaging, very interested in what other people were doing. It really struck a chord with me that this guy that was like a hero to me also turned out to be a really great person.

Did you ever meet Steve Prefontaine prior to his tragic death?

No. I never met him. He passed away a year before I arrived in Eugene. He died in May of '75, and I arrived on campus at U. of O. in September of '76.

You talked about the things that made you aware of Ron Clarke. What were the things that made Pre your top boyhood hero?

I guess it was kind of his fearlessness. Clarke had a different way in that he would go out way in front by himself. It was very risky in races to go out there that hard. Pre didn't necessarily go out way in front on his own, but was just very fearless, a brave runner. The toughness and fearlessness were the things that impressed me. It wasn't just that they ran good times because there were lots of people that ran good times. Lasse Viren, for instance, won a lot of races. He was a great guy, a great tactician. They could just beat people at the end and were very tactically smart. But, a lot of us just gravitated towards Pre and Clarke because they not only won, but the way in which they won. It was really appealing.

You are coaching current U.S. distance star Galen Rupp, who told me that one of his boyhood idols was Steve Prefontaine. Does that surprise you when you consider Pre wasn't even alive when Rupp began to learn of his achievements?

Well, Pre wasn't even alive when Galen was born. No, not really because I started coaching Galen when he was a freshman in high school. Obviously, Galen must have read about him, but I'm sure that I talked about Pre. I talked about the legend—what he was like and how tough he was. Certainly from the beginning, and I would say *definitely* by the end of Galen's freshman year, Galen had a goal—that I supported—to break Pre's state record in the 2-mile. So, yes, he knew about Pre from things that I had said having gone to the U. of O. and from Galen reading up on it on his own. So, no, I'm not surprised at all.

Since you were his coach even when I talked with Galen a few years ago, I asked him if he considered you to be one of his boyhood idols, and he said you were not. You were more of an inspiration to him than an idol. How do you react to hearing to that?

It's good. With Galen and my other athletes, I always sort of caution them in terms of idolizing people. They are very aware that a lot of athletes do things and should not be idolized. These fantastic athletes aren't necessarily the people that you would want to emulate in our daily lives. Not that I'm leading a bad life or whatever, but with Galen, it was always I was this person that was just a normal, regular person. I wasn't this heroic figure. I would rather teach him to be a good person and teach him life lessons than have him idolizing me. For one thing, I wasn't as great a runner as Pre was—by any means. I always make sure not to set myself up as an idol to Galen or talk about myself. I talk about experiences and things that I thought could help him. I taught him about a lot of mistakes that I made that shortened my career and ruined my career. I think that Galen would naturally have idolized people that he really didn't know—rather than me with all the warts. (Laughs) At the same time, I think Galen knew about Pre and his whole personal character, and—like everybody—Pre wasn't perfect. But, no, I'm not surprised that I wasn't Galen's idol. I would rather have been an inspiration like his dad—perhaps a role model of some sort—but not an idol.

In the early 1980s when you won three straight New York City Marathons and a Boston Marathon, and when you were on the cover of Sports Illustrated, you were the idol of distance runners around the nation. Did you think about that when you were being hailed as the top distance runner in America?

Well, certainly I noticed that at the time. I was just so driven in my running. It's not like I really sort of sat back and derived pleasure from it in any way. The way I was driven, running was just so important to me. No matter how well I did—even if I just broke a world record—I never sat back and thought, "Wow. I'm pretty good. I'm the best in the world right now. I'm kind of on this pedestal. All these people think I'm great. I *am* great." or "I'm cool." I was so driven towards my next thing that I just didn't really take time to think about it. Only years later, like *now*, when people tell me that, do I say, "Well, huh. That's interesting." I wouldn't say I derive pleasure from it. The only pleasure I derive from hearing people tell me that I was their idol is if it was something good for them, you know, if it helped inspire them to run. Somebody will tell me, "I never ran at all, but because of you I started running, and I still run all the time now." I'll go, "Wow. Thanks for sharing. I'm glad that my career was able to help you." Somebody yesterday told me they read my book and how it helped them. I said, "Oh, that's great."

It's not like, "Oh wow. I'm cool. Somebody likes my book or liked my career." It helped somebody, and it's like, "You know what? It's good. It was worth something." So, basically, I didn't really think about it at the time. It kind of just flitted in and out of my mind. But, now, I see that if something I did in the past or what I'm doing now can help some other people, then there's a value to it. Otherwise, it doesn't really matter. I'll be gone someday, but if my career helped somebody, then maybe it lives on a little longer.

Career Notes: When Alberto Salazar won his first New York City Marathon, he did so in 2 hours, 9 minutes and 41 seconds. It was a course record and the fastest debut in a marathon in history. The next year at New York, he broke the world marathon record in 2:08:13. Salazar's third straight New York victory, in 1982, stood as the last time an American won the New York City Marathon until Meb Keflezighi won in 2009.

*   *   *

26

A Long Shadow

A.C. Green is pro basketball's version of baseball iron man Cal Ripken, Jr. The 6-foot-9 forward, who played 16 seasons with the Lakers, Suns, Mavericks and Heat, holds the NBA record for consecutive games played with 1,192. Green, an NBA All-Star in 1990, won three NBA championships with the Lakers during the "Showtime" era.

A.C. Green grew up in Portland, Oregon, and won a high school state championship at Benson Tech prior to playing four years at Oregon State University. He was All-Pac-10 First Team for the Beavers as a sophomore, junior and senior. His junior season, Green was named 1984 Pac-10 Men's Basketball Player of the Year.

Even as a young man, A.C. Green had deep faith. He understood the difference between right and wrong. Early on, A.C. made a commitment to abstain from sex until he was married. While playing in the NBA, Green actively campaigned for sexual abstinence, citing the importance of having self-respect, values and virtue in one's life. Initially, he received a lot of kidding by his Lakers' teammates, but once they came to understand his sincerity and commitment to his beliefs, the kidding stopped. Green proudly remained a virgin until he married at age 38. Even now, A.C. Green is often approached by parents who thank him for being an example they can point to when talking with their kids about making good choices in life and having the courage to be true to themselves. I spoke with A.C. Green by phone on January 15, 2015.

Is there somebody in particular that you considered your first boyhood idol?

No, it was a merry-go-round. It all depended upon who we liked in our house. I was the youngest of four kids, so it all depended on what my brothers and sisters were talking about. Then, once I went outside the house, it depended on who my friends were all talking about or imitating. So, you go from the likes of The Jackson Five to Tom Jones to JoJo White—and shooting jump shots like him. You go to Doctor J, Kareem and Muhammad Ali. I mean, it starts just going across the spectrum when you think of that time.

It sounds like there must have been a lot of music in your home when you were growing up.

Yeah, I think, more than anything, the genre was more of the blues. Then, Little Richard was one that we were pretty much raised on. It was definitely a diverse upbringing.

One of the guys you mentioned was Kareem Abdul-Jabbar, captain of the Lakers, and a guy you played with after you were drafted by Los Angeles coming out of Oregon State. Since you had grown up watching him, what was it like to find out you were going to be his teammate when you joined Pat Riley's Lakers?

Being drafted by the Laker team was just nostalgic from that standpoint. There's no preparation for something like that. During my senior year at Oregon State, you were seeing him as well as some of his teammates on your Wheaties box when you had breakfast every morning—the champions of the world! Lo-and-behold, you wind up being drafted in the NBA and selected by that same team that you were having breakfast with for so long. It was just weird. It was also exciting. I was really looking forward to it—a goose-bumps kind of feeling knowing training camp was going to be coming. As much as Coach Riley and Jerry West tried to prepare me what things were going to be like and

369

how to anticipate things, you still knew that—sooner or later—you were actually going to get face-to-face with the guys. You were going to actually start hearing a ball bouncing. It was very cool when that finally did take place.

Seeing Kareem—well, I actually *heard* him. I heard his footsteps before I saw him. I was just doing my prepping before our very first training camp opened. I was just getting shoes laced and socks pulled up and all that kind of stuff. Then, I heard footsteps coming in my direction, and the next thing you know, the *shadow* comes. It's a long shadow, and it just keeps moving past. You think it's a solar eclipse, but it's Kareem walking by. It was just, "Wow! There's the Cap. There's the Cap." It was fun.

Kareem was viewed by outsiders as a rather surly guy. What about as a teammate? Was he a good teammate? Was he good to you?

Yeah. He was extremely patient—a good teacher and communicator. We had fun around each other and just learning about one another. He really was a good teammate. He was quiet to the outside world, but amongst those that he was familiar and comfortable with, he had his own personality and fit right in. He wasn't the jokester in the locker room where every day you count on something he's going to do or say—life of the party time. But, at the same time, he was engaged. He was around. It was fun, and we had talks just about life itself. We talked about faith. We talked about how to prepare for games and just a little bit about everything. I really appreciated and valued the time I had with him.

Another of your former teammates, Magic Johnson, was worshipped by many future NBA players. Was he also a good teammate?

Yeah, I would almost echo the same things that I said about Kareem, except Magic *was* the center of attention. His personality was such that he really tried to get to know everybody and make everyone feel comfortable and involved. He was just a super, super teammate who was real passionate about playing and about winning. He was just an example setter. I was really, really fortunate to have him being sort of the leader of the team.

You talked about discussing faith with Kareem. You were one of the first openly-religious players in the NBA. You wore your Christianity on your sleeve. You sort of led the way for other athletes who wanted to publicly observe their faith. Do you feel you were somewhat of a trailblazer in that regard?

A lot of people had faith and have religion. Some were able to allow their religion to turn into a faith that they can express. I was more about demonstration and leading the conversation. I was kind of this only guy talking about faith. I didn't mind speaking on it, but I always felt it's really about what you do, not what you say. Because of that, it got a lot of attention. It inspired a lot of people I've come to find out after the fact. It raised a lot of eyebrows, got a lot of attention and created a lot of conversation inside of certain circles.

You won a high school state championship at Benson. You were a huge part of Oregon State's success during your years in Corvallis. You won championship rings with the Lakers. You clearly established yourself as a success on the basketball court. Have you had people come up to you and tell you that you were their boyhood idol?

Yeah, countless times that has been said. Even to this day, there are a lot of parents sharing with their child or grandchild about how much inspiration they received because of someone taking a stand and being true to who—or what—they are. That still happens, which is still cool. It really is. I think it just makes me even prouder knowing that I come from Portland and come from small beginnings—a small city and small state. My mom is one that always echoed that it's not where you come from. You can still accomplish and walk a certain path of influence and impact. I'm always proud to say where I'm from and what I represent.

Career Notes: When he played, A.C. Green was an excellent defender (NBA All-Defensive Second Team in 1989). Although he was never asked to be a huge scorer in the NBA, he still averaged 9.6 points and 7.4 rebounds over the course of his career. Green was inducted into the Pac-12 Men's Basketball Hall of Honor in 2012, nine years after he had been inducted into the State of Oregon Sports Hall of Fame. Green's Oregon State University jersey number (#45) has been retired.

* * *

27

Like Father Figures

Ed Dickson is an NFL tight end who played the 2014 season with the Carolina Panthers. In 2015, Dickson re-signed with Carolina, agreeing to a multi-year contract. Dickson was an All-Pac-10 player at the University of Oregon in his junior and senior seasons. His sophomore campaign in Eugene, Dickson set a school-record for receptions by a tight end with 43 (for 453 yards and 3 touchdowns). As a junior, in 2008, he was second on the team with 508 receiving yards on 35 catches with 3 touchdowns. Dickson was named Second Team All-Pac-10 following his junior season. As a senior, he again finished second on the team with 42 receptions for 551 yards—a school-record for tight ends— and six touchdowns. Dickson also set a school-record for receptions by a tight end in a single game when he made 11 catches against California. Dickson was named First Team All-Pac-10 his senior year.

Ed Dickson, who had interest from multiple teams as an unrestricted free agent, chose to remain in Carolina and signed a 3-year contract with the Panthers in March of 2015. That might have been a surprise to some considering Dickson—with Carolina in 2014—set new career lows with 10 receptions for 115 yards and one touchdown. The Panthers had planned to use Dickson in a two tight end set with Pro Bowl tight end Greg Olsen. However, Dickson was called upon to do more blocking than originally anticipated after Carolina fullback Mike Tolbert went down with a knee injury. That meant fewer passes being thrown in Dickson's direction. He had only four receptions for 36 yards through the Panthers first 10 games.

But, once Tolbert returned, Dickson's numbers improved. He made six catches for 79 yards in the final six games of the regular season. He had three receptions for 67 yards in the Panthers two playoff games.

I talked with Ed Dickson on March 9, 2014, at the Oregon Sports Awards program in Beaverton, Oregon.

Who was your first boyhood idol?

I was from Southern California, and we didn't really have a pro team to follow. In basketball, I was a Laker fan my whole life. But, in football, we didn't have a pro team, so I watched the Cowboys on TV. They always showed the Cowboys. So, my idol was probably "Prime Time," Deion Sanders, or one of those Cowboys back in the day like Troy Aikman or Michael Irvin.

But, my childhood memories of my idols had to be my coaches. My dad was in and out of my life a bit, so my coaches were like father figures in my life. I hang close to my coaches. That's why I can appreciate the coaching that I had. Whenever I experience something like getting a championship ring, I go back and show it to those coaches and let them know that they laid a path in the way for all my success today.

Are you talking about all of your coaches collectively, or was there one that stood out?

As I was growing up, one of my high school coaches, Brian Mustang, was very influential. My travel team coach, Joe Irving, he basically gave me everything that I needed. Money was no thing to him. Time was no thing to him. He put his arms around me, and he showed me what it was to have a father that cared about you. My biggest fan, though, is my mother. My mother is my biggest fan and my biggest supporter. I love my mom the best.

Did you ever get a chance to meet Deion Sanders or any of those other Cowboys?

I met Deion once. I'll tell you a funny story. This is recent. I'm a diehard Lakers' fan, and I went to the Blazer-Laker game the other night. You know, I could meet Damian Lillard. I could meet all those NBA stars. But, I got butterflies because I met Kobe Bryant for the first time. I've met Michael Jordan before. But, as I mentioned, I'm a diehard Laker fan, and I met *Kobe*. That's the first and only time I got butterflies from meeting somebody. I've met all kind of actors like Jamie Foxx and Meagan Good. Kobe was the only person to give me butterflies. He was really a nice, down-to-earth guy. I had my championship ring on, and the first thing he said was, "Go get another one of those." He was busy, but I sat there talking to him for about five or ten minutes. I can mark it off my bucket list as one thing that I experienced.

Having played at Oregon and now that you're in the NFL, you have a lot of young fans who might be looking up to you in some fashion. Do you think about that?

Yeah, I think about it all the time. It's a responsibility being a role model. I got two kids of my own, and being a role model—being a stand-up guy—I take it as a responsibility in showing the people that is coming after me the right way to go. If they ever need any advice, my door is always open. And, once a Duck, always a Duck.

Career Notes: Ed Dickson was the most prolific pass-catching tight end in University of Oregon history. He finished his career with 124 receptions for 1,557 yards and 12 touchdowns. After being picked in the third round of the 2010 NFL Draft, Dickson played four years with the Baltimore Ravens. He won a championship ring with Baltimore following the 2012 season. When the Ravens beat the San Francisco 49ers in the Super Bowl on February 3, 2013, Dickson had two catches for 37 yards. Dickson's most productive season was 2011 when he hauled in 54 passes for 528 yards and five touchdowns. Dickson set a Ravens' record for receptions by a tight end when he had 10 catches (for 79 yards and two touchdowns) at Seattle on November 13, 2011.

In the first five years of his NFL career, Dickson totaled 121 receptions for 1,293 yards and eight touchdowns.

*　　*　　*

Michael Holton played parts of six NBA seasons with the Phoenix Suns, Chicago Bulls, Portland Trail Blazers and Charlotte Hornets. He was a starter his rookie season in Phoenix, and he started for the Hornets in their inaugural season. Holton grew up in Pasadena, California, and attended Pasadena High School. He played basketball at UCLA for Larry Brown and went into coaching for a time once his playing career ended. Holton now works for Comcast SportsNet Northwest as a sideline reporter and studio analyst for Portland Trail Blazers' games.

Although I had covered UCLA games when Michael Holton played for the Bruins, I first met him when he played for the Trail Blazers from 1986–88. A role player for Portland, Holton was always well-spoken and a good interview. Later, when I saw him working as an assistant coach at the University of Portland and then at Oregon State, I thought it was just a matter of time before he would become a collegiate head coach. He finally got his chance at the University of Portland, but he found—like many before him and after him—that UP is a difficult place to coach. Few quality players are willing to play at the small private school, and admission standards are high. Holton was fired after five difficult seasons. I thought it said something about Holton's professionalism when he was hired by Comcast SportsNet to work with me during broadcasts of Portland Pilots' basketball games just a few years after he had been fired by the school. Viewers would have had no idea that Holton had been let go by the university. He handled his assignment with true professionalism.

I talked with Michael Holton at the Caddies 4 Cure charity golf event in Oregon on June 13, 2011.

Who was your very first boyhood idol?

At first, I think my boyhood idol was Doctor J (Julius Erving). He was just bigger than life as a basketball player and represented something to reach for. But, as I got a little older and continued to move forward in basketball, I think George Gervin became more that person for me. I was able to play with him and learn some lessons and have some conversations about being a professional. Those things kind of stayed with me. So, from a player's standpoint, I think Doctor J, and then it was George Gervin.

But, if you want to say *boyhood* idol—going back to high school—it's my high school coach, George Terzian. A great man. We won the championship. He was a very principled Christian guy that stood for those standards and values. He spoke into my life and gave me what really became the backbone of my life in the bigger picture.

Coaches often play a significant role in the lives of young boys and girls. Coaches have a huge impact on a young person's life.

I think coaches are *teachers* first. I'm old enough to remember when coaches really were teachers. That was a requirement. Coaching was what they did to augment teaching. So, they stood for things and principles. It wasn't about just winning or just putting together an all-star type of team. It was about the fundamentals of learning. At my high school, we had a basketball fundamentals class two hours a day in the summer for credit. We did jump-stops and ball-handling and form and technique and defensive slides—all of the nuts and bolts of the fundamentals of basketball. The way those things were taught and graded—and the *accountability*—really is what stayed with me, not just in basketball, but in life. When you get transferable skills from sport, that's when you really have been given something.

So, you learned many life lessons from your high school coach, George Terzian.

Yes. Great man. He coached at Pasadena High School for many, many years. He coached Michael Cooper. He coached Jim Marsh. He coached a lot of guys. Then, he went on to Pasadena City College, and I actually got my coaching start with him at Pasadena City College. I was his assistant. I remember one time we were coaching an intra-squad game. I didn't know anything about coaching. So, my team made some mistakes, and I called timeout. I was emotional. I was irate. I spent the timeout telling them how bad their mistake was. When the day was over, Coach Terzian pulled me to the side and said, "When you have a timeout, you don't need to tell them that they've made mistakes because they already know that. You need to tell them what they need to do coming *out* of the timeout."

Let's talk about your NBA idols. What are your memories of meeting Julius Erving?

I remember two things about Doctor J. My rookie year I was starting for the Phoenix Suns and he was coming up the court in an open-court situation. I was sure I could take the ball from him because he was tall and he had a high dribble. I reached in with my inside hand, and he grabbed my wrist while he reverse-spun. So, I actually went the other direction while he went towards the basket. That was my first lesson that it's not as easy as it looks.

My most memorable Doctor J story was when I was playing with the Chicago Bulls. It was late in his career, and he was playing the big guard position. I had a chance to play a significant number of minutes against him, and I had a good game—21 points. At the old Chicago Stadium, when the game was over, you exited the court behind the basket. We looked at each other and made eye contact. He motioned me to meet him at half-court. He told me, "Good game," and told me that he thought I could be a good pro. That just really encouraged me because I was a journeyman player. When somebody that I looked up to like Doctor J told me to stay the course, it just really meant a lot to me.

When you were at UCLA and in the NBA, I'm sure there were kids that looked up to you. Were you cognizant of that as you went about your daily life?

Yeah, I always felt a sense of responsibility, particularly in the area of being available when asked to speak at a camp or speak to a kid or speak to a high school team. I just always wanted to make sure that I kept a spirit of availability because to me the one thing everybody always remembers in life is who encouraged them. You don't remember wins and losses. All that stuff fades, and trophies get tarnished. But, people that encouraged you, you know, it stays with you. So, I've always tried to maintain a spirit of availability so that when I can maybe encourage somebody else, I make sure that I'm available.

Michael, when you became the head basketball coach at the University of Portland, did you think about the important part you would play in the lives of the young men you were coaching?

Yeah. What I did feel was the weight of responsibility to try to be for them what other coaches had been for me, which was a teacher and a model and consistent and fair. When I became the head coach at the University of Portland, one of the most humbling things said to me was by Larry Brown, my college coach, at a coaching retreat he held every year. He asked me, "As a head coach, what are you going to do to move the game forward?" It was an overwhelming statement. I mean, "What am *I* going to do to move the game forward?" But, I think what he was saying to me is, "You do have a responsibility, a large responsibility." I was humbled by that, but I always remembered it.

Career Notes: Michael Holton averaged 6.2 points and 3.0 assists in 325 NBA games. His best pro season was 1988-89, when he averaged 8.3 points and 6.3 assists for Charlotte.

Holton spent time an assistant coach at the University of Portland, Oregon State University and UCLA prior to being named the head men's basketball coach at the University of Portland in 2001.

*   *   *

Gary Cunningham was a three-year starter at UCLA for Hall of Fame basketball coach John Wooden in the early 1960s. As a senior in 1961-62, the Inglewood, California, native averaged 13.4 points and a team-best 6.9 rebounds on the first Wooden-coached team to reach the NCAA Final Four. In 1965, Cunningham coached a seven-foot future Hall of Famer on the Bruin's freshmen basketball team. Cunningham later served two seasons as UCLA's head basketball coach and recorded the best winning percentage in school history.

Even though it didn't count in the official records, Gary Cunningham was the first basketball coach to win a game at Pauley Pavilion. Cunningham was hired as a UCLA assistant coach in 1965, and he was responsible for coaching the Bruins' freshman team. At the time, freshmen were ineligible to play in varsity competition. One of the players he coached was a 7-footer named Lew Alcindor, who later changed his named to Kareem Abdul-Jabbar. In November of 1965, the freshmen played the UCLA varsity—ranked number one in the country—in the very first game played at Pauley Pavilion. Alcindor, his freshman teammate Lucius Allen and the rest of the BruBabes beat the varsity, 75-60. Against the two-time defending national champions, Alcindor scored 31 points and pulled down more than 20 rebounds—a sure sign of things to come. In his very first coaching assignment after being hired by Coach Wooden, Cunningham had beaten his mentor.

I talked about childhood heroes with Gary Cunningham during a phone call on December 7, 2011.

When I ask you to name your very first boyhood idol, what name pops into your head?

When I was a kid there wasn't a whole lot of television for professional sports or college sports. We learned about players through the newspaper, and it was mostly local coverage. And, we learned about players through trading cards, believe it or not. I wanted to be a football player, and I wanted to be a baseball player. Those were two important sports to me. I always felt like I wanted to be a quarterback, so the guy's name who pops into my head is Norm Van Brocklin with the L.A. Rams. I grew up in the L.A. area. We didn't have Major League Baseball when I was a kid. The Dodgers came in 1958. We had Pacific Coast League baseball, and we had big-time NFL football. Basketball, we didn't have. The Lakers weren't there; they came later. So, basically it was football we followed. Norm Van Brocklin was the quarterback, and the Rams had good teams. They were fun to watch.

You played and later coached at UCLA. Did you ever consider that kids might be idolizing you or looking up to you in some manner?

No, I never considered myself an idol. I've never been into that. I'm not into the ego thing. But, I always felt like I had to set an example for young people—and for other people. I made myself accessible. If a young kid would come up and want an autograph or something, you know, I'd talk to them a little bit. I would say, "What's your name?" But, I always felt like I wanted to be a good role model for people, and I wanted to be accessible. It disturbs me today when people ignore the fans. I'm not saying you should sit there like Coach Wooden and sign autographs for half an hour, but at least be cordial to people because you are a role model. I never considered myself a role model, but—in all actuality—I was a role model. Young people are very impressionable. I felt like I needed to present a good image and be real, be genuine. A lot of that, I got from Coach Wooden. Those are the kinds of things that all of us learned from Coach. He did so much good for humanity and even *more* after he finished coaching. But, he had to have the base of coaching—and the success—in order to accomplish the things that he did afterwards. He wasn't a one-dimensional guy. I mean, he was so knowledgeable in so many areas, and he was a good person. Frankly, I miss him. I really miss him.

There are many athletes now who try to avoid the fans. Why have things changed so dramatically?

Today, it's money-driven and ego—all of those things. It's changed drastically. I was very naive. I always felt that athletes didn't smoke, didn't drink, were clean-cut and on and on and on. Then, when I became an adult, I realized that that wasn't always true. I remember going to a Los Angeles Angels game in the Pacific Coast League. I came out after the game and here's a guy that pitched that night smoking a cigarette. I thought, "Holy cow! He's an athlete. How can he do that?" That's how naive I was.

Career Notes: Gary Cunningham still holds the UCLA record for free throw percentage in conference games over the course of a season (1.000). He was a perfect 28 of 28 from the line in conference games in 1959-60. Cunningham was picked in the seventh round (58th overall) of the 1962 NBA Draft by the Cincinnati Royals, but never played in the NBA.

Cunningham was an assistant under John Wooden from 1965 until the "Wizard of Westwood" retired after winning the 1975 NCAA title. Feeling burned out on coaching, Cunningham did not pursue the job and accepted a position as UCLA's director of alumni relations. Gene Bartow succeeded Wooden and went a combined 52-9 in two seasons before bolting to begin the athletic program at Alabama-Birmingham. Just two years after Wooden's retirement, UCLA again needed a new coach. UCLA approached Cunningham and offered him the job, which he accepted. Following his first season, he was named 1978 Pac-8 Men's Basketball Coach of the Year. Cunningham was head coach for only two seasons and guided UCLA to conference titles both years. The Bruins had a combined record of 50-8 under Cunningham. His overall winning percentage (.862) remains the highest in UCLA men's basketball history. Cunningham later served as a college athletics administrator. He was the Athletic Director at Western Oregon, Wyoming, Fresno State and UC-Santa Barbara.

*   *   *

Jack Ramsay,
in 1943, was a college basketball player at St. Joseph's College in his native Philadelphia. But, Ramsay—feeling an obligation to defend his country—left school to serve in World War II. Ramsay was a Navy underwater demolition diver—a precursor of the NAVY Seals. He was in the last demolition team to be commissioned. In fact, Ramsay was at sea heading to be part of an invasion at the very time the atomic bombs were dropped in Japan. The planned invasion was put on hold and then cancelled once the Japanese surrendered. Ramsay always expressed great disappointment that he didn't get to use his frogman skills after training long and hard for battle. Eventually returning to a more normal way of life after the war, Ramsay returned to St. Joseph's and played for the school basketball team from 1947–49.

Ramsay enjoyed a Hall of Fame coaching career, first in college at St. Joseph's, then in the NBA. Later, Ramsay became a broadcaster and continued working as an NBA analyst on radio and TV at an age most people would have long been retired. For years, "Dr. Jack" was the lead analyst on ESPN Radio's NBA coverage. He was teamed with the late Jim Durham, a long-time friend. The two were engaging and entertaining—one of the best pairings in sports broadcasting history.

A physical fitness buff, Ramsay competed in triathlons until he was 70. Ironically, Ramsay spent more than a decade fighting off various forms of cancer. He continued to work even as cancer ravaged his body. This was the one battle the ultra-competitive Ramsay couldn't win. Jack Ramsay died on April 28, 2014. He was 89.

I had the privilege of knowing Jack Ramsay for nearly 34 years. He was the head coach of the Trail Blazers when I arrived in Portland in 1980. In the six seasons Ramsay coached the Blazers while I was working in Portland television, Ramsay guided his club into the playoffs five times. Even the year they didn't make it to the postseason, the Blazers still had a winning record.

I was the person that broke the story in the summer of 1986, when Jack Ramsay was fired by the Trail Blazers. A source, who was very close to Jack, gave me the heads-up about the dismissal. I called Ramsay at home to confirm his status. A part of me felt bad about making that call. I also felt bad when I announced Ramsay's dismissal on my local sportscast later that night. You see, after six years, I had developed a great working relationship with Jack. In addition, I felt we had a sort of kinship since his son Chris— who now works for ESPN.com—was a news producer at my TV station. When I contacted Jack, I apologized for having to phone him at home under these difficult circumstances. He confirmed the news of his firing and immediately attempted to make me feel better about calling him at home to ask about his job loss. On the air that night, I felt like I was reporting on a death in the family when I delivered the news to Portland viewers that the man that had guided the Trail Blazers to the 1977 championship was now out of a job. Jack showed true class that day, which should surprise absolutely no one who knew the man.

Jack Ramsay was a Hall of Fame basketball coach, but he was an even better person. Trust me when I tell you that he loved his family. He cared about his players. He cared about his friends. He even cared about people he barely knew. Jack was a great conversationalist. He listened when you talked with him and always responded appropriately. Jack could engage you in conversation on any number of subjects. I miss our conversations. I miss Jack. But, knowing how much he had to endure in the last decade of his life, I know that he is at peace and in a better place.

I talked by phone with Jack Ramsay about his childhood heroes on August 25, 2011.

Who was your very first boyhood idol?

I was a big baseball fan when I was a kid. I lived in Connecticut, close enough to New York to be a New York Giants baseball fan. In fact, I saw a World Series game in 1933 between the Giants and the Washington Senators. My idol was the Giants right fielder, Mel Ott, a little guy with a great stroke. The Polo Grounds, where they played their games, had a short right field. My father used to take me to games every so often, and the day was complete when Mel Ott would line the ball just over the right field wall into the stands and get a home run. I remember after a game, waiting outside the clubhouse until the players came out. I saw him come out. He had on what was called then a polo shirt—like a golf shirt. He looked so youthful and energetic. I never got a chance to talk to him, but I did get his autograph at one point. He was my first idol as far as sports were concerned. Then, when I got interested in basketball, Hank Luisetti was at Stanford, and they made a movie about him in which he acted. He was the first basketball superstar and the innovator of the running one-handed shot. So, I started following him and that got me more interested in basketball than baseball. Those were my two guys.

When you were coaching, and certainly now that you are on radio and TV, there are people who look up to you with envy. Do you ever consider the fact that there are people who might be idolizing you from afar?

Yeah, I do, and I feel blessed to have had that through my life. I've really gone through my whole life—except for summer jobs—without having to *work*—at least in my understanding of what work is. Coaching was a pleasure. The radio and TV stuff has been more of the same. So, I feel I've had a very unique and blessed kind of life. I'm very appreciative of it.

Career Notes: Jack Ramsay began his coaching career at St. Joseph's. He guided the Hawks to the 1956 NIT Final Four and the 1961 NCAA Final Four. His record in 11 seasons at St. Joseph's was 234-72 (.765 winning percentage). He guided the Hawks to five straight NCAA Tournament appearances and nine straight postseason bids, both of which are school records. Ramsay took his skills to the NBA, first as general manager of the 1966-67 Philadelphia 76ers. That team won the NBA championship. Ramsay soon returned to coaching and spent more than 20 seasons as an NBA head coach in Philadelphia, Buffalo, Portland and Indiana. His teams went to the playoffs 16 times. In 1977, Ramsay guided the Trail Blazers—led by Bill Walton and Maurice Lucas—to the NBA title. Ramsay's overall record as an NBA head coach was 864-783. Jack Ramsay was inducted into the Naismith Memorial Basketball Hall of Fame in 1992.

*   *   *

28

A Lot Of Eyes Are On You

Bill White played outfield and first base in the majors for 13 years with the New York/San Francisco Giants, the St. Louis Cardinals and the Philadelphia Phillies. He helped the Cardinals win the 1964 World Series championship. White was the first African-American to hold a high-ranking executive position in Major League Baseball. He was named the President of the National League in 1989 and held that position until he retired in 1994.

In 2011, White authored, *Uppity: My Untold Story about the Games People Play*. In the book, he told of his encounters with racism during his life in baseball. White was a pioneer in the early days of integration in baseball. When White played in the minors for Danville, Virginia, he was the only African-American in the Carolina League. He experienced blatant racism firsthand. Still continuing to be a pioneer, White became the first full-time African-American broadcaster in the majors and spent a number of years calling games for the Yankees.

As mentioned earlier, I was thinking of writing about the 1964 Cardinals—a book I hoped to complete before their 50th anniversary season. That book did not come to fruition, but I was able to talk about that magical season—and about childhood heroes—with Bill White. White was a huge part of that championship team in '64. While talking with him about the Cardinals' remarkable comeback that season, I began to feel like a little kid again. I was ten years old when the Cardinals won it all in '64. I felt ten years old again as I talked with Bill White on the phone from my home. I can still remember seeing White—a powerful, left-handed hitter – bang a few home runs at Busch Stadium in games I attended with my family. Those memories last a lifetime. So will memories of my phone conversation with Bill, as we discussed idols, baseball and more. I talked to Bill White on April 21, 2011.

Who was your boyhood idol growing up?

I'm from Warren, Ohio, and we stressed football there. The Cleveland Browns were my favorite team. Those guys were my idols. In '47, they won the championship of the All-America Football Conference, and three years later, they merged into the National Football League. In '47, they had Marion Motley and Bill Willis. And, they had Horace Gillom, a punter. He could kick the ball six miles. (Cleveland won the AAFC championship all four years of the league's existence, 1946–49.)

The only way for me to be able to afford to go to college was to play football, and I wasn't very good. But, I was offered a scholarship to play at Columbia in New York and at Western Reserve, which is now Case Western Reserve, in Cleveland. But, both of those cities were too big for me, (laughs) a little kid from Paxton, Florida, and Warren, Ohio. I ended up at Hiram College, a little college about twenty miles from Warren. We had 400 students.

As far as baseball, my childhood idols were Jackie Robinson and Larry Doby. Later, one of my heroes was Martin Luther King. He went through hell, and he was responsible for great changes in this country.

Did you ever meet Martin Luther King?

No, I never met Dr. King. But, I did meet Jackie. I met him at first base when I was playing for the Giants in 1956. Jackie hated the Giants so much he didn't speak to me on the field. He'd walked and got on first base, and he didn't say anything. I found out he just was that kind of competitor. He did *not* like the Giants. Of course, Jackie was with

Brooklyn. He didn't speak to anybody in a Giant uniform. I went to the Army after the 1956 season, and the Giants traded for Robinson—to play first base until I'd get out of the Army in two years. Jackie refused to be a Giant. He retired from baseball.

There have been several people I've talked with who have told me their idols were Willie Mays or Stan Musial. You were a teammate of both and should be able to provide some real insight into the kind of men they were. Were they good guys?

Willie was like a father to me. I lived with him and his then-wife, Marghuerite, in New York and then in San Francisco for a few months when I got out of the Army. He's a man I really admire. I admired Musial as a hitter. He was an excellent hitter. We on that Cardinal team were a lot younger than Stan—(Ken) Boyer, myself, (Dick) Groat, (Bob) Gibson, (Curt) Flood. You *respect* a Musial. And, I have a great amount of respect for Willie because I owe my career to Willie. Willie was just one heck of a person. He was a father figure for me, and he actually *was* a father for me because he taught me all I know about baseball.

I am a third-generation Cardinal fan and was a very happy 10-year-old boy when you and your teammates won the 1964 World Series. You were one of my many heroes on that team. What do you best remember about that time with the Cardinals?

Well, I remember '61 as well as '64 because that's when we integrated spring training in Florida. All the players, including Musial and Boyer, lived in a motel that was leased by the team in St. Petersburg. We couldn't stay together as a team at any other hotel or motel in St. Pete. We got to know each other. Our families got to know their families. Our wives got to know each other. Our kids got to know each other. I got to know Ken Boyer and Stan Musial and Red Schoendienst and their families. We had Bob Gibson. We had Curt Flood. We had myself and a big guy named George Crowe. We (blacks and whites) were like family. We had barbeques together. We ate together. We swam together.

We did everything together there at the motel. In '63, we came within a few games of winning the National League pennant. In '64, we won the whole thing, and I think we did that because we became closer and were like a close-knit family. We played together. We knew each other, and we *liked* each other.

Maybe it was the family atmosphere that helped the Cardinals win in '64, but they also had a little help from the Phillies, who lost 10 straight and blew a 6½ game lead with only 12 to play. Starting with a doubleheader sweep of the Pirates on September 24, the Cardinals won eight straight games and eventually won the pennant on the final day of the season to cap one of the greatest comebacks in baseball history. Bill, be honest. Did you really believe the Cardinals could win the pennant?

No, I didn't. I thought we had lost it when we traded (Ernie) Broglio for Lou Brock (June 15, 1964). At the time, nobody liked that trade, (laughs) but we wouldn't have won it had it not been for Brock. So, no, I didn't think we could win. I don't think *anybody* thought we could win.

The 1964 World Series was your only postseason appearance. Although you struggled at the plate for much of the series, you had two hits and scored a run to help the Cardinals win the deciding seventh game. What jumps into your mind when you think about the '64 Series against Mickey Mantle and the Yankees?

Well, the Yankees didn't scare us because we played them in spring training. We both had spring training in St. Petersburg. We always beat them because we hustled, even in spring training. The Yankees just got ready for the American League because they were a cinch to win every year. Of course, they were older in '64. But, they didn't awe us, at all. We knew—at least we *felt*—that we had a better team. We had a younger team. We had a closer team. We just thought we were gonna win.

Now, I had a bad World Series because I kept trying to hit home runs. But, I called my hitting guru, Harry Walker, who was home in Leeds, Alabama. He said, "Hey, quit trying to hit home runs. Hit the ball back up the middle." I finally got a base hit. But, basically, we won because we were a team. Boyer got a big home run (Game 4 grand slam). Tim McCarver got a big home run (10ᵗʰ-inning 3-run homer in Game 5). Mike Shannon played well.

When you won the 1964 World Series, it was as if you had shown the world that blacks and whites could work together towards a common goal. In a sense, you and your teammates were part of the Civil Rights movement.

I'm not sure we were part of the Civil Rights movement, but I think we changed a lot of things, including desegregating spring training in Florida and in Arizona. People of all colors could see us play every day. They saw, first of all, a *team*. They saw nine guys out there helping each other. They saw nine guys hugging after a win. They saw nine guys just getting along. I think that was very important.

Career Notes: A slick-fielding first baseman, Bill White won seven consecutive Gold Gloves for his defensive prowess (1960–66). White hit 201 homers and drove in 862 runs in his eleven full seasons in the majors. He ended his career with 202 homers, 870 RBI and a .286 batting average.

Bill White was routinely on the National League All-Star team in the early 1960s. He was at first base in the 1963 All-Star Game when the entire Cardinal infield started for the National League. In the 1964 championship season, White batted .303, with 21 homers and 102 RBI to help St. Louis win its first National League pennant in 18 years.

*   *   *

Mychal Thompson was the number one overall selection in the 1978 NBA Draft. He played for the Portland Trail Blazers for seven seasons. Thompson also played one half-season for San Antonio and 4½ seasons for the Lakers. He was on the Lakers' squads that won NBA titles in 1987 and 1988.

Thompson isn't the only member of his family to play professional sports. His oldest son, Mychel, played basketball at Pepperdine University, had a brief stint in the NBA with Cleveland and is now playing pro ball in Italy. Another son, Klay, is an All-NBA guard for the Warriors and helped shoot Golden State to the 2015 NBA championship. A third son, Trayce, is an outfielder with the Chicago White Sox.

After retiring from the NBA, Thompson has worked in radio and TV in Portland and Los Angeles. He is now a color commentator on Laker radio broadcasts.

I have known Mychal Thompson since my first winter in Portland in 1980 when he was beginning to show why the Trail Blazers had drafted him with the #1 pick of the '78 NBA Draft. Mychal was coming off a season in which he did not play because of injury, and he bounced back with a good season (17.0 points and 8.7 rebounds).

When he was done playing, Mychal worked for a few years as a talk show host at the radio station where I worked in Portland. He also hosted the Fifth Quarter after the Trail Blazers' games. Mychal occasionally worked on TV, once serving with me as the color commentator on an Oregon high school state basketball championship game. I can tell you with absolute certainty that—on and off the air—Mychal is an engaging fellow, armed with snappy patter and a quick smile. I'm happy to see him and his sons all having success in their current endeavors.

I talked with Mychal Thompson in Portland on March 3, 2014.

Who was your very first boyhood idol?

C'mon. There's only one guy that was my idol, and he probably was the idol of millions and millions of people around the world. That was Muhammad Ali. My all-time favorite athlete, I love the way he competed. I loved what he stood for, how brave he was, and how he stood up for equal rights for everybody. He actually put his life and his career on the line for his beliefs and for his convictions. I idolized him because of that, not just his talents in the ring, but because of his convictions and what he stood for. That's what I admire him for the most.

Did you ever have the opportunity to meet Ali?

I met him in New York. I was 14 years of age. We were on vacation, and he was staying in the same hotel we were. We were able to talk with him. He stopped and he was very nice to me and the family. He called us his Bohemian Family, his family from the Bahamas. I'll never forget that.

Mychal, you were idolized by a lot of young fans during your playing days. Did you think about that back then?

Oh, yeah. You know that there are fans—especially the kids—who look up to you. You have to understand that that's part of your job—to be a role model and to realize that a lot of eyes are on you. You have to watch how you conduct yourself because you're a public figure.

As you would expect, more than a few people have indicated one of their role models growing up was Magic Johnson. You were Magic's teammate on the Lakers. He was special.

Oh, yeah. He's my second favorite athlete of all time even though he was a peer of mine. I liked the way he competed. He was a winner. And, he was just so nice to everybody. No matter what you did in life, Magic treated everybody with respect.

Career Notes: Mychal Thompson was born in Nassau, Bahamas, but his family moved to the United States when he was young. Thompson

393

attended high school in Miami, Florida, and played college basketball at the University of Minnesota. He was a consensus First-Team All-America selection in 1978. Thompson scored 12,810 points (13.7 PPG) over 12 NBA seasons. He averaged in double-figure scoring in each of his seven full seasons in Portland. His best NBA season was 1981-82, when he averaged 20.8 points and 11.7 rebounds.

*   *   *

29

The Word Is Humble

Brooks Robinson spent his entire 23-year career with the Baltimore Orioles. Considered by many to be the greatest defensive third baseman in MLB history, "The Human Vacuum Cleaner" won 16 consecutive Gold Gloves for defensive excellence. His series of spectacular defensive plays in the 1970 Fall Classic are often mentioned when great plays in World Series history are discussed. In addition to his stellar defensive play, Robinson batted .429 and hit two home runs in the 1970 Fall Classic. Not surprisingly, he was named the 1970 World Series MVP. With Robinson playing a key role, Baltimore played in four World Series over a six year span. They won two championships.

Robinson now works on behalf of former players in the role of president of the Major League Baseball Players Alumni Association.

I interviewed Brooks Robinson on my radio sports talk program in 1990. I was thrilled to talk with him 25 years ago, and I can confirm that I was just as thrilled to visit with him when I contacted him more recently to ask about his childhood heroes. Both times I interviewed Robinson he was very generous with his time. He was another one of those sports legends that I would have enjoyed talking with for hours. When we got around to discussing his boyhood idol, Brooks surprised me when he said his first sports idol was the same as mine. By the way, the other athletes in this chapter also considered "Stan the Man" to be a pretty special guy.

I talked by telephone with Brooks Robinson on December 2, 2013.

Who was your very first boyhood idol?

If you're talking about baseball, it was Stan Musial. I was always a Cardinal fan because that's the only game that we got on radio. Stan Musial was the best player on the team. He was always my boyhood idol. I grew up in Little Rock. Bill Dickey, the great Yankee player, grew up about ten blocks from where I lived. He wasn't living there at that particular time, but I knew he was born there and had spent his childhood there. I used to have a paper route, and I used to go by his house. I knew he was not there and that he didn't live there then, but I used to flip that paper a little extra hard to get it up on the porch. Bill Dickey was another idol of mine.

You played in the major leagues for a few years while Musial was still playing for the Cardinals. You were in the American League. He was in the National. But, I'm sure you crossed paths at some point. Do you remember the first time you met "Stan the Man?"

I do not remember, but it was probably at a spring training game or an All-Star Game. He retired in '63, so I had a chance to meet him somewhere along the line, but I'm not sure where.

Many have talked about what a great person Stan Musial was. No doubt, you've heard those same kinds of things mentioned when Stan's name is brought up.

Well, I heard that. Sure. And, you could see that by that outpouring of love when he passed away. I understand it was really just an unbelievable scene when he passed away. He liked people. He liked to be around people. He enjoyed himself. To see him come out on the Hall of Fame stage every time and take that little stroke—that swing of his—we got a big kick out of that. Then, he'd be down in the bar playing his harmonica. He was just an outgoing, wonderful person.

You were one of the brightest stars in Baltimore during your playing days, and many youngsters idolized you. Did you think about the fact that you had become the same kind of hero to kids that Stan Musial had been for you?

It didn't really make an impact on me until I started getting letters and people were telling me they named their son, Brooks. I have a whole list of Brooks' people. We send them a picture and say, "I'm honored that your name is Brooks." But, we got that, letters and things, I'm sayin' a hundred times over all these years. And, it still happens. I was at a store doing a little signing here not too long ago. A lady came up to me with her husband. She was pregnant, and she said, "Well, this is little Brooks," because they knew it was a boy. I love that.

You played in Baltimore for a long time. Fans in that city love you, and I know you love them back.

Absolutely. Absolutely. You know, I practically came here with the team. I signed in '55 out of high school. The Orioles—the old Browns—came here from St. Louis in '54, so I practically came with the team. I played longer with one team than anyone in the history of baseball—along with Yastrzemski. He played like 23 full years with the Red Sox. I played *part* of—or *all* of—23 years with the Orioles. I guess it's just like John Unitas in this town. We were here about the same time. We stayed here. We lived here. We raised our families here. They went to school here, and they work here.

Since you ended up with a team that had been based in St. Louis, and because you had grown up a Cardinals' fan, was there ever a time you said, "Darn! I would have rather signed with the Cardinals than the Browns?"

No, not really. The Cardinals didn't really show an interest in me as a player. I had a basketball scholarship offer to the University of Arkansas, and there was a scout—the Cardinals' chief scout for the area—Fred

Hahn, who had told the Arkansas basketball coach, "If you're wanting Brooks to play basketball, you better just go after him because I don't think he's gonna be a big league baseball player." So, the Cardinals didn't really pursue me. The teams that did were the Cincinnati Reds and the Orioles. There were seven or eight teams I had contact with, but it came down to Cincinnati and Baltimore. Both of them offered me major league contracts. That meant you skipped a couple or three options than if you signed a minor league contract. That just meant they couldn't control you as long, and they had to make a decision on whether they wanted you on the roster or not. But, anyway, Little Rock was a Detroit farm team. You went from Little Rock, up to Toledo, and up to the Detroit Tigers. I used to go out and shag balls and take infield a few times. Ray Winder, who was the owner of the Little Rock Travelers, he thought that he had a good chance to sign me. But, it worked out that Baltimore was my quickest way to the major leagues. That's what they impressed on me.

Brooks, a number of athletes have indicated that Willie Mays was their boyhood idol. You would have played against Mays at some point, most likely in spring training. Can you tell me what you and your contemporaries thought about Willie Mays back in the day?

Well, I just went to a Gold Glove Awards ceremony in New York with Rawlings Sporting Goods. They honored Willie, and he came. I know he's had some health problems—vision problems and things—but having Willie Mays there, he *made* the show. I don't care if no one else showed up. (Laughs) Willie was there, and he made the show. He's in the same breath with Mantle and Aaron. You talk to the Milwaukee players, and they say, "Oh, Hank Aaron's the best." You talk to the Giants, "Mays is the greatest." That's a conversation that will go on and on. But, Willie was exciting. He could do everything—hit, hit with power, run, field, throw. I mean, he had all the tools. He's simply one of the greatest. Someone said players go up a hill and there are only a small number of players who reach the top of that hill. You'd have to say that Mays is right at the top.

You have been called perhaps the greatest defensive third baseman in baseball history. The mental picture I have of you is you making those spectacular defensive plays in the 1970 World Series when you ranged far to your right and dove to your left to rob Cincinnati batters of hits. In particular, I recall that play behind the third-base bag where you backhanded the ball in foul territory and threw out Lee May at first base. It's still a fresh image in my mind although it happened many years ago. It's an image that I suspect will last in the minds of anyone who saw it live or has seen the videotape. Are those the moments for which you are still best remembered?

Oh, sure. Absolutely. Being in the World Series and winning the World Series, it's really like a springboard to the Hall of Fame. That series of defensive plays was like a once-in-a-lifetime happening and it happened to be in the World Series. You can play for a week and never get a chance to make an outstanding play.

Career Notes: Brooks Robinson made his major league debut in 1955. After his final season in 1977, Robinson had amassed 2,848 career hits, 268 home runs and 1,357 runs-batted-in. His best season offensively was 1964. That year, he batted .318, with 28 home runs and a league-best 118 runs-batted-in. Robinson won the 1964 American League Most Valuable Player Award. He was runner-up to teammate Frank Robinson in the AL MVP voting in 1966, the year the Orioles won their first World Series. Brooks Robinson was the American League's starting third baseman in 15 consecutive All-Star Games. He was voted as the All-Star Game MVP in 1966 after going 3-for-4 at the plate, with a triple and a run scored. Robinson was inducted into the Baseball Hall of Fame in his first year of eligibility in 1983. He was selected to Major League Baseball's All-Century Team. Brooks Robinson is also a member of the Baltimore Orioles Hall of Fame. His jersey (#5) has been retired by the Orioles.

*   *   *

Rod Thorn has spent a lifetime involved with professional basketball. He has been an NBA player, coach, team executive and league executive. Thorn retired from his position as the NBA's president of basketball operations in August, 2015. It was his second stint in the league office. Thorn earlier spent 14 years as head of basketball operations under then-commissioner David Stern, primarily serving as the NBA's chief disciplinarian. Thorn has also been general manager or president of basketball operations of the Bulls, Nets and 76ers.

Thorn has been an NBA executive for so long that some might not remember he played in the NBA for eight years after being selected with the second overall pick in the 1963 draft. I never forgot because I have a couple of his basketball cards from the '60s in my collection. Thorn has held a lot of jobs and accomplished many things during his decades involved with basketball, but in Chicago, he will always be remembered as the guy that drafted Michael Jordan in 1984. As detailed in an earlier chapter, Thorn can thank the Portland Trail Blazers for selecting Sam Bowie with the second pick in the draft, allowing Jordan to slip to the Bulls.

I spoke with Rod Thorn in Portland, Oregon, on March 19, 2011.

Who was your first boyhood idol?

Hands down, it was Stan Musial. My father was a baseball player. He played in the Cardinals' system for a while. He played with Stan Musial when Musial started as a pitcher in Class D ball. KMOX Radio—the 50,000 watt "Voice of St. Louis"—we could get in West Virginia. So, I used to listen to a lot of Cardinal games. I loved Stan Musial. I grew up in the '40s, so starting from about 1951, I used to listen to the games—not all of them, but a lot of them. I became a big Cardinal and Stan Musial fan.

So, it was pretty much because of those radio broadcasts that you followed Musial and the Cardinals?

That is correct. Harry Caray, who was the "Voice" of the Cardinals for so many years, would do the games. He was exciting. He made the games sound very exciting.

Did you ever have a chance to meet Stan the Man?

Never. Never. And, I was in St.Louis as a coach in the ABA for a time. I ate dinner at his restaurant. He had a restaurant called *Stan and Biggie's*, but he was never there when I ate there.

As you got older and became affiliated with basketball, was there anybody that stood out for you in that sport?

Jerry West. He was a big star at West Virginia when I was in high school. West Virginia went to the Final Four and got beat in the final game by California his junior year. So, I went to West Virginia, and I was a freshman when he was a senior.

Career Notes: In 2015, the Naismith Basketball Hall of Fame honored Rod Thorn for his contributions to basketball by presenting him with its John Bunn Lifetime Achievement Award. Thorn, a native of Princeton, West Virginia, was the 1963 Southern Conference Athlete of the Year while at West Virginia University. With the Mountaineers, he played on two basketball teams and three baseball teams that appeared in NCAA tournaments. A high school basketball All-American, Thorn also earned All-America honors after his senior season at West Virginia. He scored 1,785 career points at WVU and set several school records.

In the NBA, Rod Thorn played for the Baltimore Bullets, Detroit Pistons, St. Louis Hawks and Seattle SuperSonics. The 6-foot-4 guard averaged 10.8 points, 3.1 rebounds and 2.6 assists in his pro career. Thorn was named to the NBA All-Rookie team after he averaged 14.4 points, 4.8 rebounds and 3.7 assists for Baltimore in 1963-64. He averaged a career-best 15.2 points in 1967-68, his first season in Seattle.

Early in his coaching career, Thorn was an assistant with the New York Nets when Julius Erving led the team to the 1974 ABA title. Also in the now-defunct American Basketball Association, Thorn spent a brief time as head coach of the Spirits of St. Louis (1975-76). He was also the interim head coach of the Chicago Bulls for part of the 1981-82 campaign.

As the Bulls' general manager in 1984, Thorn was responsible for drafting Michael Jordan. Later, as GM of the Nets in 2002, Thorn was named NBA Executive of the Year for orchestrating the Nets' turnaround that led to their first appearance in the NBA Finals. Thorn assembled a Nets' team that reached the NBA Finals in 2002 and 2003.

*   *   *

Harry Gallatin starred nine years for the New York Knickerbockers in the 1940s and '50s before ending his career with the Pistons in 1958. Nicknamed "The Horse" because of his size and strength, the 6-foot-6 Gallatin was one of the early NBA's top rebounders. Gallatin played in 610 consecutive games with the Knicks, a record that still stands today. After his playing days, Gallatin spent parts of three seasons as the head coach of the St. Louis Hawks. He was named the very first NBA Coach of the Year in 1963. Gallatin later coached the Knicks for parts of two seasons. He was enshrined in the Naismith Basketball Hall of Fame in 1991.

Trust me when I tell you that Harry Gallatin spent his entire life involved with sports. Harry's first season with the New York Knickerbockers was 1948-49, when they were part of the Basketball Association of America (BAA). It was the BAA's third season—its last before merging with the National Basketball League (NBL) to form the National Basketball Association (NBA). The first year of Gallatin's pro career, the teams in the BAA were the New York Knickerbockers, Washington Capitols, Baltimore Bullets, Philadelphia Warriors, Boston Celtics, Providence Steam Rollers,

Rochester Royals, Minneapolis Lakers, Chicago Stags, St. Louis Bombers, Fort Wayne Pistons and Indianapolis Jets.

I first met Harry Gallatin after I transferred from SIU-Carbondale to SIU-Edwardsville in January, 1974. Harry was the school's golf coach. He was also teaching a golf class at the university. Needing to sign up for an elective class, I signed up for Harry's "Introduction to Golf" class. He was a gentle giant of a man, yet quite calm and extremely patient. I can still hear Harry telling me, "Keep your left arm straight!" Despite Harry's best efforts, I never became a very good golfer.

I was saddened by the passing of Harry Gallatin on October 7, 2015. He was 88.

Harry Gallatin was at his home in Edwardsville, Illinois, when I got him on the phone on January 16, 2014.

Harry, who was your very first boyhood idol?

I would say Stan Musial of the Cardinals. He just seemed to be the type of guy that I liked. He had great ability, and he was sort of an honest, sincere-type person that I like a lot.

You grew up in Roxana, Illinois, which is close to St. Louis. Did you get to Sportsman's Park very often to see him play?

Yeah, my dad liked baseball, and he always wanted me to be a baseball pitcher. He and I played catch an awful lot in the vacant lot behind the house. He'd take me over to St. Louis, and we'd sit in the bleachers there in Sportsman's Park. So, I became a baseball fan, but I also loved basketball.

Did you ever get a chance to meet Musial?

Oh, sure. In fact, there were a number of occasions where I was with Stan. He had a golf tournament in Branson, Missouri, and I still have his jacket from when I played golf down there. It was a tournament where he invited an awful lot of people who are in the Hall of Fame in Missouri. Through that association, I became good friends with Stan. Any time I saw him, he'd say, "Hey, what are you doin', big guy?"

I've asked a lot of people if their idols lived up to expectations. I bet that Stan lived up to your expectations?

Yes, there's no question about that. Let me tell you about one time I got together with Stan. Arnold Palmer dedicated a golf course over here in Alton, Illinois, which is just north of here. We had a scramble for the opening of the Spencer Olin Golf Course. Stan came, so I have a picture in my family room of me standing with Arnold Palmer and Stan Musial and Joe Magrane, who was a pitcher for the Cardinals at the time.

Stan Musial seemed to have a down-to-earth, everyman quality about him. That was a little unusual for a big star like that.

The word is humble. He thought everybody was a good person, and he wanted to come across as being one of those. He'd just sign every time a kid would ask him for an autograph. Or, if anybody else would ask him to do something, he'd bend over backwards to try to make people happy.

I knew that Stan had been in declining health for some time, but it saddened me when he passed away. It almost felt like my father had died. How did Stan's passing affect you?

Well, it was a big, big disappointment to me. But, this had been coming on for a while. He always came out for the opening ceremonies for baseball and that kind of thing. It was obvious that Stan was moving to the point in his life that he may not be around. He did so many things for the people in St. Louis. He's just an idol that will never be forgotten here.

Let's talk about your career. You go back to the early days of the NBA. In fact, you played in the first NBA All-Star Game. Was it a big deal back then?

Well, *yeah*. It was a big deal. It had never happened before. It was in Boston. If I remember, I think I got a hundred dollars for playing in that All-Star Game. (Laughs) But, it was quite an honor. Walter Brown was the owner of the Celtics at that time. He was a great guy. The All-Star Game was something that he thought was important to kind of bring the league up in visibility. Basically, that's what we were trying to do in the early days—trying to get people interested in the league and the cities that participated. That was one thing that Walter Brown thought was important. Yeah, that was quite an occasion for me.

Harry, you played in seven straight All-Star Games, so it's pretty clear that you were one of the very best players of your time. You must have been an idol for kids who looked up to you in the same way you had looked up to Stan Musial. Do you ever think about that?

Well, yeah, I do think about it because I idolized Stan, and I don't think he ever turned down anybody for an autograph. I certainly feel that way, too. In the mail every day, I get one or two letters from kids seeking an autograph. I don't think I've ever turned any of them down. It's just one of the things I think is important. If people think that much of you that they want your autograph, you certainly have to give it to them.

I happen to know that you never missed a game during your playing career. You have to take great pride in that fact.

Yeah, (laughs) it's one of the things I'm very proud of. And, I was also very lucky. I don't think I ever missed a practice or a game in grade school, high school, pro ball. I can never remember missing anything. It was the same thing at the university (SIU-Edwardsville) in the time that I served here. I don't think I ever missed a day of work. In fact, I remember when I left the university. I got a check for $10,000 for not missing sick days. I pray every day that I'll remain healthy like that. I've always said that the number one priority for everyone should be their health. It is the one thing that I talk about all the time to people.

Here's another thing I'm sure you're proud of. You and Willis Reed still share the Knicks' record for rebounds in a game with 33.

That's a story, too. We played in Madison Square Garden on Saturday night. We always took a train to Fort Wayne, Indiana. The next day, Sunday morning, I remember walking from the train station down to the gym there in Fort Wayne—with the church bells ringing. I was tired, *really* tired. We buckled up in the *afternoon* for crying out loud. We had lunch and put on the suit again. It was the best game I ever played for the Knicks. I scored 30 points and had 33 rebounds. I remember that one well. I don't know why it happened. I was really tired at the time, so you just never know.

Harry, what was it that allowed you to be successful? You were only 6-feet 6-inches tall, a little undersized for a center even back then, wasn't it?

Yeah, it was. Well, I always played hard and never let up. As far as rebounding is concerned, it's effort that makes a difference. I always thought if I was going to do something, I'd do it to the best of my ability and play as hard as I could. It paid off for me.

Have you ever had anyone tell you that "Harry the Horse" was their favorite player back in the day?

Oh, yeah. From time to time, there have been some people that have come up and talk to me about that and mention "The Horse." But, the older you get, the fewer people come up. (Laughs)

Career Notes: During his NBA career, Harry Gallatin averaged 13.0 points and 11.9 rebounds. He led the NBA in rebounding in 1954 (15.3

boards per game) and was named First Team All-NBA. Gallatin played in seven consecutive NBA All-Star Games, including the first All-Star Game in 1951. Gallatin had five points and five rebounds for the East in a 111-94 victory over the West. The Celtics' "Easy Ed" Macauley earned MVP honors by scoring a game-high 20 points and holding George Mikan of the Minneapolis Lakers to only four field goals on 17 attempts.

Harry Gallatin was the head basketball coach at Southern Illinois University in Carbondale for four seasons. He later was hired as the first athletic director at Southern Illinois University in Edwardsville and also spent three seasons as the school's head basketball coach. Gallatin served as SIU-E's men's golf coach for 24 years.

*   *   *

30

She Walked The Path

Paula Creamer is one of the most popular players on the LPGA Tour. Well-known for her pink golfing attire, Creamer has been nicknamed the "Pink Panther." Although she struggled a bit with her game in 2015, Creamer remains a wonderful player. She is one of the most sought-after product endorsers in women's golf.

Creamer has been a strong supporter of The First Tee youth program and hosts an annual event—Paula 4 Kids—which benefits the First Tee of Sarasota/Manatee (Florida).

Sometimes star players—in any sport—won't speak out on issues because they don't want to offend anyone or be too controversial. That is not the case with Paula Creamer. In April of 2015, Creamer received notoriety for suggesting that Augusta National host a female version of the Masters each year in addition to the men's tournament. While the idea was quickly dismissed by club chairman Billy Payne, who cited the inconveniencing of Augusta National's members, Creamer still believes it's a sound idea. A highly-coveted product endorser, Creamer has graduated from being a teen sensation to a young woman with enough celebrity, credibility and courage to become an advocate for women's golf. She has reached out to connect with thousands of young girls and inspired them to play the game. Golf needs more champions of the sport, champions like Paula Creamer—a visionary with game.

I talked with Paula Creamer in a phone interview on August 12, 2011, and also during a news conference at the LPGA Tournament in Portland, Oregon, on August 28, 2013.

Who was your first childhood idol?

I have a couple actually. I don't really have just one. I met Kathy Whitworth when I was about 14 years old. Kathy Whitworth has always been a big inspiration to me. She's helped me along. I've definitely had some really good talks with her, and I still keep up with her to this day. But, I've also always looked up to Nancy Lopez and Juli Inkster. I think they're grinders. Juli and I have become very, very close. It's pretty neat that you can say one of your role models is now your Solheim Cup partner and you play against her every week. That doesn't really happen much in sports. But, those are three women that I've always really, really looked up to.

What was it that made each of them a childhood idol of yours?

Well, their demeanor. All three of them are fighters. They're grinders. They're champions. Kathy Whitworth has won 88 times. (Laughs) I mean, you've gotta learn things from her; that's for sure. Just mentally, they're all so strong, and they've done so much for the game of golf. For me as a kid, I was really the only girl, and to see that these women were champions and were the best players in the world, I thought, "Wow! If they can do it, maybe I can." It was just that whole fighting concept— and practicing—that kept motivating me to get where I am today.

In talking with a number of women's professional golfers, it becomes clear that Nancy Lopez has been an inspiration to many players in women's golf. She's really special, isn't she?

She's just an incredible person on and off the golf course. That's what I like. You can really let your golf club do the talkin'. Then afterwards, she's just a normal down-to-earth woman. She's done *so* much for the game, yet she's so humble. That is something that I really admire and that I try and take into my golf life, and my personal life as well.

The first time you met each of these three women who have meant so much to you and to women's golf, was it all just a little unbelievable?

Oh, definitely. Of course it was. It's just incredible when you meet people that you've looked up to and there they are talking to you. Memories like those you cherish forever.

You are a hero to many young girls today. Do you think about that often?

(Laughs) It's amazing. I've never really considered myself a role model or anything like that, but I am. It's hard. I have to pinch myself. It's people like Nancy and Kathy and Juli that have given me the opportunity to be a role model because they have taught *me* so much. If I can get little boys and girls involved in the game of golf in a positive way, then I'll take it. It's a big role, but I cherish it. I think it's incredible that I just turned 25 and have all these little boys and girls look up to me. It's pretty special.

There is a young girl here in attendance, Audrey Ward, who became your fan for life when you walked over to her on the 18th green last year here in Portland. You removed your watch and handed it to her. Do you remember that, and how often do you do something like that?

I do remember. And, I try to do it as much as I can. I think it's pretty cool to give back to junior golf. They're the future of the LPGA and golf in general. I've always found that I love kids. I love giving back, especially with First Tee and being an ambassador for them. It's just a fun part of what I can do. I have great sponsors. They allow me to do that kind of thing. If I can help one person out there to just get involved a little bit more than they have before, then I feel like I'm doing a good job out here.

We've talked before about childhood idols. You are now obviously Audrey's idol as a result of your act of kindness last year. How important is that to you?

It's kind of hard for me to embrace that I am an idol. I came out here on tour when I was 18 years old. I was playing against my role models and am still playing with my role models to this day. With Juli Inkster the first couple years, I would even hit balls next to her on the range. I'd be just watching her. I was so excited to be out with people that had influenced me to pick up a club. To realize that I have that effect on someone else, I can't quite grasp it. I still am learning so much that hopefully I can be of help. I love what I do. I take big pride in coming out here and trying to conduct myself well. It's a great game that we have. Like I said, I just hope that I can—whether it's wearing the color pink or whatever it is—get girls involved in this game.

Career Notes: Paula Creamer won 11 American Junior Golf Association tournaments and was the nation's top-ranked amateur in both 2003 and 2004. She was named the 2003 AJGA Player of the Year. Creamer played in ten LPGA tournaments as an amateur and finished in the top-20 in half of those events. A 17-year-old Creamer fired a 7-under-64 in the second round of the 2004 ShopRite LPGA Classic. She finished that tournament tied for second, one stroke behind Cristie Kerr. Later in 2004, Creamer qualified for the LPGA Tour, winning the qualifying tournament on her first attempt. She was the 2005 LPGA Rookie of the Year after winning a then-LPGA Tour rookie-record $1.5-million. Creamer won more than $1-million dollars in each of her first five LPGA seasons. Her most successful year was 2008 when she won four tournaments and nearly $2-million. Through late October of 2015, Creamer has career earnings on the LPGA Tour of nearly $11.5-million. She has ten LPGA Tour victories, including the 2010 U.S. Women's Open at Oakmont Country Club. As a member of the United States Solheim Cup team, Creamer went a combined 12-6-5 in 2005, 2007, 2009, 2011 and 2013. In August, 2015, she was named a Solheim Cup captain's pick by Juli Inkster. The following month in Germany,

Creamer came through in the clutch. She won the final singles match to lift the United States to a remarkable come-from-behind 14½ -13½ victory after the Americans entered singles play on the final day trailing 10-6. Creamer is now 4-2 in Solheim Cup singles for her career, and she has been part of four Solheim Cup championship teams.

* * *

Brittany Lincicome is one of the top American players on the LPGA Tour. The Florida native has won more than $7-million on the women's professional golf tour since her rookie year in 2005.

I think the first time I ever heard Brittany Lincicome's name was in 2004. As an 18-year-old amateur, she fired a 5-under-par 66 to grab the first round lead of the 2004 U.S. Women's Open at the Orchards Golf Club in South Hadley, Massachusetts. She didn't win that weekend, but her performance put everyone on notice that a new American women's golf star was on the horizon. Lincicome hasn't disappointed since turning professional. She's won six LPGA tournaments—two of them majors—and she played for Team USA in her fifth straight Solheim Cup in 2015.

I talked with Brittany Lincicome by telephone on August 8, 2011.

Whatever the sport, many of us had a favorite player while we were growing up. Can you think about those days where you were just a kid? Who was your first childhood idol?

It's going to have to be somebody in golf. I actually played baseball myself for five years growing up, but I didn't really follow baseball too much. Being in the golf setting, it would be either Nancy Lopez or Annika Sorenstam. They always kind of seemed to be in the limelight— especially Annika—when I came through junior golf. It would probably have to be Annika Sorenstam because she did so much for the game. Just watching her play golf, you know, she could hit it right-to-left. She could hit it left-to-right. She always seemed to come up with the shots, and I thought that was very cool.

Did you ever get to meet her when you were a kid?

No, but either my rookie year on Tour or my second year on Tour, I was paired with her in the final group and shot like a 78 or something. I was so nervous! But, you know, live and learn, and it was a great learning experience. We miss her very much on the LPGA Tour.

Do you remember which tournament that was?

Yeah, I believe it was out in Arizona because desert golf was something I wasn't used to. And, then playing with somebody so famous, it was very challenging. (Laughs)

What went through your mind when you first learned you were going to be paired with Annika?

It was very nerve-wracking. (Laughs) My rookie year, I remember going to the driving range, and I wanted to hit golf balls next to somebody that was really super-famous. So, I always looked for Annika or Juli Inkster—or players that were really, really great—just so I could hit golf balls next to them. (Laughs) When I got paired with Annika, it was one of those things where I went into it not expecting anything great in case something went wrong. And, I was just kind of taking it all in and enjoying the day.

What was she like? Did she meet your expectations?

Oh, yeah. She was above and beyond. She was very serious on the golf course, but off the golf course—very chatty, very nice. If you needed anything, she was there and normally had the answers.

You mentioned Nancy Lopez. Almost every woman golfer I've spoken with has brought up her name, if not as a childhood idol,

certainly as someone that just about everyone respects. What was it about Nancy that drew you towards her?

She's like a Juli Inkster—just very mothering. She always seems to be there and has the right things to say. At the beginning of this year, at the Founder's Cup in Phoenix, I bogeyed the last hole to finish second. I would have been in a playoff if I would of made par. I was crying. Nancy was there, and she was very comforting. She always has the right things to say. Obviously, being in the spotlight as much as she was, you take her advice and you run with it.

Now you are being idolized by a lot of young golfers. Do you think about that, and if so, does it make you want to toe the line and do the right thing all the time?

Absolutely. We live day to day on and off the golf course, and I try to be respectful. I am always thinking in the back of my mind that some child somewhere might be watching and to make sure I do the right things like the idols that I idolized always did. There are getting to be more, but there are just not enough girls playing golf. So, anytime I see a young girl playing, I'm always excited. I put in the extra effort to go over and sign an autograph and encourage them to play golf and go to college and see if they can turn pro.

Career Notes: Brittany Lincicome has won six LPGA tournaments, including a pair of majors. She won the 2009 Kraft Nabisco Championship by one stroke after eagling the final hole. In the 2014 LPGA Championship, Lincicome had a chance to win her second major title. However, she bogeyed the final hole of regulation and lost in sudden-death to Inbee Park. She was able to claim her second major championship in April, 2015, when she won the ANA Inspiration (the former Kraft Nabisco Championship). She again eagled the 72nd hole of regulation to force a playoff with Stacy Lewis. She won on the third hole of sudden-death.

*   *   *

Cristie Kerr is living proof that patience and hard work can lead to something good. Kerr did not win a tournament in her first five years on the LPGA Tour. But, once she secured her first professional victory in 2002, Kerr became one of the toughest competitors in women's golf. Kerr has finished in the Top 10 of 158 LPGA tournaments in her career (as of October 30, 2015). Cristie has won 17 tournaments, including two majors (2007 U.S. Women's Open and 2010 LPGA Championship). After winning the 2010 LPGA Championship by a record 12 strokes, she became the first American player to be ranked #1 in the Rolex World Golf Standings.

While working as a sportscaster in Portland, Oregon, I was privileged to cover the city's annual LPGA tournament. Each year, from 1980 to 2013, I saw how great women's golf can be when played at the highest level. I noticed that Cristie Kerr was one of those players who worked tirelessly at the driving range trying to master her craft. Obviously, her hard work paid off. I was on hand to witness one of her 17 career victories—the 2013 Portland tournament.

Cristie Kerr was ranked number one in the world when I talked with her during a news conference at the LPGA tournament in Portland, Oregon, on August 18, 2010.

You talked about dreaming of this day when you were a little kid and practicing a six-foot putt to win a tournament to become the best in the world. When did you first seriously believe that you could be the best player in the world?

It might sound bad to say but I have always felt like I had the ability, the talent. I always felt like I could be number one. I think if you're a professional golfer and you don't think that way, you'll probably never get there. I feel like I've had that within me forever. It's what I've always wanted to do. I've always known how good I am, but it's taken me time to mature a little bit as a person along the way over the years. Now, I'm ready to be able to handle all that stuff.

When you first picked up a club early in life, who was your idol?

I think I wanted to be Nancy Lopez. She was one of my idols growing up. All the great American golfers—Juli Inkster, Beth Daniel, Meg Mallon, Rosie Jones—I envied them so much. I wanted to be them. That's how I got involved in wanting to play golf. I watched those players play and win tournaments on TV. That's how I got exposed to professional women's golf. It's fitting that I'm here now saying I wanted to *be* them, and I *am* them. It's a great honor.

You mentioned several players there, but the first time you met Nancy Lopez, what did that mean to you?

It was an amazing experience for me. I think I might have been 14-years-old. I played in Orlando. I had qualified for the LPGA tournament, and I got paired with her. I was terrified. She was my idol, but—at the same time—I was a kid, and I was playing with her in a tournament. Many years later, she said I didn't look terrified at all, that I was very focused and all this stuff. That's *me*, but I was a kid back then. I was so excited, but—at the same time—scared to be playing with my idol, Nancy Lopez.

Career Notes: Cristie Kerr has career earnings of nearly $16.8-million on the LPGA Tour (as of October 30, 2015). She is the highest-earning American woman in the history of the women's pro tour. Kerr has been a member of the United States team in every Solheim Cup competition since 2002. In 2015, she played in her eighth Solheim Cup and posted a singles victory on the final day to help Team USA stage a remarkable comeback to beat Team Europe.

* * *

Natalie Gulbis is one of golf's most popular players. A native of Sacramento, California, Gulbis consistently attracts some of the largest galleries at LPGA tournament stops around the world. Not only has she been highly competitive since her rookie year on the LPGA Tour (2002), the attractive blonde has been featured in numerous photo spreads. She has appeared in several Sports Illustrated swimsuit issues and Golf Magazine's "Most Beautiful Women in Golf." Gulbis has embraced her physical attributes and has issued her own photo-calendar. Without question, she has become one of the most marketable players in women's golf.

Gulbis is very good for the LPGA Tour. She is fan-friendly, bright and articulate. Also, Natalie's active participation in social media makes her one of the LPGA's most popular ambassadors. Gulbis has been involved in charitable causes for many years. She founded the Natalie Gulbis Foundation in 2005. And, after volunteering for the organization as a teen, Natalie remains very involved with the Boys & Girls Club. She now has a Boys & Girls Club bearing her name in Henderson, Nevada, near Las Vegas.

I think it's safe to say Natalie Gulbis would have many more tournament wins and ever greater career earnings' numbers if she hadn't battled health issues for much of her career. Gulbis has fought painful back problems for years, but she played valiantly through extreme discomfort. She was forced to undergo back surgery in 2010. In 2013, Gulbis contracted malaria while playing in the LPGA tournament in Thailand. Bedridden for a time, she missed more than a month of the LPGA season. The lingering effects of the disease clearly affected her play throughout the year. Gulbis also played with a painful hip injury in 2014 and missed nearly four months in the back half of the season. She went through physical therapy in an effort to avoid surgery. Finally, she finally relented and had surgery the week of Thanksgiving. After the procedure, Gulbis avoided golf for more than a month before slowly starting to work her way back into playing condition.

The physical problems have been a real challenge for Gulbis, who looks forward to again being in good health and in contention to win every Sunday. She's done so much for women's golf, I hope she can avoid any more health issues and regain command of her game. She deserves some good things to happen for her after all that she's done to promote the women's game.

I spoke with Natalie Gulbis by phone on August 19, 2013.

Who was your first childhood hero?

My first idol was Nancy Lopez because I had played golf at a young age and my dad used to be a fan of Nancy Lopez. I used to love to watch her on TV. My dad would always take me to LPGA events. Nancy Lopez was always so nice to me. I have a pretty big collection of things that she signed for me as a kid.

Then, when I got to play on the LPGA Tour, the most nervous that I had been *ever*—more than a Solheim, more than a major—was the day I got to play with Nancy Lopez in a tournament as a professional. It was probably my fifth year on Tour. She was my childhood hero, and I really looked up to her and idolized her. I got to play for her when she was captain of the Solheim Cup team. It was just the greatest week. I loved every moment of it.

That first time you played in a tournament with Nancy, it had to seem a little surreal.

Absolutely! It was surreal! It's surreal now that I'm happy to call her a friend and have gotten to know her very well. I still idolize her, and I remember how much I wanted to do things like Nancy Lopez. I remember just how wonderful she was every time that I met her. It's really important. I remember how, when she did sign something for me, how much that meant to me. I looked up to a lot of professional athletes. I was a big Niners' fan growing up, and we were a big fan of

Joe Montana. We used to go to training camp, and I remember when he would sign something. It was really a big deal. Those professional athletes made such a positive impression on me as a young athlete. I just wanted to be like them and to be able to do that someday. So, it's something that I love to do now.

Do you think about the fact that there are young girls and boys who watch you and look up to you?

Every day. I do every day. I was in a golf shop in Las Vegas yesterday getting my clubs worked on, and a couple came up and asked me to sign some stuff. They asked me, "Do you ever get sick of people coming up asking you?" I said, "No! I love it!" I love that the Tour has so many fans and people are excited to meet us. It's gonna be really sad when that doesn't happen anymore. (Laughs) I'm gonna miss it!

I think about the fans constantly. At the end of the round, whether it's a good day or a bad day, these fans are so excited to meet you. I've had some really tough days on the golf course, then there's this group of fans in the gallery that is waiting to meet you and spend a couple moments with you and get your autograph. They don't care that you bogeyed the last hole and that you shot a high score. They are just excited to see you. One of the best parts about being a professional athlete is getting to do something that you love and getting to do it in front of fans that are excited to come out and watch you.

Career Notes: In 2005, Natalie Gulbis had Top-10 finishes in three of the four major championships. She finished tied for 17th in the fourth major that year and was sixth on the money list with more than $1-million in earnings. The following year, Gulbis again finished in the Top-20 of all four majors. She and her former University of Arizona teammate, Lorena Ochoa, were the only LPGA players to accomplish that feat in 2006.

Natalie Gulbis has won four professional tournaments. She captured the LPGA's 2007 Evian Masters with a birdie on the first hole of a playoff with Jeong Jang. She was also part of three winning LPGA teams in the Wendy's 3-Tour Challenge (2007, 2009, 2013). Gulbis has played on three winning U.S. Solheim Cup teams (2005, 2007, 2009).

Displaying great determination and mental toughness, Natalie Gulbis has played brilliantly at various points in her career, especially when she has felt good physically. As of October 30, 2015, she has amassed nearly $4.9-million in career earnings on the golf course, and that does not include what she has earned in her lucrative endorsement deals.

*   *   *

Suzann Pettersen has been one of the more successful players on the LPGA Tour over the last nine years. A winner of 15 LPGA tournaments and nearly $13.5-million in prize money, the young woman from Norway has been relentless in her pursuit of excellence. Despite her solid play over the last decade, she has never been ranked number one in her career.

I saw Suzann Pettersen win the Portland LPGA event in 2011 and 2013. Her game looked very good, as it has throughout much of her career. It is a little hard to believe she has never been ranked number one in the world. She won five tournaments in 2007 and four in 2013, but neither year could she achieve her goal of being ranked number one. Pettersen has been ranked as high as number two in the world, but the number one ranking has eluded her. Perhaps injuries have had something to do with it. Like several other LPGA players, Pettersen has been bitten by the injury bug more than a few times. She missed five events at the start of 2004 after undergoing elbow surgery. She had back surgery in 2005 and only played in nine events. In 2015, she has been bothered by a shoulder injury, however she did pick up a victory. If she can stay healthy, she could be able to make one more run at number one.

I talked about childhood heroes with Suzann Pettersen in Portland, Oregon, on August 29, 2013.

Who was your first childhood idol?

Obviously, being Norwegian, I looked up to a lot of our skiers, a lot of our big-time skiers. Kjetil Andre Aamodt is probably the biggest Olympian with the most medals in World Championships and Olympics in Norway. It's such a small country, so it's so easy to kind of see him as a role model. Then, when you grow up, you actually get to know him. You get to kind of put their personality to their name in the real world. So, I would say a lot of the Norwegian skiers. But, obviously, then Annika Sorenstam was one of my big role models.

What was it like when you met them for the first time?

Yeah, you know it's kind of weird how it goes, especially when you grow up and you're kind of competitive yourself. For me, it was just nice to get to know them, like get to know them off the camera. You usually have an image of what they're like on the camera, and to meet them in person and get a personal relationship to them, it gives it just a little bit different edge, I guess. For me, it was quite neat. I remember the first time you meet them you ask a lot of questions— everything you've wondered for years. They're so genuine and so nice to sit there and take the time to answer. Then, from there, I mean, a lot of them now are very good friends of mine. It's kind of fun.

You say Annika was one of your role models. With the success that you have had in golf, do you think that there are young girls and boys that might be looking up to you in the same manner you looked up to Annika?

No, I don't really think about that. Annika was an idol for me, obviously, because she's from Sweden and I'm from Norway. What she did showed me. She walked the path for me. I took a lot from what she did in taking all the challenges there are when you play golf up in Scandinavia, especially during the winter time. Now, I've been on Tour for a long time, and I'm probably one of the older players. There are a lot of younger players on Tour now that might have looked up to me when they grew up. I tried to be as real as could be. You can only be you. I am aware of it, and you try to think of that when you take actions. It's kind of hard because, as long as you're competing, you don't really look at it that way. I don't know. I just think it's surreal to think that people look up to what I do as special. I still don't think of myself as an idol.

I'm trying to remember. Did your LPGA career overlap with Annika's?

Yeah. Yeah. And, I got to know her.

Have you told her thanks for paving the way for you?

Yeah. She's become a very good friend of mine. I still stay in touch with her—still see her and play all different kinds of sports with her these days. It's a nice link for me to still have that. Even up to this date, I can give her a call if I have questions. It's always nice to have someone to kind of play ball with—someone who's done it and who has experience. Obviously, she did it her way. You gotta find your own way, but getting good advice never hurts.

Career Notes: Suzann Pettersen was a five-time Norwegian Amateur Championship winner (1996–2000). She won the 1999 British Girls Championship and the 2000 World Amateur Championship. Through October 20, 2015, Pettersen has won 15 LPGA tournaments, including two majors (2007 LPGA Championship, 2013 Evian Championship). She won for the first time in more than 19 months in June of 2015, when she won in Ontario, Canada. Suzann Pettersen has represented Europe eight times in the Solheim Cup, most recently in Germany in 2015.

* * *

31

My Own Sports Illustrated Poster

Jordan Poyer is an NFL defensive back, currently playing for the Cleveland Browns. An All-America cornerback in 2012 at Oregon State University, Poyer began his pro career with Philadelphia in 2013, but moved to Cleveland midway through his rookie season. In 2015, he is entering his third season with the Browns.

There are people in Oregon who will tell you that they expected Jordan Poyer to be playing professional baseball rather than pro football. Poyer was a multi-sport star at Astoria High School. Yes, he was very good in football. He was named Oregon's Class 4A Offensive and Defensive Player of the Year as a senior. But, he also led Astoria to a pair of Oregon high school state baseball championships. Poyer was named Oregon's High School Baseball Player of the Year and was drafted by the Florida Marlins. He was seen primarily as a baseball prospect coming out of high school, but he chose to play football for Mike Riley at Oregon State. Poyer was sure fun to watch at OSU. He had an uncanny sense of knowing when the football was being thrown in his direction. He intercepted 13 passes in his career, seven of those in his stellar senior season. Interviewing him throughout his career, I found Jordan to be polite, accommodating and well-spoken. I'm pulling for him to have a long and successful NFL career.

I talked with Jordan Poyer at the Oregon Sports Awards in Beaverton, Oregon, on March 9, 2014.

Who is the person you would consider your very first boyhood idol?

423

Man! I had so many, man. Some people might feel some sorta way about it, but I loved Michael Vick. I loved watching him play when he was at Virginia Tech and when he came out and went to the Atlanta Falcons. He was my favorite player to watch. I modeled my game after him a little bit. It was kind of crazy 'cause I was able to actually meet him and sit down and talk with him about life. He talked with me about his whole situation and how the whole dog-fighting thing changed his life. He kind of gave me a different perspective on the world and just how to look at it. I could probably sit here and think about my idols for hours, but he was definitely one that meant a lot to me.

What was it like to sit down with him? You might have had his football cards and posters, and now you were talking with him man to man.

It was crazy, man. I used to like Joe Haden, too. You see a corner come out of Florida. I'm in college still, and I'm watchin' him play. I want to see what he's about. Then, I'm lining up and giving him a call at safety. It's unreal, you know? Playin' guys like Tom Brady, it's been crazy, man. It's just been a crazy journey, but definitely I still get star-struck when I see a lot of those guys around the locker room.

The dog-fighting thing with Michael Vick that resulted in him serving time, did that change your image of him?

At first, when it happened, it did. But, then I saw his process through it—how he came out of it. It made him a better man. I don't want to get too much into it because we shared a lot of personal talk, but it made him a better man. I think his story changed my life, too. It gave me a different look on life. I respect him as a man. Obviously, we all make dumb decisions in life, but it's what you do after that dumb decision— how you fix that and how you become better and learn from it. I think that's important.

Obviously, Oregon State fans loved you when you played for the Beavers in Corvallis, and Browns fans love you now in Cleveland. You are an idol for a lot of kids. Do you ever think about that?

I do, and I think that helps me keep my head on straight. There's a lot of opportunity out there to mess up. There's a lot of opportunity out there to do some dumb things. But, at the end of the day, I do it for the people I love—my family and my fans. I play this game because I love it. I've been getting support from people since day one. I couldn't thank them enough because everybody else around me makes me do what I do. I don't do it for anything else. The money's gonna be there, but I do it for the love of the game.

So, I guess you sign a lot of autographs for kids?

Oh, man. Yeah. Yes. Lots of those!

Career Notes: Jordan Poyer received All-Pac-12 recognition in 2011 and 2012. As a senior, he was a consensus All-American, Oregon State's first since 1967. Poyer was drafted in the 7th round of the 2013 NFL Draft by Philadelphia. After playing three games for the Eagles, he was claimed off waivers by the Browns. Poyer played nine games in Cleveland in 2013. He served as the team's primary punt returner the final six games and averaged 14.3 yards per return. Poyer played in all 16 games with the Browns in 2014, forcing one fumble and making 21 tackles—15 of them solo.

*   *   *

Neil Lomax was a record-setting quarterback at Portland State University who went on to become a two-time Pro Bowl quarterback in the NFL. Lomax started 101 games for the St. Louis/Arizona Cardinals from 1981 to 1988, but was forced to retire at age 29 because of a bad hip. Lomax might have become one of the NFL's legendary quarterbacks if he had not been with a mediocre Cardinals' team and had he been able to stay healthy. Lomax had a ridiculously strong arm and put up incredible numbers at Portland State. He held 90 NCAA passing records when he graduated from Portland State in 1980.

I've known Neil Lomax since the very first month I arrived in Portland to work at the local NBC television affiliate in fall of 1980. Lomax was about to begin his senior season as the Portland State quarterback, and he was the toast of the town. Playing in the "run and shoot" offense of then-PSU head coach Mouse Davis, Lomax had already been putting up video-game type numbers. They would become even more ridiculous by the time his days as the Vikings' quarterback were complete. During his career at Portland State, the home-grown Lomax passed for a (still) school-record 13,220 yards, with a school-record 106 touchdown passes on 938 completions—yet another PSU record. Lomax passed for more than 300 yards in a game 28 times. He passed for more than 400 yards ten times in college.

You almost could not comprehend the things Lomax accomplished on the football field. He once threw seven touchdown passes—in a single <u>quarter!</u> He threw eight touchdown passes and ran for a TD in a <u>105-0</u> win over Delaware State in 1980. In a 1979 game, Lomax set a PSU-record with 77 pass attempts and a school-record 44 completions at Northern Colorado. He still owns Portland State records for most yards of total offense in a season (4,157 yards in 1980) and a career (13,345 yards). I could hardly wait to see what Lomax would do as an NFL quarterback.

I was invited to be with Neil on NFL Draft Day in 1981. Lomax had been told by two NFL clubs that he would be their choice in the first round if he was still available. There was also a chance one of the other NFL teams would select him, so my cameraman and I were focused on Neil as each pick was made. Neil could not disguise his disappointment when pick after pick was made and he did not hear his name. Even the two teams that had told Neil he would be their selection picked other players instead. Lomax, sitting in the middle of a room filled with friends, family and a television crew, sat in stunned silence. After raising an eyebrow and smiling ruefully, Lomax said, "Well, [I'm] still in Portland." The entire first round passed with Lomax sitting there in front of the camera, trying hard not to show his frustration. Finally, ESPN announced the Cardinals were taking him in the second round with the 33rd overall selection. Lomax, though disappointed he wasn't a first round pick, was obviously relieved to see his ordeal come to an end. I will admit to you these many years later that I felt a little embarrassed after unwittingly becoming an intruder in what had become an uncomfortable situation for Lomax. I always think about Neil Lomax's draft day when I see NFL and NBA prospects sitting in front of the TV cameras, trying not to look nervous while waiting to hear their names called on draft night. I suspect that if Neil Lomax is also watching, he, too, has flashbacks to his awkward draft day experience.

I spoke with Neil Lomax by telephone on January 5, 2015.

Thinking back to when you were a young boy, can you remember your first boyhood idol?

My earliest memories were probably in the late '60s or early '70s when I was nine, ten, eleven years old. I would cut out the pictures in Sports Illustrated of Bart Starr, Roman Gabriel, and NFL quarterbacks. Also, I always loved golf, though I didn't play a whole lot. I would cut out golf pictures—Jack Nicklaus and anything from Augusta National. I thought watching the Masters back in those days on our color TV was the most beautiful thing in the world. I cut out a bunch of pictures of Jack Nicklaus.

Have you ever met Nicklaus or any of your other boyhood heroes?

I have not met Nicklaus. I met Arnold Palmer and Bob Hope. I met Roman Gabriel when we played Cal Poly Pomona my junior year at Portland State when he was the head coach at Cal Poly. He criticized our whole offense all week long saying, "These guys are like a playground team and no one knows how to put a defense together." We rolled 93 on him. (Laughs) He did not shake Mouse's hand after the game (a 93-7 Vikings' win). I really was upset about it. I went over there and shook his

427

hand. He kind of grabbed me and said, "Hey, great game, great game. But, that was terrible you guys running up the score like that." He said something like that. And, I met Bart Starr about 20 years ago at some NFL function. That was really cool. I would say those two guys, Starr and Gabriel, were my boyhood idols. I just remember watching them on TV when they were with the Packers and the Rams.

Then, when those Sports Illustrated posters started coming out—those big three by four foot posters—I started buying those. I got all the Blazers, Bill Walton, Kareem Abdul-Jabbar, Jerry West. When I got in high school, I finally stopped ordering those and cutting them out.

What was it like to meet Bart Starr? Do you remember where you first met him?

Absolutely. He was the head coach of the Packers. I was flown in during the NFL (Scouting) Combines. Back in those days, they didn't have just one Combine in Indianapolis. Each team, if they were going to draft you, they flew you in. I flew in to about 15 different cities that year before draft day. One of them was Green Bay, and Bart Starr was the coach. It was 1981. He only lasted more two years, and then they fired him.

Even though you were meeting in a professional situation, you had to be a little amazed to be sitting across the desk from one of your boyhood heroes.

Yeah, I was in total respect and awe of him. And, he was the most gentle, honorable, kind, humble man that I've ever met—for a head coach. He was just so kind, so thoughtful. You wouldn't picture him as an aggressive, tough head coach. He was so calm. He had a lot of Tom Landry in him. But, I don't think he had that aggressive side to deal with spoiled millionaires. He just couldn't cope. I don't think he ever coached in college or anywhere after that. He's a great, great man.

When you were quarterback at Portland State, you directed a high-scoring offense. Kids all over the Northwest were pretending to be Neil Lomax and the PSU Vikings. Then, you made it to the NFL, and you had your own football card. Did you think about the fact that you had become an idol, too?

No, not really. It was later, when so many of these kids—that are dads now—would tell me they came to one of my football camps or a Fellowship of Christian Athletes camp or a Multnomah Athletic Club camp. They'd say, "You and Greg Barton put on a camp, and I came to it," or, "I was an eleventh-grader, and I went to your All-Northwest Football Camp with Kenny Easley." Then, they'll show you the pictures. There we are, me and Fred Biletnikoff and Kenny Easley and Jim Zorn, and there's this little kid—who's now 40 or 45 years old. It's kind of interesting to go back.

I think the first time that I thought I made it was when I had my own Sports Illustrated poster. It came out in 1981. I thought this is the coolest thing in the world that they have this and I can order my own poster now. You know you've made it when you open a Sports Illustrated, and you can order your own poster.

Career Notes: In the NFL, Neil Lomax passed for 22,771 career yards with 136 touchdowns and 90 interceptions. In 1987, he led the NFL with 272 completions in 463 attempts for 3,387 yards. His most productive season was 1984 when he established career highs with 345 completions in 560 passing attempts. He completed a career-best 61.6% of his passes for 4,614 yards, which was another career high. Lomax twice was an NFL Pro Bowl selection.

*　　*　　*

Derek Anderson, a veteran NFL quarterback, enters the 2015 NFL season as a reserve QB with the Carolina Panthers. While at Oregon State University, Anderson set numerous school passing records (most since broken), including most career touchdown passes and most passing yards in a season.

In 2002, when Anderson became the starting quarterback at Oregon State as a sophomore, Beaver fans were anxious for a return to a major bowl game. Just two years earlier, Jonathan Smith had quarterbacked the Beavers to a Fiesta Bowl win over Notre Dame. OSU fans looked at Anderson's NFL-size body and strong throwing arm and believed great things were in store. However, Anderson struggled his first two seasons as the starter. Anderson completed only 47% of his passes as a sophomore and threw 24 interceptions as a junior. While some fans did remain supportive, there were quite a few fans who booed Anderson's inconsistent play. The postgame call-in show was often an Anderson bash-fest. In addition to hosting the postgame radio show, I was calling TV play-by-play of the Oregon State games. I remember feeling bad for young quarterback. It was obvious that the booing was affecting him and shaking his confidence. There was no mistaking the pain in his eyes when he met face-to-face with the media for postgame interviews. I wondered if the negative fan reaction might cause a complete loss of confidence and ruin his chance to one day play in the NFL. Anderson had shown he possessed great arm-strength. He threw for more than 4,000 yards his junior season. It was the occasional poor on-field decision that drove some Oregon State fans batty. But, in the end, Anderson had the last laugh. His senior season, he completed 54% of his passes for 3,615 yards and 29 touchdowns with 17 interceptions—a high number of picks, but seven fewer than the previous year. When his career was over, Anderson owned a number of school passing records and had led the Beavers to three straight bowl games as their starting QB. Now in his 11th NFL season, I think it's safe to say Derek Anderson has proven to the doubters that he had what it takes to be paid to play at the highest level.

I spoke with Derek Anderson at the Caddies 4 Cure charity event in Beaverton, Oregon, on June 12, 2011.

Who was your boyhood idol?

I liked Troy Aikman. He was obviously one of the quarterbacks I watched. And, former Washington State quarterback, Drew Bledsoe. He was huge, you know, just him being close to Oregon. Somehow, I started watching him and collecting his football cards and stuff like that. I was a big basketball guy, too. I used to like Shawn Kemp and the Sonics.

Have you ever met Aikman?

Yeah, I have. It was kind of funny. He's a super nice guy, and he's a good golfer who loves to play. I actually met him at Tahoe. It's fun to watch him now. He does a good job on TV as a broadcaster.

Have you met Bledsoe?

Yeah, I did. Actually, I went to Drew's football camp when I was 16. That was pretty cool for me. He and his dad helped me a lot when I was there. I stayed in touch with him and his brother, Adam, throughout the process.

When you were at Oregon State, many young fans were wearing your jersey number. Did you think about being an idol back then?

Not really, but yesterday we had my football camp at Scappoose, and it's pretty cool. A lot of those guys have known me since I was little, so it's a little bit different. I know their parents, and I know their brothers. Trying to be a good role model and a good citizen for those guys is obviously something that means a lot to me.

Since you've been an NFL quarterback, have any college players come up to you to say that you were his boyhood idol?

Yeah, I have some guys that are at school, and they all say they watched me all through college or when they were little. It makes me feel old. You know, I'm not really that old, but it sometimes makes me *feel* old.

Career Notes: Derek Anderson grew up in the tiny town of Scappoose, Oregon, located about 20 miles northwest of Portland. He was a high school All-State player in football and basketball. In both his junior and senior seasons at Oregon State, Anderson led the Pac-10 in passing attempts and completions, total passing yards and total yards. The 6-foot-6 right-hander passed for 11,249 yards during his college career, which was an Oregon State record and—at the time—put Anderson in the number two spot on the Pac-10's all-time list behind USC's Carson Palmer. Through the 2014 season, Anderson still ranked in the top 50 of all FBS quarterbacks in career passing yardage.

Anderson was drafted in the sixth round of the 2005 NFL Draft by the Baltimore Ravens. He never played for the Ravens, but has played for Cleveland, Arizona and Carolina. With the Panthers, Anderson has primarily served as Cam Newton's backup. In 2014, Anderson started—and won—two games for the Panthers when Newton was unavailable due to injury. Anderson played in six games for Carolina in 2014 and finished the year with five touchdown passes and no interceptions. He completed 65-of-97 passes (67%) for 701 yards. Anderson played in the NFL Pro Bowl in 2007. For the Browns that season, he completed 298-of-527 passes (56.5%) for 3,787 yards, with 29 touchdowns and 19 interceptions.

*   *   *

Brady Quinn is a former Notre Dame quarterback who has played in the NFL and spent 2014 as a Fox Sports football analyst. Quinn received the Maxwell Award as the nation's best college football player in 2006, becoming the first player from Notre Dame to win that award since Ross Browner in 1977. He also won the Johnny Unitas Golden Arm Award as the nation's top quarterback.

At the time I talked with Brady Quinn, he told me he was still hoping to get another chance to play in the NFL. Now in his early 30s, Quinn feels he could be an effective NFL quarterback, especially now that he has analyzed quarterback play from the high elevation of the broadcast booth. Hoping to impress an NFL team, Brady went to the first NFL Veteran Combine in March, 2015. He is still waiting for a team to call. Even though he hasn't played in a regular season game since 2012, Quinn hasn't ruled out a return to the field. Is his return improbable? Yes, but it's not entirely out of the realm of possibility. There are plenty of marginal quarterbacks in the NFL. But, whether or not Quinn gets a call from an NFL team, he doesn't have to worry about being unemployed. Brady has shown great promise in the broadcast booth. And, if all of the Fighting Irish fans tune in to watch Brady work the game, ratings will soar!

I talked with Brady Quinn by phone on January 5, 2015.

Who was your very first boyhood idol?

I think a lot of young men always look up to their father. But, besides my father, as far as a sports idol goes, that would be Joe Montana. I was born in 1984, so my earliest recollections of Joe are of him winning his Super Bowl titles with the 49ers and Bill Walsh and Jerry Rice. Really, Jerry Rice and Joe Montana were my two favorite players because of their whole connection. I started playing football at seven or eight years old, so that was who I always mimicked and kind of idolized growing up. That was because I was looking back on the history of the Super Bowl and "The Catch" and all that. We had the Cincinnati Bengals, an Ohio team, so I followed them. We had family out on the West Coast. I remember flying out there as a young child and getting a 49ers jacket and being pretty stoked about it. I always followed Joe Montana in his career.

Did you ever meet Joe Montana when you were a kid?

No, I never met him when I was a kid. However, I did once I went to Notre Dame. The first time I met him, I met him with his family my true freshman year. We were playing USC at home, and he had come in town for the game. One of his daughters apparently went to school there at the same time I did. His kids were all on the field for our walk-through. Afterwards, I got to meet with him and talk with him a little bit. Then, his kids were throwing around this little mini-football. They threw it to me. I caught it and threw it back. All of a sudden, Joe ran over and was like, "No. No. No. Don't throw that! Don't throw that!" I was like, "What do you mean?" He's like, "You got a game tomorrow. You don't want to mess up throwing a small ball like that and then having to throw a bigger ball tomorrow. No. No. No." I guess he was kind of concerned about me messing up bad the next day (laughs)—not that we were able to really compete with USC that year. It was just kind of interesting. That was my first recollection of meeting and talking with Joe Montana.

Wow. Do you think he was worried about you getting hurt throwing a different size football?

No, I don't think he was worried about me hurting myself. I think he just—for whatever reason—didn't want me to get into a funk and get used to throwing a small ball versus a big ball and allow it to affect something in my throwing motion the next day.

Did the fact that you had idolized Montana, a former Notre Dame star, influence your decision to play for the Fighting Irish?

Um, I don't think so. Well, I guess, actually, in a way it did because when I was deciding between Ohio State, Michigan and Notre Dame, I did take into account the fact that when someone asks you, "Who was the best NFL quarterback from Ohio State?" it might be hard for you to think of an answer. Michigan's got more guys—like Tom Brady. As I grew older and was going through high school, Brady was really somebody who I kind of idolized at that time of my life. I thought I had a similar skill set and similar size stature, so that came to mind as I was going through high school and possibly wanting to go to Michigan and follow his footsteps. But, I think it just personally was a better situation and a better fit for what I wanted to get out of my life experience going to Notre Dame.

Do you now have any kind of relationship with Joe Montana since both of you were successful quarterbacks at Notre Dame?

Yeah, I do. We don't talk that often. We talk maybe a couple times a year—just kind of keep in touch and usually run into each other here and there. He's a great guy. He's very, very laid back—one of the more fun-loving guys. The times when I got to know him most and saw him a lot more was when his kids were going to Notre Dame. He was pretty excited about their opportunity to go to school there and experience some of the things that he experienced. But, he's very laid back—just a cool guy. That's the only way to describe him. He's just a very down-to-earth, cool guy.

Being the starting quarterback at Notre Dame, you had to have been aware that there were young fans that wanted to grow up just like you similarly to you growing up wanting to be like Joe Montana. Did you think about that at the time?

Um, I don't know. It was tough when I first got there to think about that. I always tried to do the right things and be respectful of people— sign autographs and do all those sorts of things. I felt like it was what my parents taught me to do—to be respectful to others and try to use the platform I was given to make others happy. I think as I got older, I started to realize that and definitely tried to conduct myself in that way, you know, to be a role model for others and to take school seriously and stay out of trouble.

Like so many current and former athletes, you have established a foundation. The "Third and Goal Foundation" makes a difference in the lives of our nation's veterans. Why was this issue important to you?

My father actually fought in Viet Nam. He was a Marine. He's been a homebuilder after he finished school and when he came home. I've always been close to the military—doing visits when I was in college and early in the pros. Around 2010, we came up with the idea to try to make homes handicap-accessible for those coming back from Iraq and Afghanistan who had suffered just awful injuries and loss of limbs. That was our way of being able to help and give back and use what we'd been given to kind of pay it forward and help others.

Whether or not your playing-career is over, you've shown outstanding ability as a football analyst. There are probably young people who now see you as sort of a TV idol.

Yeah. (Laughs) I never thought about it like that. I grew up in the Columbus, Ohio, area—Dublin, in particular. Somebody who I was close with who was doing that business back then more locally was Kirk Herbstreit. I grew up having a relationship with him because I saw him every other week while receiving some sort of high school award and talking with him on the radio. As his career continued to develop and got him more into college football, I went to Notre Dame and started to have some more success there. It was interesting how our relationship kind of built through that. Now, all of a sudden, I'm going in that route at this point in my life. I guess he was one of those idols, or one of those mentors coming along the way because he does such a fantastic job. But, I'm way too early-on in my career to think about that. I've got too much work ahead and too many things to get polished-up on before I think about that. I'm still working on it. It's definitely different. I wish I could go back and play—now more than ever—because I've had the opportunity to see it from this side. I think I would allow more of my emotions and more of who I am as a person to come out instead of hiding so much. You grow up in this New England Patriots' style of coaching and organizations. They really coach you to not give anyone anything and be very vanilla and vague. It doesn't do a whole lot for you, especially for those who work on the TV side. I've started to learn

436

that, and I wish I could go back and do it all over again knowing what I know now.

Career Notes: Brady Quinn set numerous passing records during his time in South Bend, including career passes (929), career pass attempts (1,602), and career touchdown passes (95). After leaving Notre Dame, Quinn was drafted by the Cleveland Browns in the first round (#22 overall) of the 2007 NFL Draft. He played in 14 games over three seasons with the Browns and passed for eight touchdowns with seven interceptions. Quinn has also spent time with several other NFL teams, but the only time he saw regular season action was with Kansas City in 2012. He played in 10 games for the Chiefs and threw for 1,141 yards, with two touchdowns and eight interceptions.

*   *   *

Sean Mannion was a record-setting quarterback at Oregon State University. Mannion was picked by St. Louis in the 2015 NFL Draft and is on the Rams' roster as the team's third quarterback (as of September, 2015).

Oregon State fans were sometimes frustrated by the play of Sean Mannion during his four seasons as the Beavers' QB. The fan frustration was understandable. Over his first two seasons, Mannion had as many interceptions (31) as touchdown passes (31). In fact, he was picked off 54 times in 47 games as OSU's quarterback. That's a big number in the interception column. But, Mannion eventually won over the OSU fans because he began posting even larger numbers on the positive side of the ledger. Mannion threw 83 career touchdown passes. He completed nearly 65% of his passes, and, boy, he threw a lot of passes. Mannion hooked up with receivers on 1,187 of his 1,838 passing attempts for 13,600 yards. He set school and Pac-12 records. More importantly, he silenced his critics.

When it came to being interviewed, Mannion was a tad shy during his first two years at Oregon State. Maybe it was because he didn't want to talk about his ongoing struggle to find his footing in the college game. He wasn't playing horribly. He was just somewhat inconsistent. During his sophomore season, he nearly lost his starting job to Cody Vaz. However, in his junior season, Sean matured into the role of college football star. He was more comfortable talking with reporters, and he was certainly more comfortable on the football field. In his junior season, Mannion threw a school-record 37 touchdowns and had only 15 interceptions. Beavers' fans were now solidly in support of their 6-foot-6 quarterback.

Mannion had a solid senior season, cutting his number of interceptions to eight to go with 15 touchdown passes. He threw for more than 3,000 yards for the third time in his four seasons in Corvallis. He had improved so much that the Rams picked him in the third round of the 2015 draft.

In the 2015 NFL preseason, Mannion completed 31-of-57 passes (54.4%) for 300 yards, with one touchdown and one interception.

Mannion entered the 2015 regular season as the Ram's third-string quarterback. I believe Mannion has what it takes to be an effective QB in the NFL. I hope he gets a chance to show what he can do. Sean is one of the nicest young men I've had the privilege of covering during my career. He can count me as one of his fans.

I spoke with Sean Mannion at the Oregon Sports Awards in Beaverton, Oregon, on March 9, 2014.

Can you think back to your very first boyhood idol? Is there one person who quickly comes to mind?

It's hard to think of just one because you always have a few favorite players from your favorite teams. But, Peyton Manning sticks out. Playing quarterback growing up and watching the NFL, you know, Peyton Manning is synonymous with quarterbacks. I appreciate getting to see him, both as a kid and now when I know more about the game.

He was someone who I guess you could say was a boyhood idol when I was younger. Now, I just appreciate how he plays the position.

Have you had a chance to meet him yet?

I have not, but I'm going to the Manning Passing Academy this summer. So, hopefully I'll meet him there. That would be a really cool experience.

Oregon State fans have appreciated your hard work through the years, and there are many young kids wearing your jersey around town. Have you ever considered that these youngsters are looking up to you in somewhat the same fashion that you look up to Peyton Manning?

I don't really think about it much, but I know whenever you have a chance to give back or meet little kids after the game, it's really overwhelming to see just how highly they think of you—and just for playing football. I always try to take as much time as I can to sign autographs or take pictures or whatever because I know a few years ago I was that little kid that wanted a picture of someone or wanted someone's autograph. It's funny how you go from being that little kid to here.

Next year, you'll be drafted and will probably be pictured on your own football card. Will that seem a little strange?

Oh, definitely. Definitely. To think that it's even an opportunity for me, it's definitely surreal.

I again contacted Sean Mannion on August 19, 2014, after he had met his boyhood idol.

Sean, I wanted to check back with you to see if you were able to meet Peyton Manning at the Manning Passing Academy last month.

Yeah, I met Peyton and Eli, their other brother Cooper and their dad, Archie. I met all of them. It was a Thursday through Sunday camp. We got to work out with them twice, and I spent a lot of time talking with them. It was just a great time.

What was it like to have the opportunity to spend time with the Mannings? When we last talked, you hadn't met Peyton, and you were thinking it was going to be a cool experience. Was the experience as good as you anticipated?

Oh, it surpassed all my expectations. It was a great, great experience. There were 1,200 campers, and I was one of about 30 or 40 college guys. We were like camp counselors for the younger kids. Then, we had a couple workouts where we could workout with Peyton and Eli. From a football perspective, it was a great place to learn from Peyton and Eli—who are synonymous with the quarterback position in the NFL. From a more personal perspective, those are two people that I've grown up watching play quarterback that I've tried to emulate my game after. I learned a lot. To get to know them a little bit, and just kind of be around them and talk with them, it was a really great experience.

How did they treat you?

They were very, very friendly. They're very approachable, very personable. They're the kind of guys that stand there talking to you for a while and you almost forget that they're two of the best quarterbacks in the history of the game. They're very easy to talk to and very approachable—anything you want to ask them.

We see the Mannings on those ESPN SportsCenter promos acting sort of goofy and silly. In your brief time with them, could you tell if they're like that in real life?

You know, when it comes to football, I'd say they're very, very serious. When we worked out with them, there was no goofiness. Everything was very focused. Everything was all about improving on the football field. Then, when you get them into a more casual setting and you're getting to know them, they joke around a little bit. I wouldn't say they're goofy. Like I said, they're very personable.

So, your meeting with Peyton and Eli was everything you hoped it would be?

Oh, yeah. Everything and more. Everything and more.

Career Notes: As a junior in 2013, Sean Mannion threw five touchdown passes against Utah to tie Derek Anderson's Oregon State record for TD passes in a game. The next game, Mannion threw six touchdown passes against Colorado to set a new school mark. That year, Mannion broke the Pac-12 record with 4,662 passing yards in a single season. Mannion ended his college career as the Pac-12's all-time leader in passing yardage with 13,600 yards. He was picked by the Rams in the third round (#89 overall) of the 2015 NFL Draft.

*　　*　　*

32

MJ Knows Who I Am

Dwyane Wade, a high-scoring guard, has led the Miami Heat to three NBA championships in his first twelve years in the league. Miami's career leader in many offensive categories, Wade has been an NBA All-Star 11 consecutive seasons (through 2015) and was an All-Star starter in nine of those games. He was named the NBA All-Star Game MVP in 2010 and the NBA Finals MVP in 2006.

I think you have to give Dwyane Wade a lot of credit for being able to put his ego aside when LeBron James joined the Heat. Together, James and Wade led Miami to four straight NBA Finals. They won a pair of championships as teammates. Wade obviously understood that having James on the team made Miami a legitimate championship contender every year. However, it's still pretty amazing that Wade—an elite pro athlete—was able to share the limelight with someone else—particularly LeBron, the league's best player. Wade was considered "the franchise" for the Heat until LeBron showed up. Wade had already led Miami to one NBA title. That Wade was willing to accept a lesser role says something about his desire to win. It also says something about the man's character.

I talked with Dwyane Wade in Portland, Oregon, on December 28, 2013.

Who was your first boyhood idol?

I grew up in Chicago. Michael Jordan. He just had it. He was one of those athletes. He had the charisma. Obviously, he had the basketball talent. He had the athletic ability, the special moments, the big games, the game-winning shots. He performed at the highest level. He just had everything. And, he was actually not too much taller than I thought I could get, you know, being six-six. I'm like, "Okay. I could see that I might grow to be his height." He just had it.

Do you remember the first time you met him?

I do. It was at All-Star Weekend. It was very cool. It was very cool, to say the least—a humbling moment for me. It was one of my first All-Star Games. To be there, and MJ comes through. It's like this big wave of people and this big crowd. You know he's coming through. And, he stops and says hi to you. It was just like, "MJ knows who I am!" We gained a relationship from there. I was with his brand for a couple years. I have so much respect for what he did for the game and also for what he continues to do years later.

A lot of kids idolize you. Do you think about it? Does it affect the way you live your life?

Obviously, I'm an idol for my kids first. But, it means a lot. You thank their parents for even letting their kids look at you that way. You carry that when you make mistakes. You're going to make mistakes. We all do. But, you also try to be that for them kids. They love the way you play basketball. They love the way you dress and all these kinds of things. You try to make sure you give them that because one day they won't be looking at you the same way. It will be someone else they're idolizing. So, while you have it, you just try to enjoy it.

Career Notes: Dwyane Wade was an All-American at Marquette prior to his selection as the fifth overall pick in the 2003 NBA Draft. Wade was a unanimous NBA All-Rookie selection his first season and has been recognized as an All-NBA player eight times in the years that followed. Despite missing some 150 games because of injury, Wade scored 18,812 points during his first 12 NBA seasons, all with Miami.

In his career, he has averaged 24.1 points, 4.9 rebounds and 5.9 assists. His most productive season was 2008-09, when he averaged 30.2 points, 5.0 rebounds and 7.5 assists. Wade was a member of the gold medal-winning USA Basketball Senior National Team at the 2008 Summer Olympics in Beijing, China.

* * *

Damian Lillard grew up in Oakland, California, and says he wears uniform #0 (or the letter O) as a tribute to the three places that have had a huge impact in his life—his hometown of Oakland, his college town of Ogden, Utah, and his NBA home in Oregon. Lillard was not heavily recruited in high school and attended Weber State University for four years (one of those a medical-redshirt year in which he played only ten games). A two-time Big Sky Player of the Year, Lillard left Weber State with one season of eligibility remaining to enter the NBA Draft. He has overcome long odds to become one of the NBA's brightest young stars.

Lillard has a signature shoe line that has gone global and is featured prominently in adidas commercials. In the summer of 2015, the multi-talented Lillard also released five rap songs under the name, Dame DOLLA (Different on Levels the Lord Allows).

Damian Lillard had a friend in high school who was bullied, and Lillard stepped up to help the young man. Partly because of that experience, Lillard became the face of a popular anti-bullying program—RESPECT: Pass It On.

When considering Damian Lillard's basketball abilities, I want to say only one thing. He is absolutely ruthless at the offensive end when the game is on the line. Lillard transforms himself into a silent assassin—the guy that wants the ball in his hands when the clock is ticking down in the final seconds. Having felt like he was an underdog much of his life, Lillard relishes the idea of being the one to take the final shot. He wants to be the one to finish off the opponent.

Even more impressive than Lillard's excellent handling of end-game situations is the manner in which Lillard handles the responsibility of being a team leader. Having spent a lot of time in the Trail Blazers' locker room conducting postgame interviews, I can tell you how it works for Damian Lillard. He always answers questions from the media—no matter what. After showering, he slowly—very, very slowly—gets dressed. Facing his locker, with his back turned to the reporters assembled behind him, Lillard methodically buttons his shirt. He puts expensive earrings in each ear. He makes sure everything is in its proper place before he turns around to face a barrage of questions from the reporters that are jockeying for position while trying to shove microphones and TV cameras in his face. It's a routine that is repeated game after game, win or lose. Portland, like most NBA teams, has had players that bolt from the locker room before the media is allowed inside. Those players do their best to hide after a bad game. That is never an issue with Lillard. He knows it is his responsibility to answer the media's questions, whether he sank a game-winning 3-pointer at the buzzer or whether he turned the ball over while trying to work his magic in the game's closing seconds. That's what real leaders do. Lillard signed a five-year contract extension with the Trail Blazers in July, 2015. It was reported by numerous media outlets that the extension is worth at least $120-million. I would be surprised if it turns out that he's not worth every penny.

Here's one additional personal note about Lillard. I wrote earlier about Coach Terry Stotts offering me encouragement in Brooklyn when I was called into action as the Trail Blazers' radio play-by-play announcer for two games in 2013. Lillard was the only Portland player who made a similar comment to me. Damian indicated he was happy I was getting a chance to be part of the team. He recalled that I had been laid off from my job a couple months earlier, and he felt good about me catching a break.

I talked with Damian Lillard about his childhood hero in Tualatin, Oregon, on March 14, 2013.

We all pretended to be somebody we idolized when we were growing up. Who pops into your mind when I ask you to tell me about your very first boyhood idol?

When I was playin' basketball, it was always Michael Jordan.

Have you ever met Jordan?

I haven't met him. I've been *near* him. I'm sure that'll be coming.

What will it mean for you to finally meet this guy who meant so much to so many young basketball fans through the years?

It's going to be a great experience. He's the person that I watched—the "Come Fly With Me" DVD, all the highlights, the greatest player to play this game and play at this level. So, it'll be crazy just to have the opportunity to meet him.

You're now an NBA star, and you've taken a very public stand against bullying with your RESPECT campaign. Because of your leadership—on and off court—many kids look up to you. You understand that you have terrific influence, don't you?

I realize how much I can affect how some kids think and how they behave based on my experience. I grew up in a tough city facing tough situations. I wasn't perfect, and I'm not perfect now. I had fights. I got mad. I got in trouble in school. Making it to the NBA, it's about me being able to show them the right way how to conduct myself—how I am on the floor and how I am off the floor—how I treat people. Doing the anti-bullying campaign makes people realize that it's important for people to see that it affects kids. Bullying can lead to bad things—low confidence, low self-esteem—even suicide in some situations. It can make people turn against their parents because they don't feel love. So, it can cause a lot of bad situations. If I can be the guy to have effect on some kids as an NBA player and show them a better way, why not?

Career Notes: Playing against the Lakers in his first NBA game on October 31, 2012, Lillard scored 23 points and had 11 assists. He joined Oscar Robertson and Isiah Thomas as the only players in NBA history with at least 20 points and 10 assists in their NBA debuts. In his first three NBA seasons, Lillard averaged 20.2 points and 6.1 assists. The unanimous 2013 NBA Rookie of the Year has been a two-time NBA All-Star and also earned All-NBA Third Team recognition. Lillard holds the NBA record for most 3-pointers made (599) in a player's first three seasons.

*   *   *

Mo Williams,

a veteran of 12 NBA seasons, has played for seven NBA clubs—the Jazz, Bucks, Cavaliers, Clippers, Trail Blazers, Timberwolves and Charlotte Hornets. A 2009 NBA All-Star with Cleveland, Williams teamed with LeBron James to help the Cavaliers advance in the NBA Playoffs in both 2009 and 2010. Mo Williams rejoins LeBron in 2015-16 in an effort to win his first—and *Cleveland's* first—NBA championship.

I wasn't surprised to see Williams sign as a free agent with the Cavaliers. He had his best seasons as a pro when playing alongside LeBron James their first time around in Cleveland. And, Williams gives the Cavaliers some insurance in case Kyrie Irving isn't 100% healthy after suffering a fractured kneecap in the 2015 NBA Finals. It will be interesting to see how the Cavs' bid for a championship plays out in 2015-16. If Irving and fellow All-Star Kevin Love can bounce back from the injuries they suffered in the playoffs, it seems to me the Cavaliers will be the team to beat.

I talked with Mo Williams in Portland, Oregon, on February 19, 2014.

Who was your very first boyhood idol?

I'd say Magic Johnson. When I was in Mississippi, the only NBA games we could catch were the Lakers. They were on TV all the time, so I grew up a Laker fan and a Magic Johnson fan.

What was it about Magic?

He was just a great basketball player.

Have you ever met Magic?

Yeah. Through the game of basketball, I have. He's a great guy. He's still a great role model, especially on the business side of things.

He truly has put together an outstanding post-basketball career, the kind of career everyone can emulate.

Exactly. He's somebody you look up to, and you look forward to being someone like him when you're done playing.

You've been a high-profile guy in the NBA, and there are kids who look up to you. Do you ever think about that? If so, what does it mean to you?

Well, yeah. You just watch how you walk, you know? You watch how you talk and watch the things you do 'cause you know they're always watching.

Some of the players I've talked with have said LeBron James was an idol for them growing up. You played with LeBron in Cleveland. He's a great player, but what kind of a person is he?

Oh, he's the ultimate role model. He's the ultimate giver. He's a great person and a great role model for kids. Even teenagers aspiring to be a basketball player or just someone coming from a difficult situation, it's great to look up to a guy like him.

Career Notes: Mo Williams has averaged 13.4 points and 5.0 assists during his first dozen NBA seasons. He scored a career high 17.4 points a game during his All-Star season in 2008-09. In the 2009 NBA Playoffs, Williams averaged 16.3 points and 4.1 assists to help the Cavaliers reach the Eastern Conference Finals. The following postseason, Williams averaged 14.4 points and 5.4 assists as Cleveland reached the Eastern Conference Semifinals.

*   *   *

Klay Thompson is an outstanding long-range shooter who

helped the Golden State Warriors win the 2015 NBA championship. Thompson teamed with fellow "Splash Brother" Stephen Curry to shoot the Warriors to their first NBA title since 1975, the year Rick Barry led the team to the title.

Klay Thompson is the son of Mychal Thompson, the first pick in the 1978 NBA Draft. I can remember seeing Klay and his brothers in Portland when they were very young boys. Although I knew they had good bloodlines, I never would have dreamed that all three would grow up to be professional athletes. What are the odds of that happening? Because of my history with Mychal—covering him as a player and then working with him at the radio station in Portland—I have kept track of Klay throughout his career. Prior to Klay's ascent to the NBA, I was excited to follow his progress at Washington State University.

On New Year's Eve, December 31, 2009, I called the TV play-by-play of Washington State's televised home game against the Ducks on the Oregon Sports Network. It was an unusual game for Klay Thompson. He led all scorers with 33 points, but made only two of ten shots launched from three-point range. Overall, Thompson finished just 6-of-19 from the field. He did, however, get to the free throw line 21 times and made 19. In the end, it wasn't enough. Washington State appeared to have the game won when Thompson dished to DeAngelo Casto for a go-ahead basket with one second left in overtime. However, a technical foul was called on the Cougar bench when players stepped onto the court while celebrating. Oregon's Tajuan Porter calmly sank two free throws to tie the score 80-all. The Ducks went on to win in double-overtime, 91-89. It was a game fans of Oregon and Washington State will never forget. I'm pretty sure Klay Thompson remembers it, too.

I talked with Klay Thompson in Portland, Oregon, on March 16, 2014.

Klay, who was your boyhood idol?

Obviously, it was Michael Jordan. But, I had a few—Kobe Bryant, Rasheed Wallace when he was on the Blazers and Reggie Miller. Also, I liked Steve McNair. I liked playing quarterback. And, Nomar Garciaparra was my favorite baseball player.

You've played against Kobe. Have you been on the court with any of your other idols?

I played against Rasheed a little bit when I was a young kid, like when I was 13 or 14. He was just fooling around with us. I went to middle school with his oldest son, so I'd see him around. I was fortunate. I still see him to this day when we go play the Pistons. It's pretty crazy.

You were a star at Washington State, and you're an even bigger star now with the Warriors. Do you think about all those kids that are looking up to you now?

Yeah, it's wild, man. That's why you always have to take time say "hey" to them and be nice. That goes a long way.

Career Notes: Klay Thompson played three seasons at Washington State University and was First Team All- Pac-10 as a sophomore and junior. He led the Pac-10 Conference in scoring (21.6 PPG) as a junior. Despite playing only three seasons in Pullman, Thompson ranks third on the WSU career scoring list.

Thompson was taken by the Warriors with the 11th overall pick of the 2011 NBA Draft. He was named to the NBA All-Rookie Team in 2012. The next three seasons, he teamed with Stephen Curry to set an NBA record for three-pointers made by a pair of teammates in a season. They combined to knock down 525 triples in 2014-15.

Klay Thompson had a breakout season during the Warriors' championship season. He made history against the Sacramento Kings on January 23, 2015. Thompson drained 11 three-pointers and scored a career-high 52 points. In the third quarter of that game, he scored 37 points, an NBA record for a single quarter. In that jaw-dropping display of shooting in the third quarter, Thompson made 9 three-pointers and went 13-for-13 from the field. Both were NBA records. Thompson represented the Western Conference in the 2015 All-Star Game. He was named Third-Team All-NBA for his play in 2014-15. In addition to playing outstanding defense, Thompson averaged 21.7 points, 3.2 rebounds and 2.9 assists in the regular season. In the 2015 NBA Playoffs, Thompson averaged 18.6 points, 3.9 rebounds and 2.6 assists. He led the Warriors in scoring in four playoff games during their championship run. Thompson scored his postseason-high—34 points—in Game 2 of the NBA Finals.

* * *

Austin Rivers has played three seasons in the NBA with New Orleans and with the LA Clippers. Austin became the first NBA player to be coached by his father when Doc Rivers—also the Clippers' president of basketball operations—acquired Austin in a mid-season deal from New Orleans. A reserve guard, Rivers emerged as key player for the Clippers in the 2015 postseason. Rivers stepped up his offensive game when the Clippers needed it most. He scored 16 points in a crucial Game 4 victory over the Spurs in the first round. He filled in for injured starter Chris Paul in the first game of the Western Conference Semifinals and scored 17 points against the Rockets. In Game 3 of the series against Houston, Rivers made 10 of 13 shots and scored 25 points in only 23 minutes. Partly as a result of his play in the postseason, the Clippers signed Austin Rivers to a two-year contract in July, 2015.

When I talked with Austin Rivers in late 2013, he was playing for New Orleans. Little did either of us know that midway through the 2014-15 campaign his father would pull off a trade to bring him to the Clippers. Doc obviously has confidence in his son's basketball ability or he wouldn't have made the trade. Austin's improved play in a few of his playoff opportunities would seem to have rewarded his father for having faith in him as a player. In return, Austin was rewarded with a new deal in 2015.

I would love to have been in the room when those contract talks were taking place between Doc and Austin's agent. We all know management will sometimes try to make a low ball offer to a player. But, how about when that player is your son? That's a different story. Doc was in a pretty awkward position. He's trying to keep costs down for the organization, but the player looking for a good deal is his son. Sometimes in negotiations, things can get a little nasty. Things can be said that create hard feelings. But, I doubt that anyone in the Clippers' front office really wanted to criticize Austin for any deficiencies in his game—not with Doc calling the shots. It all got worked out to the tune of a two year deal worth a reported $6.4-million. Austin should be able to afford to buy the Thanksgiving turkey when the Rivers all get together for the family's holiday meal.

I talked with Austin Rivers in Portland on December 21, 2013.

Who was your first boyhood idol?

Tracy McGrady. Tracy McGrady. He was the man! He was the *man*! My dad coached the Magic, so that's why I was naturally around the team. I used to watch T-Mac every single day, man, *every day!* That's who I wanted to be like when I grew up. I wanted to be just like T-Mac. I used to wear his arm bands. I used to get every Tracy McGrady sneaker. I used to have tank-tops and draw #1 on it and put "McGrady" on the back and lower the rim to like 6½ feet and do all of his moves. Every day! Then, my dad would yell at me, "Play on ten feet! Play on ten feet!"

How old were you when you were idolizing Tracy McGrady?

I'd say ages like 10 through 15. That was my dude, man.

A lot of people never meet their heroes, but you were up close and personal with your idol. What was that like?

I didn't get to talk to him that much. I just knew him. People think I was around NBA players a lot. I really wasn't. I kind of did my own thing. I wanted to do my own thing—kind of just work out on my own and make it on my own. But, I did have a chance to meet him. I was very fortunate to meet him multiple times. It was amazing every time I met him. I mean, that was my guy.

Was he honored to know that Doc's kid idolized him?

Nah, I mean, he was used to it. To be honest, T-Mac was *every* kid's guy. Most of these guys in the locker room, if you ask who their favorite player was when they were 15 or 16, I think most of them would say T-Mac. T-Mac or Kobe Bryant or Allen Iverson, those are the three guys that every guy wanted to be. It was T-Mac, A.I. or Kobe.

Without a moment's hesitation, your dad told me his boyhood idol was Muhammad Ali.

Yeah, Muhammad Ali. He has like a million Ali items. He has like seven Muhammad Ali signed gloves. Muhammad Ali wrote notes to him. In every apartment or house he's had, my dad has had four or five Muhammad Ali posters with sayings that Ali said. That's like his dude. They're cool. You see Muhammad Ali, and it's just like, "Man, that's Muhammad Ali." It's kind of cool.

And people might not know this, but your dad told me you were named after former NBA star, Austin Carr.

Yeah, my parents named me after him, and I got to meet him last year for the first time—which was an honor for me. He's an announcer for Cleveland. So, when we played Cleveland, he came up to me. He knew I was named after him, so he was excited. I got to talk to him, and I told him, "Man, I'm named after you. I just want to let you know you were my dad's favorite player growing up." It was cool to get to meet him.

You are now an idol to a lot of kids who watch you play and collect your basketball cards. What's that like for you?

I mean, it's crazy. Today I signed a little kid's jersey. Every day I go out and take pictures with fans. It's just an honor to know that hard work pays off. You hope one day you gonna be the one that someone says, "Hey, you were this for me." You never know how big of an impact you have until you meet someone. I had a Make-A-Wish kid two weeks ago. The kid's dying wish is to come meet me. That's one of the coolest things that's ever happened, that I got to spend time with him for two days and hang out with him. The kid's in a serious condition and all he wanted to do is come hang out. That was amazing. It was huge. It shows you that you never know. That's why you always gotta act the right way because you never know who's watching you.

Career Notes: Austin Rivers played one season for Mike Krzyzewski at Duke before turning pro. Rivers was picked by New Orleans in the first round (#10 overall) of the 2012 NBA Draft. In his first three NBA seasons, Austin Rivers averaged 7.0 points and 2.1 assists.

*   *   *

Austin Carr was a scoring machine. Before entering the NBA as the number one overall pick in 1971, Carr had an outstanding amateur career. A 1967 Parade All-American at Mackin High School in Washington, D.C., Carr then attended the University of Notre Dame, where he twice received All-America honors. He remains Notre Dame's all-time leading scorer.

After being recognized as the 1971 National College Player of the Year by the Associated Press and United Press International, Carr soon showed he could also score in the NBA. Carr averaged 21.2 points for Cleveland during his rookie season and was named to the NBA's All-Rookie Team. He was an NBA All-Star in 1974, a year in which he averaged a career-high 21.9 points.

Ever popular with Cleveland fans, Austin Carr is affectionately known as "Mr. Cavalier." He remains involved with the Cleveland franchise as the color commentator on the Cavaliers' television broadcasts. Carr's jersey (#34) was retired by the Cavs in 1981.

I was a big college basketball fan when Austin Carr was playing at Notre Dame. Really, anybody who liked offense was a fan during that time. Carr played in an era when many players could put the ball in the basket. While Carr was at Notre Dame, "Pistol" Pete Maravich, Calvin Murphy and Rick Mount were lighting it up for their respective schools. Maravich is the NCAA's all-time leading scorer at 44.2 points per game. Murphy and Mount both averaged more than 32 points a game over their respective careers. But, Carr was capable of scoring with the best of them. Carr scored 42 or more points 23 times for the Irish. Nine times, he scored at least 50 in a game. Carr still holds the NCAA tournament record for scoring average in one year with a minimum of three games played. He averaged 51.3 points in the three games he played in the 1970 NCAA tourney. Keep in mind, Carr was a good outside shooter and was playing prior to the three-point field goal. Had the three-point line existed when Carr was playing, he likely would have scored 40 or more points in a game dozens of times!

I spoke with Austin Carr in Portland, Oregon, on January 15, 2014.

Let me start with what Doc Rivers told me. He said he named his son after you because you were his idol." What does that mean to you?

It means a lot because Doc used to come to my basketball camps when he was a little tyke. For him to name his son after me, it really was an honor. I felt honored that he thought enough of me to do that.

That's what this book is all about—idols—and the impact that certain people have on our lives. I know Austin Rivers eventually caught up to you and said, "Hey, I'm named after you." How cool was that?

It almost made me cry. To actually meet him after watching him on TV for so long—and how he's progressed and become a man now—it was really quite an experience.

Let's talk about you now. Who was your first boyhood idol?

When I was growing up in D.C., Elgin Baylor and Dave Bing, those were my two idols. I used to go watch them play on the playground. I always wanted to be like them, especially Dave. I wanted to be like Dave Bing. He was the guy that I always tried to emulate.

I know you played against Bing late in his NBA career. What was that experience like for you to play against your boyhood idol?

He was with the Washington Bullets then. That was really an out-of-body experience. (Laughs) Dave definitely knows that he was my idol. He was a Hall of Famer. I wanted to emulate him on and off the court. That's the way I was raised. My family raised me not to be one dimensional, and Dave was not one dimensional. I always wanted to be successful off the floor as well as on the floor.

Fans still consider you "Mr. Cavalier". Did you think about the fact that you were an idol for youngsters when you were playing in Cleveland?

I never thought about it that way, but I always respected the fact that I had to carry myself a certain way. I always tried to reiterate that whenever I spoke to kids. I always tried to help them understand that even if you're not in the public eye, you are an idol to someone—be it your little brother or your sister. You might be an idol to someone, so you gotta carry yourself in that proper way.

Career Notes: Although Austin Carr last appeared in a Notre Dame jersey in 1971, the six-four shooting guard remains the school's all-time scoring leader. Since freshmen were not eligible for varsity competition at the time, Carr played only three varsity seasons and scored 2,560 career points. He averaged 22 points per game as a sophomore, 38.1 as a junior and 37.9 as a senior. His career scoring average of 34.6 points remains one of the highest in NCAA history. Carr's offensive production in the NCAA tournament is even more impressive. His 41.3 career scoring average in NCAA tournament games ranks number one all-time. Carr also holds the NCAA tournament single-game scoring mark—61 points vs. Ohio University in March of 1970.

Austin Carr played nine seasons with the Cavaliers (1971–80) and played for both Dallas and Washington in the 1980-81 campaign. Over Carr's 10-year NBA career, he averaged 15.4 points per game. His scoring average likely would have been much higher had he not been hampered by numerous knee injuries. Austin Carr was inducted into the National Collegiate Basketball Hall of Fame in 2007. He was inducted into the Notre Dame Basketball Ring of Honor in 2011.

*　　*　　*

Dirk Nowitzki is one of the greatest forwards in NBA history. The longtime Mavericks' star led Dallas to the 2011 NBA championship and was that year's Finals' MVP. A native of Germany, Dirk Nowitzki was recognized as the NBA's Most Valuable Player in 2007.

Few big men have been blessed with the skills of Dirk Nowitzki. During his prime, few teams could contain the seven-foot star. He could score on the low blocks. He could shoot the three. He had a ridiculously effective fadeaway jumper—a shot that was almost impossible to block even though defenders knew it was coming. It's no surprise Nowitzki has been an NBA All-Star 13 times in his 17 seasons with the Mavericks. The only thing that is a bit of a surprise is that he only has one NBA championship ring.

I spoke with Dirk Nowitzki in Portland, Oregon, on April 21, 2011.

Tell me about your boyhood idol. Does someone come immediately to mind?

Uh, obviously, Detlef Schrempf was a big guy for German fans. He was the first German to really make it in this league and have an impact in this league. Then, I started playing basketball in the '90s, so I was a huge Chicago Bulls fan. It was the Jordan era—MJ. And, I loved Scottie Pippen's game because he was so smooth. He could do anything on the court, and that's what I loved. He played defense. He could block shots. He could shoot. He could put the ball on the floor.

I'm trying to remember. Did you play against any of those guys at some point in your career?

When I first got in the league, Pippen was in Houston. They had Hakeem Olajuwon, Charles Barkley and Pippen on that team, which was amazing. I walked in, and I was like, "Oh, my God! Three of the all-time greats on one team!" My whole rookie year was kind of awkward in that way. I was always playing against idols. Then, Jordan came back in Washington a couple years later. I got a chance to play against him, which was amazing. It's been a great ride, and hopefully, I can top it off with a championship.

You are an idol now for so many young kids. Do you think about that at all?

I try to play my game and have fun and help the team win. I'm not a guy that goes in there and dunks over two people. But, hey, if people like my style and they like that a big guy can move and shoot—if that's what you like—then that's great. But, if you're looking for some high-flying dunks, I'm not the guy to watch. (Laughs)

Career Notes: Dirk Nowitzki has played in more games than any player in Mavericks' history. Through the 2014-15 season, he is the franchise leader in points (28,119), rebounds (10,051) and made three-pointers (1,575). Nowitzki was recognized as an All-NBA performer 12 straight seasons (2001–11). He was named All-NBA First Team four times. When he was named All-NBA First Team in 2005, he became the first European player to receive that recognition. Nowitzki also was the first European player to score 20,000 points in the NBA. Nowitzki averaged eight points as a rookie, but has scored in double-figures every year since. In 1,265 regular season games, he has averaged 22.2 points, 7.9 rebounds and 2.6 assists. Nowitzki always seemed to step up his game in the postseason. He has averaged 25.4 points and 10.2 rebounds in 140 NBA Playoff games.

*　　*　　*

33

An Honor For Me To Have Raced

Bobby Rahal is one of the owners of the Rahal Letterman Lanigan Racing team. The team has won races in CART/Champ Car, the IndyCar Series, the Indy Racing League, Indy Lights and the American Le Mans Series. Bobby's son, Graham Rahal, drove the #15 Steak 'n Shake IndyCar for Rahal Letterman Lanigan in 2015, and finished fourth in the Verizon IndyCar point standings.

In his own 18-year driving career, Bobby Rahal competed in the top racing series in the world, including Formula 1, Le Mans/IMSA and CART/Champ Car. And, he's done more than his share of winning.

In the 1980s, Bobby Rahal was one of the most successful drivers in the Championship Auto Racing Teams (CART) circuit. Rahal really seemed to enjoy racing on the road course in Portland. He won in Portland in 1987, the year he captured his second straight CART championship. Bobby had three other podium finishes in Portland between 1989 and 1995. He was always a guy that racing fans kept their eyes on because he was as competitive as anyone racing at the time and willing to do whatever was necessary to win.

As a driver, Rahal was serious about the racing game. It showed every time he was approached for an interview. I can tell you that I always braced myself before asking Bobby if I could talk with him. He just seemed to be a little annoyed about having to spend time being interviewed. During the interviews I conducted with him, yes, he answered the questions. But, I always felt like he couldn't wait to wrap things up and get back to his racing team. I understand that now—there is almost always work to do—but at the time, I would think to myself that he could have been a little friendlier.

Now, as an owner, Bobby appears to me to be much more relaxed, particularly around the media. He has been extremely generous with his time, and he's been just as friendly as can be. Maybe the pressure is off now that Bobby no longer has to worry about being behind the wheel of a race car going 200 miles an hour. Or, maybe it's just that I understand the racing game a little better than I did in the 1980s when I was a young sports reporter. In any case, I can tell you that over the last ten years or so, every conversation I've had with Bobby has been as enjoyable as you could imagine. I talked with Bobby Rahal by phone on July 10, 2013.

Thinking back to the days you were a kid, can you remember who you would consider your first boyhood idol?

My idol in racing was Jim Clark from Scotland. He won the Indy 500 in '65. He was a two-time world champion, and in my mind, he was one of the greatest if not *the* greatest driver ever. And, Dan Gurney was a close second. I really admired Dan Gurney for doing so many things. He helped pioneer building his own cars—really taking on some risks—to try to improve his opportunities in racing, and I really liked that. He was always such a gentleman—or at least you thought that. Of course, now I *know* that to be the case after having been with him many times over the years. I'd say those two were certainly my boyhood idols, Jim Clark and Dan Gurney.

Did you ever meet either of them when you were a young boy?

No, not as a kid. No. I met Dan, of course, later on when I was in racing. Of course, Jimmie Clark was killed in '68, so I never had the chance to meet him. But, to me, the two of them really epitomized what a race driver—what a *sportsman*—should be all about, which is being first class, giving credit where credit is due and being humble. I really liked how they went about their craft. So, while I would love to have met them when I was a kid, I never had the chance.

When you did meet Dan Gurney later in life, was he everything you expected?

Oh, yeah! (Laughs) You're always a little awestruck. Even today, I'm a little awestruck when I'm around Dan. He taught me so many things in such a short period of time, and he is such a wonderful man.

You were obviously idolized by youngsters and racing fans when you were driving. Did you ever think about that? Did it affect the way you interacted with fans knowing that kids might be watching?

Oh, sure. I think you have an obligation to reach out to them. They're cheering you on. They're your fans. They're your advocates. I think you owe it to them to share some of that time with them. At times it can be difficult, for sure. You got so many things going on on race weekend. But, I don't think you can ever forget the fans because without fans you wouldn't have racing.

Career Notes: Bobby Rahal won 24 races in USAC and CART. He was the CART champion three times (1986, 1987, 1992). He also won the 1986 Indy 500, the 24 Hours of Daytona in 1981, and the 12 Hours of Sebring in 1987. Buddy Rice won the 2014 Indy 500 while driving for Rahal Letterman Racing.

* * *

Graham Rahal, son of three-time CART champion and Indy 500 winner Bobby Rahal, finished a career-best fourth in the 2015 Verizon Indy Car Series point standings in the #15 Steak 'n Shake car, while driving for his father's racing team. The youngest driver to win an IndyCar race, Rahal has three victories on the IndyCar circuit—two of those wins coming in 2015.

I first met Graham Rahal when he was 17. He was testing a Champ Car at Portland International Raceway. He was still in high school, and he looked and talked like a teenager. Yet, he was behind the wheel of a Champ Car. It was a little disconcerting.

The following year, the likeable young guy from Ohio was no longer just testing. He was driving in the Champ Car World Series. He did not win in 2007, but won a race the following year after the two premier U.S. open-wheel series merged to form the IndyCar Series. He then went more than seven years before getting his next IndyCar victory. Every time I talked with him during those seven years, he seemed to be feeling pressure to get back to victory lane. It looked like it might never happen. However, it looks like Graham and his crew figured things out in 2015. Even though disadvantaged because he drives for a racing team that has only one car (compared to the big-money teams that sponsor two or more), Rahal was in the hunt for the championship. Only when another car made contact with him late in the season finale at Sonoma were his championship hopes dashed. It was a disappointing finish to the season, but a great season nonetheless.

Having watched him go from being a teenager to a mature, young man— seemingly in the blink of an eye—I have to admit I root for Graham every race day. (Please note—it has little to do with the fact that one of his primary 2015 sponsors, Steak 'n Shake, happens to be my favorite fast food restaurant!)

I talked with Graham Rahal by phone on July 11, 2013.

Who was your very first boyhood idol?

Boyhood idol? It's probably different based on how you interpret the question. In racing, it was always Dad who I looked up to most. You can say, though, that I was also exposed to a lot of other drivers. Dad retired when I was still pretty young. I'm a big golfer, so I always loved watching guys like Phil Mickelson or Tiger Woods. Then, later in my life, a guy like Paul Newman. He had such an effect on my life, particularly on the charitable side and that sort of thing. He's a guy that you can't anything *but* look up to. So, various different types of idols, but they were equally as important.

You told me you've never met Phil Mickelson or Tiger Woods, but Paul Newman you knew well. Tell me about your relationship with him. When you first met him, did you think "movie star" or was he just another guy you knew from racing?

Well, I knew who he was, of course. Dad drove for him in the early '80s. I knew who he was—one of the best names in acting *ever*. But, when I raced Formula Atlantic, every time I won a race, he was the very first guy that I would see in Victory Lane. I wasn't driving for him or wasn't involved with him, really. He was just an extremely friendly guy. That relationship developed into me driving for his team for four years—unfortunately, for only a couple of those years was he alive. But, it was a very special relationship that I had with him.

You are obviously idolized by young racing fans who want to do what you do. Do you think about that when you are out and about?

You definitely do. I think you always have to set a good example in everything that you do in life. It's hard to accept that or understand why people would look up to you, but you know that there are people and kids that do. You have to take that as part of your responsibility.

How does it go when you interact with kids? You're only 24. It wasn't that long ago that you were one of these kids.

And that's why I try to always be extremely friendly because you know how it was being in that same spot not that many years ago. At the end of the day, our sport is 100% fan-supported. If we don't have them, we don't do what we do. So, it's extremely important. Kids, in particular, are the future of this sport.

You mentioned your dad as being one of those you looked up to and said he retired when you were pretty young. Do you have memories of him leaving the house to go racing?

Yeah! Of course. Of course. He was always extremely busy. Some of our fondest memories as a family were going to the race track together. I think that's why we still all love doing what we do now. Even those in my family who aren't involved in the racing, they really enjoy coming out and being at the track and being a part of it. Without a doubt, I do remember. I was nine or almost ten when he retired, so I was pretty young. But, I still spent time around the track.

You mentioned earlier that you were around other drivers. Was your father your favorite driver at that time?

Oh, yeah. Of course. He was my dad.

Career Notes: Graham Rahal began driving in the Champ Car World Series at age 18 in 2007. The following year, after the series merged with the Indy Racing League to form the IndyCar Series, Rahal was a winner in his very first IndyCar race (2008 Grand Prix of St. Petersburg). With the win on the streets of St. Petersburg, he became the youngest winner (19 years, 93 days) of a major open-wheel auto race. Rahal did not win again—suffering through a drought of 124 winless races—until he drove the Mi-Jack Honda to a win at Fontana on June 27, 2015. Then, just five weeks and three races later, he picked up his third career win at Mid-Ohio on his hometown track. Rahal was still in contention for the 2015 IndyCar championship during the final race of the season, but was hit from behind by Sebastien Bourdais and spun out. Rahal finished 18th in the race and fourth in the season point standings. Though he struggled for a period of time in IndyCar, Graham Rahal did drive into Victory Lane in 2011. He co-drove the winning car in the 2011 Rolex 24 Hours of Daytona.

* * *

465

A.J. Foyt is considered one of auto racing's all-time best drivers—maybe *the* best. Foyt was the first driver to win the Indianapolis 500 four times. Only two drivers, Al Unser and Rick Mears, have been able to equal A.J.'s four victories at the Brickyard. Incredibly, Foyt drove in the Indy 500 a record 35 straight years (1958–92) and has competed in 58 consecutive Indy 500 races as a driver or owner (1958–2015).

A.J. grew up in a racing family. His father, Anthony Joseph Foyt, Sr.—who went by the name Tony—owned midgets and ran race cars out of his auto repair shop. He raced midgets at Buff Stadium in Houston. For years, little A.J. would tag along with his dad to Buff Stadium and other short tracks in the area. A.J. would get his earliest driving experiences on those small dirt tracks around Texas. In 1965, when A.J. was driving Indy Cars and had already won a couple of Indy 500s, he also became the owner of his racing team. For years, A.J. and his father ran A.J. Foyt Enterprises out of the family shop. A.J. has often said that his final Indy 500 win (1977) was his favorite because it came in a car he had designed with his own motor. He is the only Indy 500 driver ever to win "The Greatest Spectacle in Racing" in a car of his own design and powered by his own engine.

It's really hard to believe the number of races A.J. Foyt won during his career. Driving nearly every kind of vehicle known to man, Foyt won 14 national titles and had victories in 172 major races. Win. Win. Win. That was seemingly all Foyt did in the '60s and '70s. Watching A.J. and his peers—Mario Andretti, Bobby and Al Unser, Parnelli Jones—that made me an open-wheel racing fan for life.

A.J. Foyt is a man who has always done things on his own terms. He's been described as many things—determined, passionate and cantankerous, just to name a few. But, he also is respected by everyone who watched him race or raced against him. That's one reason he has been inducted into numerous Halls of Fame—Motorsports Hall of Fame of America, International Motorsports Hall of Fame, National Sprint Car Hall of Fame, National

Midget Auto Racing Hall of Fame. The list goes and on and on—as does A.J., who turned 80 in January, 2015.

I spoke with A.J. Foyt on September 25, 2013.

Who was your first boyhood idol? Did you have one?

I really didn't. Well, I guess I told you wrong because back in the years when my daddy run midgets here at Buff Stadium, one of my idols was Doc Cossey. He never went on the circuit or nothin', but he ran the local tracks. I'd have to say he was my idol.

What was it like the first time you met him?

Oh, I met him as a kid. I can't remember how old I was. My daddy built me a car and painted it the same color as his number 8. At the Buff Stadium, I guess I was probably five or six years old, I went around the track with him and they took some pictures. After I won my first Indy 500, he sent me a telegram. It just said "Congratulations!" I still have it.

You—along with Mario Andretti and Parnelli Jones—were an idol to many in my generation. Did you ever think about that when you were out there racing?

Well, not really. I was kind of a loner to a point. I just tried to do the best job I could, and if I got beat today, I couldn't wait to return tomorrow and try to win. All I did was eat and sleep racing. A lot of these guys today, if they get beat, they just go on about their business. But, you take like Parnelli and myself—and Jim Hurtubise—hell, if we didn't win a race, we didn't eat too damn good. (Laughs) So, it's a lot different today.

Career Notes: A.J. Foyt won the Indianapolis 500 in 1961, 1964, 1967 and 1977. A native of Houston, Texas, Foyt was named—along with Mario Andretti—as the Co-Driver of the (20th) Century by the Associated Press. Foyt still holds IndyCar/USAC series records for most career victories (67), national championships (7) and victories in a single-season (10, tied with Al Unser). A.J. holds the record for highest winning percentage in a season (77%) with 10 wins in 13 races in 1964. He is the only driver to have won the Indy 500, Daytona 500, 24 Hours of Le Mans, 24 Hours of Daytona and the 12 Hours of Sebring. He also won back-to-back championships while driving in the International Race of Champions (IROC) series in 1976-77. Though he retired as a driver in 1993, *owner* A.J. continues to remain in the game. His racing team won Indy Racing League championships in 1996 (Scott Sharp) and 1998 (Kenny Brack), and Kenny Brack won the 1999 Indy 500 while driving for Foyt. In 2015, AJ Foyt Racing ran two cars in the IndyCar series—the #14 of Takuma Sato and the #41 of Jack Hawksworth.

*   *   *

Jack Hawksworth drove for AJ Foyt Racing in the Verizon IndyCar Series in 2015. In his second season in IndyCar, Hawksworth suffered through a frustrating season. The 24-year- old British driver was unable to post a Top 5 finish. He finished in the Top 10 only five times in the season's 16 races.

My only personal interaction with Jack Hawksworth occurred in St. Petersburg, Florida, three days before his first race for A.J. Foyt in March, 2015. While I wanted to inquire about Hawksworth's boyhood idol, I also wanted to get his thoughts on driving for one of racing's legends. I could tell Hawksworth was tremendously excited, and why wouldn't he be? He was joining a racing team that had more resources than his previous IndyCar team. It was quite clear that Hawksworth was honored to be driving for AJ Foyt Racing.

I speculated that he might be feeling a bit of pressure. After all, it's natural for a person to want to impress a new boss. But, Hawksworth told me he wasn't feeling any extra pressure just because his boss is a legend in racing. The young Brit said the only pressure he felt was the pressure he puts on himself to do his very best while behind the wheel. After a 2015 season in which the results were not what anyone on the team desired, Hawksworth is looking to be much more competitive in his second season behind the wheel of the # 41 car in 2016.

I talked with Jack Hawksworth on March 26, 2015, during Media Day at the Grand Prix of St. Petersburg.

Thinking back to your earliest days, can you recall your very first boyhood idol, the person that had the biggest impact on you as a kid?

Growing up in England and Europe, I was following Formula One from a young age. For sure, growing up my hero was Michael Schumacher, the German race driver. I always admired him. At the time when I was younger, I liked him because he was winning races, and he was in the red Ferrari. Years later, I actually began to like him because of his work ethic and the things he did with the team. So, he's always been my idol, but the reasons for why he was my idol kind of changed as I got older. Certainly, he was my boyhood hero.

Did you ever get a chance to meet Michael Schumacher?

I never got a chance to meet Michael. I got a card from him saying "Best Wishes" and stuff. Somehow, somebody managed to get me one from him. But, I never managed to meet him. I would have liked to. Maybe someday.

How old were you when you got the card from him?

It was actually not long ago. It was like 2010. I think it was a sponsor of mine who managed to get the card. He'd met Michael, and he got him to sign me a card. It was pretty cool.

A lot of kids are now fans of yours as you drive the #41 IndyCar. Do you ever think about the fact that roles are now reversed and you are the driver being looked up to by young racing fans?

(Laughs) I'll be honest. That sounds a little bit crazy. I just want to do the best job I can. I want to go out there and win races for A.J.'s team. We know we can do that, and if people like that, then perfect. Honestly, it sounds very strange to think that the role would be reversed in that circumstance. It's nice, and if that's the case, that's great.

You are now working for a man who was a boyhood idol for many racing fans. How would you describe A.J.?

A.J. is a character. That's how I'd describe him. He's a great guy. He's a racer. If you ever get down to the core of A.J., he's a really good guy, and he's a racer. He's very passionate about this sport—probably more passionate than anyone I've ever come across. I've only known him for a short while, but from what I know about him and from every time I've spoken to him, he's genuinely a very nice guy. He loves his racing. What I will say about him is that when he walks into a room, there's an aura about him. Even at the shop—even with all these guys who've worked for him and known him for years—when he walks in and starts speaking, everybody listens. He's got that kind of aura about him.

Was there any hesitation on your part to drive for him because you knew you would be driving for a racing legend?

It's pretty awesome. It's still surreal to think I'm driving for him. The Foyt name has won so many races—Le Mans, Indy 500, Daytona 500, multiple Indy Car championships. He holds the record for Indy Car wins, and I'm driving for him now. So, that's extremely special. I think it's more of a motivation than anything because as a team, we want to put the Foyt name back at the top. It's not been there for a few years since the time A.J. retired. Obviously, we want to get it back up there.

I think that's the target—to get us winning races and maybe even winning an Indy 500 championship in the next few years.

Even though you haven't been in this situation for a very long period of time, A.J. is your boss. Would you consider him a tough boss?

I don't know. I guess I'll find out if I do any stupid stuff, right? But, so far, he's been very easygoing. I think that he expects you to perform because that's what you're here to do. You're here to do the best job you can for the team, but I also think he understands the necessary workload and everything which goes in to it. He's a racer. He wants to win. He's going to demand a high level of performance from me, and that's expected. That's what my job is. So, I look forward to that.

Career Notes: Jack Hawksworth, who is from the United Kingdom, got his start racing karts in his native country. Setting his sights on the Verizon IndyCar Series, he quickly moved up the ladder. Hawksworth dominated the 2012 Star Mazda Series and captured the championship after winning eight of his 16 races. The following year, he moved to Indy Lights and finished on the podium in half of his 12 races. He posted three Indy Lights victories in 2013. Hawksworth moved up to the Verizon IndyCar Series with Bryan Herta Autosport in 2014. During his rookie IndyCar season, Hawksworth immediately turned heads by qualifying in the Firestone Fast Six three times in the first six races. He qualified second and led the first 32 laps at the inaugural Grand Prix of Indianapolis. Hawksworth's best 2014 finish was third place in the Grand Prix of Houston. After driving for AJ Foyt Racing in 2015, Jack Hawksworth is still looking for his first IndyCar victory entering the 2016 season.

* * *

Will Power won the 2014 IndyCar championship while driving for Team Penske. The Australian-born Power won races at St. Petersburg, Detroit and Milwaukee in his championship season.

In 2015, despite winning only one race—the Grand Prix of Indianapolis—Power was in contention for a second straight title entering the final race of the season. However, at Sonoma, teammate Juan Pablo Montoya made contact with Power in a turn and effectively ended the championship hopes of both Penske drivers. Thanks to seven finishes in the Top 5 during the season, Power finished third in the point standings.

In late 2015, the 34-year old Power published his autobiography, *The Sheer Force of Will Power.*

I met Will Power for the first time in 2006 when he was driving a Champ Car for Team Australia. I interviewed him before the race and thought it would be nice if this mild-mannered, young guy from Australia did well on race day. He did not. He finished last. In Portland's final Champ Car event the following year, Power finished seventh in a race won by Justin Wilson.

Power won a few races in Champ Car and in his first year in IndyCar, but we would not see Power's true ability behind the wheel until 2010. That year, he won five races for Penske Racing. He won six races the following year. It's somewhat stunning to look back now and realize that he did not in a championship either year, despite having a two-year stretch during which he won eleven races.

I was able to arrange a short visit with Will just before the start of the 2015 IndyCar season so that I could ask him about his first childhood hero. Despite not having interviewed him since the Champ Cars left Portland after the 2007 race, I found Power to be the same quiet guy I had interviewed years earlier. I wasn't at all disappointed when it appeared Power might come from behind to win the 2015 championship in the final race of the year. I was disappointed, however, when his teammate, Montoya, smashed into Power's car, ending both of their championship hopes.

I talked with Will Power on March 26, 2015, prior to the Grand Prix of St. Petersburg (Florida).

When I talk about your first boyhood idol, is there a name that immediately pops into your mind?

Yeah, it's Nelson Piquet—Formula One driver.

What was it about him that attracted you to him?

I don't know. It was the name or something. It was kind of funny. When you're a kid, you just latch onto someone for a reason—what he looks like or his name or the car he was driving. I liked the look of the Williams race car at the time. But, yeah, he was definitely a guy that I remember was my favorite as a kid.

Did you ever meet him?

I never met him, but I actually got to race against his son, Nelson Piquet, Jr., in British F3, so I saw him at the race track. He was there. I would like to have met him, but I was just too shy. (Laughs) I just was watching him, thinking, "Yeah, that was the guy that I loved when I was a kid, and now I'm racing against his son."

Young racing fans now look up to you the same way that you looked up to Nelson Piquet. Do you think about that?

I actually think about it more now than I used to because you kind of put yourself back to when you were a kid, and you're like, "Oh yeah. I loved that." You want to interact with the kids and give them a signed hat or show them the cockpit or show them a steering wheel because they *love* it. As a kid, it's the type of thing you remember forever when that sort of thing happens. It's like "Oh, this guy let me sit in the racecar.

He showed me his steering wheel." So, I think it's good to do that. I do that more now. Before, I had the blinders on. I was so focused. I couldn't interact with anyone.

It has to warm your heart to be able to do that for kids.

Yeah, it does! Absolutely! One of my biggest fans is a kid. He's got Cerebral Palsy. He can't talk. He's in a wheelchair. His whole life is *me*. He's flying to Indy this year. He's gonna come to the 500. He's never *ever* been on a plane. It's very difficult for him because of his situation. He's in a hospital having to have surgeries because his bones are growing together. He watches my races almost every day. He just keeps watching my race *wins*. So, I feel I gotta win more races for this kid (laughs) 'cause that's what makes him feel better. You think about his life. He's confined to a wheelchair. You think about life and how blessed you are just to have a normal life. You just feel so blessed. This kid is so mentally tough to deal with the pain that he has to go through every day. Man, it breaks my heart.

Career Notes: Previous to racing in IndyCar, Will Power drove in the Champ Car World Series. He was the Champ Car Rookie of the Year in 2006, finishing sixth in the point standings despite going without a win. He picked up his first Champ Car race victory at Las Vegas in April, 2007. He also won that year in Toronto. Power won the last-ever Champ Car race, which was held at Long Beach in 2008. He then joined Roger Penske's team as a part-time IndyCar driver in 2009 and earned his first IndyCar victory at Edmonton that year. In 2010, Power won five IndyCar races. He won six in 2011 and three more in 2012. He finished second in the IndyCar Series point standings three straight years (2011–13) before finally breaking through to win the IndyCar championship in 2014.

*   *   *

Helio Castroneves is a three-time winner of the Indianapolis 500 and the only driver to win "The Greatest Spectacle in Racing" in his first two tries. He won in 2001 and 2002, then again in 2009. Castroneves has also finished second in the Indy 500 on two occasions, both times finishing less than a second behind the winner. Remarkably consistent in IndyCar's premier event, he has thirteen Top 10 finishes in his fifteen Indy 500 races.

Castroneves has made news—both good and bad—away from the track. He teamed with dancing partner Julianne Hough to win television's *Dancing with the Stars* competition in 2007. In a much more serious matter, Castroneves was charged with conspiracy and income tax evasion in October, 2008. However, in mid-April of 2009, Castroneves was acquitted of the tax evasion charges. Prosecutors dropped the conspiracy charge the following month.

Even though he has won the Indy 500 three times, it would be safe to say that his victory in court was the most significant of all the wins in Helio Castroneves' life. His reputation and career were saved. It also would have been a huge public relations blow to the IndyCar Series if one of its most popular drivers had ended up serving time in jail.

Castroneves is clearly one of the top drivers of his generation. He's one of only ten drivers to win three or more Indianapolis 500s. It is not a stretch to think he could already have become the first five-time winner in "The Greatest Spectacle in Racing." In the two Indy races in which he finished as the runner-up, Castroneves finished less than a second behind Gil de Ferran (in 2003) and Ryan Hunter-Reay (in 2014).

You might not know that it was the tragic death of a fellow driver that gave Helio Castroneves his big break in racing. In 1999, a short time after Castroneves learned the CART team for which he was driving—Hogan Racing—was ceasing operation, he was selected to drive for Penske Racing. Penske had originally signed talented Canadian driver Greg Moore to drive the #3 car, but Moore was killed in the final CART race of 1999. Penske then offered the job to Castroneves.

I spoke with Helio Castroneves on March 26, 2015, at the Grand Prix of St. Petersburg.

Who was your first boyhood idol?

Ayrton Senna. For us Brazilians in my generation, he was the guy we were always watching, waking up in the morning and seeing him winning races. That was the inspiration for my generation to become a race car driver.

Did you ever get a chance to meet him before he perished in a crash while leading the 1994 San Marino Grand Prix?

Yeah, I did. I actually raced against him in a go-kart in 1990. He was doing some type of event. It was Wheel Life. I was invited to do it. It was a great experience I will never forget.

What was it like to race against your hero?

It was incredible. It was just among friends, uh, nothing professional. On the qualifying, we did something. I took pole position, and he said, "Okay, fast guys start in the back." He was starting right beside me in the back. So, we started, and we moved up through the field. I won, and he finished third. I was like, "Yeah! I *got* him!" That was super cool!

You have been an idol for many people, whether for racing or for winning *Dancing with the Stars*. Do you think about the fact that people look at you and have fond feelings?

I think I have so much to learn in life. I'm glad about the position that I got. But, I don't see myself being that kind of person yet—and I might never be. Or I might never think about it because, always, what I want to be is just be myself. My mom always told me to be myself. As long as

I have fun, the people that are watching know they can have fun, too. It doesn't need to be racing, but any kind of a job. Enjoy. Have fun. If they get that from me, my message is accomplished.

Career Notes: Since 2000, Brazilian-born Helio Castroneves has won a total of 29 races in CART and IndyCar for Team Penske, but he has never won an IndyCar championship. Castroneves is the last driver to win back-to-back Indy 500s.

*   *   *

Dario Franchitti won three Indianapolis 500 races, making him one of just ten drivers to win as many as three times in IndyCar's premier race. Franchitti was just the second Scottish-born driver to win "The Greatest Spectacle in Racing," following Jim Clark, who won in 1965.

One of the most popular drivers in auto racing, Franchitti was forced into retirement in November of 2013 after he was seriously injured in a crash in Houston. Doctors who assessed his head and spinal injuries advised Franchitti to give up racing because the risks of more extensive injury were too great. Having lost best friend Greg Moore and former friend and teammate Dan Wheldon in fatal racing accidents, Franchitti accepted the medical advice and ended his driving career. Still with Target Chip Ganassi Racing in 2015, Franchitti worked as a consultant for the four Ganassi drivers (Scott Dixon, Tony Kanaan, Charlie Kimball and Sage Karam).

Dario Franchitti ranks alongside Jim Clark and Jackie Stewart (Franchitti's first race car owner) as Scotland's most famous racing legends. To pay tribute to his late countryman, Dario drove Clark's Lotus-Ford 38/1—the car that won the 1965 Indy 500—around Indianapolis Motor Speedway prior to the start of the 2015 Indy 500.

Franchitti married American actress Ashley Judd in December, 2001, and she often accompanied him to races when her schedule allowed. The couple divorced in 2013.

I talked with Dario Franchitti at the Grand Prix of St. Petersburg on March 27, 2015.

Who was your first boyhood idol?

I'm a big Jim Clark fan. Jim Clark is my hero. I have a room in my house that's full of his memorabilia, and I have one of his old race cars. So, he's my hero. But, that happened later. I wasn't a kid by any stretch. I was probably 17 when Jim Clark became my hero. When I was four or five years old, the guys I used to love watching were Gilles Villeneuve and Mario Andretti. When he was driving the Lotus in 1978, Mario was the guy I wanted to meet.

Mario is a living legend, and he's still around IndyCar.

Yeah, I was just with him yesterday.

Do you still have the same sort of feeling? Do you say to yourself, "This is the guy that was my boyhood idol?"

Mario, I'm lucky enough now to count as a friend. I go out to dinner with him and that kind of stuff. He's a great man. He's my friend's (Marco's) grandfather and my other friend's (Michael's) father. You know what I mean? But, he's still Mario Andretti, and there will always be that bit of me that has that hero worship of him. The great thing is this paddock is full of people like that. A.J. Foyt, Rick Mears, Michael Andretti, all these guys. The paddock is full of them, and you can see them at any turn. It's fabulous that they're still around and still love the sport.

You were obviously an idol for so many during your driving days. How do you feel about that?

Um, it's nice to know you were appreciated. That's the thing. There's no more to be said other than that. It's nice to know you're appreciated.

Career Notes: Dario Franchitti drove to Indy 500 victories in 2007, 2010 and 2012. A four-time IndyCar Series champion, Franchitti won titles in 2007, 2009, 2010 and 2011. His four IndyCar Series championships tied Mario Andretti for second most all-time in USAC/CART/IndyCar. Scott Dixon joined Andretti and Franchitti when he won his fourth IndyCar title in 2015. A.J. Foyt, with seven championships, is the only driver to win more. In 2007-08, Franchitti became the first professional driver to win, consecutively, the 12 Hours of Sebring, the Indy 500, an open wheel series' championship (IndyCar) and the 24 Hours of Daytona. Foyt and Andretti are the only others to win all four, but neither were able to do so in succession. Prior to joining Target Chip Ganassi Racing to drive in the NASCAR Sprint Cup Series in 2008, Franchitti drove in the CART and IndyCar series for Hogan Racing, Team Kool Green and Andretti Green Racing. After just one season in NASCAR, Franchitti returned to IndyCar in 2009. He picked up right where he left off in 2007—winning the IndyCar championship. His total of 31 CART/IndyCar victories left him tied for eighth-most at the time of his retirement.

*　　*　　*

James Hinchcliffe is a popular Canadian race driver, currently employed by Schmidt Peterson Motorsports in the Verizon IndyCar Series. Hinchcliffe, who has driven an IndyCar since 2011, has four career wins. Fans voted him IndyCar's Favorite Driver of the Year in 2012. He remains one of the most popular drivers on the IndyCar circuit.

I spent a few minutes talking with James Hinchcliffe on Media Day just prior to the season-opening 2015 Grand Prix of St. Petersburg. The affable Hinchcliffe was quite generous with his time, extremely friendly and quick with a smile. While I believe many of the modern pro racing drivers talk with the media mainly because sponsors expect them to do so, I truly felt that James enjoyed talking with us members of the press. I remember thinking Hinchcliffe is just a terrific young man, a likable guy that anyone would enjoy talking with about any number of subjects. Interestingly, as I left the Media Day festivities, I had a momentary feeling of melancholy—a very brief moment when I considered the fact that all of the drivers I had just interviewed are involved in a very dangerous profession—one that could take their lives in the blink of an eye. Perhaps I thought about the danger they face because I had interviewed several drivers who have been killed in racing accidents—Greg Moore, Dan Wheldon, Scott Brayton. One of my favorite drivers, Alex Zanardi lost both legs and nearly his life in a horrific crash just months after I had sat down with him for a lengthy conversation. As I left the 2015 St. Petersburg Media Day—for just a second or two—I thought to myself how tragic it would be if one of the drivers I had just interviewed was seriously injured or killed on the race track. It was probably because of his sunny disposition, but I thought to myself how horrible it would be if Hinchcliffe happened to be involved in a bad crash. Was it a premonition or pure coincidence?

Hinchcliffe was seriously injured May 18, 2015, during practice for the 2015 Indianapolis 500 after he had qualified 24th on the starting grid. Hinchcliffe lost a great deal of blood and suffered injuries to his pelvic area and upper left thigh. He spent eight days in the hospital before being released. The personable Hinchcliffe missed the remainder of the 2015 Verizon IndyCar races while recovering from his injuries. He plans to resume his racing career in 2016. I can't tell you how glad I am that the 28-year-old Toronto-area native is alive and well. Sadly, another driver I spoke with in St. Petersburg that weekend, Justin Wilson, tragically lost his life in a freak accident during the 2015 race at Pocono late in the season.

I talked with James Hinchcliffe on March 26, 2015, in St. Petersburg, Florida.

Who was your very first boyhood idol?

The first one was Jacques Villeneuve. One of my earliest memories of watching a motor race was when Jacques won the 1995 Indy 500. It helped that he was Canadian. It helped that my favorite color was blue (the color of Villeneuve's Player's Ltd. Indy Car). For a young kid, it was kind of easy to fall in love with his story—his dad (Canadian F1 driver Gilles Villeneuve) being who he was. Jacques comes up to Indy Car and wins Rookie of the Year his first year. He wins the championship and the Indy 500 the second year. It was this cool story. Then, I really followed him when he went to Formula One. It was the same thing— top rookie first year, championship his second year. It was cool. So, he was the first one I idolized as a boy. But, I think the one that had the most impact a little bit later was his Player's replacement. It was Greg Moore. For me, that was the guy that really stood out. He really resonated with me above and beyond a lot of guys. There's a lot of bad-ass racing drivers. It's a lot harder to find one of those who's a bad-ass human being as well. That's what Greg was.

Since Greg was Canadian and a guy you looked up to, what did his death in a 1999 crash mean to you? How difficult was that for you to process?

It was devastating because at that point I'm a young kid who's racing karts and wants to be an IndyCar driver. I watch the guy that I wanted to be the most get killed doing what I'm putting all my effort—and everything in my life—towards doing. Even at a young age, it gave me pause, a bit of a reflection on what I was doing. I know it freaked my parents out a good amount as well. Ultimately, they left the decision up to me, which I'm sure was very difficult for them. Greg's death definitely gave me a bit of a jolt, for sure.

Did you ever have the opportunity to meet Greg Moore or Jacques Villeneuve?

I met Greg once, very briefly, at the Toronto race in '99. It's a funny story. I had the steering wheel off the Formula Ford 1600 that Greg raced back in '91, and I wanted him to sign it. So, I stood outside his trailer for three hours and ten minutes. One of his mechanics saw my sister and I standing out there for hours. Eventually, one of them walked up and goes, "Do you need something? What's going on?" I showed him the wheel and told him the story. He said, "That's the coolest thing I ever heard. Wait right here." He runs into the trailer, and he pulls Greg out. Greg sat there, and he chatted to my sister and I for like ten minutes. To get that kind of face time with him—at a *race*—in *Canada!* I mean, I've now been in that position, and I've never had ten free minutes at the race in Toronto. (Laughs) That was such a special moment for me. My sister did most of the talking. I could barely get a word out. I was just so in awe that I was actually getting to meet him. That first meeting was short, but it had a big impact on me.

Obviously, he lived up to your expectations.

A hundred percent. You know, it's funny. I wrote an article for the 15th anniversary of Greg's passing. One of the comments I made near the end of the article was, "There's this saying, 'Don't meet your heroes'." I call B.S. because I met mine, and he was a *legend*. He was a *great* guy. And, to me what makes a hero is not if a guy hits a lot of three-pointers or wins a lot of races or throws a lot of touchdown passes. It's a guy that can do that and still be a humble, honest, decent human being. And, that's what Greg was.

Knowing how you felt about your childhood idols, do you think about the important role you now play with kids since you have become one of the best race car drivers in the world?

A hundred percent. I was a fan of this sport long before I was involved in it. I know what it means to have a Sharpie in one hand and a hero card in the other and to stand outside your guy's trailer for three hours trying to get an autograph. Yeah, I take every spare second I have to be with fans. It doesn't just have to be young fans. It can be middle-age fans, old fans, teenage fans. It doesn't really matter. A fan's a fan. I don't for a second assume that I have the kind of impact over anyone that Greg had on me. But, even if it's a tenth of that, that's a big day, you know, a big moment in that kid's life. It makes so much sense to spend a moment with fans.

Whether or not an athlete is deserving of idol worship it seems that you believe the athlete must understand the responsibility that goes with being a high-profile person in the world of sports.

That's just it. You can't control who a kid looks up to. My biggest hero in my life is my dad. But, at the same time, Greg was also a big hero to me and a big influence on me. You're super-conscious of that in the way you behave at the track and the way you react to certain things. I want to be the guy that Greg was because it's so easy to be a jerk and do this job. It would be easy to be flippant about some of the extracurricular stuff that goes along with this job. It's really hard to be, you know, a good, honest, humble person, but that's what I want to be.

Career Notes: The Canadian-born James Hinchcliffe began racing at a young age, karting in Canada and the United States, before patiently working his way up the North American open-wheel racing ladder. After spending more than five years in various racing series, Hinchcliffe reached the Firestone Indy Lights series in 2009. In 2010, he won three Indy Lights races and finished second in the championship. Hinchcliffe received the Greg Moore Legacy Award as the rising star in Indy Lights. Hinchcliffe was hired to drive an IndyCar for Newman/Haas in 2011 and captured IndyCar Rookie of the Year honors that year. In 2012, Hinchcliffe moved to Andretti Autosports and made his second career start in the Indianapolis 500. He qualified on the front row and finished sixth in the 2012 Indy 500. Hinchcliffe won three races for Andretti Autosport in 2013, but did not win in 2014. That led to a move to Schmidt Peterson Motorsports in 2015. Hinchcliffe earned his fourth career IndyCar victory when he won the second race of the 2015 season in New Orleans. However, he appeared in only three more races in 2015 because of the injury he suffered in practice at Indianapolis.

*   *   *

Simon Pagenaud drove the #22 IndyCar for Team Penske during the 2015 season. A four-time winner in IndyCar competition, Pagenaud did not produce a victory in 2015, which was his first season driving for Roger Penske. The charismatic Frenchman with an engaging smile spent the year getting up to speed and working with the three other drivers in the Penske stable—Juan Pablo Montoya, Will Power and Helio Castroneves.

When I talked with Simon Pagenaud prior to the start of the 2015 season, he was incredibly excited about joining the famed Penske racing family. Pagenaud realized going in that he was going to be the fourth car in a four-car stable, but he was still wildly enthusiastic about joining one of the top teams in motorsports—a team with the kind of money to have top of the line equipment. I watched every race in 2015 and occasionally wondered if Simon still felt the same about his opportunity. Sure, he had a very competitive car. He finished in the Top 5 four times. But, he was clearly paying his dues with the new team. The three other Penske drivers all competed for the series' championship right down to the final race of the season. Pagenaud ended the year 11th in points. His three teammates all finished in the top five. I'm sure Simon is still excited about his affiliation with Penske. But, I'll bet he won't be satisfied to just be the good teammate in 2016 and beyond. I think he'll be putting most of his energy into getting back into the win column.

I talked with Simon Pagenaud on March 26, 2015, at the Grand Prix of St. Petersburg.

Who was your first boyhood idol?

That's pretty easy. Ayrton Senna. I was four years old. (Laughs)

What was it about him that made him your favorite?

I don't know. I think it was the passion, the aggressiveness. He was flamboyant, very flamboyant at the wheel. At the time, I found that very intriguing and fascinating.

You were nine years old, nearly ten when he died. Did you ever have a chance to meet him when you were a young boy?

No, I never had the opportunity. I've read every book about him. I've seen every movie, but I didn't get to meet him.

You are someone that young kids look up to today and probably say they want to be just like you when they grow up. What does that mean to you? Do you every think about that?

I don't think about it because I still think of myself as the kid living his dream. I'm 30 years old, but I'm walking into Team Penske now and realizing my lifetime dream. I'm still living this. It's hard for me to imagine people looking at me and wanting to be me. I'm actually living that life. I want to become something. I'm not there yet. I know what I want to become, and I'm working at it. Maybe once I achieve what I want to achieve, maybe I'll realize that kids look up to me.

So, you're saying that you're still just a little kid living the dream?

I am. It's a funny thing, you know. I'm very mature, very calculated, but deep inside I'm still a little kid living his dream.

Since you still consider yourself a little kid, how does it feel to be around the IndyCar Series where you get to see Mario Andretti, A.J. Foyt and other racing legends on a daily basis? Do those names mean something to you? I know they're American drivers, but I assume you know their history.

Yeah, Mario—and A.J. Foyt, as well. Those guys, they've won in every series, which is very unusual nowadays. I would love to be able to say that I won all the races they've won. I would love to be able to say that

I won the 24 Hours of Le Mans, the IndyCar championship, the Indy 500s. You don't get to see drivers doing that anymore. I just have a lot of respect for those guys. At the time they were winning, it was a different time for racing. It was a lot more dangerous. The competition was different, also. There weren't as many teams as good as there are now. So, it was a very different time. But, uh, I enjoy it so much, you know?

A.J. and Mario are considered living legends. You can pretty much sense that when they're walking around, can't you?

Yes. I gotta tell you. I'm part of this industry and this racing world, and I've been lucky to be in the Top Five every year since I got to IndyCar. But, when I see Mario, I'm still shy. And, when I see A.J., it's the same thing. I'm still shy underneath. It's an honor for me to have raced with Dario Franchitti and to race Tony Kanaan. Those were my heroes when I was a kid. I would have loved to race with Mario and A.J., too. But, I'm just very proud to be racing with them still being involved.

Career Notes: Simon Pagenaud has driven many different types of race cars in various series over the last 15 years. He finished eighth in points in the final Champ Car season in 2007. Pagenaud then drove for four years in the American Le Mans Series and was the American Le Mans Series champion in 2010. Pagenaud drove to a second place finish in the 24 Hours of Le Mans in 2011. He also made his IndyCar debut in 2011. Driving for Schmidt Peterson Hamilton Motorsports, Pagenaud finished in the top five in the IndyCar point standings in 2012, 2013 and 2014. He won two IndyCar races in 2013 and two more in 2014.

*   *   *

Scott Dixon has placed himself smack dab in the middle of the conversation when people are discussing the best race car drivers of his generation. In 2015, the New Zealand native won his fourth IndyCar championship for Target Chip Ganassi Racing. The 2008 Indy 500 winner became just the fourth driver to win as many as four championships, joining Mario Andretti (4) and Dario Franchitti (4) and the all-time leader A.J. Foyt (7).

I enjoyed watching Scott Dixon race in Portland during his first two seasons in CART. He finished seventh both times he raced a Champ Car in the Rose City—in 2001 (with PacWest Racing) and 2002 (with Chip Ganassi Racing). You could see that Dixon had the talent to go a long way in the sport. Unfortunately, we saw no more of Dixon in Portland after he raced there in 2002. In 2003, Chip Ganassi was among those who took his racing team to the Indy Racing League. That was the beginning of the end for CART. Five years later, CART/Champ Car was bankrupt, and the teams that had managed to survive until the bitter end were folded into the new IndyCar Series. I'm happy that Dixon—one of the truly good guys in racing—is having so much success in his career. Selfishly, I just wish we could have seen him a few more times in Portland.

I talked with Scott Dixon on March 26, 2015, at the 2015 Grand Prix of St. Petersburg Media Day.

Who was your first boyhood idol?

Uh, I think, as strong and serious ones, probably Ayrton Senna. From my era, he was huge. But then, sort of having the understanding of motor sports in general, Denny Hulme and Bruce MacLaren. There were a lot of good, young drivers back then. But, you know, in Europe, you also had your rugby stars and your sailing stars. But, in racing, those three were definitely the ones for me when I was young.

Did you ever have a chance to meet any of them?

No. No, I didn't, unfortunately.

Without a doubt, there are youngsters driving go-karts today who consider you as an idol. What does that mean to you?

Oh, I can't say I think about it too much. I feel I am just a regular guy doing what I love. I feel very privileged to be doing what I'm doing. It is cool to go to go-kart races or to watch smaller categories race and see the response—the passion and the love that they have for the sport. It feels kind of strange in a lot of ways, but kind of cool, too.

Career Notes: Scott Dixon started out in karting. He gained experience by winning a pair of Formula Vee championships in his native New Zealand. After being successful in other racing series, Dixon moved to America to race Indy Lights. He won the 2000 Indy Lights championship for PacWest Racing. He advanced to CART in 2001 and picked up his first major open-wheel victory when he won at Nazareth, Pennsylvania. At the time, he was the youngest winner of a major open-wheel race. Dixon earned CART Rookie of the Year honors after finishing eighth in points. Dixon joined Target Chip Ganassi Racing when the PacWest team folded after the third race of the 2002 season. The following year, Target Chip Ganassi Racing moved to the Indy Racing League (IRL). Dixon won his very first IRL race (at Homestead, Florida) and went on to win the IRL championship. Dixon also won IndyCar championships in 2008, 2013 and 2015. Through 2015, the 2008 Indianapolis 500 winner has won 38 CART/IndyCar races, fifth most all-time and more than any other active driver. He stands one victory behind Al Unser and four victories behind Michael Andretti. The two retired drivers will be in Dixon's crosshairs in 2016. In addition to his IndyCar success, Dixon has twice been part of the winning team in the 24 Hours of Daytona. He teamed with Dan Wheldon and Casey Mears to win in 2006, and he teamed with Tony Kanaan, Kyle Larson and Jamie McMurray to win Daytona in 2015.

* * *

34

Kind Of In Awe

Doug Collins grew up in Illinois and was an All-State basketball player prior to playing at Illinois State University. In 1972, while a junior at Illinois State, Collins averaged a career-best 32.6 points a game. The 6-foot-6 guard averaged 29.1 points during his three-year college career. Collins was the first overall pick in the 1973 NBA Draft and played eight seasons for the 76ers. An injury shortened his playing career, but Collins stayed in the game by becoming a coach and a broadcaster.

Having grown up just 45 minutes from Illinois State University, I had the chance to see Doug Collins play several times when he was starring for the ISU Redbirds. He was an outstanding college player, with a beautiful stroke and a quick first step to the basket. The world learned about Doug Collins when he stepped into the spotlight at the 1972 Munich Olympics as a member of the U.S. men's basketball team. In the gold medal game, Collins made two free throws with only three seconds remaining to give the Americans a 50-49 lead over the Soviet Union. However, because of confusion over a timeout and a mix-up with the game-clock, the Soviets were given a total of three chances to inbound the ball and steal the game—and steal it they did. On the third try, a length-of-the-court pass and ensuing layup lifted the Soviet Union to a 51-50 victory. The controversial finish resulted in the United States men's basketball team suffering a loss for the first time in Olympic competition. Collins and his teammates steadfastly refuse to accept their silver medals because they still believe they earned the gold.

Collins remains the best player to have worn an Illinois State uniform. He was a basketball All-American and an Academic All-American following all three of his seasons with the Redbirds. Collins is a member of the Academic All-America Hall of Fame, a somewhat rare feat for a high-caliber athlete. To honor its most decorated basketball player, the basketball floor at Illinois State's Redbird Arena has been named Doug Collins Court. A statue of Collins posing alongside his ISU coach, Will Robinson—the first African-American head coach in Division I—is located outside the Arena's north entrance. Collins left Illinois State decades ago, but he clearly has not been forgotten.

I spoke with Doug Collins—then the 76ers' head coach—on March 19, 2011, in Portland, Oregon.

Who was your boyhood idol?

Pete Maravich. He was just making his name in the SEC, and we were fortunate growing up in Benton, Illinois, that we got the SEC Game of the Week on TV. So, I got to see a lot of Pistol Pete. I grew my hair like him in college. I wore his floppy socks, and I did all his ball-handling drills. So, Maravich was my idol. Also, Jerry West and Walt (Clyde) Frazier. Walt Frazier was playing at Southern Illinois, which is about thirty miles from my house. Being a guard, I watched those guys play and tried to emulate a lot of what they did.

Frazier played at Southern Illinois prior to your arrival at Illinois State, so you didn't play against him until you faced off in the NBA. Is that correct?

I did not see Clyde until we got in the pros together. We played against each other when he was with the Knicks.

What about Maravich? You got a chance to play against him in the NBA. What was that like for you?

It was surreal. I think probably the most surreal moment I had was when I made my first All-Star team. I walked into the locker room and shared it with those guys that we're talking about. Then, my second year making the All-Star team, Pistol and I started the game together. That was a real dream come true for me, too. I've had an amazing life. I can't even put it into words. I was very blessed. I grew up in a town, a very small southern Illinois town, where basketball was king. I had a high school coach, Rich Herrin, who was so far ahead of his time. He gave me a chance to be where I am today.

Did you ever tell Maravich he was your idol?

Oh, yeah, sure. Absolutely! I learned so much from him and the way he handled that ball and how much he loved the game.

And, I know for a fact that when you played at Illinois State and in the NBA, there were young players who idolized you the way you had worshipped "Pistol Pete". Did you ever think about that?

I did not. You know what? I just played. And, what I wanted people to always see with me was this is a guy who loves to play basketball. That's the way I played the game. So, if anybody saw me and emulated me, I really hope it was the passion and the joy that I got in playing the game I love.

Career Notes: The season before Doug Collins was selected by Philadelphia with the first pick in the 1973 NBA Draft, the 76ers won only nine of their 82 games, still the NBA record for futility. However, by Collins' fourth season with the team, the Sixers were able to reach the NBA Finals. In the 1977 NBA championship series, Philadelphia won the first two games at home. But, the 76ers then lost four in a row to Bill Walton and the Trail Blazers, handing Portland its only NBA title. Collins played all eight of his NBA seasons with Philadelphia and averaged 17.9 points per game. He appeared in four consecutive NBA All-Star Games from 1976 to 1979. Collins made his NBA head coaching debut in 1986 when he took over the reins of the Bulls, who were led by a young Michael Jordan. Collins later coached the Pistons, Wizards and 76ers. He coached in the All-Star game in 1997 and guided the Eastern Conference to a 132-120 win over the West. As a broadcaster, he has worked as a basketball analyst for TNT, NBC Sports and ESPN. Doug Collins was named a recipient of the Naismith Basketball Hall of Fame's Curt Gowdy Award in 2009.

*   *   *

Rick Carlisle is one of only 13 men to win an NBA championship as both a player and a head coach. The head coach of the Mavericks since May, 2008, Carlisle coached Dallas to the 2011 NBA title. He has also been the head coach of the Pistons and the Pacers.

I gained a lot of respect for Rick Carlisle in the wake of his 2003 firing by the Pistons. I was stunned when he was let go after seeing what he had accomplished in his first two seasons in Detroit—NBA Coach of the Year in his first season and a trip to the Eastern Conference Finals in year two. Carlisle's Pistons won 100 regular season games in those first two seasons. How in the world could Detroit fire him? It was shocking. It was also a surprise when Carlisle showed up at the Pistons' news conference announcing his dismissal. Not only did he not rip the team for firing him, he graciously thanked many in the organization for giving him the opportunity. I immediately likened Carlisle's handling of the situation to that of Rick Adelman, who handled his 1994 dismissal by the Trail Blazers with similar class. Like Adelman—who went on to win 1,000-plus games in the NBA—Carlisle has gone on to prove his value as a coach. Carlisle has won 59% of his games as an NBA head coach (619-431 through 2014-15). Most importantly, he has coached an NBA champion.

I interviewed Rick Carlisle in Portland, Oregon, on April 21, 2011.

Who was your very first boyhood idol?

I have a wide spectrum of different guys. Bill Bradley was a big hero of mine, and then, Dr. J—Julius Erving—was my favorite player. Those guys are pretty diametrically different. (Laughs) Those were my two playing idols, but that's going back several decades.

What was it about those two guys that made them special to you?

In Bradley, I just saw a guy that was extremely resourceful and could get the most out of his ability. He was a highly skilled guy that was extremely successful. Dr. J was just a breathtaking player and one of the most fun guys in the history of the game to watch. They're both terrific people. I've had a chance to meet both of them in later years.

Others have indicated it was a little strange to meet their childhood heroes. Was it for you?

It was. You always wonder if that's ever gonna happen and how it would happen. I actually ran into Dr. J before a game when both teams were out shooting around on the court. We were playing Philadelphia when I was with Boston. It was my rookie year. My ball kind of bounced over toward him, and he just said, "How ya doin', Rick?" And, you know, (laughs) it was just like, "Yeah, geez, that's Dr. J." It was pretty cool. I've had cool experiences with both of those guys.

Do you recall the details of your first meeting with Bradley?

I just met him briefly. It was back when I was playing with Boston. He was a class guy and everything that I hoped and expected.

Career Notes: Rick Carlisle played two years of college basketball at the University of Maine before transferring to play his final two collegiate seasons at the University of Virginia. He was a co-captain of the Virginia team that reached the NCAA Final Four in 1984. Carlisle was selected by the Celtics in the third round of the 1984 NBA Draft. He played three seasons in Boston, and the Celtics reached the NBA Finals all three years. Boston lost to the Lakers in the 1985 and 1987 Finals, but beat the Rockets in six games in the 1986 NBA championship series. Carlisle played just eight minutes in the 1986 Finals. He attempted only three shots and made them all. Carlisle was a role player during most of his playing career. He averaged only 2.2 points in his five NBA seasons with the Celtics, Knicks and Nets. In New Jersey, Carlisle played briefly for head coach Bill Fitch, but gave up his playing career when Fitch offered him an assistant coaching position. Carlisle worked as an assistant with the Nets, Trail Blazers and Pacers before getting a chance to become a head coach.

In 2001, Carlisle was hired as head coach of the Pistons. He was named the 2002 NBA Coach of the Year after his first season. Detroit won 50 games and a Central Division title in each of Carlisle's two seasons as head coach. The Pistons reached the Eastern Conference Finals in 2002-03. However, because of friction between Carlisle and the team's front office, he was fired shortly after the season. Soon after, on September 2, 2003, Carlisle was named as the head coach of the Pacers. Carlisle again had immediate success. In his first season at Indiana, the Pacers won a franchise record 61 regular season games, cruised to the Central Division title and reached the Eastern Conference Finals. But, in 2006-07, Carlisle's fourth season with the Pacers, they went 35-47 (the only time in Carlisle's first 13 years as an NBA head coach that his team has finished the year with a losing record), and Carlisle stepped down after the season. He worked as an ESPN studio analyst until he was hired to coach the Mavericks. Entering the 2015-16 NBA season, Carlisle has won 338 regular season games as coach of the Mavericks, just one behind the franchise's all-time leader Don Nelson.

* * *

Jeff Hornacek, a former standout in the NBA as a player, is now an NBA head coach with the Phoenix Suns. Hornacek will be challenged to be as successful in coaching as he was as a player. The six-four shooting guard had a distinguished playing career, most of the time spent with the Suns and Jazz. One of the NBA's all-time best free throw shooters, Hornacek shot nearly 88% from the line over the course of his career. Longtime fans will recall that Hornacek lightly stroked the side of his face three times before each free throw attempt. He later revealed that was his way of saying hello to his three children during the game.

Jeff Hornacek was one of the athletes who indicated to me that he did not have an actual boyhood idol when he was young. However, he did have an interesting story about how a future Hall of Fame player taught him a trick that helped him become a better player. Hornacek's father was a coach and school administrator at St. Joseph High School in Westchester, Illinois (where Isiah Thomas was a star player). Hornacek, who went to Lyons Township High School in LaGrange Illinois, revealed that—even though he attended a different high school—he learned something from Thomas.

I talked with Jeff Hornacek in Portland, Oregon, on February 25, 2013.

Who was your very first boyhood idol?

I never really had one guy I looked at as an idol. But, the one guy I tried to watch as I was getting to an age where I could really make use of it was Isiah Thomas. My dad was one of the coaches and Dean of Students at the high school Isiah went to, so I watched him go through high school. I don't know if he was an *idol,* but it helped me out in my career—seeing what he does, watching him play and playing against him in pickup games when I was young. I think I was a freshman when he was a senior.

What was it about Isiah that you liked? Was it his overall game?

Well, yeah, obviously his game. Back then, there was such an excitement at St. Joe's when NBC would put his games on TV. There was one thing I learned from playing in those pickup games with Isiah in that little high school gym. I was just a little kid out there—the young kid. I was cutting underneath the basket one time and just happened to look up and saw this ball out of the corner of my eye. I put my hands up, caught it and laid it in. I was like, "I didn't even think I was open." What I learned from that one play was what I did all through college and when I made passes in the pros. Simply, when a guy is cutting or running down the court and his man's not looking, he's really *open*. That's one thing I think really helped me in my career.

It's interesting that the guy you mention as being important to you, even though you didn't consider him an actual idol, was only in high school at the time.

Well again, I never thought I had an idol. I grew up watching Jerry Sloan and the Bulls' teams. I was a baseball guy and loved watching hockey. I watched all the professionals on all the different levels, so I never really picked one guy out. Isiah is the closest to an idol that I could say.

You eventually found yourself in the NBA and were playing against Isiah Thomas and the other stars that you had seen on television. What was that like, especially considering you had already played against Thomas when you both were in high school?

I think it helped me. A lot of guys get starry-eyed when they get in the NBA. They've watched guys on TV for years, and all of a sudden they're playing against them. For me, it was, "Hey, if I could play against Isiah in high school," then I never feared playing in the league and getting nervous. So, in that respect, it really helped me.

When you played for the Jazz, John Stockton and Karl Malone might have received more of the headlines, but all three of you had huge fan followings. Did you ever think about being an idol to young kids?

Well, of course. You know the little kids are out there watching you. Being a coach's son—and the way John played and the way Karl played—we always felt that we played like basketball is supposed to be played. As a team, you do little things to try to help your teammates. You may not get the glory. You may not get the stats, but you're just doing whatever it takes to win and doing it the right way. I think we all knew that. Watching our style of play—the way Coach Sloan had us playing—the way we'd go ahead and set picks on the biggest guy out there no matter what, then maybe all the young players out there could look up at us and say, "Hey, that's how you play."

You said earlier you watched Jerry Sloan on TV when he played for the Bulls. You wound up playing for him with the Jazz. Did that seem a little strange?

That seemed the strangest thing for me—to have watched Jerry playing as a Chicago Bull when I was a little kid—then I get traded to Utah. Even before that, I saw him across the court coaching when we played against the Jazz. That was great to be mixed up in his group. He's such a great guy. So, that was nice.

Career Notes: Originally a walk-on point guard at Iowa State University, Jeff Hornacek ended up an All-Big Eight Conference player. Hornacek helped the Cyclones reach the 1986 Sweet 16. In their first game in the tournament, Hornacek hit a shot to send the game to overtime and then hit a long jumper at the overtime buzzer to beat Miami University 81-79. It was Iowa State's first NCAA tournament victory in 42 years. Two days later, Hornacek helped Iowa State upset second seed Michigan 72-69. Hornacek had his #14 jersey retired by Iowa State in 1991.

Selected by Phoenix in the second round of the 1986 NBA Draft, Hornacek played 14 years in the NBA. He played with the Suns, 76ers and Jazz. Hornacek went to the playoffs six times with Phoenix and seven with Utah. He teamed with John Stockton and Karl Malone to lead the Jazz to the NBA Finals in 1997 and 1998. Hornacek averaged 14.5 points and 4.9 assists in 1,077 NBA regular season games. A 1992 NBA All-Star, Hornacek twice won the NBA Three-Point Shootout. He shot .403 from beyond the arc during his NBA career. The Utah Jazz retired his #14 jersey in 2002. Hornacek won 48 games his first season as coach of the Suns and 39 games in 2014-15.

*   *   *

Bob Weiss is a former NBA player and coach. The well-travelled Weiss played 12 seasons with the Philadelphia 76ers, Seattle Supersonics, Milwaukee Bucks, Chicago Bulls, Buffalo Braves and Washington Bullets. He spent most of his playing career with Chicago. Weiss has served as head coach of the Spurs, Hawks, Clippers and Sonics. In the 2015-16 NBA season, Weiss is an assistant coach with the Charlotte Hornets.

Bob Weiss served as an analyst with me on a few basketball games I called on TV for the University of Portland. I appreciated Bob's expertise and humor. In my opinion, he could have a great career in broadcasting if that was something he wanted to pursue. He could also be a standup comedian. The guy is witty and can tell a great story.

I talked with Bob Weiss by phone on January 5, 2015.

Who was your very first boyhood idol?

I grew up watching the Celtics with Bill Russell and John Havlicek, the Lakers with Jerry West, and Oscar Robertson of the Cincinnati Royals. They were some of the bigger names that I watched when I was a kid. I was fortunate enough to get to play with Wilt Chamberlain. He got me a ring in Philadelphia. And, I got to play against and defend Jerry West and Oscar Robertson. I think Bob Cousy was another one who caught my attention when I was growing up. I got to go to a basketball camp that he ran in Camp Graylag in New Hampshire. I got to meet all of those guys who were big sports heroes for a kid.

I remember the first time I saw Jerry West. I was playing for Penn State. We were playing at Syracuse University. The Syracuse Nats were in the

NBA at the time. I was leaving the hotel, and I heard an announcement, "Paging Jerry West. Paging Jerry West." I immediately did an about-face and walked back to the lobby. Jerry West was walking at a quick pace towards the front desk. That was the first time I got to see Jerry West face-to-face.

Did you go over and talk to him?

Oh, no. No. No. No. (Laughs) I just got to see him go by. That was it.

What did it feel like to become a peer and play against these guys you had grown up idolizing?

I don't know. You're just kind of in awe. It's a very, very exciting thing to have happen—to be able to walk out there on the court with them and play. I can't really remember any other emotions—just great excitement and being in awe. It was quite a thrill when you come into the league and some of those guys that you had watched were still playing.

Another thing I remember was when I first started into coaching. I was with the Dallas Mavericks, and I went up to a camp in Cincinnati. One of the agents used to run a camp up there where some of his players would play. K.C. Jones was on that Celtic team too, and now years later, he was up there scouting. We went to a bar. I had about three beers, which at that time would make me pretty tipsy. (Laughs) I remember just walking back to my room, stopping and saying, "Wow! I just had beers with *K.C. Jones*."

Here's a good Wilt Chamberlain story. I was a rookie, and we were playing exhibition games in North Carolina. In those days, we would fly into a city and rent five cars for the team. I was in a car with Wilt. I was riding shotgun, and Wilt was driving. We pulled up in front of the coliseum, and there are some cars parked there. Then, there was a half of a space and then a police sawhorse barrier. So, Wilt pulls up there, and he says, "Rook. Move that barrier, and I'll park right there." I look at the barrier, and I look over, and there's like 30 cops having their pregame meeting about 40 yards away. So, I look at the barrier. I look at the cops. I said, "Wilt, they aren't going to want me to move that barrier or they wouldn't have put it there." He says, "Rook. Move the barrier! I'm gonna park there." I look at the cops again. I look at Wilt again and said, "Wilt, they're not gonna let me move that thing." He says, "Rook!" I say, "Okay! I'll move it!" So, I get out and close the door. I no more than put two hands on that thing and start to lift it up—three cops come jogging over. They're gonna give me heck. Wilt's rolling down the window, and he's sticking out his head, so I'm thinking, "Oh, okay. Wilt's gonna save me." Wilt sticks his head out, and he says, "Officer, I *told* that dummy not to move that thing!" (Laughs) I climbed in the car, and we went around and parked in the back. (Laughs)

You played in the NBA for a number of years and had fans in a lot of cities that knew your name and maybe even collected your basketball cards. Did you ever consider the fact that you might be a childhood idol for some of the younger fans?

Definitely *not*. (Laughs) I never reached idol status. It was really funny. When I got out of Penn State, I didn't even consider playing in the NBA. It was kind of like maybe being a movie star or something. You just never got to do that kind of stuff. I had a good career at Penn State, but it wasn't in a big city. It wasn't a major program. So, I didn't really think that much about it. Then, all of a sudden, I heard I might get drafted. I was drafted in the third round. I still didn't know if I had much of a chance to make the team. In fact, the first few years, I didn't. In 1965, I made the team and then got cut. I played in the Eastern League. The next year I had a really good training camp, but the 76ers had signed two guards—Matt Guokas and Billy Melchionni—from Philadelphia schools. They both had no-cut contracts. That made five guards, so I got cut again even though I had a great camp. I went back and played in the Eastern League. Then, towards the end of the year, Larry Costello tore an Achilles. I got to come up. That's when they won the championship. I didn't get to contribute, but I got to watch it.

It was fun. After that, I was in the league for ten more years. But, no, I was never a boyhood idol. But, it was fun playing against my idols.

Career Notes: Bob Weiss was drafted by Philadelphia in the third round (#22 overall) of the 1965 NBA Draft. He played in 783 regular season games in 12 NBA seasons and averaged 7.6 points and 3.7 assists per game. As a head coach, Weiss compiled a record of 223-299 over seven NBA seasons. He twice guided Atlanta into the NBA Playoffs. In 2008, Weiss coached the Shanxi Zhongyu Brave Dragons in the Chinese Basketball Association. Weiss was prominently featured in the book *Brave Dragons: A Chinese Basketball Team, an American Coach and Two Cultures Clashing*, which was written by author Jim Yardley.

*   *   *

35

He Walked Off That Baseball Card

Steve Garvey was a 10-time All-Star first baseman, who played a total of 19 years with the Los Angeles Dodgers and San Diego Padres. Long before Cal Ripken, Jr. established Major League Baseball's all-time mark by playing in 2,632 consecutive games, the durable Garvey had been nicknamed "Iron Man" after setting the National League consecutive games record with 1,207 straight. Garvey was the recipient of many honors during his career. In 1981, he received the Roberto Clemente Award, MLB's highest honor for humanitarian service.

Steve Garvey was such a productive baseball player that many have forgotten he was a two-sport standout at Michigan State University. He was an All-American baseball player and a defensive back on the Spartan football team. Though he was not eligible to play on the varsity football team as a freshman, Garvey played a key role in helping the Spartans prepare for the so-called 1966 "Game of the Century" between top-ranked Notre Dame and second-rated Michigan State. Coach Duffy Daughery took advantage of Garvey's high school experience as a quarterback to have him play the role of Fighting Irish quarterback Terry Hanratty in practice the week before the game. Future Hall of Famers Bubba Smith and George Webster—stars of the Spartan defense—pounded away at Garvey all week. On game day, a battered Garvey stood on the sidelines and watched the two teams play to a 10-10 tie.

I spoke with Steve Garvey by phone on April 12, 2013.

If I ask you to tell me about your first boyhood idol, is there someone who immediately pops into your mind?

I was lucky to be a batboy at the age of seven for the Brooklyn Dodgers. I loved all of them—Jackie Robinson and Pee Wee Reese and the rest. But, the guy that stood out was Gil Hodges. He was six-three, six-four, big hands—a big guy. He was soft-spoken, a lot like my dad. They were the same size. Dad was a semi-pro football player. But, I really liked Gil. I watched Gil and his demeanor—how he handled the fans. He was my first real idol.

He walked off that baseball card. I watched him that first day as a batboy. I sat on the bench, and he sat next to me with Pee Wee Reese. We were talking about how the Yankee pitcher was holding the ball for a curveball one way and a fastball the other. I'm listening to them, and all of a sudden another player is trying to sit down. Almost sitting down on top of me is Jackie Robinson. I was a seven-year-old, but, not only did they treat me well—kind of as a son—but I watched how they treated the fans. It was a different time back then. It was simpler. Guys had second jobs in the off-season. They played for six or seven thousand dollars a year. It was a great time to get to know these gentlemen and grow up with your heroes. Gil epitomized that era.

I know that when you played, you wanted to portray a positive image for the fans. Was that because you realized kids were looking up to you the same way you looked up to Gil Hodges and those Dodgers?

Absolutely, I was blessed. To be a kid—at seven—batboying in the spring for the World Championship Dodgers, it doesn't get any better than that. I batboyed for the next seven or eight years until my high school schedule got tough. Then, all of a sudden I'm drafted by the Dodgers. It's almost a Hollywood script (laughing)—batboying for the Dodgers, growing up with them, now getting drafted by them. It was a philosophy that the Dodgers had—the organization and the O'Malley family—about the national pastime. It was about being part of it and being honored to be part of it—and having respect for the fans. I was lucky. I had more of an in-depth understanding. I always said, "If I'm a major leaguer someday, I'm gonna be like Gil." When the time came, I just tried to make a difference. I just tried to be the player that was available—sign the autographs and love the game. I went out and played with migraines and hairline fractures and all that stuff in reverence to these men that were before me.

Career Notes: A native of Tampa, Florida, Steve Garvey played in five World Series—four with the Dodgers and one with the Padres. He batted .417 in the 1981 Fall Classic as the Dodgers beat the Yankees in six games. In 55 career postseason games (including NLDS and NLCS games), the right-handed hitting Garvey batted .338, with 11 home runs and 31 runs-batted-in. Garvey was voted the 1974 National League Most Valuable Player. He was the All-Star Game MVP in 1974 and 1978. He was twice voted MVP of the National League Championship Series. Garvey was a lifetime .294 batter, with 272 home runs and 1,308 RBI during his 19-year major league career. He won four National League Gold Gloves for being the best defensive player at his position. He is the only first baseman to have played an entire season without committing an error (1984 with San Diego). Ironically, Garvey did not win the Gold Glove that year he played error-free baseball.

* * *

Michael Conforto was a three-time All-American baseball player
at Oregon State University before being drafted by the New York Mets in the first round of the 2014 amateur draft. After spending only a calendar year in the minors and without spending a day in Triple-A, Conforto made his major league debut with New York in July of 2015. He impressed the Mets so much that it appears he is in the majors to stay.

I had the pleasure of covering Michael Conforto when he was starring for Oregon State. A tremendous hitter in college, Conforto reminded me in a lot of ways of another former Beavers' great, Jacoby Ellsbury. The son of former Penn State football player Mike Conforto and 2-time Olympic gold medal-winning synchronized swimmer Tracie (Ruiz) Conforto, Michael arrived on campus swinging a hot bat and never cooled off.

Michael Conforto played in the Little League World Series in 2004. He led Oregon State to the 2013 College World Series. And, in 2015, in his first year in the major leagues, he played a key role in helping the Mets reach Major League Baseball's World Series.

I talked with Michael Conforto on May 20, 2013, not long before he and his OSU teammates were headed to Omaha to play in the College World Series.

Who was your first boyhood idol?

As far as baseball, I think probably Mickey Mantle. My dad got me a couple Mantle baseball cards, and I always liked Mickey Mantle. I watched movies and documentaries on him. I just thought he was an amazing player.

What was it about Mickey? Was it the baseball cards or was it because of the amazing things he was able to do on the baseball field?

I think it was a little bit of both. Him playing for the Yankees during that sort of Murderer's Row era and him being the best player on that team, I thought that was pretty cool. I liked that movie *"61"* with him and Roger Maris, the two of them going after each other for Babe Ruth's home run record.

Mantle's last year in the majors was 1968. What year were you born?

1993, so I didn't ever get to see him play. I just thought that he was a really cool player and just a great athlete.

Oregon State fans have loved watching you play for the Beavers. Do you possibly consider yourself an idol for young Beavers' fans?

That's an interesting question that I haven't had to answer before. I guess, when I was growing up, I would watch college baseball players and hope that I could be them one day. I was at the College World Series when the Beavers won it in 2007. I met Darwin Barney and Joey Wong. So, yeah, I looked up to them and thought, "Wow! They're pretty old." I think it's crazy that I'm in their place today. It's kind of crazy how time passes. Yeah, I guess to all those kids that want to be a Beaver someday, maybe they do look up to me. Thinking about that now, it actually means a lot to me. I just hope I'm doing a good job being a good model for them.

Michael, if you do make it to the major leagues and get your own baseball card, do you think there might be kids who are born 25 years after you retire that might one day see you on a baseball card and learn about your career in the same fashion that you learned about Mickey Mantle on his bubble-gum card?

(Laughs) Yeah, I hope that someday I'll have those baseball cards. That would just be a trip to be in that position—almost flip-flopped—where someone else is looking at my card and saying that they want to be like me. I'll see; gotta get there first. But if I do, I think it is something that I would think about. I'd definitely cherish that. I'd definitely make sure that I pay it back—talk to as many kids as I could and give them as much advice as I could because everyone should experience it if they can. What I'm going through right now with my college ball team is just a blast. It's the best time of my life. I hope as many kids as possible can experience it.

When I initially asked you about your boyhood idol, you hesitated momentarily as if you were trying to decide who to say was your first boyhood idol. Did you have someone else you were thinking about mentioning?

Well, now that I about it, Ken Griffey, Jr. was someone that I watched and really modeled my game after. Obviously, he was *the* guy in Seattle for a while there. Then, him coming back to Seattle later on to end his career was pretty cool. I never met him, but I went to watch him play, I don't know how many times I saw him, but *a lot*. He's got that sweet swing and made those incredible plays in the outfield.

Career Notes: After batting .349, with 13 home runs and an Oregon State University single-season record 76 RBI (in 58 games), Conforto was recognized as an All-American and the 2012 Freshman Hitter of the Year by the National Collegiate Writers of America. In 2013, he was named Pac-12 Baseball Player of the Year and a first-team All-American by the American Baseball Coaches Association after he batted .328, with 11 homers. That was the year he led Oregon State into the College World Series. In his junior season—his last at OSU— Conforto was again recognized as an All-American and named the 2014 Pac-12 Baseball Player of the Year. He hit .345, with seven homers and 56 runs-batted-in.

Conforto, the 10th overall pick in the 2014 June amateur draft, caught the attention of New York fans when he went 2-for-2 and threw out a runner at home in the All-Star Futures Game in Cincinnati in the U.S. team's 10-1 victory. Playing in three levels of minor league competition over 12 months prior to joining the Mets, Conforto batted a combined .308, with 34 doubles, 15 homers and 73 runs-batted-in. Called up from Double-A Birmingham in late July of 2015, Conforto quickly showed he could hit major league pitching. Through his first five weeks in the majors, Conforto was batting .293, with 4 home runs and 14 runs-batted-in in 82 big league at bats. His on-base percentage was .392 and his slugging percentage .537. He hit five home runs in September and ended the 2015 campaign with nine homers and 26 runs-batted-in. He hit .270 in 174 at bats. In October of 2015, Conforto became one of the few major league players to hit a home run in his first postseason at bat. In the 2015 World Series, Conforto batted a team-best .333 among the Mets' regulars and hammered two homers in Game Four.

Initially, it was believed Conforto would be sent back to the minor leagues once the injured Michael Cuddyer came off the disabled list. However, the Mets appreciated Conforto's approach to hitting, his solid defense in left field and that he had delivered several times in the clutch in late game situations. Conforto remained on the Mets roster and was a key contributor as New York won the National League East. He also started in left field against right-handed pitching throughout the 2015 postseason.

* * *

Tony Gwynn played his entire 20-year major league career with the San Diego Padres. The popular outfielder, nicknamed "Mr. Padre," was arguably the best hitter of his generation. Loved by baseball fans in San Diego and around the country, the affable Gwynn saw his #19 Padres' jersey retired in September of 2004. The next spring, a street near Petco Park in San Diego was named Tony Gwynn Drive. Gwynn was further honored when a statue of him was unveiled at the stadium in 2007. Tony's younger brother, Chris Gwynn, played in the major leagues, and Gwynn's son, Tony Gwynn, Jr., has also spent time in the majors.

After retiring as a player in 2001, Tony Gwynn became the head baseball coach at San Diego State University, his alma mater. Not everyone knows that when Gwynn was a freshman at the school, he did not play baseball because he was on a basketball scholarship. A five-eleven point guard, Gwynn tied or set several school records, including a few that remain—assists in a game (18), assists in a season (221) and assists in a career (590). Playing college basketball for a Division I school might have been enough for most people. But, Gwynn wanted to play baseball in addition to basketball. He got his chance only after future major leaguer Bobby Meachem—then a freshman shortstop at San Diego State—convinced baseball coach Tom Dietz to give Gwynn a tryout. Meacham had played on teams with and against Gwynn when they were in high school, and Meacham gave the coach a glowing scouting report on Tony. The sweet-swinging Gwynn ended up as a two-time All-American in baseball, batting over .400 in his junior and senior seasons at SDSU. In 1997, San Diego State's baseball field was named Tony Gwynn Stadium in his honor—not bad for a guy who was a basketball star at the university. The gifted two-sport standout was drafted by two of San Diego's major league teams—the Padres (MLB) and the Clippers (NBA)—on the same day, June 10, 1981.

Sadly, Tony Gwynn began a long, arduous battle against cancer in 2009 when a malignant tumor was removed from his right cheek. Gwynn said the cancer in the salivary gland was the result of his longtime habit of chewing tobacco. He would seem to get better for a time, but the cancer would return. Each time, Gwynn bravely fought back. Gwynn took a medical leave of absence from SDSU in March, 2014 to undergo additional cancer treatment. He hoped to be able to recover and get back to his job as the school's head baseball coach—even signing a one-year extension with the Aztecs in June. But, just days later, on June 16, 2014, Tony Gwynn died of salivary gland cancer. He was 54.

It was a sad day for anyone who ever had the pleasure of meeting the congenial Hall of Famer. I was fortunate to have had the chance to interview Gwynn several times. I always found him to be very friendly—just a terrific fellow. Although I had contact with him only during our occasional phone conversations through the years, I considered him to be extremely likeable and the kind of guy you would like to hang around with to talk about baseball or family. I had enjoyed watching him when he served as a baseball analyst on television. When he died, I remember thinking how sad it was that nobody would ever hear his voice again—that wonderfully magnetic voice—so full of energy, enthusiasm and life. Sometimes, a person's death hits you hard, even if you weren't particularly close. For me, the passing of Tony Gwynn was one of those times.

The last time I talked with Tony Gwynn was when we talked on the telephone about his boyhood idol on February 20, 2013.

Tony, who was the guy that you first idolized as a kid?

I grew up in Long Beach, California, and my first boyhood idol as a kid was a guy by the name of Willie Davis. He was a centerfielder with the Dodgers and a left-handed hitter—like I was. Boy, I tried to emulate everything I saw Willie Davis do. So, growing up, he was the first guy that I really tried to emulate and really liked a lot.

Once you start playing the game, you start to realize that you can have certain characteristics of certain guys that play. So, once I started playing, I realized I wanted to be a guy like Rod Carew. Growing up, I really tried to emulate the things that he did. Then, when I got to the big leagues, I got an opportunity to meet Rod Carew. Those two guys were huge in my development as a younger player.

Did you ever get a chance to meet Willie Davis?

I did. I was already in the big leagues when I got a chance to meet him. We had a day here in San Diego where we were honoring one of the older Padre teams, and Willie Davis played for the Padres for one year. So, I got an opportunity to sit down and talk to him—pick his brain a little bit. For me, it was a big thrill. He couldn't understand why. (Laughs) He couldn't believe that he was my favorite guy growing up. He was having some trouble in his life at that particular point, but for me, it was a big thrill getting a chance to meet him.

You might have had some preconceived notions of what he would be like. Was he everything you expected?

As a kid, I just loved him as a baseball player. Maybe I was different. I didn't really think of him as a person. I just thought, "This guy is a really good baseball player." He really doesn't get a whole lot of credit because he played on a team with a lot of other good players—Sandy Koufax, Don Drysdale, Don Sutton—you go right on down the line of guys that he was playing with. I just admired him as a baseball player.

Kids ask that same question, "Who was your role model growing up?" I tell the truth. Honestly, it was my parents. My parents were there every day. If there were questions I needed to have answered, I would ask them. They would give me their best answer. But, when it came to playing baseball, Willie Davis was the guy. I loved his game. I loved the way he played.

We used to get to the ballpark early at Dodger Stadium. We'd sit there, and we'd catch the end of their batting practice. Back in the days when they used to take infield-outfield, we'd be sitting in the pavilion out in centerfield. There's Willie Davis—right in front of you taking infield. I would just be watching the way he did things. I don't think I had any notions of what kind of guy he was, so when I eventually got to sit down and talk to him, I wasn't disappointed. I was pretty thrilled about having the opportunity to meet him.

There's a whole generation of Padres fans who grew up idolizing you. Did you ever think about that?

Every day. Every day I used to think about trying to set a good example. I knew that kids were looking up to me, and—other than chewing tobacco—I consciously thought of trying to do the right thing.

My dad used to tell this story about how hard it must have been for Jackie Robinson when he broke into the big leagues, and I thought about that every single day. I was just trying to do the right thing— trying to treat people right, trying to make good decisions and conduct myself in a manner in which my mom and dad would be proud.

511

I think I did that—other than using chewing tobacco. I even took the can out of my pocket and started leaving it in the dugout after I really thought about it. I tried not to go to the plate with it. Other than the tobacco aspect, I thought I did an okay job.

Career Notes: Tony Gwynn accumulated 3,141 hits in his career, 19th most in baseball history. He was an eight-time batting champion, tied with Honus Wagner for the most National League batting titles. Only American Leaguer Ty Cobb has won more batting crowns. A 15-time National League All-Star, Gwynn batted .370 or better three times in his career. He finished with a lifetime batting average of .338. One of the first players to closely examine video of his swing in an effort to improve his batting stroke, Tony Gwynn batted over .300 in each of his last 19 seasons. Gwynn batted .371 in his two World Series with the Padres (1984 & 1998). While known for his hitting, Gwynn was also an outstanding defensive outfielder. He won five National League Gold Gloves for his defensive prowess. A man of outstanding character and a person committed to serving his community, Gwynn was the recipient of baseball's highest off-field honor, the Roberto Clemente Award, in 1999. He was inducted into the National Baseball Hall of Fame in 2007.

*   *   *

George Culver is one of those fortunate men who spent a lifetime working in a career he loved. Culver played baseball at the game's highest level and then spent more than three decades trying to help other young men live the same dream.

Culver pitched in the major leagues for nine years. After his playing days ended, Culver spent 30 years working in a variety of positions in the minor leagues—manager, pitching coach, roving instructor. You name it, Culver likely did it. While he never made it to the World Series as a player, he was the pitching coach of the 1983 Portland Beavers when they won the Pacific Coast League crown and played in the Triple-A World Series.

In 1964, Culver pitched for the Triple-A Portland Beavers, a Cleveland Indians' farm team at the time. The '64 Beavers' pitching rotation—Culver, Sam McDowell, Luis Tiant, Sonny Seibert and Steve Hargan—was once recognized by Baseball America as the greatest minor-league pitching staff ever assembled (based on appearances in the major league World Series, MLB All-Star Game, total big league wins and other selected criteria).

When I talked with George Culver in 2010, we were sitting inside PGE Park—the Portland ballpark that was known as Multnomah Stadium and Civic Stadium during the years (1964–66) he pitched for the Beavers. Culver enjoyed reminiscing about his days in the Rose City. He recalled how incredible Beavers' fans were in those days and said he had never experienced that kind of enthusiasm in his baseball career until he arrived in Portland. Culver said some of his fondest baseball memories involve his time pitching for the Beavers. He said the Portland players in that era called it "baseball heaven" to be in a minor league city that loved its team as much as Portland fans loved the Beavers. We both expressed disappointment that the current Beavers' owner, Merritt Paulson, was selling the team to make way for an expansion MLS franchise. The Beavers left town after the 2010 season, leaving a void for the Portland fans who loved Triple-A baseball.

I interviewed George Culver on August 13, 2010, when he was a roving pitching instructor for the Dodgers. Unbeknownst to me at the time, he would retire from a remarkable life in professional baseball just ten days later.

My first boyhood idol was former St. Louis Cardinals great Stan Musial. Can you think back and name your very first boyhood idol?

Well, no doubt it was Mickey Mantle. But, the first major league player I actually was *told* about was Stan Musial. He was on the Wheaties box when I was a kid in the early 1950s. My cousin told me, "That's the greatest baseball player in the world right there." That was my very first introduction to baseball. When I was a kid, we had no TV. Hardly anybody did in those days. But, we had the big, tall stand up radios, and my uncle would have a baseball game on. Usually, it was a Pacific Coast League game. I'd listen to the Seattle Rainiers, the Portland Beavers, the Hollywood Stars, Los Angeles Angels and Sacramento Solons. That was my first *real* introduction to baseball. Then, as I started becoming a player, a lot of those PCL guys had become coaches or managers of teams I played on. So, I knew them by name, but not necessarily by sight.

After seeing him on the Wheaties box, I always remembered Stan Musial. Then, when I played for the Cardinals in 1970, Stan was a guest instructor in spring training. Every day after practice, I don't know why but he picked me to stay out and play pepper with him. I'm looking around, and there's nobody out there but me and him. What a thrill just to be on the same field!

Then later, I pitched against Mickey Mantle. What a thrill that was! Then—as the Dodgers moved west—I started idolizing Sandy Koufax, Don Drysdale, Maury Wills and Vin Scully. Now I work with Maury. He works at times in the Dodger minor league system. The whole thing has been like a dream for me.

What was it like to pitch against Mantle? Do you remember the first time you faced him in the major leagues?

Oh, I was scared to death. You'd just assume he was going to hit a home run off of you. I was with Cleveland, and we were playing at Yankee Stadium. Before the game, I went out to watch Mantle take batting practice. I was the first guy out there. I said, "I want to watch him take batting practice." I got to walk up pretty close to the cage and watch Mantle hit. I just tried to act like I belonged there, you know? Guys are lookin' at me, saying, "What are you doin' out here? Go back to the dugout, kid." He didn't start this particular night, and the Indians brought me in, in relief. They announced my name, "Now pitching..." When they announced my name, it sent chills all up and down my spine. Then, I hear this big, loud yell. I'm thinking, "Why are these people clapping for me?" Well, the cheers were for *Mickey* coming out of the dugout to pinch-hit. I went, "Oh no!" He's swinging about 14 bats over there warming up, and I'm going, "Oh, my God! How am I gonna handle this?" My knees were actually shaking. I didn't come close to throwing a strike on the first three pitches. I never dreamed he'd swing three and oh, so I just threw a strike—thinking I'd be able to get a strike on him. He swung and hit a fly ball out by the monuments. Our centerfielder, Vic Davalillo, ran it down. So, I looked around, and said, "That wasn't so hard after all." It was about a 500-foot fly ball! But, what a thrill—kind of like all your bubble gum cards coming to life around you.

George, you've been one of the fortunate few to get a chance to actually compete against some of your boyhood idols.

Incredible! I've been in baseball for almost 50 years now. I look back on my career, and I just think about how fortunate I am to have traveled this road. It gets me emotional. All the guys I idolized as a kid, I ended up playing a lot of them. And, even if you didn't play with or against them, sometimes they were now coaches. As I was a young kid coming up, Early Wynn was my first pitching coach. He won 300 games. I had to pinch myself and say, "Stop looking at the guy. Go ahead and do your work." I'm idolizing all these guys, and I'm supposed to be playing. Same thing when you're facing Willie Mays. I'm thinking, "God. Look at Willie Mays. No! Get to work here! Let's go! We gotta pitch to this guy! Quit idolizing him!" (Laughs) That's what I always tell the young kids when they go to the big leagues, "Respect them, but don't fall in love with them. You still gotta get them out."

Career Notes: George Culver was a multi-sport standout at North High School in Bakersfield, California. He played baseball for two years at Bakersfield College before signing as a free agent with the New York Yankees. Culver never pitched in the majors for New York, but pitched nine years in the big leagues with the Indians, Reds, Cardinals, Astros, Dodgers and Phillies. In a major league career that lasted from

515

1966 to 1974, he had a lifetime record of 48-49, with a 3.62 ERA. Culver had one shining moment as a big league pitcher. As a member of the Cincinnati Reds, the right-hander pitched a no-hitter against the Philadelphia Phillies in the second game of a twilight doubleheader on July 29, 1968. Culver's battery-mate that night was future major league manager Pat Corrales, who provided offensive support by going 2-for-5 with two runs batted in. The leadoff man for the Reds was baseball's all-time hit-king Pete Rose, who went 2-for-5 with a pair of runs scored.

*   *   *

Dan Wilson was the starting catcher for the Seattle Mariners when they made four trips to Major League Baseball's postseason from 1995 to 2001. An excellent defensive catcher, Wilson batted .262 during his 14 years in the majors with the Reds and Mariners. Dan Wilson is currently the Mariners' Minor League Catching Coordinator. He also spends part of his time as part of the Mariners' broadcasting team.

I was always a fan of Dan Wilson when he was catching in Seattle. For one thing, he was an Illinois native, same as me. But, more importantly, Wilson truly was an outstanding defensive catcher. He also hit well enough that he wasn't a huge liability at the plate—most of the time. However, Wilson himself will acknowledge that he struggled mightily in postseason play. I covered all of the Mariners' home games during their postseason trips in 1995, 1997, 2000 and 2001. Like the Seattle fans, I could not believe how ineffective Wilson was at the plate. Behind the plate, he was great. At the plate, he just could not seem to come through with the bat in his hands. In Wilson's 30 postseason games, he had only eight hits in 88 at bats (.091). The Mariners didn't hold it against Wilson. He was inducted into the team's Hall of Fame in 2012.

I talked with Dan Wilson by telephone on January 26, 2012.

Who was your very first boyhood idol?

I actually had two. One was a catcher with the Cincinnati Reds named Johnny Bench. He was a guy that when I was growing up in the '70s, the Big Red Machine was the dominant baseball team. They were led by Johnny Bench, a guy not only who was a great player, but really changed the art of catching. He was the genesis of the one-hand catcher and the hinged (catcher's) glove and that kind of thing. He was a guy I looked up to. And then, when winter rolled around and it was hockey season, I'm from the Chicago area, so my boyhood idol then was Tony Esposito, who was a great goaltender for the Blackhawks for so many years. He was a guy that I wanted to be. If I couldn't have been a baseball player, I would have wanted to have been Tony O.

So, you were always paying close attention to catchers and goaltenders?

Yeah, (laughs) I guess I liked masks or something. But, both of those guys were the guys that I wanted to be growing up.

Did you ever get a chance to meet either one of them when you were a kid?

Not when I was a kid, but I did get a chance to meet Johnny Bench in Cincinnati. I came up with Cincinnati and had a chance to meet John in spring training one year. What a thrill that was for me to finally meet the guy that I looked up to for so many years. There was the famous picture of him on the cover of Sports Illustrated holding eight baseballs—or whatever it was— in one hand. I mean, his hands were huge! I felt small as it was because he was my boyhood idol. But then, when he shook my hand and swallowed up my entire elbow, I remember feeling really, really, *really* small at that point.

Was he everything you expected? As a young player, did he treat you well?

I didn't really have a chance to talk to him for too long, but we did have a chance to shake hands and say hello. He was very cordial. I think we talked a little catching—again, just a guy that I was able to relate to a little bit. That was great. I didn't have a chance to get to know him personally beyond that, but it sure was a great experience to finally meet him.

During those seasons when the Mariners ended up playing in the postseason, you were an idol for a lot of little kids in the Northwest. Did you think about that?

Yeah, you know, it's a strange feeling. I get it a lot of times when I meet kids now that they're in high school. They say, "You were my idol growing up." Not only does it make me feel old, it makes me feel kind of strange at the same time. But, I think that's part of the deal when you're talking about professional sports—especially baseball—when there's so many games on television. It's night after night, and your face becomes very familiar to a lot of people. That's just kind of part of the deal, so you have to take it in stride. But, it is kind of a strange juxtaposition to sort of look at things in that perspective.

Career Notes: Dan Wilson was the seventh selection in the 1990 amateur draft. He was picked by the Reds and played his first two major league seasons in Cincinnati. After being traded to Seattle, Wilson soon became the Mariners' regular catcher. Wilson was an All-Star for Seattle in 1996, a year in which he batted .285 and established career highs with 18 homers and 83 runs-batted-in. Wilson ended his career with a .995 fielding percentage, at the time, the highest for any catcher in American League history. His 1,281 games behind the plate are the most for any Seattle catcher.

* * *

Michael Morse is a powerfully-built first baseman/outfielder, who just completed his 11th major league season, his first with Pittsburgh.

Morse played a key role in helping the San Francisco Giants become baseball's champion in 2014. He hit a dramatic game-tying, pinch-hit home run in the bottom of the eighth in the deciding Game 5 of the 2014 National League Championship Series against the Cardinals, a game San Francisco won in the bottom of the ninth on Travis Ishikawa's three-run homer. Then, in the deciding Game 7 of the World Series, Morse singled home the tiebreaking run in a 3-2 win at Kansas City. Giants' fans will long remember the important contributions Morse made during San Francisco's run to the 2014 championship.

Michael Morse had a pair of stints as a Seattle Mariner. He started his major league career in Seattle in 2005. He played in the Northwest for four years, left to play for the Nationals for four years, then returned for a partial season in Seattle in 2013. It was during his second stint with the Mariners that I had a chance to ask him about his childhood heroes. Let me tell you this. Morse is a big guy. They say he's 6-foot-5 and about 245 pounds. His head-to-toe muscles make him look even bigger. I could see how he would have been capable of putting together a 30 home run season like he did with Washington in 2011. Until we talked, I had forgotten that Morse came up to the majors as a shortstop. I visited with Michael Morse in Seattle on August 10, 2013.

Who was your very first boyhood idol?

I'd say, A-Rod. When I was drafted, I got to meet him. It was a great experience because I got drafted as a shortstop, and he was a shortstop at the time. It was pretty neat.

What was it about Alex Rodriguez that made you look up to him?

The fact that he was a big guy. He and Cal Ripken were big guys playing shortstop, a position where typically big guys don't play. One of the coolest things that he told me was, "No matter what happens, don't let your ability take you away from playing short. If you end up playing another position, make it because of your power and your size." I really took that to heart, and I still do.

Tell me a little bit about your first meeting with A-Rod. Where was it and when?

I think it was in 2000. I think he just signed with Texas. I was at a restaurant, and he was there. He walked by, and I stood up. I said, "Mister Rodriguez, my name's Michael Morse. I just got drafted by the Chicago White Sox." He said, "Let me guess. You're a pitcher?" I said, "Nope." And, he's like, "An outfielder?" I'm like, "Nope. I'm a shortstop." He's like, "Wow!" So, he walks by, and then he came back. He paid for my meal with my friends. He said again, "No matter what you do, don't let them tell you you're not good enough to play your position." I took that to heart, especially when I was in the minor leagues. I made it up to the majors as a shortstop, which was one of my goals.

Since he was your boyhood idol, what do you think about everything he's been going through in terms of his alleged use of performance enhancing drugs? (Rodriguez later admitted to using PEDs)

It's tough. It's tough for a guy like him. He's a role model to a lot of people. He's also one of the best baseball players that I've ever come across. It's unfortunate that it's happening. He's a competitor, so it's gotta be tough for him.

Did you collect A-Rod's baseball cards? Were you a card collector?

I was a card collector early on. But, when I got drafted, it was all business. I gotta get up. I gotta get up there to the big leagues. It was pretty cool 'cause I got to meet him when I got up to the big leagues. I got to introduce myself *again* to him, this time as a *big leaguer*. It was pretty cool.

The first opportunity you had to play against A-Rod, was it a cool experience?

Yeah, absolutely, but not just playing him—*a lot* of guys—Derek Jeter and all those guys, but *especially* him. A-Rod was a guy that I always looked up to as a kid, and now I'm on the same stage as him. It was almost where I felt he was larger than life.

Without question, there are young kids collecting your baseball cards and idolizing you. Do you think about that, and does it affect how you act?

When you have a bad day and things aren't going your way, I think if you put things in perspective—what we're doing and with kids looking up to us—it really humbles you. It makes you thank God for giving you this opportunity. I love it. I try to present myself the best way possible because you never know who's at the game that day.

Career Notes: Michael Morse has played 11 years in the majors with the Mariners, Nationals, Orioles, Giants, Marlins and Pirates. Through the 2015 season, Morse had a career batting average of .276, with 104 HR and 352 RBI. His most productive season was 2011 with Washington. He batted .303 that season and hit 31 homers, while driving in 95 runs.

*   *   *

Doug Drabek pitched 13 years in the major leagues with the Yankees, Pirates, Astros, White Sox and Orioles. He was a Cy Young Award-winner with Pittsburgh and an All-Star with Houston.

In 2015, Drabek completed his sixth year in the Arizona Diamondbacks organization. For the third straight season, he worked as pitching coach of the Class-A Hillsboro Hops Northwest League team in Hillsboro, Oregon. The Hops won the 2014 and 2015 Northwest League championships.

A lot of times when people lose their jobs, it is said say they're stepping away to "spend more time with the family." Well, in Doug Drabek's case, he truly chose to walk away from baseball because he wanted to spend more time at home. Drabek says playing baseball was no longer fun for him, so when was offered a chance to coach his two sons in Little League, he decided it was time to hang up his spikes. He also was able to spend time attending his daughter's cheerleading competitions. Once his children were grown, Drabek pursued a coaching job in professional baseball. He's been in the minor leagues working in the Diamondbacks organization since 2010.

I talked with Doug Drabek on January 31, 2013.

Who comes to mind when I ask you to tell me about your first boyhood idol?

Growing up and pitching, it would probably be Nolan Ryan. You heard all the things about him and maybe you happened to see him on TV with the Angels. Then, he gets to Houston—and you're a little older—you appreciate what he's doing even more. Growing up as a pitcher, you always want to throw hard and get strikeouts. So, he was probably my first idol.

Also, there was Joe Rudi. Ever since he made that leaping catch against the wall against Cincinnati in the 1972 World Series—kind of a backhand, jumping up against the wall and catching it—that's in my mind. I used to like to watch him hit because he had a little different stance there—that left leg out in front of the right leg. I actually was hitting like that in high school. I kind of emulated his batting stance.

I got to meet Joe Rudi once. I did a charity softball game a long time ago. You had Vida Blue and Joe Rudi there. I walked up to Rudi and just told him he was one of my favorite players growing up, and I told him why. He kind of laughed at it, but at least I got to meet him. My first thought was, "Oh, he's gonna be there. That's great!" And, then it's like, "All right. Should I go up and tell him?" (Laughs) People always come up to me and say, "Hey, I remember watching you in grade school." It's like, "Oh, gee thanks! That makes me feel real young." I didn't want to do it that way. So, I was sitting there, and it was, "All right, now's my chance. You gotta do it."

I got to meet Nolan when I was with the Astros. He had a legend that was associated with him. Just meeting him and listening to him talk, you could see where his demeanor on the mound was kind of his demeanor off the mound, too. I saw him laugh and joke and stuff, but you could see what he took out to the mound when he went out there. You could see it just talking to him. That's kind of neat to kind of get that feeling from somebody that you watched.

You were a hero for a lot of kids in Pittsburgh when you pitched for the Pirates. Did it ever soak in that you were an idol for them?

Uh, not at the beginning. It was more that you're a baseball player and people have got cards or pictures they want signed. But, when you're in it for a while, you have a better understanding. It might be different now because they really stress to players that, "Hey, look. These kids are watching you." Back then, you *kind of* know, but you didn't think about it. Then, after a few years, guys began to think about it more. They were told, "Look. Watch your actions," and all that. Then it kind of sunk in. Then listening to some of the kids and some of the parents, you really understand they are watching. You have to take yourself back to when you were a kid and you emulated somebody on TV or somebody you saw at a game—like I did with Joe Rudi. Then you realize it, and for me, it made me think—beforehand—before I did stuff. After you kind of put that in your mindset, it becomes a habit, and you don't have to think about it as much.

Even my wife said, "Do not ever turn down a signature or anything like that." I remember as a kid trying to get an autograph at the Astrodome, and I was the next one at the railing—the very next one! And, the player said, "Sorry, guys. I gotta go." Aw, my heart just dropped.

After going through that, you sign stuff, and you try to sign as much as you can. There are times you just gotta go or you just can't do it. Or you might be able to get a couple signed and that's it. You do your best to say, "Look, I'm sorry." But, I think you just realize people are watching what you're doing.

Career Notes: Doug Drabek had a record of 155-134, with a 3.73 ERA in 13 major league seasons (1986–98). Drabek, the father of major league pitcher Kyle Drabek, spent six years with Pittsburgh and had a record of 92-62 with the Pirates. He won the 1990 National League Cy Young Award after going 22-6, with a 2.76 ERA for the Pirates. Drabek made a total of seven postseason starts for the Pirates in National League Championship Series games in 1990, '91 and '92. His NLCS record was only 2-5, though he had an excellent ERA of 2.05. With the Astros, Drabek was an All-Star in the strike-shortened 1994 season, a year in which the right-handed pitcher went 12-6, with a 2.84 ERA.

*   *   *

Jason Bay played eleven major league seasons and hit 222 career home runs with the Padres, Pirates, Red Sox, Mets and Mariners. Bay, the 2004 NL Rookie of the Year, was the first Pittsburgh player ever to garner Rookie of the Year honors.

In 2015, Bay worked as a baseball analyst on ROOT SPORTS Northwest, primarily involved in coverage of the Seattle Mariners.

I became acquainted with Jason Bay in 2003, when he played for the Padres Triple-A franchise in Portland. Bay played in 91 games for the Portland Beavers and led the team with 20 home runs. He was a favorite among the fans at PGE Park (the former Civic Stadium/Multnomah Stadium). However, he was traded before the end of the season. Portland's loss was Pittsburgh's gain. Bay joined the Pirates in August and finished the year in Pittsburgh. The next season, I kept a close watch on Bay. I was not at all surprised when he came off the disabled list in May and began supplying pop in the Pittsburgh lineup. He was a runaway winner in the National League Rookie of the Year voting after hitting 26 home runs.

The next time I talked with Bay was ten years after he left Portland. I caught up with him prior to a Mariners' game in Seattle. I had to wait for him for a few minutes because he was busy signing autographs for fans. I didn't realize that day that Jason Bay would be out of baseball just four months after I spoke with him on April 27, 2013.

Who was your very first boyhood idol?

It was Cincinnati Reds outfielder Eric Davis. I was a baseball player from six years old. That's what I wanted to do. I loved it. Eric Davis was a five-tool guy coming up. He could hit, run, throw and all that stuff. It was kind of tough for a guy in Trail, B.C. to get some Eric Davis coverage, but he was my boyhood idol. And, still to this day, he's a favorite athlete of mine. He's still my guy.

Have you met him?

I have met him. He was at Cincinnati Reds spring training. He goes every year. I know a lot of guys on that Reds' team, and they speak very highly of him. He was a class act.

He didn't disappoint you? He was pretty classy?

I don't think I got all "googly" and told him, "Hey, I followed you and had your poster on my wall and all that." It was just, "Hey, nice to meet you." Even so, I was like, "Man, I followed that guy." But, I didn't get all "fan-ish" on him, so I was proud of myself.

Many athletes have said that meeting their childhood idol was a little strange, but exciting.

Absolutely, but I think just because he was a baseball player, it was a little different because we meet a lot of baseball players. Had it been outside of the realm of what I do for a living—if it was Eddie Vetter or somebody out of the baseball realm—I think there might be a little more doting goin' on.

You undoubtedly had a lot of kids idolizing you during your Rookie of the Year season. Did you think about the fact that you were suddenly being idolized by kids in Pittsburgh?

Sometimes you have to stop and think. You get so caught up in the daily grind and what you're doing. Then, all of a sudden, you sign an autograph for a kid. I've got three kids now, and you go to school with them and someone kind of looks at you in a certain way. It puts things in perspective as far as that you made that kid's day. Like I said, sometimes you lose sight of that when you play baseball all the time. Then you have little moments like that to bring you back. That's why you still do it.

Career Notes: Jason Bay, who grew up in Trail, British Columbia, played for Canada in the 1990 Little League World Series. He played college baseball at Gonzaga University and was drafted by the Montreal Expos in the 22nd round of the 2000 amateur draft. The Expos traded Bay to the Mets in 2002. The Mets dealt him to the Padres later the same year. Playing for San Diego, Bay homered in his major league debut on May 23, 2003. However, he spent much of the 2003 baseball season with the Padres Triple-A team in Portland. Traded to the Pirates in late August, he finished the year in Pittsburgh, batting .291, with three homers in 27 games. Still considered a rookie, Bay started 2004 on the disabled list due to offseason surgery. But, after being activated in May, he set a Pirates' rookie record with 26 home runs. Bay batted .282, with 82 RBI in 120 games and was voted 2004 National League Rookie of the Year. Bay's first opportunity for postseason play came with Boston in the 2008 American League Division Series. Bay homered in the first two games of the ALDS and ended the series batting .412, with 2 doubles, 2 HR and 5 RBI as the Red Sox advanced past the Angels. Bay also homered in the 2008 American League Championship Series, but the Red Sox lost in seven games to Tampa Bay.

In 2009, Bay won a Silver Slugger Award after setting career-highs in home runs (36) and runs-batted-in (119). In late 2009, Bay signed a 4-year, $66-million free-agent contract with the Mets, but injuries impacted his effectiveness at the plate. After three disappointing seasons in New York, Bay and the Mets parted ways. Bay signed with Seattle, but was released by the Mariners in August, 2013. He announced his retirement from baseball in spring of 2014. Jason Bay slugged more than 30 home runs in a season four times and finished his career with 222 homers. He was a three-time All-Star.

* * *

Jamie Burke is a retired catcher who spent a majority of his career in the minor leagues attempting to earn a spot on a big league roster. Burke spent eight years in the minors before getting his first opportunity to play in the majors. Even after he was finally given the opportunity to try on a major league uniform, Burke only saw very limited duty. He played parts of eight seasons in the majors, but spent far more time in Triple-A than the big leagues. Burke spent 18 years as a professional baseball player, but played in only 191 major league games. He had 390 at bats as a big league hitter.

Some of you might be wondering why Jamie Burke is included in a book that features a number of Hall of Fame players and many other star athletes. Well, I believe Burke represents the thousands of professional athletes who toil in relative obscurity while hoping to one day get a chance to wear a major league uniform. Burke is a success story. He made it to the majors. It is true that his major league opportunities were limited, but Burke is a testament to perseverance. He continued to pursue his dream of playing in the majors. In the process, he was able to fashion an 18-year career as a professional baseball player. Also, players dream of seeing themselves on a baseball card wearing a major league uniform. It took some time, but

Burke finally saw that dream come true. He was pictured on a Topps card in 2007, when he was in his 15th year in pro baseball!

In the minor league towns in which he played, there were undoubtedly many fans who respected Burke's effort and dedication to the game. The young baseball fans in Cedar Rapids who cheered for Burke when he played for the 1994 Midwest League champions might well have moved on to other childhood heroes, but—for a time—Jamie Burke might have been their number one guy.

Fans who remember Jamie Burke as pro baseball player might not know that he played two varsity sports at Oregon State University. He was the kicker on the Oregon State football team and a 1993 Pac-10 All-Northern Division third baseman on the Beaver baseball team. Burke, who grew up in Roseburg, Oregon, also played in three high school state championship games (2 football, 1 baseball). In a small town like Roseburg, Burke and his high school teammates, no doubt, were idols for a lot of kids around town.

I talked with Jamie Burke on August 21, 2012, when he was managing in Cedar Rapids.

First of all, did you grow up wanting to be a pro athlete, and if so, were you thinking about football or baseball?

I wanted to be a running back when I was younger. But, once I got older, I realized it wasn't going to work. I was blessed with a good leg. I could throw the ball a little bit, so going through junior high, I tried playing quarterback. I was just trying to find my niche. Then, I tried receiver and defensive back, kicker and punter. Baseball-wise, I never thought about it much, but I did always want to be a big league baseball player when I was playing in the back yard as a kid during the summertime or when I was playing Wiffle ball. You know, you imitate people. Cal Ripken, Jr. was my huge idol. I wanted to play shortstop like him.

Why were you attracted to Ripken? What was it about him?

Just his ability and the things he would do out on the field—him being an All-Star and still going out there and playing hard. He was just a hard-nosed player. That's the way I looked at myself. Obviously, he was more talented than I was, but that's who I wanted to be like. I always had to have an Orioles cap all the time. He's an ironman. Just watching him, you can see he's a hard-nosed player. Those are the type of players I really enjoy watching.

Did you ever meet Cal as a kid or later on in your life?

(Laughs) Yeah, it was later. It's kind of funny. I always said if I get a chance, I will walk up to him, introduce myself to him and let him know what I think about him. In 2001, I got called up, and I was in the big leagues with Anaheim. We're going to Baltimore, and I'm nervous about going to Baltimore. I go out on the field right off the bat and just watch him take batting practice and field ground balls. But, I'm a big leaguer, and so is he. That's his last year, and he's going to be retiring after the year. So, to get to the batting cages, you gotta go through their dugout. The batting cages are up there behind their dugout. When it's time for me to go in the cage, I walk down there, and there he is talking to pro golfer Phil Mickelson. All of a sudden, I just kind of froze up. Then, I caught them taking a break in their talking, so I was like, "Mister Ripken. Jamie Burke. You've been my idol. I appreciate watching you play. It's sad to see you go. You are a true ironman, and I just appreciate what you've done on this field." I shook his hand, met Phil Mickelson and went and hit. They'll never remember me, but I'll always remember that.

Was Ripken gracious? Was he everything you expected in that brief moment?

Oh yeah. He had hands of steel, too. His shake about broke my hand. (Laughs) He was very cordial. He was nice to me. He talked to me a little bit and asked about me. I told him where I was from. It was a great moment for me.

When you joined the Mariners, I know you were an idol for some kids in the Northwest. Did you think about that when you were signing autographs for kids?

No I didn't. For me, I just enjoyed it. For me, it was like being on that other side of the fence from where I was as a kid. You know, when I kept close track of the Legion program, those guys were my idols. Being able to watch them play, you're like, "I like this guy or that guy." You remember their names. But, for me to be able to come back home as a major leaguer, it was hard. After the '07 season and the '08 season—my first two seasons in Seattle—we'd try to go to the grocery store and grab something. You would get stopped by 10 or 15 people. Everybody asked me to go do these autograph signings or to come to their baseball practice. It caused a little wear and tear on my wife because I started sending her to the grocery store alone. But, for me, it was great to be able to be that person someone could look up to, especially in a small town like Roseburg.

Career Notes: Jamie Burke wore the uniform of the Angels, White Sox, Mariners and Nationals. After reaching the big leagues in 2001, Burke appeared in only nine games for the Angels that year and went just 1-for-5 at the plate. He then appeared in only 64 major league games over the next five years. Burke spent all of 2006 in the minors before making it back to the majors with the Mariners in 2007. He spent parts of three seasons in Seattle. Then, he played for the Nationals, but appeared in only seven games over a season and a half in Washington. In his major league career, Burke batted .277, with 3 home runs and 39 RBI. It was with the White Sox in 2004, that Burke established career highs in games (57), at bats (120), RBI (15) and batting average (.333). Jamie Burke tried managing after he put away his catcher's mask. In 2012, Burke managed the Class-A Cedar Rapids Kernels. Eighteen years earlier, Burke had played on Cedar Rapids' Midwest League championship team. After just one season at Cedar Rapids, Burke left to manage the Class-A Burlington Bees. He decided to end his managing career after the 2013 season in order to spend more time with his wife and three young sons.

* * *

Ozzie Smith, a Hall of Fame shortstop, played a total of 19 years for the San Diego Padres and St. Louis Cardinals. Nicknamed "The Wizard" for his wizardry at shortstop, the defensive whiz won the National League Gold Glove Award 13 consecutive seasons from 1980–92. With Smith starring at shortstop, the Cardinals played in three World Series in the 1980s. Ozzie earned a championship ring when St. Louis beat Milwaukee in the 1982 World Series.

One of Ozzie Smith's most memorable moments came on October 14, 1985, when he hit a game-winning home run in the bottom of the ninth off the Dodgers' Tom Niedenfuer in Game Five of the 1985 National League Championship Series. The unexpected blast prompted Hall of Fame broadcaster Jack Buck to call, "Go crazy, folks. Go crazy!" It was the switch-hitting Smith's first-ever home run from the left side of the plate.

I loved watching Ozzie Smith play. It was not unusual to see Ozzie dive to backhand a ball hit in the hole, then bounce to his feet a split-second after hitting the ground to make a strong throw to first in time to retire the batter. He was—without question—the best defensive shortstop I ever saw.

One of my biggest thrills in life was being able to take my parents to a World Series game in 1982. After the many trips mom and dad made to St. Louis to take me to Cardinals' games while I was growing up, I felt pretty good about being able to get us tickets to see Ozzie Smith and the Cardinals take on the Brewers in Game 1. It stunk that Milwaukee won the game that night 10-0, but I think mom and dad enjoyed themselves as they soaked in the festive atmosphere. I'm pretty sure our seats in the upper deck in center field were the worst seats they had ever occupied, but we took consolation in the fact that we weren't the only ones sitting far from home plate. Hall of

Fame pitcher Gaylord Perry (then with the Mariners) was also sitting out in center field just a few seats from us. Dad thought if Gaylord couldn't get seats closer to home plate, then it was understandable that we couldn't get seats closer to the field.

I talked with Ozzie Smith on June 17, 2008, and again on June 6, 2011, when he was participating in the Caddies 4 Cure charity event in the Portland area.

Who was your first boyhood idol?

I grew up in Southern California, but I had to catch the bus out to Dodger Stadium when the Pirates came to town because I loved Roberto Clemente's style of play. I loved watching Roberto do his thing out there. He's not a person you can really pattern yourself after, but the energy that he brought was something that I was impressed with as a young man. He was just one of those people that caught your eye when you went to the ballpark.

Sadly, Clemente was killed in a plane crash on December 31, 1972. Did you ever get an opportunity to meet him?

No, I didn't, but I did admire him from afar.

Obviously, you were an idol for many Cardinal fans. Did you think about that when you were playing?

No, not really. It was all about having the opportunity to play professionally. I think that was the goal for all of us. People now talk about the Hall of Fame a lot, but everybody's dream that played professionally was like Joe Carter's dream of 1993—being at the plate in the bottom of the ninth with two outs to get the big hit for your team to win. That's the real dream. Making the Hall of Fame became a by-product of trying to be the very best you could be day in and day out.

Legendary Cardinal announced Jack Buck had many memorable play-by-play calls, but one of the most memorable was the call he made when you hit the game-winning home run against the Dodgers in Game Five of the 1985 NLCS. I'll bet you've heard that a few times.

(Imitating Jack Buck) Smith corks one into right, down the line. It may go...(pause) Go crazy, folks! Go crazy! It's a home run, and the Cardinals have won the game by a score of three to two on a home run by the Wizard! Go crazy! (stops imitating Buck) That's a part of Cardinal lore now. To be a part of that is just wonderful.

Ozzie, am I right to assume that was your biggest thrill in baseball?

I had some great individual moments, but my greatest *accomplishment* had to be that I played from 1985 to 1996 with a torn rotator cuff. It's easy to play when you're healthy, but it's totally different for anybody who's ever had a serious injury, especially a torn rotator cuff. You don't realize what an important part that little muscle is in the back of your arm until something happens to it. I'm talking about just driving or opening a car door—any of those little things that sometimes we take for granted. That certainly was—and had been—the biggest challenge for me. There were some days I went out on the field I *knew* that there was only one long throw *in* me. I had to keep myself in a position to be able to still make a play and, hopefully, it wasn't a play that was going to cost us a game. Through all of the things that I did, I think it was my ability to protect that secret and cover-up that injury. That was really one of my greatest feats.

Have you had major league players approach you to tell you that you were their boyhood idol?

I've had a lot of the young shortstops come up to me and say, "You were the guy that I watched when I was growing up. You were an inspiration."

And, anytime that that happens, I don't know if you can be paid a greater compliment. It's special when they do.

You've often credited Cardinal GM/manager Whitey Herzog with being the guy that salvaged your career after you had struggled at the plate with the Padres.

There are so many people in our lives that play a part in helping you succeed. From a baseball standpoint, the person that probably gave me the opportunity to do what I did was Whitey Herzog. We all need somebody to believe in us. He certainly was that person for me. I don't think that I would have made it to the Hall of Fame if he had not rescued me from San Diego.

Final thing, Ozzie. At the beginning and end of every season, you would do a back flip when taking the field at the start of the game. Since I had grown up a Cardinal fan, I was always happy that you never hurt yourself doing that.

It took me years to realize that that was pretty dangerous. Let me tell you a quick story. We had orientation for the Hall of Fame, and they wanted to get a picture of me flipping with the Hall of Fame in the background. Well, I went out early—about 7:30 in the morning—and on my first pass, I pulled a calf muscle. So, to make a long story short, when I left there, I was in a boot and a wrist-cast. That *was* the final flip.

Career Notes: Ozzie Smith was a National League All-Star 15 times. Not considered much of an offensive threat early in his career, Ozzie flourished under manager Whitey Herzog following Smith's trade to St. Louis. From 1985 through 1993, Smith batted at least .270 eight times in nine seasons. In 1987, the speedy Smith batted .303 with a career-best .392 on-base percentage, 40 doubles and 43 stolen bases. He earned the Silver Slugger Award at shortstop following that 1987 season. In his career, Smith would compile 2,460 hits and 580 stolen bases. Ozzie Smith was inducted into the National Baseball Hall of Fame in his first year of eligibility in 2002. He was also included in the inaugural class of inductees into the Cardinals Hall of Fame in 2014. Ozzie's jersey (#1) has been retired by the Cardinals. Fittingly, Ozzie Smith was honored with 1995 Roberto Clemente Award. Like his boyhood idol—for whom the award is named—Smith was singled out for best representing the game through positive contributions on and off the field.

*   *   *

36

Keep Trickling This Down

Gary Payton was recognized in 1996 as one of the "50 Greatest Players in NBA History," and he is a member of the Naismith Basketball Hall of Fame. Payton played for five NBA teams, but spent a majority of his 17-year career in Seattle. The SuperSonics made Payton the second overall pick in the 1990 NBA Draft, and he remained with the team until 2003. He retired as the franchise leader in points, assists and steals.

As a Portland sportscaster, I covered Oregon State University basketball during the four years Gary Payton played for the Beavers. A tough kid out of Oakland, California, Payton played his first three seasons in Corvallis under Hall of Fame coach Ralph Miller. Payton—whose immense basketball talent came packaged with a heavy dose of attitude—was a lot to handle. But, the gruff Miller was up to the task. The legendary coach taught Payton there was more to the game than just offense. Miller urged the athletic guard to play tight man-to-man defense, saying it could lead to quick offensive opportunities. Payton responded by becoming a lockdown defender. He played with an intensity and fire that few others—in any sport—have ever exhibited. Payton's tight, suffocating defense would inspire others to call him "The Glove." After coaching Payton for three seasons, Miller retired in 1989. Long-time assistant Jim Anderson became the new head coach, and Payton's 1989-90 campaign under Anderson turned out to be his best. The senior averaged 25.7 points, 8.1 assists and 4.7 rebounds.

In March of 1990, Payton was featured on the cover of Sports Illustrated as "The Player of the Year." You've probably heard the saying, "A picture is worth a thousand words." Well, that still-photograph on the S.I. cover truly told a thousand words. In the photo, Gary's cocky attitude and toughness that had been instilled in him by his father—Al "Mr. Mean" Payton—was on display for all to see. Sports Illustrated captured Payton's swagger, which always included a steady dose of trash-talking.

Payton's son, Gary Payton II, was a standout for Oregon State University in 2014-15. GP II was named First Team All-Pac 12 and the Pac-12 Conference Defensive Player of the Year. Only two Oregon State players have ever recorded a triple-double. They are Gary Payton and Gary Payton II.

I talked by phone with Gary Payton on January 15, 2015, just minutes before he left to watch his son play a game against the University of Washington in Seattle.

Gary, go back as far as you can remember and think about your first boyhood idol. Was there somebody that was special to you at a very young age?

Yeah. George Gervin. George Gervin was very special to me. I used to watch him when he played for the San Antonio Spurs and how he used to do the finger-roll. I had all the pictures of him up on the wall. He was sitting in the ice chair, and I had all his basketball cards and everything. I used to sneak into the Coliseum in Oakland and sit up in the third deck and watch him play. I just had a ball watching him because I thought he was so smooth. He would *score* a basketball, and that's what I was thinkin' about when I was young.

I know the "Ice Man" had retired by the time you reached the NBA, but did you ever have a chance to tell him how you felt about him when you were growing up?

Yeah. Ever since I got into the pros and got a chance to meet him, I have had him induct me into a lot of Hall of Fames. I had him induct me into the Hall of Fame at Oregon State. I had him come to my high school when they retired my jersey. He inducted me—with John Stockton—into the Hall of Fame in 2013. He's like a father to me. I see him everywhere. We go to all the All-Star Games. We always go to the Legends stuff. He's with me in a lot of places. We talk a lot. We talk on the phone. I call him. When I told him that he was my idol—and I broke down and just told him—he was amazed by that. Ever since then, we've been really tight.

A lot of people never get to meet their childhood heroes, but you have become friends with yours. Do you feel fortunate that your boyhood idol is now a pal of yours?

Yes, I am. I'm very happy that I got a chance to meet George Gervin because I did idolize him for a long period of time. I'm happy to see what kind of person he is as a man. Especially him being older than me and him telling me how he used to watch me play—how I used to do things—it was just a big joy. It made me feel really happy—for him to feel that way about me—when he didn't really know how I felt about him. It's always great. It's a pleasure for me to still have a relationship with him now, and he's like a father figure to me, too.

You had a lot of people who looked to you for inspiration when they were kids. A couple of longtime NBA guys—Jason Kidd and Jason Terry—told me you were a guy that meant a great deal to them when they were young. Kidd, of course, grew up in the Bay Area like you, and Terry was a high school star in Seattle when you were with the Sonics. What does it mean to you to know that you were important to those guys when they were growing up?

It's really big because the simple fact is Jason Terry still calls me "Dad." Every time I see him, he is like, "What's up, Dad? What's up, Pops?" I gave him tennis shoes when he went to the University of Arizona.

He was wearing them at Arizona. When I was in the pros, I gave him shoes. With Jason Kidd, it's the same thing—sort of helped to raise him since he was 14 years old. To hear that about those kids lookin' up to me, it's just like what I did with George Gervin. It's just amazing that kids respect you like that. I had two of the guys, Jason and Jason, who had a good sense about themselves. They wasn't that guy where he had too much of a big ego, like, "I'm the bad dude. I'm good. I don't need to talk to you. I don't need to do this." I had kids that understood and were grateful for what they were gettin' from being around me. And, that was it. Jamal Crawford is the same way. I raised him, too, since he was a little pup in Seattle. These kids that have looked up to me, it makes me feel good because I showed them the right way. And, look what they're doin' now.

You've had kids idolize you for your basketball skill, but now that you're a broadcaster for Fox Sports, there might be kids looking up to you because of your broadcasting skills.

Yeah. (Laughs) You know, I've been getting that a lot. You got this social media now. You go back to the Twitter. You go back to Facebook. You gotta be on it now. I see some of the comments that some of the guys post when I'm at Fox. They post what they want to be. Some of them sit on the streets, and a lot of them say, "Man, I want do to the same thing you do. You've done it in a great way. After basketball, you're doing more things. You've been an entrepreneur. You're doing bigger things, more things for yourself." I want kids to want to do that because I want them to grow up and try to do the same things I do. I want them to do that for the kids that's coming up, too. I've got younger kids, and they idolize a lot of these basketball players. But, I want them to see the right things about these basketball players so that when they come up—and young kids see *them*—they can do the same thing. We keep trickling this down to other kids—and *other* kids—because these kids need a little guidance. It's a great feeling for me to do more things and not be out there in bad situations or in a bad way or having negative press against me. If these kids want to idolize me like that instead of them idolizing a negative person, that's great. That's what I want.

Career Notes: Gary Payton was the 1987 Pac-10 Freshman of the Year before making the All-Pac-10 Team his next three seasons. He remains Oregon State's all-time leader in scoring, assists and steals. Payton averaged 16.3 points and 6.7 assists in his 17 NBA seasons with the Sonics, Bucks, Lakers, Celtics and Heat. He led Seattle into the 1996 NBA Finals and played for the Lakers when they made it to the 2004 NBA Finals. Payton won his first NBA championship ring with Miami in 2006. A tenacious defender, Payton led the NBA with 2.85 steals per game in 1996. He retired with 2,445 career steals. Payton is the only point guard that has won the NBA Defensive Player of the Year award. Payton made the NBA's All-Defensive First Team nine straight years. He was a nine-time NBA All-Star and received All-NBA recognition nine times. Gary Payton played on gold medal-winning United States Olympic teams in 1996 and 2000.

* * *

Jason Terry grew up in Seattle watching Gary Payton work his basketball wizardry with the Sonics. Terry's overall game doesn't really compare with Payton's, but there is one area where Terry is much better. Jason Terry can seriously shoot the three-ball. In his first 16 seasons, Terry made 2,076 shots from beyond the arc, third most all-time behind Ray Allen and Reggie Miller. Terry has played for five different NBA clubs. He spent five years in Atlanta and eight in Dallas before playing for the Celtics, Nets and Rockets. He started all 17 games for Houston in the 2015 NBA Playoffs at age 37. And, Terry will be back with Houston in 2015-16.

While working in Portland, I had heard a little about Jason Terry when he was a high school sensation at Franklin High School in Seattle. However, I didn't see him play until he went to the University of Arizona. He played four years for the Wildcats and was part of an NCAA championship team his sophomore season. Terry really wasn't much of a scorer his first three years in Tucson, averaging no more than 10.6 points a game. However, Terry exploded offensively in his senior season to average 21.9 points and 5.5 assists. He earned All-America honors. Suddenly, he looked like the real deal.

In the NBA, Terry averaged eight points as a rookie, but the next season he averaged a career-high 19.7 points. A consistently good scorer, he averaged in double-figures 13 straight seasons. One of the reasons for that was his superior three-point shooting. Man, the guy could light it up from downtown! He made more than 100 three-pointers in each of those 13 straight seasons he scored in double-figures. Terry has never been an All-Star, but he has had longevity. And, he has shown there is always a place for a shooter in basketball.

I talked with Jason Terry on April 21, 2011, in Portland, Oregon.

Did you have a boyhood idol?

No question. Gary Payton was my boyhood idol. I'm from Seattle and grew up in the inner-city. He would come in to the inner-city and do basketball camps. He'd pull us to the side and talk to us about what it meant to be a professional.

I think he hung around the NBA long enough that you got to play against him, didn't you?

I got to play against him. Some of my greatest games I've ever played were against Gary Payton going back home and playing in Key Arena.

What was it like to play against him since he was your idol?

It was a surreal moment. It was like father-son, little brother-big brother. He *talked* to me the whole night, and you know GP's one of the best at trash-talkin'. He didn't let up on me, and I didn't let up on him. I had some of my best performances.

Obviously, there are some young people today who say, "Jason Terry is my guy." Do you often hear that?

Oh, all the time. No question. I have several people playing here tonight that might say that. Brandon Roy is a young guy that I used to work out. He used to be at the other end shaggin' balls for me. As you get older in this league, guys that you have tutored and mentored along the way seem to start comin' in to the NBA.

Career Notes: Jason Terry has averaged 14.8 points and 4.2 assists during his first 17 years in the NBA. The 6-foot-2 guard was named NBA Sixth Man of the Year in 2009 when he averaged 19.6 points off the Mavericks' bench. Terry won an NBA championship ring with Dallas in 2011. That season he averaged 15.8 points and 4.1 assists.

*   *   *

Brandon Roy had a chance to be a great guard in the NBA, but injuries forced him from the game far too soon. Known in basketball circles as B-Roy, the former University of Washington standout earned NBA Rookie of the Year honors with the Portland Trail Blazers in 2007. Roy was an NBA All-Star the next three seasons. He was on a path to greatness. However, bad knees allowed him to play in only 47 games his fifth season in Portland. Unable to continue his career due to a degenerative knee condition, Roy announced his retirement on December 10, 2011. He sat out the 2011-12 season before attempting a comeback with Minnesota in 2012-13. But, Roy played in only five games before deciding he could no longer perform. What started out as such a promising NBA career was over.

It was so difficult to see Brandon Roy have to call it quits after playing less than five full seasons in the NBA. He was one of the good guys. Everyone liked him—his teammates, the media and the fans. In Portland, a town with only one major league sports franchise, B-Roy had everything a guy could want. He was all smiles all the time. Then, seemingly overnight, it was all gone.

Perhaps the Blazers should have known Roy was a gamble. He had knee problems when he played for the Huskies in Seattle. But, after the way Roy began his NBA career, nobody was faulting the Blazers for acquiring him on draft night from the Timberwolves (who had taken Roy with the sixth overall pick in the 2006 NBA Draft). Certainly, nobody faulted Roy either. It was just so disappointing for everyone—the organization, the fans, and particularly for B-Roy.

I first saw Brandon Roy play when I called a game involving the Washington Huskies during his freshman season. I didn't know much about him, other than that he had been an outstanding player for Seattle's Garfield High School and that the Washington coaches absolutely loved him. He didn't show me much that first night. I really couldn't see what the coaches saw in him. I'll admit it. I was absolutely wrong about him. Roy led UW to three straight NCAA tourneys. He became a Husky All-American, the Pac-10 Player of the Year and an NBA All-Star.

A quick back story about the interview you are about to read. I spoke with B-Roy prior to a playoff game against Dallas—a game in which he came off the bench to score 16 points in a Portland victory. Coincidentally, Jason Terry—whom Roy had admired when Terry was a Seattle high school star—scored 29 points off the Mavericks' bench that night. Two nights later, Roy had his last big game in the NBA. Roy scored 18 of his game-high 24 points in the fourth quarter to lead the Blazers to a victory that evened the playoff series at two games apiece. I wondered to myself if Terry's brilliant performance two nights earlier might have inspired Roy to display his own on-court brilliance one last time.

I talked with Brandon Roy on April 21, 2011, in Portland.

Who was your boyhood idol?

543

Mine growing up was Michael Jordan. It was MJ. Being a kid and having dreams of playing basketball, he was the standard. I admired just the way he carried himself on the court. He was so smooth. He could dribble. He could shoot. Just the way he accepted every challenge that came to him, I really looked up to him when I was a kid.

Have you ever had a chance to meet Michael Jordan?

Yeah, I did have a chance to meet him. Our Trail Blazers president, Larry Miller, is good friends with Jordan. He set up a chance for me to meet him during All-Star Weekend in Arizona. My kids came into town, so I got delayed picking them up from the airport. I had to cancel, and I was so upset that I had to cancel on Michael Jordan. But, the weirdest thing was later we're in Charlotte. I used to go to use the bathroom right before the game starts, and I was running back to use the bathroom. I heard this voice talkin' kind of loud, and I thought, "That sounds like Jordan." He was coming my way, so I got nervous and went to hide. (Laughs) I always wanted to meet him, but I got nervous right at my chance to meet him. He saw me right before I could hide, and he said, "B-Roy! What's up, man?" I became eight years old again. (Laughs) I turned, and I gave him a hug. It was the coolest thing in the world for me just to be able to embrace Michael Jordan, a guy that I had admired my entire life. It was really cool.

Since your days at the University of Washington, and especially now that you're an NBA All-Star, you have become an idol to a lot of young kids. Do you think about that?

Yeah, at times I do think about it. I think about it mostly when I'm signing an autograph. Maybe you're a little tired or maybe you're busy, and you don't really feel like signing an autograph. I always think, "Man! When I was that kid's age, if I saw Michael Jordan or Kobe Bryant or Shaquille O'Neal, I wouldn't think about what he was doing. I would just want *so badly* that autograph and a chance to meet him." To be able to give that back to kids—no matter what I'm doing—is something that I always try to do. If I can, and it's not against any rules, I try to make sure I sign autographs for the kids.

You mentioned Kobe Bryant. He must have been a guy you idolized along the lines of Jordan. What was it like the first time you had to go on the court to play against him?

Yeah, actually Kobe was another guy I admired. After Jordan retired, Kobe came around. I was still about middle school going into high school. I was a huge fan of Kobe. He's a guy that I really watched closer because I was getting older myself, and I understood a little more. I went to a Sonics' game when I was in college just to watch him play. I had nose-bleed tickets. I'm sitting up high, and I'm watching him and how he moves. I want to see how he carries himself—how he goes to the bench, how he interacts with his teammates—just all the things that don't show on TV. I went home and told my dad, "That was just the coolest thing in the world. I wish one day I'll have a chance to play against him." My rookie year I had my first opportunity to play against him, and man, I was nervous. (Laughs) I was like, "Okay, man. On TV, he looks extremely quick. Am I that quick? Can I guard him? Can I score on him?" But, it was fun. He was somebody that I've also admired. I put him up at that level of Jordan. To be able to play against him was special. To score on him, I was like, "I scored on *Kobe!*" I was kind of laughing. So, it's always been a blessing of mine to be at this level and play those guys. For young kids, it's like, "Have those dreams." And, don't think that just because I'm at this level that I don't get excited about playing against some of my favorite players, too.

B-Roy, you're now an NBA veteran. Are any of the rookies saying they looked up to you when they were younger?

(Laughs) You know, it is funny. Some of the young guys are like, "I remember your rookie year when you did this." All those guys come in and say they remember when I was at the U-Dub and when I scored

545

30 points or when I did this move or hit this shot. I'm like, "Wow! Am I getting older or should I be flattered?" (Laughs) All those things are kind of cool, but at the same time, it's just such a blessing. I'm just so fortunate to be able to say that I accomplished things and met some of the people that I always wanted to meet as a kid.

One of the Mavericks, Jason Terry, told me he was a guy you looked up to when you were young. He remembers you rebounding shots for him when you were a young guy. True story?

Yeah, man! I remember that like it was yesterday. Jason Terry was the *man* where I was from. I remember when Arizona went to the NCAA Tournament. Everybody in Seattle was so happy. I wasn't an Arizona fan, but I loved Jason Terry. My dad would take me to games when JT was in high school. I would go to the game with my dad, and me and my brother would sit there and watch Franklin and Garfield play. My dad's like, "That's Jason Terry, one of the best players in the state." I would sit there and be like, "Wow! These dudes are great!" And, they were in *high school*. (Laughs) I've always been a fan. Then, Jason goes to college, and he would come and would work out. A coach of his was also a coach on my team, and he would have us come in and rebound for JT. I was happy just to rebound for him. I was like, "Man, he's going to the NBA. This dude's great!" He set the standard for how I wanted to progress in basketball. When he went to college, I was like, "Wow! I want to go to college. Jason Terry went to college." He was one of the first guys to go to college that I knew and had seen up close. I was like, "College is enough for me. If I go to college like JT, that's good enough." Then, JT went to the NBA. I was like, "JT's in the NBA! I know this guy. I know a guy that's in the NBA. I can do it, too." He made it realistic for me to feel like I can make that goal—he, along with another Seattle guy, Jamal Crawford. They're the two that really took me under their wing, worked with me and gave me that talk, "You can make it to the league. You keep working." Working with them helped elevate my game. It was good. I owe those guys a lot. They did a lot for me.

Career Notes: Brandon Roy averaged 18.8 points, 4.8 rebounds and 4.7 assists in his NBA career. He scored a career-high 52 points against Phoenix on December 18, 2008. Roy was inducted into the Pac-12 Hall of Honor in 2014.

*   *   *

37

Totally Changed My World

Bill Walton is one of the most decorated players in basketball history. A multiple-time champion at the high school, collegiate and professional levels, Walton has been a winner—on the court and in life. The Naismith Basketball Hall of Fame is just one of the many Halls of Fame that count Bill Walton as a member. He earned seemingly every accolade a player can receive—national player of the year in high school and college, as well as Most Valuable Player in the NBA. Some consider Walton to be the best-ever high school and college basketball player. Injuries were the only thing that prevented him from becoming one of the best pro players in history. Walton missed three entire seasons because of foot injuries. Only one time in his ten NBA seasons did he play in more than 67 games. During his NBA career, Walton actually played in fewer games than he missed due to assorted injuries.

Many years after his retirement, incredibly painful back problems left Walton unable to sit, stand or walk. In October of 2009, Walton told reporters in Portland that he once considered suicide as a means of ending his arduous ordeal. Walton said, "I was lying on the floor, a pitiful, helpless ball of flesh. I could not walk, think, talk, sit, stand, sleep or do anything. I had unrelenting, excruciating and debilitating nerve pain from my chest to my knees." Convinced to undergo spinal fusion surgery in early 2009—his 36th orthopedic operation—Walton literally got up off the floor and began to battle back from the depths of despair. Following the surgery, Walton proclaimed himself, "Back in the game of life." Finally experiencing relief from the pain, the native of La Mesa, California, resumed a more normal life. He returned to television in his role as a basketball analyst. One of the most sought-after analysts in the game, Walton has worked for nearly every TV network during his broadcasting career. When basketball season is in full bloom, you will see Bill Walton working a game at least two or three times a week.

It should not surprise you that Bill Walton pulled himself up off the floor when times were tough. In basketball, the guy simply never quit. He was always trying to win. Winning was the only thing that mattered to him. I was at that news conference in 2009 when Walton reflected on his darkest days and talked about regaining his life. You could see that he had turned the corner when he said, "I went from thinking I was gonna die, to wanting to die, to being afraid that I was gonna live—to now seeing rainbows, calliopes, clowns and dreams of a better tomorrow."

Most of us did not know Walton had been going through such physical and mental turmoil. In fact—unbeknownst to me—it was while he was recovering from his spinal fusion surgery that I emailed Bill and asked if he would provide a blurb for my first book. In true Walton form—and without ever mentioning his health issues—Bill wrote several pages of complimentary things about my book. I only had space on the back cover of the book to use a few lines, but I will forever be grateful to Bill for his generosity and friendship.

I talked with Bill Walton by phone on December 29, 2013.

Who was your very first boyhood idol?

I've been really, really lucky in my life in that the world of sports—which has been my life—was totally different than the family that I grew up in. My parents are not involved in the world of sports—not as participants and not as spectators. That's just not their world at all. But, my very first coach was my best coach. He's one of the major reasons why I loved basketball and why I loved sport. It was because of my first coach. His name was (Frank) "Rocky" (Graciano). He was our town's fireman, and he was a volunteer. He started the athletic program at our school because he saw a need for young children to be organized and involved with positive things once school got out. I started playing for him shortly thereafter. All of his children, my older brother, and I were all about the same age and went to school together. It was just a fantastic life for me that I did not have on my own. I was a lifelong stutterer, a terrible stutterer. I was a very reluctant, very quiet, reserved young man. Sports became my religion. Sports became my shield. That all started when I was eight in 1960.

Then, in 1961, two incredible things happened to me. I found Chick Hearn on the radio. 1960-61 was when Chick started doing the Lakers, and I fell in love. I had a little transistor AM radio, and I listened to Chick call the games. That totally changed my world because then my world went beyond what I could see and touch.

Also in 1961, the San Diego Chargers of the AFL moved to San Diego from Los Angeles, and their practice facility was about a half a mile from our family home. They practiced at a public park. It was called Sunshine Park. I would ride my bike or ride my skateboard—which I had hand-made—up to the park, and I'd watch these heroes and legends play. Sid Gillman was the coach. In the '60s, I'd watch Ron Mix, Jack Kemp, Paul Lowe, Keith Lincoln, Earl Faison, Chuck Allen, John Hadl, Lance Alworth, Tobin Rote, Ernie Ladd, Gary Garrison. It was just awe-inspiring to see these great AFL champions play and practice. Then, I would go to the games, which were in downtown San Diego. I'd ride my bike downtown, and in those days, we never even locked our bikes. We never had a ticket. We'd just sneak in. We were just children. The ushers would just say, "Go on in." It was fantastic. Later on, I got to meet all those guys. I got to meet Chick Hearn. I got to meet the Chargers.

In the mid-60s, my mom was our town's librarian. My mom brought home from the library Bill Russell's first book, and she said, "Billy, this just came in, and I thought it might interest you." It was the first sports book that I had ever read. It was Bill Russell's, *Go Up for Glory*. It totally changed my life, and Bill Russell became my hero. Now, listening to Chick all the time, I had known about Bill Russell. But, it was a Laker broadcast, so it was always about Jerry West and Elgin Baylor and some other Lakers. Ultimately, it became about Wilt Chamberlain. But, the way Chick would talk with such reverence, awe and respect for Bill Russell—and to be reading this book about Bill Russell—it just blew my mind. It opened up a whole new world.

I grew up in a household without a television. Television was not our life. So, now in the newspapers and on the radio, I also find UCLA basketball and Johnny Wooden. Then, Johnny Wooden comes into my life. Johnny Wooden was a great promoter of the game of basketball. He came to San Diego in the mid-'60s to put on a basketball clinic with Bill Sharman. They were very good friends. My first coach, Rocky, he made it possible for me to go to this clinic and sit there in the crowd and listen and watch. I knew about UCLA. I listened to their games on the radio and read about them in the newspaper.

Then, I started high school in 1966. I was a very good basketball player, and because of that, I was able to ultimately meet all these heroes. I got to meet all the Chargers. I got to meet Chick Hearn. I got to meet Jerry and Elgin and Wilt and Bill Russell. And, I got to meet John Wooden. Every one of them was a nicer person than I ever dreamed and imagined. When that happens in your life, it is affirmation of the hope—and *belief*—that this is a wonderful world full of beautiful people.

Bill, earlier you mentioned your very first coach. You said Rocky was your best coach. Why do you consider him the best coach you ever had?

When I first met Rocky, I was eight years old. He made it fun. I was so lucky that every coach I had as a child was a John Wooden disciple.

551

Coach Wooden spent his whole life teaching, building, promoting the game—the sport of basketball. He was always doing clinics, always doing programs, always doing interviews, always writing books. Not for money! He did it because he loves to teach, and he loves to make other people's dreams come true. So, here was Rocky, who loved life and who loved family and loved team and all the things that I believe in. We couldn't wait to get to practice every day. In school, it was like, "Okay, we're kind of caged up here. We want to get out and start runnin' and playin'. Where's Rocky? What time does he get here?" And, Rocky would be waiting outside the door when we burst out at three o'clock every day. He's say, "Let's go, guys." He organized our whole school, and he got the other firemen around town to organize the schools in their neighborhoods. We had games and practices and tournaments and championships in every sport. It didn't matter what the score was. It was just all so *fun*. Rocky was the key. We loved that guy.

I was really lucky in that my parents loved me more than they cared about themselves. I had fabulous parents. I had Rocky. We had great teachers in all our schools that we went to. I had Bill Russell—and then, Muhammad Ali. I used to listen to his fights on the radio and read about them in Sports Illustrated all the time. And, what he did for the world is just absolutely incredible. If you ever have the chance, you have to go to the Muhammad Ali Center for Peace Museum in Louisville. It will blow you away, all the things that that guy did in his life. You walk through this museum, and it's a journey through the history of our lives. Ali was another incredible hero of mine.

In the social and political world, my heroes were Bobby Kennedy, Martin Luther King and Sargent Shriver. I got to know Sargent Shriver through my relationship with the Kennedy family. I was 15 years old when Bobby Kennedy and Martin Luther King were shot. Here were my heroes—just dropped down in front of me—and things were never the same again.

And, then I had all my musical heroes—Jerry Garcia and the Grateful Dead, Bob Dylan, Neil Young, Carlos Santana, Crosby Stills Nash & Young, John Fogerty, John Lennon, The Beatles, The Rolling Stones. All these guys were my musical heroes, and I got to meet all of them, too. It was just all so fantastic. And, every one of them stood for something. They played with purpose and passion in their life. They were not about stuff. They were not about material accumulation and fiscal gratification. They were about making the world a better place. My heroes have been the shining star, the beacon of hope and moral compass in my life. I'm just hoping beyond hope that one day I can become a tiny fraction of what they have become and try to do something to make this world a better place—as they have already done.

When you were at UCLA and when you were starring for the Trail Blazers in the NBA, you had young fans worshiping the ground you walked on. Did you ever think about that?

No. I never think about that. I wish that I had been able to do something with my life. But, the injuries, the failures and the inability to get it done—it's frustrating, disappointing, embarrassing and shameful. I've tried to do my best. I just wish I could have done something. I wish I could have done more.

I think you're being a little hard on yourself. Trail Blazer fans will never forget their only NBA championship which you helped deliver in 1977. But, going back to what you said a moment ago, I've talked with other athletes who saw their heroes die young. I understand the devastating effect that has on someone to lose someone who means so much to you. When Bobby Kennedy and Martin Luther King were gunned down, how did you deal with the anguish you felt?

Well, we also lived through Jack Kennedy's assassination which was four a half years before the assassinations of Bobby Kennedy and Martin Luther King. You're going along through life, and you think everything is good. You think that, "Okay. We're moving forward. We're moving forward." Then, these unbelievable events—these incredible events—happen. It's awful, a tragedy—world-changing and history-defining. How do you recover from that? I was 11 years old when President Kennedy was assassinated. I was 15 years old when they assassinated Bobby Kennedy—who was going to become president—and Martin Luther King—who was doing so many positive things to try to make the world better. It casts a pall over everything that you have because it makes you no longer believe that the game is on the level.

I'd like to take a moment to ask you about the first time you met Bill Russell. When you first met him, did you have a flashback? Did you think to yourself, "This is Bill Russell. I read his book when I was just a little kid?"

Absolutely. Absolutely. I met Bill Russell when I was in college. Going to a school like UCLA in an incredible cultural center like Los Angeles in the early 1970s, I mean, c'mon! Bill was living in Los Angeles. He was such an active person. But, I felt that way about *all* the guys. Every time I met one of these guys, I'd always just say to myself, "Oh, my gosh. This is my hero." When you meet them, it's like a sunrise. It's like a sunrise where there's not a cloud in the sky and the sun is coming up behind Mount Hood. You look, and it's, "Oh, my gosh. I'm the luckiest guy in the world."

Bill, I want to thank you so much for sharing your boyhood idol stories with us.

I have some more important names for you—Chris Waddell, Lance Weir and Chase Boyd. Chase Boyd, Lance Weir and Chris Waddell are all in wheelchairs. They're all people who we know and love—and live with—and work with—in our work in the *real* world. They are my heroes today. All of their stories are so incredible.

Lance Weir is from Arkansas. He was named after Lance Alworth, and he was a great sports star growing up in Arkansas. He went to Arkansas State University where he walked on to the football team. He goes there. He joins the Marine Corps Reserve. He becomes a fantastic Marine and is just on top of the world. Then, he becomes a quadriplegic in a canoeing incident in 1993. He has spent the last 20 years in that chair. I've been a best friend with him for the last 12 years. What he has been able to teach me in the course of my life—about what really matters in life—has made him *my* hero.

Chase Boyd is now 19 years old. He is the oldest child and only son of Andy and Caroline Boyd—Southern California natives. They are the epitome of the American Dream—hugely successful in business, a great family, everything perfect. And, when Chase is a young boy, he gets diagnosed with progressive Muscular Dystrophy. They tell him he's got a couple years to live. That was like 13 years ago. For the last few years, he's been bolted into a wheelchair. He can't move any part of his body. He can blink, and he can talk. His parents, Andy and Caroline, have given up everything in their lives to make this young man's life— his world—as good as it can be. Today, Chase is lying in a hospital bed and may never get out. To see the fight, the spirit, the drive, the determination of this young man—doing everything he can to do *what* he can. And, then to see his parents, who once had everything. Their son has never had the chance to live a normal life that we all take for granted. And, now they're going to lose their son. To see their sacrifice, they are my heroes.

(Note: Chase Boyd passed away on 1/2/2014, just four days after my interview with Bill Walton.)

Chris Waddell has an incredible story. He was a skier (for Middlebury College in 1988) when he was in a terrible accident during competition and became paralyzed from the waist down. He can still use his arms, and he is a dynamic professional public speaker. He has this program where he goes around and talks to people about the world and life and everything. Two of the main themes that he has are, number one, "Who are *your* heroes? Who is inspiring you to make this world better?" And, number two, he tells his own story, his own journey, about how when he was lying there at the beginning after his accident. Now, whenever that happens, the first thing that goes through the person's mind is, "I'm going to kill myself because my life isn't worth living." And, *I've* been there myself during my ordeal with my back. Chris Waddell is lying there, but then he works his way out of the funk. He starts to come back, and he starts to say, "Okay. I want to do something. I want to make a difference here." So, he makes the commitment, "I'm gonna be the first guy in a wheelchair—the first paraplegic—to ever climb Mt. Kilimanjaro." Now, Mt. Kilimanjaro is not a technical climb in terms of mountain-climbing. It's a long walk up, a long walk uphill. So, Chris Waddell builds this very special contraption that's gonna allow him to go by himself under his own power all the way to the top of Mt. Kilimanjaro. He's getting really near the top. He has a team of support guys with him, but he's doing all the work—with this special contraption. When they get there, right near the top, there has been a recent rock slide on the top of the mountain that has blocked the path. With his challenges and limitations, he cannot get over this rock slide. So, he thinks it's over. He's just really bummed. He's really devastated. His team is all right there, and his team picks him up and puts him on the other side of the rock pile. It was not that big of a rock pile, but he couldn't do it by himself. He's on the other side, and he continues on and finishes the climb up to the top of Kilimanjaro. They're up there. They're all happy. They're all celebrating—with the exception of Chris, who is demoralized, frustrated, disappointed, ashamed, embarrassed. One of the guys comes over to him and says, "What's wrong, Chris? You did it! This should be the grand crowning moment of achievement and accomplishment." And, Chris—through the sadness—says, "I wanted to do this on my own. I wanted to make it by myself." And, the guy looked at Chris and said, "Chris, you don't get it at all. *Nobody* makes it to the top of the mountain by themselves." Chris has this whole speech that brings you to tears. And, *Chris* is one of my heroes.

These are people who fight that daily struggle, that daily struggle to make it, which is so hard and so fragile. That's why heroes are so important. When times are tough, who's gonna pull you through? How many times—when things were really tough—did Bobby Kennedy or Bill Russell or Martin Luther King or Sargent Shriver or Muhammad Ali or Bob Dylan or Neil Young or Jerry Garcia stand up and say, "Let's go!" Or my dear friend (and former Trail Blazer teammate) Maurice Lucas whose favorite saying was, "I'll take care of this." How many times have all of those people stood up and said, "I'll take care of this?" The culture that I grew up in was, "We can do better. We can do better than what is going on right now, and I've gotta do something about it." That's the approach I take to my life each and every day.

Career Notes: Bill Walton won two California high school championships at Helix High School before winning a pair of NCAA crowns at UCLA under John Wooden. He won two NBA titles, with Portland (1977) and Boston (1986). Walton was named the NCAA Division I National Player of the Year in each of his three varsity seasons at UCLA. The Bruins were 30-0 in each of Walton's first two seasons. The 6-foot-11 center led UCLA to national titles in 1972 and 1973. He had 24 points and 20 rebounds against Florida State in the 1972 title game. In 1973, Walton put on the greatest display in championship game history. He made 21-of-22 field-goal attempts while scoring a championship game record 44 points in an 87-66 rout of Memphis State. Walton led the Bruins to an NCAA record 88 consecutive victories before he experienced a loss in college. In Walton's three varsity seasons, UCLA went 86-4. The big redhead averaged 20.3 points and 15.7 rebounds. The Portland Trail Blazers made Walton the first pick in the 1974 NBA Draft. In 1977, he averaged 18.6 points and led the league with 14.4 rebounds and 3.2 blocked shots to power Portland to its only NBA championship. Walton was named the 1977 NBA Finals MVP. The following season the Blazers started 50-10, but Walton was then injured, and Portland finished 58-24. Even so, Walton was recognized as the league's Most Valuable Player that year. An All-Star in 1977 and 1978, Walton's injuries prevented him from continuing to play at an All-Star level. Walton spent time with the Clippers and the Celtics, winning a championship with Boston in 1986. He was voted NBA Sixth Man of the Year after playing in a career-high 80 games, 78 of those off the bench while earning a championship ring with the Celtics. Walton retired in 1987, with NBA career averages of 13.3 points and 10.5 rebounds.

*   *   *

38

The World Is Your Oyster

Mariel Zagunis is USA Fencing's version of Michael Jordan. A true champion of her sport, the native of Beaverton, Oregon, has won two Olympic gold medals and a pair of individual World Championships. At the 2004 Olympics in Athens, she won the first Olympic gold medal for an American fencer in 100 years. Zagunis remains the only U.S. women's sabre fencer to hold the Olympic title.

Mariel Zagunis might have been destined for greatness from the time she was born. She is the daughter of former U.S. Olympians Robert and Cathy Zagunis. Her mom and dad were rowers, but Mariel wasn't all that interested in rowing. However, the first time she picked up a sabre—at age 10—she was hooked on fencing. Mariel began winning competitions at a young age and has kept right on winning into adulthood.

Mariel was only 19 years old when she won the gold medal in Athens in 2004. Since she was one of Portland's local athletes, she was really big news in the Rose City. Everyone scrambled to get an interview with the teenage fencing sensation. It seemed unlikely that Mariel would ever be able to top being an Olympic gold medal winner. But, it turned out she was just getting started. She soon won a pair of individual World Championships and more gold in the 2008 Olympics. Even when she was failed to medal in the 2012 Olympics, she still came away with a once in a lifetime experience. Zagunis was chosen to be the American flag bearer during the Opening Ceremony of the 2012 London Games. Her smile illuminated the stadium, and she was seen—worldwide—on social media and traditional media as she carried the flag, proudly representing her country.

I have had the chance to interview Mariel several times, and I find her to be a delightful young woman. Just don't pull out a sword and challenge her to a duel. If you do, she has the ability to promptly cut you down to size. I talked with Mariel Zagunis by phone on October 22, 2014.

Who was your very first childhood idol?

It's hard for me to really pinpoint it because I was involved in so many different sports. Whatever sport I was playing, I looked up to idols in that sport. Because I was a really big soccer player, a big influence on my life was all the women soccer players from the '99 U.S. team—Brandi Chastain, Julie Foudy—all those women. I really looked up to them because they were coming around and having such success at a time that was making a really big impact on me and a lot of my friends. We saw these amazing athletic women doing such amazing things and achieving these really incredible accomplishments like winning the World Cup. Those were a lot of the women that I looked up to when I was a kid.

Then, outside of them, I really looked up to Iris and Felicia Zimmerman, the Zimmerman sisters. They're still involved with the fencing world—not competing or anything. They were a generation ahead of me. They were very successful foil fencers. Sisters out of New York, they were making really big strides in our sport when I first got started in fencing. I looked up to them like, "Oh, my gosh! They're so cool. They've done so much, and they're going to the Olympics!" So, I really looked up to them when I first started fencing.

Of course, I always looked up to my parents because my parents were both Olympians. They were both rowers. Both my mom and dad were on the '76 rowing team for the U.S. I think that my passion for wanting to be an Olympian—that aspiration and inspiration—came from them. It was something that I knew was a big part of their lives. I always remember them telling me stories about them trying out for the Olympic team—and making it—and their experiences at the Olympics. That was always something that was very fascinating and special for me to know that both of my parents had been there and done that before.

Let's talk about the first time that you met some of your idols. Did you ever get a chance to meet any of the U.S. Women's soccer stars?

I first met Julie Foudy just a couple years ago. It was at a Women's Sports Foundation event that I met her. I met Brandi Chastain back in 2007 or '08 through a Nike event. And, then I met her again at the London Olympics this year. I haven't really met a lot of them in person. But, just as a young girl growing up playing soccer—remembering those magical moments of Brandi Chastain scoring the winning shootout goal and ripping her shirt off and just being really powerful. It was just a great moment for sports' victories and for women and empowerment, just feeling so, "Oh, my gosh! Look at her do that! I want to be in that position someday where I have this moment of victory, this moment of celebration." Sure enough, for me, it came about a decade later when I got to win the Olympics. Although I had a lot of layers on and couldn't really rip my shirt off, it was still that type of moment where you really feel something for the athlete. And, you really are excited that you were able to experience something so monumental.

With all the success you've had, there's no question that you are an idol to young fencers around the country. I know even there in Portland where you train, there is a young fencer—2013 World Junior Champion Sage Palmedo—that is having success due, in part, to your support and mentoring. Only 13 years of age, she trains with you at Oregon Fencing Alliance. Do you think about the fact that you are an idol to the next generation of fencers?

Yeah, I think about it off and on. With Sage and all the young girls that I have the pleasure of training with, it's a little bit different because I see them every day. We work together all the time. I know that in past years when they were much younger, they definitely looked up to me. But, now we're working together. Sage, for example, we've known each other and been in the same class for a really, really long time. But, now, Sage is trying for the Rio Olympics. We work together every single day. We practice against each other and motivate each other. I know that when she was much younger, I may have been this intimidating-type role model fencer that happened to be in her same class. But, now, it's really, really cool to have this camaraderie with her and have this relationship where we're both motivating and inspiring each other to be better each and every day.

And, when it comes to other fencers around the world that I'm inspiring, I really do enjoy being a role model. When it first started, I didn't really realize it or ask for it. I was still very young, and I was just kind of doing my thing and not really realizing the true impact I was having on our sport around the nation and around the world. Now that I'm older, I realize that. It's really fun to show up at national competitions and meet these young female saber fencers that tell me that they started fencing because they saw me win the Olympics on TV. That is really inspiring to me. It's really awesome to hear that I'm giving back to the sport in that way. By doing what I love, I'm inspiring other people to fall in love with the sport as well. I'm really proud of that, and I'm proud to be a really good role model with my actions on and off the (fencing) strips.

You appeared so proud when you entered the Opening Ceremony at the Olympics carrying the American flag. There had to be thousands of little girls watching you carry the Stars & Stripes and saying to themselves, "Wow! She's great! I want to be like her someday."

It's so weird to think about, but it's also very humbling and really, really cool. I'm very proud that I was able to be granted that opportunity to be the flag-bearer—just being a female athlete and showing these other young girls who are aspiring to be the best that they can be in their sport or in whatever their passion, to say, "Yeah! Girl power! We're gonna take it as far as we can go and just have fun doing it."

You are the last person to be heard from in this book. By this time, readers will have learned that nearly all of their sports idols had idols of their own when they were young. You have the final say. Is it possible to sort of summarize what having an idol might mean to a child in terms of goal-setting and reaching for the stars?

It's incredibly important to have idols, to have mentors, to have role models—all of those things—whether it's coming from one person or a group of people, or one coach or your parents. It's so, so important because when you're a kid, the world is your oyster. You can really believe in anything. You look at these kids today, and they have such great imaginations. When it comes to goal-setting, when I was ten years old, I said that I wanted to be an Olympic champion. Although that may have sounded crazy for a ten-year-old, the people in my group—my parents and my coach—all believed in me. Everyone around me was really supportive of that dream—even though at ten years old, it's like, "Oh, my gosh! There's so much that has to be done in order to even get close to having a chance at the Olympic team!" The people around me really inspired me. They encouraged me. They kept me on the right track. It was something that throughout my formative years—and especially through fencing—made me believe that I could do anything if I put my mind to it. I never believed that I couldn't do everything that I wanted to do. So, having idols—and having people that believe in you that you can look up to and that trust in you and you can trust in them—is so, so important to put you on the path to success. If you believe in yourself, that's one thing. But, it's important to have a whole community of people around you—mentors and coaches and parents who are gonna help you every step of the way, let you stand on their shoulders and teach you everything that you need to know. To have them really keep you on track to be the best that you can be, I think that that's a really powerful thing.

Career Notes: Mariel Zagunis won individual gold medals at the Olympics in 2004 and 2008. She won individual World Championships in 2009 and 2010. She warmed up for the 2016 Rio Olympics by claiming the individual gold medal in the 2015 Pan American Games.

*   *   *

ACKNOWLEDGMENTS

I would like to extend a sincere thank you to the many athletes who shared memories of their childhood heroes for this book. Without their willingness to tell their stories, this project would never have gotten off the ground. Also, many of the athletes I interviewed had a media contact or personal representative that helped facilitate the interviews. I thank them for helping me get together with the athletes and coaches.

I also learned late in the process that I was required to have written permission from each interviewee (or from his or her agent/ representative). That meant I had to go back—in some cases several years after conducting the interviews—to try to receive written consents from nearly 200 athletes. My sincere thanks to the athletes who quickly granted their consents and to everyone who played a role in helping me get back in touch with these sporting legends.

Sadly, I was unable to reach several dozen athletes; therefore, their interviews are not included in the book. To those athletes—and to the athletes who may have sent their consents after the manuscript was turned in to the publisher—my apologies. Know that I would have loved to have your story in the book. If there is a *Sports Idols' Idols II*, I promise that you will be included in that edition (if you will get in touch and let me know you want to be part of it).

Most disappointing was when my requests for consent were denied—in some cases by an athlete's management team. I struggled to understand why consent would be denied since the athletes and coaches had willingly talked with me about their early childhood heroes. Since no specific reason for denial was provided, I can only guess that the various management teams determined their clients should not be associated in any way with their first childhood idols because those childhood heroes later had legal issues. I understand the desire to distance a client from anything controversial, but shame on anyone who revises history simply for the sake of someone's public image. We can't change who we first idolized even if that person turns out to be flawed. It seems to me that including those interviews in the book would have served as a cautionary tale rather than to be a negative for the athletes who had once looked at a sports idol as someone who could do no wrong. I could be wrong about the reasons consent was denied, but in most cases, the childhood idols that had been mentioned had legal problems later in life. I doubt it's just a coincidence that consent was denied.

This book would not have been possible without the support and guidance of many people—family, friends and business associates. I can't possibly name everyone, but please know that I appreciate what each of you did to help this book become a reality. While I appreciate every effort that was made to help me, there were a few media relations people who went far beyond the call of duty to help me when I required their assistance. I offer special thanks to Jim Taylor, Colin Romer, Rachel Levitsky, Mike Kitchel, Brian Breseman, John Blundell, Chris Romanello, Anna Wildish, Raymond Ridder, Brett Winkler, Matt de Nesnera, Matt Tumbleson, Tim Donovan, Michael Lissack, Seth Burton, Sarah Melton, B.J. Evans, Taylor Jacobson, Chris Metz, Mark Nelson, Katie Simons, Tracey Hughes, Julie Fie, Lori Cook, Dan Levy, Jason Amberg, Shawn Shoeffler, Ryann Rigsby, Kathi Lauterbach, Kelby Krauss, David Hovis, Anne Fornono, Monica Hilton, Tim Hevly, Kelly Munro, Jeff Hoffman, Reid Hutchins, Meghan Flanagan, Nick Parker, Kevin Hopkins, Jeff Chilcoat, Jason Wallace, Kerri Harper, Rob Schreier, Katherine Brackman, Joe Jareck, Audrah Cates, Shawn Novack, Kathy Baarts, Rhonda Pullens, Christopher Hastings, Patty Reid, Robbie Bohren, Nate Horgen, Ben Cafardo, Alli D'Amico, David Kaplan, Brian Berger, Graham Kendrick and dozens more.

A project this large required a huge amount of time, leaving me with less time to be with family and friends than I would have liked. Thank you for understanding I was totally consumed by this project, particularly in the two years since my layoff from the radio station in Portland. Working to complete this book kept me going through what could have been a far more difficult time. Thanks to you, my family and friends, for your love and support. With your help, the book is now complete, and I can move forward. Many of you patiently listened to me talk about the project these last few years. Please know that I appreciate your willingness to listen even as I told you the same stories about the book time and again.

A few who deserve special recognition for being willing to spend time with me (even if I wasn't very good company) include William and Jan Thun, Mark and Angie Kattelman, Genevieve Smith, Carl Click, Rita and Larry Arnold, Russ Bauman, Leanne Christenson, Debi Sonne and family, Eileen and John Biggio, Rich and Debbie Patterson, Kathleen Gaylord, Terry Durham, Brad Newgard, Dave Anderson, Mark Mason, Michael Anthony, Mike Oaks, Michael Nettleton, Bobby Corser, Ron Quant, Shirley Skidmore, Dave Barbaris, Curt and Waynetta Blaum, Raymond Blaum, Jim and Joanne Hawes, Linda and Joe Borgia, Jack Eich, Tom Kolbe, Brian Ericksen, Angie Machado, Joe Becker, Joey Johnston, Mike Barrett, Kerry Eggers, Mike Tokito, Ken Goe, Anne Peterson, Paul Linnman, Bob Miller, Rick Nafe, Mike Rich, Michelle Wortner, Josy Ansley, Matt and Shelby Thompson, Janis Struebing, Jean Dowell, Wayne and M'Lou Thompson, Carlos and Claudia Ward, Audrey Ward, Bryant Ward. Fred Wehking, Duncan Reid, Jon Warren, Mike Parker, "Dream" Weaver, John Lashway, Tim Roye, Jim Patton, Blake Timm, Jon Simmons, Chuck Charnquist, Steve Brandon, Al and Andrea Egg, Tom and Pam Herbage, John and Gail Strubberg, Rick Labasan, Joanne McCall, Greg Jarrett, Joel Blank, Tim Clodjeaux, Clint Sly, Mike Lund and dozens more.

Four people were instrumental in the book being published in its current form. My good friends Wayne Thompson and Al Bell, my son,

Adam Betzelberger, and my wife, Sharon Betzelberger, all spent time reading portions of the book at various stages of its development. They provided me with sound writing advice and wonderful editing tips. Their suggestions helped me improve the format to make it far more interesting to the reader. I know the end product isn't exactly what any of them suggested, but I incorporated several of their ideas. Without question, these four wonderful people spent more time talking with me about this project than anyone, and they made the book better. I thank them for their valuable input.

Thanks to the late Maurice Lucas for inviting me to participate in his celebrity golf outings. Because of Luke, I was able to spend some time with one of my boyhood heroes, Bob Gibson.

My thanks to my broadcasting mentor, Jay Randolph, who helped propel me into the sports journalism business.

Also, I want to thank Bob Costas for his blurb on the back cover of the book. I've been one of Bob's fans ever since he was the "Voice" of the Spirits of St. Louis. Thanks to Pam Davis for getting my request to Bob in such a prompt fashion.

And, finally, my thanks and love to my wife, Sharon, and to our children, Adam and Kelsey, for their constant support and love. I couldn't have done it without you all these many years.

ABOUT THE AUTHOR

Scott Lynn has worked in radio and television for nearly forty years, covering amateur and professional sports in Portland, Oregon; Tampa, Florida; and Decatur, Illinois. The trusted journalist was named Oregon Sportscaster of the Year seven times and earned three prestigious Edward R. Murrow regional awards. The Lincoln, Illinois, native has called the play-by-play of hundreds of high school, college, and professional games on regional and national television. He has called the action on the radio networks of the Portland Trail Blazers and Oregon State University Beavers. Now in semiretirement in the Tampa Bay area, Lynn calls basketball and baseball games for the University of Tampa on TampaSpartans.TV.

Scott Lynn's first book—*THORNRIDGE: The Perfect Season in Black and White*—was highly acclaimed. This is the second book he has written since surviving stage 3 colon cancer in 2008.

Made in the USA
San Bernardino, CA
25 April 2016